B Mom

Lovely Weeds

Crissy Shreve

AuthorHouse™ LLC
1663 Liberty Drive
Bloomington, IN 47403
www.authorhouse.com
Phone: 1-800-839-8640

Published by AuthorHouse 02/15/2014

ISBN: 978-1-4918-4794-7 (sc)
ISBN: 978-1-4918-4795-4 (hc)
ISBN: 978-1-4918-4793-0 (e)

Library of Congress Control Number: 2013923786

CONTENTS

DEDICATION

When someone just fits with you, you say that you are of an ilk. This is for you, my "ilks." You know who you are.

I've seldom chosen you; you've just appeared like brightly colored packages next to my plate on birthday mornings. Some of you have been in my life for a long time; others have floated in and out. You've stood by me, held me up, and pushed me back out there when it was time.

You are the ones who shared my despair and cried my tears when my marriage fell apart and when Jason died. Sometimes you cried in my stead—in those times when I couldn't get close enough to the pain to cry for myself.

You are the ones whose hearts were as touched by Larry's return as mine was. You grabbed onto the joy and called it your own—because I am your own. In that, you made Larry your own as well. It's just who you are.

You are the ones who, over many years, have finally convinced me that I might actually be lovable. I must be, because you love me. I thank God for you. I thank you.

You are the ones who wrote and called to say that Larry is lucky to have me as his mom. On this eve of Larry's and my first meeting, I am afraid. Not terrified, not panicked, just a little scared.

This is for Judy, who saved me long before I met Jesus.

This is for Larry, who never gave up.

This is for Mike, whose wise counsel saves me from myself more often than I like to admit.

Above all, this is for Jason, the best "ilk" ever. He's waiting for me in heaven. Baby, I miss you every day.

This is also for one other person. I don't know who you are, but I'm praying that God will find you, put this book in your hands, and open your heart to His special message meant just for you.

BMom
Larry Eve
29 July 2010

Lovely Weeds
Crissy Shreve

My weeds get deeper every day,
I look around me in dismay,
Through them it's hard to see a way,
To grow.

I'm planted here on rocky ground,
I feel so stuck, my roots are bound,
And up till now I haven't found,
A way to grow.

My leaves are parched, my throat is dry,
And I have no tears left to cry,
The raindrops seem to pass me by,
No way to grow.

The sun invites me out to play,
But I in sadness turn away,
And cower in the light of day,
Afraid to grow.

And yet, and yet, what can that be?
A flower sprouting out of me!
Oh, dandelion, oh, lovely weed,
I watch it grow.

I look around me and I see,
Hundreds, thousands, just like me,
We all will be what we will be,
And we will grow.

I raise my head, I spread my seeds,
Creating other lovely weeds,
Trusting God to meet my needs,
In Him I grow.

Illustrations

Lovely Weed—Calligraphic Dandelion By OCAL
http://www.clker.com/clipart-14537.html

Baby in Arms, Crissy Shreve, ©1997

Praying Boy, Crissy Shreve, ©1995

THE CAST

Me: Cristina, Crissie, Kris, Cris, Crissy, at various stages of my life.

My mother: Laura.

My grandfather: Edward. I called him Dadum; cousins called him Pup-up (by various spellings).

My grandmother: Laurena. Known to us all as Nana.

Aunts & Uncles: John and Ruth (AKA Grandma Ruth), Austin and Audrey, James (Jimmy) & Rebecca.

Cousins: Judy, Jan, John (Ruth's children); Johnny (Jimmy's son), and Bobby (Audrey's son from a previous marriage, raised by Austin but never adopted).

Bill: Laura's husband, who may be my father.

The other man who may be my father.

Larry: my son placed for adoption.

X1: my first husband.

Mike and Jason: my sons from my first marriage.

X2: my second husband.

Step-Mike and Rick: my stepsons.

Various grandkids.

Introduction

I quickly realized as I began writing that this has to be the story of my life. For one thing, it's the story I know. For another, it's a way to help Larry know me—who I was, who I am now and how I got here. As I recall the experiences that made me, I gain new understanding of myself—never a bad thing. Finally, if this is to be a book, it will require material. I've got a lot of material, but it's mostly about me. So it has to be what it is, I guess.

I believe this book is one of God's intentions for reuniting Larry and me—along with doing it just because He loves us, and, the biggie, sharing the unusual and wonderful joy of our finding each other again. It's God putting back together the shattered pieces of my life and my soul. I hope you will see His fingerprints—they're all over it.

A favor, please. There are many different stories, themes, and ideas in BMom. You may get bored in places; you may disagree with me in others. Please skip ahead a bit if that happens. There are so many great stories that you will miss if you just put the book down. Trust me.

So, what's up with the BMom thing? When Larry and I were first emailing, I suggested that he might just call me Cris. I hold his adoptive mother in highest esteem, and I didn't want to encroach even a little on the name she's earned—the name Mom. Larry, however, said, "Oh, no, you are Mom. I will call you Mom." And he does. So, we created A(doptive) Mom and B(irth)Mom.

I am thrilled to be BMom.

ROSEBUD ON THE ALTAR

Donna Dickey Guyer [1]

A child is born. And in this flower's shaft,
the petals sleeping with a gentle nod,
a human being has been autographed,
"To the whole world with all my love,"
from God.

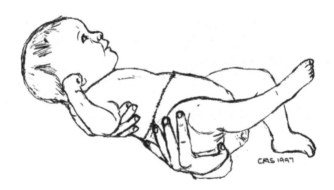

---

[1] Donna Dickey Guyer is deceased. I tried without success to find a copyright holder through her publisher and at various addresses I found on the Internet. Her dear friend at Poets of the Palm Beaches assured me her family had discarded her work and that it should be no problem for me to quote her poem with credit. I do so in honor of a wonderful poet.

CHAPTER ONE

HELLO AND GOODBYE

On July 13, 1965, my son was born. My mother asked that I call him Larry, for her. Her name was Laura. A few days later, I left him in the arms of new parents I couldn't know, and with no real hope of ever seeing him again.

For forty-five years, I carried my baby boy as a scar on my heart. I could not know whether he was alive, whether he was healthy, whether he was being loved and cared for. The hardest part was not having a way to know if he needed me.

Once I was married and had a home, I wrote a letter to the attorney who'd handled the adoption, just wanting her to know how to find me if it were necessary. Sadly, she had died, and I was unable to find out whether anyone had taken over her practice or had her records.

I couldn't have kept him. I was sixteen years old when Larry was born. His father was not a bad guy, but I could see no likelihood of his being able to support us. I didn't want Larry to be raised in the same near-poverty in which I'd grown up, nor did I want to go on living in it myself. I'd seen friends who, in the same circumstances, married too young. The novelty wore off very quickly. They weren't ready to be wives and mothers; they were still children themselves. One of them, when the baby was only a few months old, was already stepping out with other guys while her husband was at work. She was still a teenager, wanting and needing to do what teenagers do.

It would have been impossible for my mother, a single mother herself, to take on another mouth to feed. She suggested putting Larry in an orphanage until I was able to take care of him. In hindsight, that day came much more quickly than I thought it would, but the idea of

1

putting him in an orphanage, even for one day, was repulsive. All I could do was trust that Larry was safe in God's hands.

Abortion wasn't available back then. I wish I could say that I wouldn't have had one, but had it been an option, I very well might have. I'm so grateful that it wasn't.

Despite the circumstances of his conception, Larry was not an accident, nor was he a mistake—not in God's economy. Larry was fearfully and wonderfully made, knit in my womb.[2] He was and is exactly who God intended him to be. God knew that one day Larry would find me, and that it would be right when I needed him.

As hard as the intervening years may have been, they were as nothing compared to the joy I felt when Larry found me. On the surface, it might seem that placing one's child for adoption is an impossible choice. And it is, except that with God all things are possible.

I was in eleventh grade when I was pregnant with Larry. I made it through the first six months of school without anyone noticing. At some point, my mother suspected, and wondered why I wasn't having periods. "Is your belly going to be swollen with a child?" she asked. Mostly, though, I think she didn't want to know, didn't want it to be true, and certainly hadn't a clue what to do about it if it was. It was my Spanish teacher who finally brought my "condition" to my mother's attention, and to the attention of the authorities at school, as well. In those days, pregnant teenage girls weren't permitted to parade around school with swollen bellies. One girl, a year ahead of me, had left school, married, had her baby, and then returned to school to finish.

Once my dilemma was known, I quickly blossomed. How I'd managed to get by in my normal clothes for six months, I don't know, but from one day to the next, nothing fit any longer. Of course I knew I was pregnant pretty much right from the start. A few close friends knew, as well. For the most part, though, I just went on with life as usual. There wasn't much else I could do. I'd broken up with Larry's father and was even dating other guys. Denial at its best.

I did give a lot of thought to how I was going to get myself through the predicament, though. I remember being very relieved to

---

[2]   Psalms 139:14 I praise you because I am fearfully and wonderfully made; your works are wonderful, I know that full well. NIV

find a newspaper ad for the Florence Crittenden Home[3]. At fifteen years old, I didn't know how to go about approaching them, and I wasn't ready for my secret to come out, anyway, so I just stored the information away in my brain until it came time to do something. Going there and giving the baby up for adoption made sense to me. My mother was rather surprised that I had a plan. Of course I had a plan. I'd had to figure out my life on my own all along—why should this time be any different? I don't think it ever occurred to me to seek help or counsel, and even if it had, I wouldn't have known from whom.

There was, of course, the fear of judgment, and knowing that I'd once again disappoint everyone in my family. I never perceived them to be people who would be there for me. That was, perhaps, a bit unfair to them, as I didn't give them the chance to prove otherwise, but I think it was largely true.

There were "standards" of behavior in my family. I was expected to be many things I simply didn't have the resources to be able to be. My mother didn't necessarily expect me to meet these standards; she herself couldn't meet them. I suppose I did more to make them ashamed of me than I did to make them proud. I don't remember anyone ever saying they were proud of me, despite how quick they were to point out my faults. Still, I can recognize that, in their own ways, they all loved me like crazy and wanted better for me than what I was capable of producing on my own. That was the rub. They had expectations of me, but they didn't engage in my process.

I never had any morning sickness, so it was pretty easy to pretend, even to myself for the first months, that I wasn't really pregnant. The first undeniable sign was when I felt those first "butterflies," Larry's movement inside me. I remember exactly where I was when it happened, and it was a precious moment. I realized that there really was a little somebody growing in there.

I don't remember being particularly scared. As I think back to that time, that surprises me. It was something I'd have to face, to deal with, but not in fear. I don't really know why that was true—perhaps I was so numbed by life by then that I wasn't feeling anything. Maybe it was because I had a plan, a way through it, and ultimately, out of it.

---

[3]   The Florence Crittenden Home closed in the mid-70's. All records were burned.

Perhaps I simply didn't have enough sense to be afraid. I know now that God was with me in it, even though I didn't know Him then. After all, He knew who was growing inside me.

My memories of my time at the Florence Crittenden Home, affectionately known to its denizens as "Flo's," come to me in bits and pieces. My Uncle Austin drove me there. We entered through the front door, which is only remarkable because, in my several months there, I never again used the front door until the day I left. There was a side door that we girls used.

Uncle Austin had apparently been a supporter of Flo's for some time, which may have been a bit of a self-fulfilling prophecy on his part. He saw me to some degree as a daughter. I wish I could say he'd seen himself as a dad and, maybe he even did, at least in his own way. In any case, I think he was afraid that one day I'd need Flo's. I did. It may even be that his being a supporter helped me get in on short notice. When he checked me into Flo's, he was mortified, and very angry with me. I'd disappointed him, and he never forgave me. He was still cordial to me after that, but it was clear that I'd lost my status as his pride and joy.

I didn't have many maternity clothes, just a few cheap items my mother had picked up for me at the dime store. It didn't matter, though; there were plenty of leftover items at Flo's. Obviously no one saw any reason to take their maternity clothes along when they left. The food was great, and nutritious. Four older girls, who'd come in early in their pregnancies, and hence would be there a while, were the cooks. They planned our meals, shopped for food, and prepared it all—three meals a day. The rest of us took turns washing the dishes and scrubbing the pots.

There were several young women who had already finished school and started working. I remember one in particular who spent hours composing fictional letters to her parents and friends, telling them about her happy life in another city. She'd copy these letters for herself before sending them, so as not to contradict herself in a later letter. There was a lot of shame in unwed pregnancy in those days.

Mornings we had chores. My job was to sweep down the back stairs with a brush and dustpan. On my first day, I hadn't yet been assigned a duty, and I was feeling like I didn't belong, so I bugged someone to give me a job to do. For some reason, I was initially afraid of the staff woman who was in charge of cleaning. She had something of a brusque voice and came off as a tough cookie. Ironically, I wound up really liking and trusting her, and it was to her that I complained several times when I felt the headmistress had treated me unfairly.

When I first arrived, there was no headmistress; the head nurse, Mrs. M., was in charge. Before long, though, we got a new headmistress. She was a bear. Shepherding a flock of unwed mothers was obviously not her gift. We all hated her.

Many of us had nicknames; I was "Knish." A friend of mine had observed one time that with my long, straight hair and my, let's say, prominent nose, I looked just like "Knish," a puppet in a children's TV show. He, well, I guess he was a he, had a darning knob for a nose and it stuck out the front of his mop head hair. *"Knish"* is a Yiddish word for a kind of bun or dumpling, and derives from the Russian *"knysh."* You pronounce the k. The new headmistress couldn't seem to say "Knish." She always said "Gnish."

In the afternoons and evenings, we congregated in a large dayroom on the second floor. We were allowed to smoke in the dayroom, and most of us did. We read or watched soap operas. I don't remember there ever being much argument about what to watch. "Peyton Place" was on twice, or perhaps even three times a week, and we were all hooked on it.

And the weather was hot. There was no air-conditioning then, and most of us slept up on the third floor, which was one big room, set up as a dormitory. I don't remember exactly, but there were at least fifteen and maybe as many as twenty of us at Flo's when I was there.

Some of us knitted or sewed clothing. I made myself a lightweight nightgown that was cool enough to help me survive the third floor, and a reversible wrap-around skirt that was a dark maroon on one side and madras on the other. I wore that skirt home the day I left and for some time afterwards. I'd actually read the instructions that came with the pattern, something I seldom do, and it turned out remarkably well.

Often in the afternoon, we'd go out walking around the area, just to get out and have something to do. There were no particular boundaries, but we weren't supposed to leave the immediate area. Mostly, we went up to W Street, a few blocks away. We had to travel in twos, and on any given afternoon, pairs of pregnant girls could be seen wandering around the neighborhood. W Street was great; one long block of trendy boutiques, a drugstore, an upscale butcher shop, that sort of thing.

A few of the older girls had cars stashed nearby. They must have used them for grocery shopping. I wasn't a cook then and I'm not a cook now, so I wasn't paying much attention, but thinking back, I realize that they must have gone to the store nearly every day. They had a lot of mouths to feed.

The night Larry decided to be born, the moon was full, and several of us went into labor at the same time. I was up most of the night, sitting in the dayroom, just feeling uncomfortable, nothing major. When Mrs. M. finally came in, I thought she'd just noticed me, but she'd known even before she went to bed that I was close to ready to go. She and I walked across the street to the hospital. I'd sort of thought we'd go in a cab, so I was surprised when we walked. It was fine, though.

Mrs. M. didn't stay with me; she had several others in various stages of labor, and I know she made at least three trips across the street that night. My mother came to the hospital, but I didn't see her until after I'd delivered.

Once at the hospital, I had maybe three hours of twingey labor, nothing too hard. They gave me something called "twilight sleep," which, as I remember it, made me sleep deeply between contractions, and I didn't even remember having them. Then, in the delivery room, I was put completely under. I remember the mask being placed over my nose and mouth, then . . . nothing. The next thing I knew, Larry was there.

There was a nurse from my hometown in the delivery room, and just as I was coming out of the anesthesia, she asked me where I was from and what my name was. I was groggy, so I told her. Afterwards, I lived in terror that she'd tell people at home about me.

My best friend from Flo's, who was only fourteen, spent nearly two days in hard labor before her little girl was born. I was lucky. The worst I remember was dealing with the stitches.

Once a girl had given birth, she typically moved downstairs to the mothers' room, which was on the second floor next to the nursery. Because so many of us had given birth at the same time, I never made it to the mothers' room, but Larry stayed in the nursery. I had to go up and down the stairs a lot. We brought our babies "home" to Flo's and took care of them ourselves for a few days. I fed Larry, burped him, changed his pants, and powdered his tiny bottom.

I suspect that this arrangement was intentional, so that we could be absolutely certain what we wanted to do, and probably so that any immediate medical problems might be identified prior to the baby's placement. Typically, back then, a baby was taken from the mother immediately after the birth, and usually the mother never saw the child, sometimes didn't even know whether she'd had a boy or a girl. They did it differently at Flo's.

Adoptions were final and records were sealed. The adoptive parents arrived at the home several hours after the mother had left. I was told that my baby was going to a certain town, but it wasn't true. Larry was actually raised only about five miles from where I lived at that time.

It may seem a cruelty, my having had to care for Larry, getting to know and love him, only to hand him away. It wasn't. It was, instead, perhaps the dearest of God's blessings in my life, right up until the moment He brought us back together. For those few days, I absorbed Larry's sweetness, counted his fingers and toes, smelled that wonderful baby head nectar, and cherished the tiny hand clutching my finger. He was magnificent.

These things I carried in my heart as I walked away from him and out of Flo's for the last time. These things, and the last line of a poem written by one of the girls:

"But, God, be kind, and let her know, her mother loves her, too." [4]

And then it was all over . . . except for the stretch marks.

THE HARDEST THING

This is the worst part of it all, and the hardest thing for me to admit. Right about the time I felt the first flutters of life inside me, I took a lot of aspirin in an attempt to kill myself.

---

[4] Know, old friend, that your words stayed with me for forty-five years, and I forgot neither them nor you. Thank you.

It was absolutely not an attempt to end the pregnancy. It was because, as a loopy fifteen-year-old, I was feeling sorry for myself over some boy who'd broken up with me. You'd think that being pregnant would have been my biggest problem, but in my mind, it wasn't. In my fifteen-year-old stupidity, all I cared about was getting this boy back. It wasn't even any real desire to die. I was simply trying to manipulate him into coming back to me.

It never even occurred to that loopy fifteen-year-old girl that taking the aspirin might harm the baby. It didn't occur to me until many years later. I'd never told anyone about this part of it, had in fact completely forgotten about it, and once I realized what I'd done, I was horrified, and terrified for Larry. I don't know that anyone had ever heard of Reye's Syndrome in the 60's, or its link to aspirin. Certainly I hadn't.

I remember exactly where I was when I finally connected those particular dots and realized what I'd done. It was an ordinary day some thirty years later. I was driving home from the grocery store, and for some reason, suddenly it hit me like a sledgehammer. I might have damaged my baby! I had to pull over to the side of the road. I couldn't bear it.

Who could I tell, who could I ask? The guilt, remorse and shame were overwhelming. Here, all these years, I'd been patting myself on the back for doing the "right thing," for not having had an abortion that wasn't available anyway, when the truth was that I was, or felt like I was, the most despicable human being on the face of the earth. The questions burned in my soul. Was Larry still alive? Had he died in infancy because of my stupidity? Did he suffer from some horrid disease and no one had a clue as to the cause? I had no way of knowing.

Despite the many, many mistakes I've made over the years, I've had very few real regrets, but this was the one thing I'd have given anything to be able to do over. The rest of my mistakes mostly affected me, but this one had affected Larry, and there wasn't a thing I could do about it.

Except, once again, turn him over to God.

When Larry found me, after forty-five years, my very first thought was that I could die happy just knowing he was alive and well. Even if we never established a relationship, just to know that God had covered my sin and protected my baby from my horrendous stupidity was enough. Oh, the unspeakable relief. This is grace—undeserved and unacknowledged for decades. I am in-a-pile-on-the-floor grateful.

Not long before Larry came back into my life, I did, finally, confide in my stepson, who is a doctor and a trusted friend, telling him what I'd done, and asking him what he thought might have happened. He assured me that Larry was probably fine, that I didn't need to be overly devastated about it.

Of course I also talked to God about it in depth, begging Him for forgiveness, but more, begging Him to retroactively take care of Larry. Although I don't present this as perfect theology, I have long trusted that God is capable of acting in (our) hindsight. God is eternal; time, as we know it, places no limitation on Him or on His ability to act. In that, then, his answers to our prayers would not be limited to our knowledge at any given time, or to our not thinking to pray at the right time. I fully believe and trust that God is capable of reading my heart and knowing that I will one day pray or would have prayed about something. Even if that's not true, the Bible says that the Holy Spirit prays for us.[5]

Either way, I am convinced that God heard my prayer decades before I prayed it, and that He acted according to His perfect will, in His perfect love for me and for Larry.

Larry, when I told him about it, was pretty much blasé about the whole thing. When I suggested he be cautious in using aspirin in case of a possible sensitivity to it, he said, "I'm a big boy, a little aspirin can't hurt me." Since he made it through babyhood, and presumably a fever or two, it appears he's right. Thank You, Lord.

---

[5] In the same way the Spirit also helps our weakness; for we do not know how to pray as we should, but the Spirit Himself intercedes for us with groanings too deep for words; and He who searches the hearts knows what the mind of the Spirit is, because He intercedes for the saints according to the will of God. And we know that God causes all things to work together for good to those who love God, to those who are called according to His purpose. Romans 8:26–28 NASU

LITTLE ONES
Crissy Shreve

"Little ones to Him belong"
I am a little one.
Oh, my legs are long and I have breasts,
And many candles on my birthday cake.
And I like to think I'm wiser now.

But I am still a little one,
So in need of all the things,
Given naturally to a child,
Weak in the armor of my grownup self.

Lord, it helps, it helps,
It's gotta help!
That this little one belongs to you.
Still,
And always.

When I was a child I sang that song,
Never knowing, never hearing,
Never seeing who I was,
Or Who You are.

Yes, yes!
Jesus loves me.

Chapter Two

First Things

I was born some time in the afternoon on January 1st, 1949. I've always said that my mother Laura never forgave me for causing her to miss the New Year's Eve party *and* the prior year's tax deduction. My Uncle John was with her when I was born.

My mother was hospitalized when I was only a few months old. She was diagnosed with paranoid schizophrenia, and received shock treatments. When she got out, she went to work. There was no one to take care of me except my grandmother Nana. Uncle Austin and Aunt Ruth considered placing me for adoption, but they "couldn't let me go."

In 1944, my mother and her husband Bill had had a baby boy whom they named Robert William. He died after only a few hours. My cousin Judy thinks that post-partum depression, coupled with the loss of the baby, caused my mother's illness. They didn't know much about that in those days. Many years later it occurred to me to that perhaps my mother had tried to hurt me when I was a baby and to wonder if that had been why she was hospitalized. I thought that maybe in her mixed up mind she couldn't deal with my being alive after having lost her little boy. Apparently this was not the case, though, because I asked Aunt Ruth and she said no.

My mother was still legally married to Bill, but they had been separated for some time. She apparently got involved with someone else and I was the result. I didn't learn about this until I was 14 or 15 years old though. Since she was still married, I grew up with her husband's name. Once I was grown and gone, my mother resumed use of her maiden name and still referred to herself in her eighties as Miss.

Nana, my grandmother, was sixty-five when my mother turned up penniless and ready to deliver. I'm sixty-three as I write this, and I can't imagine having a baby foisted on me to take care of. I wouldn't do it. Further, sixty-five in 1949 looked a lot different than it does today. I wear jeans. Nana was an old lady who wore housedresses and those black old lady shoes—you will either know what I mean or you won't.

Apparently Ruth had enough to do with her own 3 children and she also had limited resources. Austin had a drunk for a wife, so they didn't see any other option but for Nana to take care of me. If I had "been there," I'd have had me live with Ruth. Austin had enough money to help with expenses and provide help for Ruth. After all, he had raised his wife Audrey's son and sent him to private military school.

I wish they could have found a way that would have been healthier for both Nana and me. She had only shortly before discovered that she had late-onset diabetes. She gave herself insulin shots and tested her urine daily with little litmus-paper-like things. I remember watching her do it. I am told that Nana had to watch her diet very carefully and that my grandfather Dadum tried to get her to eat properly. That caused a lot of friction between them. There may have been other friction as well, I don't know, but I guess he wasn't being very nice to her at that time, or at least not from her perspective. I can imagine her not being too pleased with having to take care of a little girl on whom her husband doted, when he wasn't being nice to her, and while she was old and tired and sick. It really wasn't fair.

I was a strong-willed child, there's no doubt about that, and I didn't like Nana much. She was the disciplinarian, but she wasn't a "mother." Her care of me was limited to only what was necessary. She didn't have time for a little kid. Nana always washed and cooked and kept a reasonably clean house; I don't remember it ever being dirty. I figured out by about age two that I had to take care of myself and I started to do so.

My mother Laura was back by the time I became aware of myself and my surroundings. I don't remember a time when she wasn't there. I always called her by her first name, Laura, and she not only never objected, she always referred to herself to me that way too. I probably called her Laura because everyone else did.

I was generally okay during the day when my mother was at work, but I always waited for her to come home. In the evenings, Dadum and I would go up to the corner and watch for her to get off the streetcar. The minute I saw her, I'd ask whether she'd "brought me something nice." I slept with Laura in a double bed, from the time I was no longer in a crib. I was on the left; she was on the right. The bedroom where my mother and I slept was called the "front room." The middle bedroom had no name; it was just Nana and Dadum's room.

Laura, on a few occasions, stayed away overnight. I must have been told ahead of time, because on a day when I knew she wouldn't be home that night, I would start right away that morning waiting for her. Even Dadum, whom I loved to distraction, wasn't enough for me when she was gone overnight. I'd wander around in a daze all day, like I was not really there—empty, incomplete. The worst was the night. I cried and cried for her and could not settle down and go to sleep. The problem could possibly have been avoided had I had my own room and been used to sleeping alone, but there was no room available since my mother had her living room furniture in the "back room," the third bedroom in the house.

One time they sent me to Aunt Ruth's to spend the night, perhaps thinking that would work better. Somehow I must have known instinctively that Laura was not at home that night (surely they weren't dumb enough to have told me), because I cried to go home and kept my cousin Janice, who was a teenager, up all night. And I wet her bed. I'd stayed at Aunt Ruth's house other times for several days at a crack and never had a problem with being there other than that one night.

One of the men my mother dated, and most likely spent those nights away from home with, sent me a tricycle when I was around three. It was red and quite the trike. I remember it had to be put together, and when it finally was finished and I climbed on, I could only make it go backwards. It took me a while to figure out how to push those pedals the right way.

I loved to sleep with Dadum (as long as I knew Laura was home) and would often go to sleep with him in his bed. We slept "back to back." After I was asleep someone always carried me back to Laura's bed. I hated that. I probably felt like I was in competition with Nana for Dadum. That may well be part of why I hated her. I remember wetting their bed one night while I was sleeping with Dadum. Nana was in the bed too. I woke up mid-stream and said to her, "This isn't your bed!"

From the time I was very little I remember my mother having her period and bleeding in the bed. I guess it was only fair; I did my fair share of wetting it.

Of course I hated getting sick and throwing up. Fortunately, it didn't happen often and my mother always assured me that, once it had, it wouldn't happen again for a long time. One time she put a bunch of tissues on the floor next to the bed for me to throw up on. It seems to me newspapers or a bucket would've made more sense. When I had a bad cough, she'd give me Terpin-Codeine. It was available without a prescription in those days. I don't know how good it was for me, or if it was meant to be used for children, but it did stop my coughing. Horrid-tasting stuff.

When Laura came home from work, she always had swollen ankles and needed to "put her feet up for 20 minutes." It probably wasn't always exactly twenty minutes, but it was what she'd always say. There were a lot of pat phrases she'd use.

If she hadn't "brought me something nice," I'd bug her to take me down to the Five and Ten after dinner to get me a "ten-cent toy." The store wasn't open most evenings, so she could say no, but sometimes we'd go anyway, just to shut me up. On more than one occasion, when it was closed, I'd stand there looking through the window with longing. Ten cents could buy some real treasures in those days.

Laura had another interesting habit. She would go to bed at night with a cross of adhesive tape on her "frown." My mother always loved adhesive tape and she used it creatively. Holes in the wall got covered with adhesive tape, loose refrigerator doors got taped shut, light fixtures that, left to their own devices, would dangle from walls got taped up. You name it, she'd tape it. Happy the day when Laura discovered duct tape; it opened a whole new world for her.

Laura always wore dresses herself, and she made me wear dresses too. I usually wore Mary Janes, those black patent leather little-girl shoes with straps and buckles. It took me a long time to learn to buckle them. And anklet socks. I hated anklet socks. I was so pleased when bobby sox appeared on the scene. I didn't get to wear long pants until later. When I was maybe four, Aunt Audrey gave me a pair of black corduroy pants and a white long-sleeved blouse with a black ribbon around the neck. I never wore those pants, and probably not the blouse, either. I know Laura didn't want me in pants, but I don't think I was forbidden to wear them. I just didn't. Instead, I cut them up or destroyed them in some fashion; I don't know why. I remember a few years later wishing I hadn't. By that time I would've given anything for a pair of pants, but of course by then, that pair would have been too small.

Laura did dress me in shorts and halter-tops in the summer. She was always bringing clothes home for me, and often tried them on me while I was asleep. I was as much a doll for her to play with as I was her child. I had lots of toys. I was spoiled when I was little, then deprived, although not necessarily by intention, when I was older. Before Dadum died, Laura was largely able to spend her money as she wished.

There was a "Mindy" doll she bought me. Poor Mindy—I cut off all her hair, down to the roots. Bad move, but typical of me at that age. I didn't take good care of things, especially toys, and I wasn't into dolls, anyway.

My mother and I used the "back room" upstairs as a living room and we had a TV in there. There was an old TV of Nana and Dadum's downstairs that didn't work. It had a small screen, maybe 6 or 8 inches, one of the earliest TVs. They didn't throw things away, and they didn't get them fixed, either.

The sofa in the "back room" was on an angle and all my toys were behind it. What a mess it was back there. One time my mother decided to get determined about my "redding up." It was a new experience for me, and I fought it tooth and nail. She didn't give in, however. I cut my finger deeply on some sharp tin thing and thought, Great! Now I won't have to finish redding up. Darned if she didn't put a Band-Aid on my finger and make me finish. That was unusual, though; normally I got my own way in things. I was stubborn and I'd stick to my guns until my mother gave in.

My grandmother would often watch TV with us in the evenings in the "back room." She would sit and bite her fingernails, and so would I. My mother said I got it from her. Maybe, but I was pretty nervous and in need of some sort of comfort.

Despite my willfulness and bravado on the outside, inside I was a scared little girl. I was particularly afraid of dogs. One time, when I was not three yet, my grandmother must've had enough of me, and she locked me out of the house. I cowered on the front porch. It was fairly safe there, and she probably knew I was entirely too terrified to go anywhere. I just peered over the rail and watched for dogs. After a little while, I had to tinkle, so I pounded on the door. Nana was down in the basement doing wash and didn't hear me. I was wearing a dress and panties and my Mary Janes, with the hated anklet socks. I wet them all. Little girls can only hold it for so long, you know. Nana finally showed up and opened the door. She was very angry at me. I don't remember whether she spanked me or not, but she was sure mad. It wasn't my fault she'd locked me out. Maybe she was just mad at herself, but little girls don't know those things.

We lived on the side of a hill. Above the house was the back alley and below it was the front "street," which was basically a wide, graded path, overgrown with grass and weeds and, in the spring, lots of beautiful violets. Below the path it was woods, all the way down the hill. I was always a dreamer, and one of my dreams was that they would pave our street and build houses below, preferably houses where children would live. When I was older, I dreamed of babysitting those children and making some money. Sixty years later, the street remains unpaved.

I remember Nana chasing me around with a yardstick, and she'd also lock me in the basement from time to time. I'd huddle crying in terror on the dark stairs. The basement was big and gloomy with stone foundation walls. It was very scary and I did not like it down there. I got to be very good at outrunning her.

Now, I certainly did things that made her mad. She wasn't abusive for no reason; her intention was to punish me for something I'd done. Years later, in a support group, someone suggested that perhaps Nana had wanted me to be strong and independent; she knew I'd need to be. I'd like to think that it might be true.

Some time before I started school, they had an electrician rewire the house. I remember watching him work at the fuse box in the upstairs hall. He replaced all the old fabric wiring with new fabric wiring that was still in the house when it burned in 1989 or so. I've always loved watching people work on things, especially house-related things.

We went to Atlantic City every summer when I was little. We ate at a place called Pancoast's that served pancakes. I was a bit confused by that. One evening in Atlantic City, my mother had me all dressed up in my pretty dress and Mary Janes, and of course the anklet socks. I think we were supposed to meet someone. We left the hotel and started walking along the boardwalk. I had to tinkle. I told my mother that I wanted to see something in the sand—the beach was down some ten or so steps from the boardwalk. She let me go down there alone; I can't imagine why, but she did. I went down and squatted and did the deed. It would've been sensible to pull down my panties first, but I didn't think of that, so I wet all over myself.

Laura had to take me back to the hotel and redo me. I think we may have just stayed there, because I have no idea where we'd been headed in the first place, or where we went if we did go back out. Perhaps we were to meet one of her boyfriends. I never did meet any of them.

The thing is, though, even though Laura had much more reason to be mad at me for wetting my pants that night, she wasn't nearly as mad as Nana had been when she'd locked me out. At least I don't remember Laura being mad at me, only upset at having to go back to the hotel. Perhaps it was all in my perception.

Laura had a two-piece red bathing suit, and I had a little yellow checked two-piece suit. It was the only time in my life I ever wore a bikini. My mother mostly (as she said) "never let go of my hand for one instant" in those days, and it was a good thing, because the beach was big and crowded. One time we saw an ice cream vendor nearby. My mother always had a passion for ice cream, so we headed over to get some. Imagine my dismay when she asked the man for two sandwiches! I was delighted to discover that there was such a thing as ice cream sandwiches, and they became a life-long favorite of mine.

Laura was never much like a mother, more like an older sister or big playmate. Nana was the authority figure. Laura took me to the amusement park, to various playgrounds, and to the zoo. We went to the car wash and we went shopping downtown. She was slim and pretty when I was little, and fun to be with. I remember hating having to wait while she tried on clothes, but if I behaved, we'd go to the toy department. At Christmas and at Easter, there was even a little train for kids to ride, right inside the department store.

There were several playgrounds around. One was where they shot off the fireworks on the Fourth of July every year, although we always watched the fireworks from the top of a neighbor's garage a ways up the alley. The whole neighborhood gathered there. Because we were so far away up the hill, we could never see the ground displays through the trees.

The first time we went to the amusement park, Laura took me on the Whip, which was a series of cars that went straight and then "whipped" around to go the other way. I screamed and screamed for them to stop and let me off. They didn't. The corners took my breath away.

When I was not much older, she took me on the big roller coaster. It started out by spiraling down through a dark tunnel, which was where the majority of local girls received their first kisses. Then there was the slow, torturous, ratchety climb to the top of the first hill. It seemed to take forever, and even paused at the top, but then suddenly you'd be screaming down that first killer hill (arms up in the air if you were brave) and back up the second with barely enough time to catch your breath. Several slightly smaller hills followed at increasing speed leading to the U-turn from hell that made you feel as though you'd be thrown from the car and into the next century.

The trick was to stay on for a second ride—sort of like falling off a horse and getting right back on. Then you were hooked. My mother had enough sense to stay on with me the second time, and I seldom rode anything else at that park from that day on. I cried when I found out that the park had been torn down.

Another place we frequented was the observation deck at the airport. My mother liked to go watch the planes take off and land. Her husband Bill had been an air traffic controller at a smaller airport when they were married, and she always had an interest in airplanes and flying. The airport was a fascinating place and I liked it too.

On Thanksgiving and Christmas, dinner was usually at Aunt Ruth's. She had what seemed to me to be a huge dining room and she had heavy glass water goblets with raised and painted fruit on them. I loved those glasses, but seldom got to use one since she only had eight and so only the adults got them. We kids usually sat at a card table, anyway. I suppose it's a good bet she didn't want those glasses broken. She also had a Copley ceramic rooster and chicken that were always on display either on the table or on the buffet. I have them now, and they are a treasured memento of the happier and more normal part of my childhood. The water goblets are still in the family, but the color has mostly been washed off over the years.

A favorite family Thanksgiving memory is about Uncle John never failing to wander into the kitchen just about the time all the food had been put away and all the dishes had been washed and saying, "Hey, Ruthie, do you have anything to make a sandwich?" My mother, of course, was famous for wandering in right behind Uncle John and asking if there was anything she could do to help.

I wasn't there for the best Uncle John story, but it is an oft-repeated family classic. My cousin Janice and her fiancé Raphael were at Aunt Ruth's for dinner. Uncle John always said grace and it went, "Heavenly Father, bless this food, to Thy glory, and our good." This time, though, just as he was about to start, Aunt Ruth realized that she'd forgotten to put napkins on the table and distracted him by saying so. Uncle John began his prayer with "Heavenly napkins . . ."

Occasionally we'd go to Austin and Audrey's on the holidays. Audrey was actually a great cook, but she tended to put the bird in the oven, make frequent visits to the basement for a nip of hidden booze, and being quite tipsy by dinnertime, she'd disappear upstairs, seldom reappearing to eat with us. I don't ever remember Aunt Ruth and her family being at Austin's for dinner, but he and Audrey would come to Ruth's sometimes. Audrey never liked us much, but she wasn't unkind to me when I was there for a week or so in the summer, and I didn't tend to misbehave there.

I was sometimes "punished" in subtle ways for just being a dumb little kid who didn't know from what. In those days people had those metal porch chairs with the rounded front legs that, when you tried to climb up, would tip you over. One day, a little neighbor boy I played with named Scottie fell while trying to climb onto one of those chairs. I don't remember whether he fell in a comical way or I was just nervous, but I laughed. Just a spontaneous giggle, something a little girl who didn't know better and who was not yet socially adept would do. He wasn't hurt at all and took it in stride and went right on playing. A little while later, I did the same thing and fell off the chair too, but I did get hurt, just a skinned knee or elbow, but it hurt and I cried. Scottie's mother told Scottie to laugh at me. But he was a bigger person than she was, even at three, because he wouldn't laugh. I guess he, being a little kid too, understood that I hadn't laughed because he fell, but just because.

One day when I was at Scottie's house playing, his mother called me by a name I'd never heard before. I'd always assumed that my last name was the same as my grandparents' name. It was the first time I'd ever heard my real last name, which was that of my mother's husband. It was a horrid name, and one that I hated and struggled with until I finally got married years later. Although I was really little then, only three or so, that may have been my first experience of feeling like I didn't fit in. I don't know that it was a conscious feeling, but I do remember vaguely thinking something to the effect that I was not who I thought I was, that I wasn't part of my own family.

I was tough and I was tender. It is not my natural tendency to be tough; it's something I instinctively became in order to survive. Inside, I was terrified half the time. All the time. I made foolish little mistakes, those things a child does and with luck learns from, but I was punished on an entirely different level, one that related to things the adults around me knew about me that I didn't know. I must have been seen as an "alley cat" or a bastard because I was dealt with as though I was. Since I didn't know what was going on, I took on these things the only way I could, believing that I must be bad. There is always an underlying woundedness in those who portray themselves as tough. I am no exception.

When I was three or four, my mother came home one day in a drab green 1949 Ford. Prior to that, the only car I'd ever ridden in was my grandfather's old black Ford. His was from the time before cars began to have the more modern and varied shapes and colors. I refused to ride in my mother's car for a long time. I'm not sure why exactly. Who knows what goes on in the mind of a three-year-old? I loved my mother and trusted her in those days, so it must have been the car itself that scared me.

Nana would listen to the Arthur Godfrey Show on the radio in the morning. It was basically a talk show, and I didn't pay a lot of attention except when Julius LaRosa would sing. I liked Julius. I wonder, though, if there wasn't some way in which I was trying to find a common ground, any common ground, with my grandmother Nana, who really liked him.

Nana was always cooking or cleaning or washing, never relating to me in any way other than the essentials, never anything personal except to let me know, directly or indirectly, that I was in her way and she had more important things to do than to be with me. I don't remember her ever touching me or hugging me or playing with me. It's hard for me to hear various family members telling me how much Nana loved me. I hear it, but I don't know if I'll ever be able to believe it. I can still hear Aunt Ruth saying, "But Crissie, she had so much to do and take care of." Yes.

Dadum must not have had so much to do. I remember him cutting the grass with a push-type mower—no motor, just rotating blades. He was also a crossing guard up at the corner, before and after school and at lunchtime. I remember going to the A&P with him regularly, so he must have done the grocery shopping. He always bought 8 O'clock coffee. I remember the red package, which was still the same until a few years ago. I recently rediscovered 8 O'clock coffee myself and it's become my favorite (and it looks like they've gone back to the red package, too).

Once Nana had taken care of my basic needs, I was with Dadum if he was at home. He didn't play with me either, but he involved me in what he was doing. We took naps, snuggled together on the glider on the back porch when the weather was nice. I recently found an old glider from the 50's, had it restored, put it on my porch, and I enjoy it in my Dadum's memory.

My mother did play with me sometimes. And she read to me. Friends of hers, coincidentally named Stevenson (the husband's name was even Bob), sent me a book called "A Child's Garden of Verses," which was written by the real Robert Lewis Stevenson. I remember thinking I "knew" a famous author. I didn't much like the poetry, though.

Mrs. Stevenson made her own Christmas cards. They were always the best Christmas cards we'd get, and I looked forward to them every year. The Stevensons had been friends of Laura's and Bill's when they were still together, and both couples had bought wooded property in a lovely rural area. The Stevensons built and lived on theirs, but my mother's lot remained vacant for years until it was finally sold when I was in junior high. My mother was never very responsible with money. She talked about paying off all her debts when the property sold. Of course when she got her share of the money, she spent it all and didn't pay the debts. We drove out to see the lot on at least one occasion, and I vaguely remember meeting the Stevensons and seeing their house. Seems to me there was a stream running behind their yard.

I also had a book of fairy tales that had a story I liked called "Snow White and Rose Red." I hated the wicked stepmother and stepsisters in "Cinderella." "Sleeping Beauty" annoyed me. It was as if I had to wait all that time till she woke up, even though it was probably all of five minutes reading time. I've never been good at waiting. When I read the book HAWAII as an adult, I skipped the first part about all the millions of years and false starts it took to form the islands.

Laura took me to see movies. I remember seeing "Bambi" and "Lady and the Tramp," and loving them both. I had some records we played on my mother's record player. It had a changer, but it only played 45 rpm records. She had a stack she listened to sometimes. The children's records I remember were "The Big Rock Candy Mountain" and "The Chisholm Trail."

I loved watching television; my favorite was "Lassie." It aired on Sunday nights, and one time I was out playing and forgot about it, then ran inside hoping it was still on. It wasn't. I sure could have used a DVR in those days.

Despite my grandfather's being there, we were a household of females. One time I walked into the bathroom while my grandfather was sitting on the toilet. I had some vague understanding that boys had plumbing other than what I had, but I just thought that Dadum "didn't have one," and that was okay with me in some way. Years later, when I married X1 and he sat down on the toilet, that image of Dadum came back to me. It wasn't until then that I figured out that of course men have to sit sometimes too.

In a lot of ways I wished I were a boy, although looking back now, I see that had I been a boy, it would have been a disaster. But I loved to play with cars and trucks and dirt, certainly more so than with dolls. I had stuffed animals, too; I can't remember any in particular that I was especially attached to, but they were important to me, and probably a source of comfort. I love stuffed animals even now as an adult. I have to be very careful about picking one up in a store. Once I pick it up, I feel bad if I don't buy it, like I'm rejecting it. I've been heard to apologize to a stuffed animal I didn't buy or, worse, I've just bought it.

I feel sorry for live Christmas trees, too, silly as that sounds. I read a story one time about a little tree that was bought and decorated and then, when the time came, was, logically, discarded. I never pass a tree set out at the curb after the holiday is over without a bit of sadness. I feel even sorrier for trees that are still in the lot on Christmas day, those that didn't get chosen. Apparently I identify with that somehow. When X2 would see a little girl somewhere pouting, he'd say, "She looks like someone ordered her and forgot to pick her up." That's exactly how I often felt as a child.

One time my mother tried very hard to build me some roads out of cement (concrete is the correct word, but she called it cement), on the hill beside the garage. She used a trowel. The roads didn't last; they broke up pretty quickly, but it was a noble effort all the same. I have always had a need for things to be complete or right or something, and I needed those roads for my cars and trucks. I probably drove her crazy until she did it.

On weekend mornings I would work on getting my mother out of bed. Apparently I was her responsibility on those days. My grandmother could then have a much-needed break from the joys and perils of raising me. Unfortunately, my mother, working full time, had only the weekends to sleep in, and so we were somewhat at cross-purposes in this. Finally, after much cajoling on my part, she would agree to get up if I would agree to eat breakfast, including eggs. I hated eggs, but I ate a lot of them just to get her out of bed. I didn't want breakfast; I just wanted someone to play with. I was looking for emotional nourishment, but got food instead. Later on, I came to love eggs and hate my mother.

When I was a little older, I ate eggs at my friend Ginger's house, and she showed me how to eat the white first and then the yellow. This worked well, since I'd never liked the white after it had been "contaminated" with the yellow. I've always been a purist when it comes to food—I don't like a lot of combinations of things. I always ate all my meat first, then my potatoes, and then as little of the vegetables I could get away with. Of course, by the time I got to them, they were cold. Someone finally suggested that I eat my vegetables first, when they were still hot, and I learned to like them that way. Now I always eat my vegetables first, but I still work on one thing at a time. Uncle Austin often reprimanded me for this, saying it wasn't polite.

I never liked nuts, especially in fudge or brownies or ice cream. My mother loved them, particularly Jordan almonds and filberts. I may have a bit of an allergy to almonds, or at least they don't agree with me in most cases. One time Aunt Audrey gave me a big bowl of what I thought was vanilla ice cream, but was in fact full of maraschino cherries. I couldn't eat it and was very disappointed. I later learned that maraschino cherries get that way from almond extract. They sell something called *"gebrante Mandeln"* in Germany, and you can sometimes find them at carnivals in this country. They're almonds toasted with cinnamon in a big stir-fry-like vat that gives them a candy coating. I love them and I don't get sick on them. Go figure.

A favorite food was "sticky buns," which were cinnamon rolls with a sticky, gooey brown honey coating. They had a few nuts, probably walnuts, stuck on the top, but those could easily be picked off.

The thing to me has always been texture. I mean, here I am happily munching away on a nice, smooth gooey chewy brownie or a piece of fudge, and all of a sudden there's a nut to contend with. I deal with nuts every day of my life—I don't need them in my brownies.

When I see a plate of brownies on someone's table, I always ask whether they have nuts in them and, if they do, I walk away. I'm actually grateful because, given that same plate of brownies without nuts, I'd eat the whole plateful. I don't need the calories.

It's easy enough to walk away from brownies, but not so easy when it comes to human nuts, especially when one of them is your mother. As nice and as sweet and even as fun as Laura could be, she was still a nut. The thing about nuts is that you have to stop what you're doing and deal with them. I had no resources to know how to do that, and I didn't have the memories of her that the rest of my family had. There was nowhere to run. The only way to get away from her was in my head.

Not having my need for emotional nourishment satisfied, yet being given food instead, might have become a serious problem, but for some reason, that's one set of dots I fortunately never connected.

Much as I love food, it's never been what I reach for in times of need. Perhaps, even at that tender age, I somehow knew that it didn't do the trick. There were other things I turned to later on, but as a little kid, I mostly just lived inside my emptiness.

But there were good things too. My family spoke English correctly and I am grateful for that heritage. It actually hurts my ears to hear people say things like "Her and I did this or that . . ." or "It was hard on my wife and I." I have intelligent, masters degreed friends who say things like this all the time. Uncle Austin would have said to them, "You speak very well English yet, haven't you?" That was his best line. I was not allowed to use ain't, and I was corrected when I said, "What?" It was "Pardon me"—or else.

My family is musical as well and, although none of us has a strong singing voice, we can all carry a tune, and have some ability to play by ear. My grandmother and my Aunt Ruth both were good at it. By the time I came along, though, there was no longer a piano in the house. I never heard my grandmother play, but Ruth could play anything you asked for, as long as she could play it in the key of C.

Aunt Audrey was a piece of work. She and Uncle Austin lived in the attic at our house for a month or so one summer. They had a large white standard poodle named Dixie. Dixie was the closest I ever came to having a dog as a kid. I loved that stupid dog and was so proud to take her for walks around the neighborhood.

They also had a 1953 or so Ford convertible. The top retracted into the trunk, which I found fascinating at the time, compared to the standard ragtop convertibles most people had. I remember Aunt Audrey taking me for a ride in that car. We went to a liquor store in the next town, and it was "our secret." I wasn't supposed to tell my uncle, and I never did until years later, after she'd died. I was close to Austin and I don't think Audrey was pleased about his feelings for me.

Another time, we were all out in the side yard, having some sort of family party or barbecue. It was dark out. Audrey announced in my hearing that she had to "tweedle." She headed for the front porch steps, ostensibly to go up to the bathroom, but she wasn't gone long enough to have made it all the way up to the second floor and back, so I was convinced that she had just done her thing in the dirt by the steps. The next morning I looked for a wet spot, but of course it had dried up by then, if it had ever been there.

After Austin and Audrey moved to their own place, I would visit them for a week or so in the summer and reconnect with Dixie. One time Audrey was drunk and we walked into town, which was only a few blocks away, and did some shopping. On the way home, she "had to sit down" and did so, right on someone's front lawn. I didn't know what to do and was a child's equivalent of embarrassed, although what I really wanted was for her to get up and take care of me because I certainly didn't know how to take care of her.

Audrey had a neighbor who liked me and took me downtown one day, just for fun. I was maybe six or seven. We ate breakfast and I had a sweet roll that had some sort of jellied fruit in it like you find in fruitcake. Apparently I didn't chew it well enough, or it didn't agree with me, because I started feeling really sick shortly after I ate it, and really weak. The lady took me to an infirmary in the department store. The nurse had me lie on a table and she stuck what I now know was smelling salts under my nose. I didn't know then what it was, and probably as a result of too much television, I thought it was meant to put me to sleep. Of course it was exactly the opposite, but I remembered that experience just as I was being put under when Larry was about to be born. After they decided I was feeling better, we got back in the car and headed home. I made it all the way to Audrey's kitchen and then threw up in her sink. She was not amused.

We lived most of the way up a hill and going "upstreet" meant continuing up and over the hill to a small shopping area. There was a grocery store, a drug store, a hardware store, a Chrysler dealer, and what everyone called the Jews' store. I don't know why, other than apparently someone knew they were Jewish, and I suppose that was something of a novelty as there were no other Jews living in our part of town. I never knew their name. They sold candy, ice cream, and baseball cards, things like that. I remember thinking, in the goofy way kids think, that stores sold goods for less than they paid for them. I eventually reasoned it out that that just didn't make sense.

When I was still real little, I was terrified of what I called "smoke trucks." They were big semis that belched black smoke as they struggled up the hill. The Interstate hadn't yet been built, and the road we took to get "upstreet" was the main route from the city to the west. My mother and I would walk "upstreet" in the evenings, and whenever I saw a "smoke truck" coming, I would run back or ahead to the closest side street and then run up it as far as I could. Being next to Laura, even having her holding my hand, was not enough. I had to get away. She couldn't hold on to me, so great was my terror. The worst part was when we first started out—we had to go about a block up the hill and I couldn't see the trucks coming up the other side. Once we'd gotten to the top of the hill, I could see them and had plenty of time to run because they couldn't get up the hill to where I was as fast as I could run away.

"Downstreet" meant going down the hill to the main town, where everyone shopped before the shopping center was built. The A&P where I went with my grandfather was there, the five-and-ten, another drug store, the movie theater, the post office, and a dairy store with a deli, where we got chipped ham. My mother always made my chipped ham sandwiches with Miracle Whip. Hellman's tasted much better to me, something I discovered at Aunt Ruth's. Once in a while someone would make "barbecues" out of chipped ham and ketchup, heated and served on hamburger buns. Awful things, but very popular with a lot of people. Certainly a cheap meal.

Many of the streets were and still are brick, or cobblestone, and sounded funny under the tires. It's a sound that always reminds me of Dadum and his old, black Ford.

There were over a hundred steps to the bottom of our hill, and a long grade down another street, none of which was bad going down, but coming back up was a killer. The steps were made out of concrete, and there were six to ten steps and then a landing, with metal handrails all along one side. I walked down and then back up those steps twice a day from kindergarten through seventh grade and most of eighth. There were other ways to go, but they were only paths through the woods, and were steep and muddy.

Alongside the steps was a sort of path, worn by us kids walking up beside the steps rather than climbing them, or running down when we were late for school. In the winter, we'd all sort of "shoe-ski" down that path, turning it into solid ice. I'd actually dream of skiing down that path beside the steps. I could "see" myself, bending my knees, leaning forward and flying straight down that hill, although I will admit I'm not sure how I dreamed of stopping at the bottom! But I never had a chance to actually go skiing when I was young enough to feel safe and comfortable doing it.

There was nothing more beautiful than walking down the steps through the woods right after a new snow. The trees would be "frosted" with ice.

"In town" was the city itself. Before they built the new bridge and started having only buses, we rode on the streetcar. It ran for several miles on its own right of way next to the road. There was a very long gentle grade that was a delight. That streetcar would rock and shimmy and rattle and clickety-clack all the way down that grade. I've never heard or felt anything quite like it since. Several years ago, I found a model of that very trolley, and had it motorized. One of these days, I will put it on some track on a shelf around the top of my office.

I was often mixed up about things, in the way kids are. My grandparents went to church, and they took me to Sunday school. My mother never went—something about not having the "right" clothes. The minister's name was Reverend Tiechert, and he would visit us at the house from time to time, sometimes bringing his wife along. I remember being told that Reverend Tiechert was coming over, but I thought they were saying Rubber and Tissue, so I figured that he must be "Rubber" and his wife "Tissue."

When I was three, I had a nice Easter coat and bonnet. Aunt Ruth told me years later that Uncle John had insisted I have a new hat and coat for Easter that year, while his own children didn't. I never felt especially close to Uncle John; he breathed a bit noisily and was a big man. I think he may have swung me up in the air when I was real little, so perhaps that's why I was always a bit afraid of him. He often brought work home from the office and wasn't very involved with me when I visited them. He loved me a lot, though, and long after he'd died, Aunt Ruth told me a story about him that makes me wish I'd known him better. I'll tell you about it later, in context.

Naturally I loved Christmas as a kid. I couldn't wait to put the cheap cellophane wreathes on the windows and get a tree. I don't remember ever being taken to pick out the tree; Dadum would just bring one home one day, always a short-needled pine. I remember the thin glass old-fashioned ornaments we had, and the large, multi-colored lights.

One Christmas someone gave us some ribbon candy. I loved it, but my mother was afraid I'd choke on it, so she hid it. It was typical of her to hide something, rather than just throwing it away. One of the side doors on the buffet was missing a handle, and she put the candy in there. I found it a year or two later, and ate it all, bit by bit. It must've been pretty stale, but it tasted good to me. I don't remember what else was inside that door, but I was the only one who ever opened it.

There were several places in the house where no one ever looked, and I used that knowledge for my own purposes. The broken buffet door was conveniently located right next to my chair. That buffet was very well fed with vegetables and the hated lettuce and tomato my mother was so fond of serving. Laura would go to the kitchen to get something she'd forgotten, and my vegetables would mysteriously disappear in her absence. She never caught on.

Catharsis

In my early fifties, I had a minor surgical procedure that was done on an outpatient basis. I came home with a catheter, which was to be removed by a visiting nurse the next day. Well! There I was with this thing attached. It hung about eight inches down the front of me and had a bag with a valve for emptying.

When I was little, my Uncle Jim, Aunt Becky, and cousin Johnny would come to visit for a week or so every summer. They lived in North Carolina, and they could sure talk funny. My cousin Johnny, only a year older than I, was as close to a brother as I ever had and I looked forward to his arrival like crazy. It was great. He knew no one else, so he had to play with me.

Every year, on the day he was to arrive, I'd be up early, and I'd sit on a log watching for their car. Of course they never showed up until late that night, after I was long asleep. Still, it was as good as Christmas the next morning when I'd wake up and he'd be there.

We'd play in the woods every day. One time we were playing by a stream and disturbed a hidden wasps' nest. Those little buggers were translucent and huge; I've never seen anything like them since. I got stung three times while cousin Johnny somehow managed not to get stung at all. I've still not forgiven him for that.

I was fascinated (and not just a little jealous) that he could "go" right there in the woods, whereas I'd have to go home to use the bathroom. I wanted that boy plumbing, so I took an empty toilet paper roll, stood in front of the toilet, held it in front of myself and peed on my shoes. My grandmother looked in and asked what I was doing. I told her I was trying to "go" like a boy. I don't remember her being particularly angry; I certainly hope she went off and laughed herself silly.

Now fast forward—there I was many years later with that catheter. Ah! It needed emptying with some regularity. I'd lift the seat, stand in front of the toilet and open the valve. The sound effects were just right. Then I'd close the valve, shake and be done.

The best part was that, since I'd be back in an hour to do it all over again, I got to leave the toilet seat up!

POET

Crissy Shreve

I am a poet, but life has never been a rhyme.
Thoughts, sounds emitted,
Falling onto deafened ears.
Love spoken to the pillow,
In my dreams.

And now, just when things begin to rhyme,
And all is so beautiful that I glow with feeling,
Must I say goodbye to dreams?

Chapter Three

Into The World

I was sent to Kindergarten when I was only four; I didn't turn five until the middle of the year. I suppose they sent me so early to give my grandmother a break. I wonder whether giving me a break ever entered anyone's mind. I was a difficult child, no doubt about it. It is also true that I *was* a child. I was not yet utterly incorrigible; there was simply nobody capable of effectively parenting me.

I learned a lot of my early history from my Aunt Ruth. She pointed out that I had been a "bratty little kid." As an adult, I came to understand the term "shaming." It seems to me that Ruth was a master at shaming, even though she loved me and always treated me as one of her own kids. I loved her dearly too, but I realize that she probably would not have been able to handle me either. She loved me in ways I could recognize, though, and probably would have gotten more involved with me than Nana did. Both her daughters turned out pretty well, but they are both much milder than I am temperamentally, and better suited to have been raised by her.

The thing about little kids who are harder to handle than others is that often they are the future creative minds and movers of the world, and when properly understood and cared for, they can make a significant impact. Conversely, when misunderstood and neglected, they are likely to misdirect their creativity as they get older. They miss out and the world misses out.

I was regularly and consistently shamed as a kid. I suppose all kids are. And I suppose all kids take it to heart in one way or another. I never actually felt ashamed of myself, though. Most of the time I couldn't figure out what was the big deal. On the outside, I just stayed that bratty little kid. Shame is a pervasive thing, though. Deep inside,

I did feel the shame and presented an even harder exterior to those around me.

My mother was overly protective in some neurotic and paranoid ways, but was basically pretty much permissive in regard to any guidance or discipline I actually needed. She'd just say, "Have it my way," and then let *me* have *my* way. That still doesn't make any sense.

My mother drove me to kindergarten the first day. I screamed the whole time, even though she stayed in the hall and I knew she was there. It was all very new and strange. I wasn't ready for it, socially, intellectually, or emotionally. My life would have been entirely different had I started a year later. There was only one kid younger than I. Everyone else was older and more sophisticated—well, if you can call kindergarteners sophisticated. I never quite fit in with my classmates, then or in the years to follow.

Then there was the issue of getting me to and from school. My mother arranged for two junior high school girls to pick me up in the morning and bring me back home at lunchtime. I've mentioned the long steps down the hill. Every morning they would each take me by one hand and they would run down those steps. My little legs couldn't keep up, so in effect they dragged me down the steps and then on through the muddy vacant lot at the bottom, which was a shortcut we all used. I don't know why my mother never noticed my scraped and dirty knees. It took me a long time to finally tell her I could find my own way to school and didn't need them anymore, which was actually true after the first day. I've always been good at finding my way around. I didn't tell her that they had been terrorizing me until years later. My instincts were working even then. I feared that she wouldn't believe me, or worse, that she'd do something that would cause them to retaliate. I don't remember whether they threatened me not to tell. They probably did.

There were kids who were driven to school. It wasn't standard procedure, though; we kids walked to school and that was that. I suppose it never crossed anyone's mind to drive me, and I suppose it wasn't possible. Nana didn't drive, my mother was on her way to work, and Dadum was on duty as a crossing guard.

Things were generally safer then, despite my mother's warnings. She never uttered the phrase, "Don't talk to strangers," although that was taught at school. No, my mother told me to watch out for "the

33

goofs" who might be copulating in the woods by the steps. When I was acting up, she'd ask me, "Did somebody slip you a Mickey?" I don't remember what behavior of mine led her to say this to me because I'd always be too busy trying to figure out what a Mickey was[6]. "Types" was another multi-purpose derogatory word my mother used a lot. I learned pretty quickly to listen to her with one ear and then go figure things out for myself.

I had red rubber boots for the winter. Dadum tried to teach me left and right by marking an "L" on the left boot and an "R" on the right. That didn't help because he didn't put "L" and "R" on my feet. (One of X2's favorite phrases was, "Right is where the thumb is on the left." He and my grandfather would have gotten along well.) At some point I finally figured out left and right by standing on the front porch and knowing which way was left and which was right. To this day, I still envision myself on that porch when I need to determine left or right, although it's now more subconscious.

I don't remember much about my kindergarten teacher, except that she was a fairly young woman compared to my other teachers. For the most part, my elementary school teachers were late middle-aged spinsters. The only thing I remember about kindergarten was the picture books.

I don't think I was terribly interested in school, even at that point. I'd already begun my life-long tendency to figure things out for myself. There are people who read about how to do things and there are people like me, who figure it out on our own. I've never been one to read instructions. That didn't always serve me well, especially when trying, for instance, to assemble a kite. My kites never flew because I never attached the line properly.

Sometime during the spring while I was in kindergarten, my mother took me to look for the house where Eddie, my "boyfriend," lived. We walked past his house, and he and I saw each other, but for some reason my mother wouldn't stop. I remember him telling me at school the next day that he'd run in to get his shoes on and when he

---

[6] A Mickey Finn, (or simply a Mickey) is a slang term for a drink laced with a drug (especially chloral hydrate) given to someone without his knowledge in order to incapacitate him. Serving someone a Mickey is most commonly referred to as slipping a Mickey. Wikipedia.

came back out I was gone. Eddie went to the parochial school after that and I didn't run into him again until high school.

My mother came and picked me up the last day of kindergarten. She was on vacation from work and we were all going to leave right away for Atlantic City. It was such a treat to have her pick me up. She was still slim and pretty then and I was very proud of her. I remember asking her if she would take me to school on the first day the next year, but she said I wouldn't need her to do that when I went to first grade.

I got another bee sting on the way home from school when I was in kindergarten or first grade. I don't know why I put my hand where the bee was; surely I wasn't trying to catch it, was I? It was a yellow jacket and it nailed me. Another time there was an ice storm while I was in school. The sidewalks were solid ice and I was so afraid of falling that I crawled all the way home.

I went to Kindergarten in the morning, but there was an afternoon session as well. Dadum told me about the "little afternoon girls" he helped across the street. I met them in first grade. They lived next door to one another. Their mothers stayed home and cooked and sewed. They always had pretty dresses and curly hair. They rode the streetcar home at lunchtime and after school. Kids who rode the streetcar were dismissed about five minutes earlier than the rest of us. Whenever I had a dime, I would ride it too, but that wasn't very often.

One time one of my friends had two nickels, and we took advantage of the crowd of kids getting on at the same time. Instead of dimes, she and I each threw in a nickel. It was my first time stealing on any level. I'd probably done my share of snitching whatever there was to snitch at home, but this was the big time. I was cool though. I nonchalantly dropped my nickel in the box and proceeded back to find a seat. Shaking in my boots. The conductor, which is what the streetcar driver was called, knew something was wrong, but he didn't know who the culprits were. He said something to someone, which caused my guilty self to start back towards the front of the car, but I realized in time that he wasn't especially looking for me, so I sat down and got away with it. My insides were churning; it was pretty scary. I had no idea what they'd do to me if I got caught.

There were three elementary schools in our town, and later we all converged into the one that also had seventh and eighth grade.

My elementary school was a two-story brick box with a huge wooden central staircase in the middle. There were cloakrooms where we put our coats and boots. I was always made to wear leggings in the winter, which were thick, padded overalls-type things. They were part of my snowsuit and actually did a pretty good job of keeping my legs warm, but I always had to take off my shoes to get in and out of them, and they were a "real pain in the neck," which is another of the phrases of my childhood, often applied to me.

Our music teacher was Scandinavian, and she talked funny. She called her car a machine and pronounced "again" to rhyme with "a pain." That may not be all that weird, but it was to us, since no one we knew ever said it that way. She made us sing the notes of songs using do-re-mi, which was very confusing because the do-re-mi would change every time we had a song that was written in a different key.

In first grade, I'd get terribly bored and sleepy in the afternoons, and not being able to tell time yet, I never knew how long it would be until it was time to go home. We had those good old Dick, Jane, and Sally readers. My mother hated phonics for some reason, and was very glad we were taught to read by rote. I think Sesame Street would've been a big help. But I did somehow learn to read.

Mostly the problem was that things were not taught in such a way as to get my attention, so I wasn't all "there" much of the time. This is one of the reasons I love the comic strip "Calvin & Hobbes" so much. I can so relate to Calvin's daydreaming in school.

The early boredom I experienced stayed with me for all my school years and for the most part, I would've rather been somewhere else, *anywhere* else. I never felt a connection with any of my teachers. I was unremarkable, just sort of there by default. I remember the boy who was always the smartest kid in our class, and another who was a talented artist, even in first grade. I didn't figure out until some time in my 50's that I have a learning disability. I don't retain what I read. I could remember things I heard, though, so whatever passing grades I managed to get must have been from what my teachers said.

I remember being terrified of having to read out loud or recite anything. I definitely did not want to stand up and get noticed, so perhaps there was some defense mechanism in place and perhaps it was just as well. It may also be that the teachers were sensitive to my timidity and didn't force me into the spotlight all that often. I was able to read when called on—not perfectly, but passably.

Occasionally my first grade teacher would have me take a note to the second grade teacher across the hall. One time she gave me a note to take home to my mother, but I didn't hear her right and I took it to the other teacher who was, of course, totally confused. For some reason, I also had a really hard time when I had to take something home, get it signed by my mother, and then return it. I think the problem was mostly getting my mother to cooperate. One time it took so long that I finally told the teacher that I'd lost whatever it was. She gave me a new one, and I managed to get it signed and back to her the next day.

There was a kid named Gordon in first grade with me. He and I sat on the merry-go-round together one day saying self-deprecating things to the effect that we were just losers. I have no idea what that was about. I don't ever remember saying that kind of thing out loud at any other time or to anyone else. I mostly kept my feelings inside, but it was because I never had anyone else to tell, or maybe no one else who ever admitted to feeling inferior. But I sure did.

My mother, on the other hand, had delusions of grandeur, however unfounded they were. One of her favorite phrases was, "Someday when we're rich," followed by, "we'll have clean sheets on the bed every night," or something similar. I loved clean sheets, but I don't know how she thought we were supposed to get rich. She had a strong sense of her own superiority, and that of our family. She was always surprised when the world didn't seem to see it. Laura insisted that we had royal blood, but she had absolutely nothing on which to base that belief. I got into genealogy years later, and it turns out that we actually are very distantly related to the British royal family and, as such, their illustrious ancestry, but I didn't make that discovery until after she'd died. She'd have been so pleased. But it still wouldn't have made us rich.

Unfortunately, her sense of superiority took the form of hatred and prejudice. I am told that she got it from her father, my Dadum. I never saw that side of him, but I was barely seven when he died. Laura hated everyone who wasn't just like us, and she had ugly derogatory words for them.

Robert Frost speaks eloquently of hate in this most beloved of his poems:

FIRE AND ICE

Some say the world will end in fire,
Some say in ice.
From what I've tasted of desire
I hold with those who favor fire.
But if it had to perish twice,
I think I know enough of hate
To know that for destruction ice
Is also great
And would suffice.

Robert Frost (1874-1963)
(*Harper's Magazine*, December 1920)
(Public Domain)

I abhor the N-word and won't even use it to quote her, but it was my mother's favorite word, and I heard it every single day. When we were on the streetcar, and we'd go through a black neighborhood, my mother would cover my eyes with her hand. She covered my eyes another time, too. Apparently there was an arm lying in the street. Laura made sure I didn't see it, but she told me about it after we were past it, as a "warning" not to stick my arm out the window of a moving vehicle. I was so mad at her for not letting me see it!

One time years later, Laura actually said to me that the reason she no longer went to Atlantic City was that the (N-words) had turned the sand black. That all-time most ludicrous of statements well defines my mother and her illness. The reason she didn't go to Atlantic City was that she couldn't afford to go, but she couldn't admit that, not to anyone else and certainly not to herself. I'm pretty sure she actually believed her own delusions.

Another time, after an elevator had fallen in a downtown office building, my mother's comment was, "Wouldn't you just know it, I saw a (N-word) standing by that elevator just yesterday."

Then there were the Hunkies, the Kikes, the Italians, the Germans, the Japs, and the Micks. She even hated southerners. Democrats, too, but I don't remember her saying derogatory things about them until Kennedy was elected. Hunkies were anyone with a Slavic background. Many of them lived in a town called Homestead and worked in the mills there. She was always railing about Homestead Hunkies and, one time when I was eight or nine, and really mad at her, I called her a Homestead Hunkie, thinking it was the worst insult I could hurl her way. Apparently it wasn't; she didn't react to it at all.

The one thing I got from all my mother's prejudices was a dislike of labeling people and then blindly assuming their traits to be true of everyone within their racial, religious, or ethnic makeup. Some things are, of course, but they're not necessarily bad things. And things change. Sixty-some years later, the prejudices of my mother's generation have become irrelevant. There've been new wars, 9-11, racial barriers have been broken, the wall came down, and technology has shrunk the planet.

Audrey's son Bobby met a German girl when he was in the service, and married her. My mother, of course, despised Helen. I spent some time with Helen when I was staying with Austin and Audrey, and she was just fine, although it turned out that she'd married Bobby primarily to get into this country, and the marriage ended fairly quickly.

I met a girl in first grade named Kris. She lived about a block from us. She hadn't gone to Kindergarten and didn't, even in first grade, believe in Santa Claus. My mother always called her Kristy and called me Crissie. My mother would take me to visit Kristy after dinner, but I was never allowed to go "in the house." I'm not sure what Laura's problem was with these people, and she never said. Laura would sit on the wall across the street and wait while I played outside with Kristy. Of course I went in her house all the time after school once we got a little older. There was nothing at all that was scary or dangerous, and her mother was nice to me.

Down at the end of the alley was a tiny building, which was the voting house. We kids would hang around there on election days and collect handouts. They were maybe 3 x 7 inches or so, printed on card stock, and had lists of candidates on them. When the day was over, no one had to worry about disposing of these handouts, because we kids had taken them all.

For my sixth birthday my mother bought me a canopy doll bed. Because my birthday was New Year's Day, it was a tradition that I attempt to stay up until midnight on New Year's Eve. I seldom made it, but that night I did stay awake, while Laura put the doll bed together. She worked on it right there at the foot of the bed, and I wasn't allowed to peek. It really was quite beautiful, and I don't think I was especially disappointed, but since I wasn't into dolls, and there was no doll to go with it, it was pretty much useless to me.

When I was in first grade, everyone in my Sunday school class at church got invited to be in the junior choir. I remember being surprised—we were so young. We had robes and choir practice and we sang the anthem once a month. We went to Sunday school first, and then church afterwards, so it was a long morning. At some point I realized that I might as well listen to the sermon, if only to pass the time, although I didn't understand much of what was said; the sermons were usually rather dry and "out-of-the-can."

STICKS AND STONES

"Sticks and stones may break my bones, but names will never hurt me." Yeah, right. Does anyone actually believe that?

I've talked about the weird "street" I lived on, and the alley we used for access to the house. In first grade, I had a little friend named Janet, who was a year younger than I, and who lived on a "real" street. We were inseparable; in fact, I probably ate more meals at her house than I did at my own. For some reason, she always wanted us to play "Scotch sisters," and we'd hold hands and skip down the street together.

Then one day, when we were walking home from school, I got squirrelly. I don't know what made me do it, but I grabbed the belt from her raincoat and starting whipping it around, and at her. I didn't hurt her, didn't even hit her with it, but she got mad at me and went home and told her mother. The mother decided that Janet could never play with me again. And she never did. Janet said her mother called me an alley cat.

Well, I forgot all about it as time went on, but these definitions of us are sneaky and pervasive, and when I got to be a teenager, I started acting like an alley cat. You know what I mean.

Now fast-forward. I saw that girl and her mother again for the first time in fifty years. They both embraced me like a long lost friend. As they did, I remembered, and I realized how much that name had hurt me. And then it struck me: "Maybe they don't really think I'm an alley cat after all."

In that moment, God healed a 50-year-old wound that had festered deep inside me for all that time without my even knowing it.

Others like to try and define us, and one of the ways they do that is by calling us names. And they aren't always nice names, either. Certainly not names that God would call us. God sees us differently than other people do, and He sees us differently than we see ourselves through the eyes of the people and the experiences in our lives.

The name Jacob means "trickster," and Jacob of the Bible lived true to his name. He tricked his uncle Laban out of his flocks, and his brother Esau out of his birthright. But then Jacob had an encounter with God. God asked him, "What is your name?" And he answered, "Jacob." And God said, "You shall no longer be called Jacob, but Israel; for as a prince you have power with God and with men, and you have prevailed.[7]

My pastor recently posed an amazing question in a sermon at church. He asked, "Whose script for your life are you living?"

In telling my story, I've discovered a whole lot of scripts that were written for me by others. Few of them were any good. The "Alley Cat" script was huge, and it was one of the scariest in that I played the role totally unaware.

Now, I don't think I'm alone in this. We've all got our scripts. For me, the question moves from which of my scripts were (and still are!) written by others, to which of my scripts were written by me, to which of my scripts are written by God. Those by others were largely written to suit their own needs without much regard to or knowledge of who I

---

[7] Genesis 32:24–28

was or what my needs were. Those I've written myself are only slightly less misguided.

Only God knows all about me and only He can reveal my true identity. In Revelation 2:17, He says, ". . . I will give each one of you a white stone, and in the stone will be engraved a new name, a name that no one knows except the one who receives it." Only God knows me and loves me well enough to be the One I can trust to rewrite the script for my life.

There's one more piece to this, and that is to consider how many scripts I've written for others, knowingly and not so knowingly. I don't think it's possible or even my job to attempt to rewrite them. Rather, my job is to tell them about the God who knows them and loves them and Who has a new name and a new script for them too.

Abba's Lullaby
Crissy Shreve

Good night, my child, Sleep well, my child,
I'll be right here with you,
Sweet dreams, my child, Hold on, my child,
My promises are true.

You're safe with Me, You're strong in Me,
I'll be here when you wake,
I see your tears, I cry with you,
In Me your comfort take.

You have my heart, You have my words,
You have my warm embrace,
Sleep well, my child, I'll stay with you,
Until we're face to face.

My plans for you, Are good and true,
There's nothing you should fear,
My ways are best, the best for you,
And I will make them clear.

No matter what the world may give,
You've found your rest in Me,
So close your eyes, and let it go,
My love has set you free.

Just close your eyes, and let it go,
My love has set you free.

Chapter Four

The Intruder

Second grade. I learned about death that year. My grandfather died shortly after I turned seven. He'd been ill for a few months, and I remember my grandmother having to take care of him, too, on top of everything else. One time she'd just gotten him cleaned up and into fresh pajamas, and he threw up all over himself and the bed.

On the February day he died, I'd come home for lunch as always, and was about to go back to school, when my grandmother made a point of telling me to say good-bye to Dadum. Although that was unusual, I didn't connect the dots. I didn't know it was forever, but when I came home after school, his bed was empty. Even the bedding was gone. He was gone.

I wandered around the house singing to myself, "I'll never forget him, he was the love of my life," to a tune I made up. I didn't know how to grieve; I don't know that I even cried much. It was so much deeper than that. A huge part of me died with him. Dadum was the only "father" I'd ever had. I still needed him. My other family members were busy with their own grief. No one really talked to me about it, or helped me through it in any way. Once again, I was on my own.

I did the best I could, I suppose, the best a lost little girl can do. But I never got over it. The emptiness of his absence stayed with me all my life. I could never replace the special love I'd had for him and that he'd had for me. I made it all the way to my sixties before I could truly entertain the possibility that anyone might love me. I suppose part of it was that his love for me was the measuring stick I used to gauge others' love. No one else was, or could ever be, my Dadum.

I carried that emptiness into all my future relationships. Nothing was ever "enough." I see now that I was unable to allow it to be enough, perhaps even as some sort of sick loyalty to Dadum. Even coming to know Christ in my early twenties, even understanding intellectually that He loves me immeasurably, didn't get through that emptiness. Nothing did.

It's such an oxymoronic concept, isn't it? To consider that emptiness, empty by definition, could so utterly block one's ability to be filled. It's said that every one of us has a God-shaped hole that only God can fill. Although Dadum was my earthly father, it is God who is my real Father, my forever Father. Abba. I am now finally able to allow Him to be just that.

Easter came as usual the spring after Dadum died. My mother bought me two baby ducks. I wanted to name them Dimples and Pimples, but my mother didn't think that was such a good idea. I never did come up with any good names, but it didn't matter much— you couldn't tell them apart, anyway. My mother got a bit of chicken wire somewhere and laid it out in a circle in the yard as an enclosure for the ducks. This was obviously ill advised; we lived right next to the woods.

I don't know where my grandmother was that day. She wasn't part of this story. I came home for lunch and found four webbed feet, no ducks attached, standing perfectly in line on the sidewalk next to our house. Their bloody carcasses were up on the porch, along with the tracks of the raccoons that had killed them. The irony was that the raccoons hadn't even eaten my ducks; they'd just killed them.

I did cry, and hysterically. I couldn't stop. I was most likely crying for my grandfather, too, although of course I didn't understand that at the time. I went back to school and still couldn't stop crying. Through my sobs, I told my teacher what had happened, and she told me to settle down and get to work. I was again alone in my grief.

Another day when I came home for lunch, I found a snake sunning itself on the landing at the top of our back steps. It was only a Garter Snake, but I didn't know that. I'd never seen a snake before, and I was scared to death. I ran around through the side yard to get to the door. My grandmother wasn't there that day either, so I had no one to tell me the snake wasn't dangerous. I never crossed that landing again without watching out for one.

I didn't see another snake until years later, when my son Mike was in Kindergarten. I did Cultural Arts for the PTA. I had a small budget, and I would hire or sweet-talk various people or groups into coming to the school and doing a show. One time I had a group from a local pet shop, and they bought a number of interesting creatures, including a snapping turtle and a king snake. Despite my recurrent terror, I made myself touch that snake. To my surprise, it wasn't slimy. Its skin was dry and cool, much like the pair of snakeskin shoes I owned. It wasn't poisonous. The man asked if I'd like to "wear" the snake and I agreed, so he dangled it around my neck, and I held its head in one hand and its tail end in the other. I fell in love with snakes, but I don't know any personally—I never know which ones are poisonous and which aren't.

Even more years later, X2 and I were heading south on vacation, but I didn't know where we were going; it was to be a surprise. I'd recently heard a friend talking about how her sister lived in Arkansas and kept a king snake in her yard to ward off more dangerous snakes. I casually said something to the effect that if we were going to Arkansas, we'd better look out for snakes. It turned out that we did go to Arkansas, and X2 admitted later that, when I'd said that, he'd nearly turned the car around.

While we were there in Arkansas fishing, we putt-putted around the lake in a little rented rowboat with a 15 horsepower motor. We went exploring up a side channel, and there on an overhanging rock was a huge copperhead or water moccasin dangling over the edge with a half-eaten fish in its mouth. X2 turned the boat around and we got out of there.

Back to my childhood, ours was not the only "street" that had been cleared but never paved. There were several others nearby, one of which was the sled path, and it ran several blocks straight down hill. It was really fast, and the bigger kids always got mad at me for dragging my feet, so I didn't use it much. The big kids would build a sled jump and some of them even went down standing up on their sleds.

I usually just sledded in our side yard, which was steep and long enough for a decent ride. I'd get to the bottom and stop, then roll off my sled and just lie there for a few minutes in the snow, as if I'd been knocked out. I was just resting, putting off hauling myself and my sled back up the hill for another run. I didn't know it, but the old lady next door was watching out her window, and apparently I fooled her, because at some point later on, she told me she was sure I *had* been knocked out a time or two. Nah.

That's a bit ironic, actually. I almost always played alone. While sledding, or at the swimming pool, I would often "show off" and pretend someone was watching. I was a latchkey[8] kid long before the phrase had even been coined. I longed for attention.

My mother never made much money, but we were not as shabbily poor as some people in our town. I think a lot of the kids' dads probably drank up their paychecks. For the most part, though, my friends had much more than I did. Not only clothes and curly hair, but things like dancing lessons.

I became a Brownie in second grade. I had the uniform and the hat, but not much else. I'd see catalogs of Brownie shorts and tops and accessories, and I'd drool over them. I wanted so much to go to camp in the summer, but there was no money for that.

Until my grandfather died, we always went to Atlantic City for a week in the summer. The Pennsylvania Turnpike was only a few years old, but it enabled us to get there in one very long day. About an hour out, I'd start my chorus of "Are we there yet?" When my own kids were little, I was amused to discover that they, too, knew that chorus quite well. As, Mike now informs me, do my grandkids, despite in-car video players, hand-held games, and ear buds.

Another trip we took was to Niagara Falls. I don't particularly remember the falls, but I remember that we stayed overnight at what would now be called a "bed & breakfast." In the room, I started singing the first line of a song, which went, "Tell me the tales that to me were so dear. Long, long ago, long, long ago."[9] I sang it over and over; it was the only line I knew. I'd heard it on the radio in the car. Someone finally told me that I had to stop, because the people in other rooms were trying to sleep. I think they just wanted to shut me up, another concept I better understood once I had kids of my own.

My cousin Judy got married the summer after Dadum died. Nana and I went; my mother didn't go. Someone drove us there, probably

---

[8]   A latchkey kid is a child who returns from school to an empty home because his or her parent or parents are away at work, or a child who is often left at home with little or no parental supervision. Wikipedia.

[9]   "Long, Long Ago," Marty Robbins

Uncle Austin. I wore a gray dress in the car, but had another to wear to the wedding itself. I don't remember that dress, but I remember Nana changing my clothes in the car. Some woman named Retta was in a car parked next to us, and she, too, changed her clothes in the car. I guess we must have driven home that night after the wedding, because I don't remember staying in a motel or being there the next day. I suppose not having a room would also explain our changing clothes in the car. I just thought it was weird. My cousin Johnny from North Carolina didn't come to the wedding, so I was the only little kid there. With no one to play with, I was mostly bored with the whole thing. For me, the only memorable thing was changing clothes in the car.

One time we all went to Cook Forest. My cousins John and Johnny were both there. John (who's six years older than I) and I walked a ways into the woods from where we were parked. I remember being absolutely certain that I knew which direction to go to get back. I have a strong sense of direction, and I tend to pay attention, but I got turned around somehow. John insisted we go the other way, and darn it, he was right. I was so sure that, as we walked into the forest, the stream was on our right. If that was true, then to go back, we needed to keep the stream on our left. Simple. But when we went out, John's way, the stream was on our right. I still don't know how that happened. Apparently we must have crossed the stream and I didn't notice. That's the only thing that makes sense.

Cousin Johnny and I thought we ought to go wading in the mountain stream. The water was ice cold, and we quickly jumped back out. Apparently I was smarter then than I was later. When I was about eighteen, I happened to be on a Lake Michigan beach one evening. It was May. The air was warm and I foolishly assumed that the water would be too. I stepped out of my sandals, waded into the frigid water, and immediately wet my pants.

My mother bought me a Betsy Wetsy[10] doll one Christmas. What's up with the doll stuff? I think she was trying to turn me into a girl. When my boys were little, and were up to no good, as little boys tend to be, I'd say to them, "I know what you're doing. I was a little boy once myself, you know." They'd huff and puff and snicker, "Oh, Mom, you're a *girl*." I suppose, but only because I couldn't help it.

---

[10]   Betsy Wetsy was a doll originally issued by the Ideal Toy Company of New York in 1935.

SHOULDS
Crissy Shreve

All the shoulds where wants are waiting,
Dazzling gems and promises
Upon those grasping fingers,
Pulling, tearing, shredding,

So little left of me.

Thank you, friend,
For seeing through!

You spread my mottled flesh
And bones apart
And found me.

And missing you, I cried.

Finally.

Chapter Five

Loss And Loving

This chapter is something of an "interlude." It doesn't fit into the timeframe of the story and isn't especially meant to.

When Shai, X2's and my second Siamese kitty, died after surgery to remove her claws, I was devastated. I had called the vet to check on her and was told that she hadn't made it. I stood in my office at work and sobbed.

Losing Squeekie, our first Siamese, had been just as devastating. X2's idea had been to get another cat right away. It wasn't a bad idea. Squeekie had chosen to be primarily X2's cat, so I wanted the new kitty to choose me. X2, Jason, and I set out to visit a local breeder. There we had five or six little ones at our feet, all of them playing with our shoelaces. I don't remember exactly how I knew Shai was the one, how she picked me, but she did.

I was still grieving Squeekie, though, and I wasn't about to fall in love with Shai like I had with Squeekie. It wasn't at all fair to Shai, but she figured it out. She loved me—like crazy. When I'd come in the door after work, she'd leap up onto my shoulder.

Shai was about two years old when we lost her. In that loss, I learned something—that much like humans, animals will compensate for a perceived lack of love by loving. I cried when Jason was born because I wanted a girl, and then I made a decision to love Jason more than I would ever have loved a girl. And it worked.

Mike had a girlfriend in high school named Beth, and she was taking a class on marriage and family. Mike got to be the "husband" in the equation. As part of the class, they made twin babies out of bags of flour—you don't dare drop a flour-sack baby! Mike and Beth each carried one twin around at school all day. The twins were called

Katie and Mikey. I still have a picture of me holding the two of them. I loved Beth as if she was my real daughter-in-law, and I loved Katie and Mikey as real little grandkids. Inevitably, Mike and Beth eventually broke up, and I was heartbroken. I missed Beth like crazy and, of course, she got "custody" of the twins.

So then Mike came home with Jenny. Like with Shai, I decided I wasn't going to risk loving her like I had Beth. And like Shai, Jenny set out to love me, and did it so well that I wound up loving her. And, of course, they too eventually broke up, and I was again heartbroken.

Having placed Larry for adoption, there was a way in which, when Mike was born, it was hard for me to wrap my head around actually keeping him and raising him. Initially, it was even a bit hard to really fall in love with him because it brought up my sadness and the unfairness of not having been able to keep Larry. I got over it quickly, but I remember having those feelings.

It didn't help that X1 and I had just moved into our first house and we were broke. Mike was born in May and it was hot out. We had no money for air-conditioning, and I needed to be able to leave Mike's bedroom door open. At that time I had a cat named Shelby, and I was afraid she'd climb in bed with Mike and smother him. She also had just had kittens, and there was no money to get her fixed. The only logical solution was to take her to the shelter along with the kittens and hope that someone would adopt her.

Of course I would not have sacrificed my baby for my cat, but it hurt so much to have to sacrifice my beloved kitty for my baby. Sometimes life just isn't fair. This was one of those times. I wish I hadn't had to choose. I wish there had been a way to keep the cat. I wish I'd been able to keep Larry. I'm glad I was able to at least keep Mike.

Another thing I learned when Shai died was that a huge piece of it was losing someone who loved *me*. I'd sure felt loved by Shai. Her death brought up my old pain of losing grandfather when I was seven. For most of my life, he was the only person I'd ever really believed loved me. When I lost Shai, and her love, I began to consider that there might be others who loved me, and that maybe I ought to recognize them as the treasures they are.

I have a friend who's been struggling with family baggage for all the years I've known her. She craves love that will never be hers, from people who were supposed to have loved her and didn't. Sometimes I get frustrated with her. Yet her stories resonate with my own, and I am just as stuck. We've both been pounding the same nail all our lives. It's a legacy neither she nor I would have chosen.

But, here's the thing: she adores me. I don't know why. I don't think it's probably about me; I'm not all that adorable. It's about her compensating for that lack of love by loving others, and she does it very well. She is immeasurably valuable to me—she, and others, who have stayed in it with me over the years, listening to me bang my hammer. It strikes me that if God turned His back on those of us who frustrate Him, we'd all be in trouble.

When I pay attention, I see that God regularly puts people in my life to bring me closer to myself, both in seeing and feeling my pain in theirs, and in using them as examples of my own behaviors that He thinks could use some work. That's always been true, but what's changed is that lately He's given me a new attitude towards them. Rather than seeing them as people I have to put up with or, worse, walk away from, now I look at them as people He wants to use to get through to me. It should be no surprise, then, that the people I have the hardest time with are the ones who are most like me. Imagine that!

At the time I was writing this chapter, I had lunch with my good friend Sue and was telling her about what I was learning as I wrote it. She made the most remarkable statement about me. She said, "You are a mixture of intolerance and extreme patience." Wow, I thought. At first I wasn't sure whether I liked that or not. I saw, though, as I thought about it, that not only was it a positive observation, but it said that I have moved towards becoming who God wants me to be. And wasn't it, in fact, a great definition of grace?

When my son Jason died, most significant for me was sadness that I'd not only lost my beloved son, but I'd also lost his love. Jason had always loved me, whether I deserved it or not, and he did it so tenderly. I never got past Jason without a hug, even if we'd had a hug only minutes before.

My Chihuahuas are good hugs too. I fell in love with the Taco Bell Chihuahua. I'd see him (although he was really a she) on the TV commercials, and I wanted one. *"Yo quiero un Chihuahua!"*

X2 and I were at a motor home rally in Georgia and I'd just had a manicure, so my nails were still wet and I didn't want to mess them up by driving the car. There was a building full of vendors offering all sorts of stuff, so I went in there, and rather than starting to the left as I would typically do, I turned towards the right.

In one of the first vendor booths I came to, there was a sign that said, "Chihuahua puppies." Oh! The woman asked me what color our motor home was. I said gray. She said, "I have your puppy." I said okay, but asked that she bring in several, because I was still operating on the concept of the animal picking me. We agreed that I'd stop back the next day.

The following morning, I mentioned to X2 that I wanted to go to the vendor building to see some Chihuahuas. His comment was that we didn't need a dog—he'd do the watching and I could do the barking. I dragged him along anyway. The woman had a crate with about seven Chihuahua puppies in it. I immediately spotted the little black and gray puppy she'd thought would be mine. He and I made eye contact and it was a done deal. He was my Toby.

Meanwhile, the breeder had been holding a tiny little brown dog, which she handed to X2 to hold while she dug out Toby's paperwork. Just that quickly, X2 fell in love—if you knew Tory, you understand. Suddenly mister "we don't need a dog" transmogrified[11] into that little boy we see at the grocery store checkout counter—you know, the kid eyeing the candy and looking up at mom with big hopeful moon eyes.

"So, which one are we going to get?" asked X2, to which I replied, "Both of them." You should have been there. His eyes lit up just like that little boy's at the checkout counter when mom says he can have a candy bar. He was right, after all—we didn't need a dog, we needed *two* of them.

As it turned out, it was good that we got them both. They were half-brother and sister, had been together their entire lives, so not only were they easily able to adjust to living in our world, they kept each other company and were never lonely when we had to leave them.

We named them Tobias and Victoria—Toby and Tory for short. They were such tiny mites; we thought they should at least have

---

[11] Transmogrify is a perfectly legitimate word meaning to transform in a magically or surprising manner. I admit I'd probably not know the word existed if I weren't such a huge "Calvin and Hobbes" fan.

dignified names. Not too long ago, though, it occurred to me that we could have named them Tabasco and Tortilla, more appropriate to their Mexican heritage, and still called them Toby and Tory. Oh, well. Being Mexican dogs, they were both little sun-worshippers and could never understand why they lived in the chilly north.

Then, as life goes, a few years later, X2 decided that he'd rather be with someone else, and we split up. The dogs were living with me, although X2 had liberal visitation and often took them home with him for a few days. The day we signed final divorce papers, I came home from the attorney's office emotionally drained and exhausted. The "kids," Toby and Tory, always slept with me. I kept a small wicker chest at the bottom of the bed so that they could jump up onto it and then onto the bed. That night, I climbed into my bed, and instantly fell asleep, something I almost never do. Tory got herself up on the bed, and for a second I noticed that she didn't seem quite right, but then I crashed. Some time during the night she died. Was she in pain? I don't know; I was sound asleep. The only comfort is in that she was close to me and, if she had to die, I was at least there with her, even if I was neither awake nor aware.

The next morning, I got up and headed straight downstairs in search of coffee. After a while, I noticed that Tory hadn't put in an appearance. As I ran upstairs to look for her, I somehow knew that she was gone. And there she was, still on my bed, but no longer there. The amazing thing was that she hadn't even soiled the bed. I picked her up in a towel and laid her in a box, which I put down on the living room floor so that Toby could see her and smell her and know that she was gone. I cried so hard. Toby was crushed.

If I speak of my dogs as if they're "people," it's because they've always been quite sure themselves that they were people. People in furry coats, perhaps, but people nonetheless. Who am I to disagree? One time a friend was holding Tory (if there was a lap to be had, Tory would be on it), and he commented that she was a "beautiful animal." I was actually a little shocked—it really had never occurred to me to think of my dogs as animals. They were "the kids." Friends would regularly ask how "the kids" were doing, or when they'd come to visit, they'd greet the dogs with, "Hi, kids."

Tory was the most magnificent of dogs. Sure, I know we all feel that way about our dogs, but she really was. Tory was a great lover, and she loved everyone. When we'd go for walks, people would stop their cars right in the middle of the street, heedless of other cars behind them, and get out to love on the "kids." I'm amazed no one ever got rear-ended. When we'd pass a guy out washing his car or a woman gardening, and that person wouldn't stop to schmooze with Tory, she'd actually be abashed. She just couldn't understand it.

I've always said that although Chihuahuas may be the least amount of dog per dollar, they are surely a bargain when it comes to love per pound.

I am absolutely certain that Tory spent her first years in heaven firmly planted on God's lap, sound asleep, with her nose in His sleeve, simply because it would never have occurred to Tory to be anywhere else. I have to smile when I imagine Jason's arrival in heaven and God's saying, "Oh, good, now I can get this Chihuahua off my lap."

I am also absolutely certain that when Jason arrived in heaven, Tory, his beloved kitty Furball, along with Sheppie, our dog from when he was little, were all there to greet him. Jason loved animals and animals loved Jason, so it's only right. You can argue, if you must, whether pets go to heaven, but if heaven is paradise, and pets are joy, how can they not be there?[12]

We'd always known that, of the two Chihuahuas, it would be Toby who would be most affected should we lose Tory. The two of them were joined at the hip, but Toby was not as needy for love and attention as Tory was. He just loved Tory. When she died, I was truly afraid that Toby would die too, of a broken heart, so Jason and I set out to look for a new little sister for him. We found Candy Girl and brought her home. Toby was so tender with her; he taught her "the ropes," and he never lorded it over her, despite his being twice her size. Of course, Candy grew to be twice his size and, typical female, from then on she proceeded to rule the roost. Toby, typical male, just took it in stride.

Jason always called Candy "Henrietta Holstein" or "half a cow," partly because she is twice Toby's size, and partly because she is white with large brown spots.

Candy loves hugs and will say, "Ooooo" when you hug her. I call it "squish-a-puppy." She doesn't care what I call it, as long as I do it

---

[12] ". . . if animals would make us happier in heaven, surely there will be a place for them there." Billy Graham

regularly. The two of them graciously allow me to share their bed as long as I'm willing to contort around them. Toby likes to sleep on my pillow, wrapped around my head. Candy is usually tucked up under the covers nestled into my back.

Candy has invented several games, one of which is the kissy game. She'll stand on the stairs with her head peeking out from between two balusters, inviting me to play. My job is to pet her, preferably on the ears. Hers is to give me nose-kisses.

Several years after Tory died, I was standing in my kitchen telling someone some story about her, and I looked down and there was Toby, who'd heard me say her name, and he had just the saddest expression on his face. He hadn't forgotten her, and he still missed her terribly. As do I.

I had a hard time warming up to Candy at first. It wasn't about her; it was that once again, like with Squeekie and Shai, I was still mourning Tory. Fortunately, Candy is, as Jason put it, a slut-puppy, and love sponge that she is, she gets her loving from anyone she can. Still, I am "mommy" and it is from me that Candy most needs love and attention. I could see the sadness in her eyes when I didn't give her what she needed. But she just went on loving me and didn't let me off the hook. Once again, I realized the value of someone who loves me, even when I'm not so in love with him or her, especially when I don't deserve it, and I grew to appreciate her and love her dearly.

While I was working on the last chapters of this book, my precious Toby Chihuahua, soon to be twelve years old, had a heart attack. As a result, one or more of his *chordae tendineae*, or heartstrings, ruptured.[13] Until very recently, this condition was curtains for a dog, but new meds are keeping him alive for now. He gets three pills twice a day. Although he's coughing a lot and he sleeps so soundly that I have to check to see if he's breathing, little trooper that he is, he takes his "new normal" right in stride. He's still mostly himself otherwise, and he still turns up every night at precisely 6 PM looking for dinner.

I know his days are numbered. I remember something X2 said when Squeekie had to be put down. He said that she was no longer

---

[13]   The chordae tendineae, or heartstrings, are cord-like tendons that connect the papillary muscles to the tricuspid valve and the mitral valve in the heart. Wikipedia

There's no way to know for sure whether or how many ruptured.

who she would have wanted to be for us and it was time to let her go. I may have to make that hard choice for Toby too, and I watch him closely. He'll let me know. But I pray that when it's time, he will be asleep in the sun, and that he will wake up to Tory licking his face. As hard as it will be to lose him, I will take comfort in sharing his joy in being with his Tory again. Meanwhile, I am grateful for every day he's still with me.

As is true of all things that happen, God allowed Tory to die too early, at only three years old. It has to be true because, if He hadn't allowed it, it wouldn't have happened. It follows, then, that the same is true of my divorce, of Jason's death, and of all the things that happen, to me personally, and in the world at large. God allows them. How am I supposed deal with that?

When 9-11 happened, several people, who knew that I love the Lord and believe He is good and that He doesn't make mistakes, asked me how God could have allowed it to happen, and what I thought about it. I firmly believe, and what I told them, was that what we don't know, usually never know, is what God *didn't* allow to happen. I remembered that when Jason died, too. I suspect there was something God knew that I didn't know, something worse that might have happened had he lived.

Despite how it looks in my own human understanding, given time, I always find that God uses what He allows. I bank on Romans 8:28[14], and although of course I grieve deeply for those I've lost, the furry ones and the not-so-furry ones, I hang on tight to the God who is in control. It has been in my times of greatest despair that He's taught me to walk through it, whatever it is, *with* Him. I can't imagine going through any of it without Him.

I'm not a theologian and I'm not equipped to explain God's reasoning for the things He allows. I don't think that's what matters, anyway. For me what matters is that, with each heartbreak, I've been drawn closer to my Lord. As Job said, the Lord gives and the Lord takes away, blessed be the Name of the Lord. We are finite, as are those we love. There is no guarantee that we, or anyone, will be here even a minute from now. There is, however, a guarantee that God will be there. Always.

---

[14] And we know that in all things God works for the good of those who love Him, who have been called according to His purpose. Romans 8:28

I don't care what they say, time doesn't heal. Time dulls. God heals.

When Jason died, God kept another promise—that with Him, all things are possible,[15] even the impossible. Navigating the death of a child is impossible. And yet, somehow, even that can be done with one's hand in His. When my marriage ended, I'd had to be taught to walk through it with God. When Jason died, I just fell into His arms.

The phone call all parents dread came in the middle of the night. I drove myself to the hospital. Either I was still asleep or I was on autopilot. I remember, about halfway there, thinking to myself, Oh! I wonder whom I might have called to go with me. Although several people came to mind, I was suddenly very aware that God was sitting right there in the passenger seat. He was with me. I had everything I needed. He carried me; my feet never touched the ground.

And then, a year and a half after Jason died, God brought my Larry back to me.

No one replaces anyone else. Shai didn't replace Squeekie, Candy Girl didn't replace Tory, Mike and Jason didn't replace Larry all those years ago, and Larry didn't replace Jason. Certainly none of the men in my life ever replaced my grandfather. I realize now that all my life I've allowed the pain of past losses to lessen my joy in the present and, in that, I missed way too much of what was right in front of me. I can finally see that love remains, and that joy, though never replaced, can be restored.

When Larry found me, after my having praised my way through the loss of my marriage and the loss of my son Jason, I at last discovered the miracle of praising God from a place of joy instead of a place of pain.[16]

I was recently standing in the shower and thinking about a good friend of mine. She's twelve years younger than I, she's skinny and gorgeous, she's healthy and energetic, she's got a cute guy who's good to her, and they travel constantly and have a lot of fun. All in all, she's got a really great life.

---

[15] Matthew 19:26

[16] There I will give her back her vineyards, and will make the Valley of [troubles] a door of hope. There she will sing as in the days of her youth . . . Hosea 2:15 NIV And I will restore to you the years that the locust hath eaten . . . Joel 2:25 ASV

These are all things I had at one time, and lost. As I was just about to get into a serious pity-party, God pointed out to me that she has nothing that she can't lose.

What do you have that you cannot lose?

SQUEEKIE AND SHAI

In the house where X2 and I first lived, there were two archways connecting the kitchen with the family room. I had installed a toggle bolt at the top of one of them and had hung a huge spider plant, complete with babies, in a large, heavy ceramic pot. Now, I know how to do a toggle bolt, but apparently I didn't have my thinking cap on the day I put that one up, because I put the little prongs into the hole facing up instead of down. The thing hung there just fine for several years.

Then one night, in the middle of the night, X2 heard a huge crash in the kitchen. The cat, our beloved Squeekie, was, as usual, asleep on X2's chest. She heard the crash and flew straight up in the air. X2 then flew straight up in the air. X2 came back down. Squeekie came back down, claws open and at the ready, landing on X2's chest. X2, after deciding that he wasn't having a heart attack, went to investigate the source of the crash.

He ventured into the kitchen to find the pot, who knows how many gallons of dirt, and the spider plant scattered across the kitchen floor. He told me he'd have taken pity on me and cleaned it up, but anyone stupid enough to put in a toggle bolt upside down could darn well clean it up herself. I, of course, slept through the whole thing. X2 just came back to bed, and before he left for work in the morning, informed me that I might want to put on some shoes before I went into the kitchen.

This was somewhat reminiscent of the night I brought Squeekie home. Some friends had bought a trimaran (a three-hulled sailboat) and were leaving to go live on it in Miami. They had several Siamese cats, all of which they'd found homes for with the exception of Squeekie. Squeekie was ten years old and blind, and no one had claimed her. Since it's not the better part of valor to take a blind cat to live on a boat, they were quite concerned about what to do with her. I had told them I'd take her if no one else did, but I wanted to wait until they were ready to leave.

The night before they left, they had a going away party for themselves, which I attended alone since X2 had spent the day moving his business to a new location and was too tired to go. At the party, I was sitting on the couch and all of a sudden I realized that I had a cat purring on my lap and had *had* a cat purring on my lap for some time. Squeekie was like that. I remembered then that I'd said I'd take her, so I said, "Guess I have to take Squeekie home tonight". My friends were so pleased and relieved, because they, too, had forgotten that I'd said I'd take her.

I had X2's car, and when it was time to go home, I put the cat in the back seat with X2's favorite leather jacket. Squeekie, who was appropriately named, squeaked the whole way home and peed on the jacket and the back seat. She continued to squeak non-stop after we got home. X2, amazingly enough, didn't wake up.

There I was, with no litter box, no cat food or dishes, and this squeaking cat, and it was 2:30 in the morning. It was October and still fairly warm out, and we had an enclosed front entry with a concrete floor, so I stuck a rug, a bowl of water, and the cat out there. Knowing I was going to sleep till noon, I wrote X2 a note saying, "When you open the front door, don't step on anything or in anything," and went to bed.

When X2 came home from work the next day, his comment was, "I'll never do anything more than feel sorry for that cat." Ha! Squeekie, knowing precisely what was going on, got right to work and had him eating out of her hand within a matter of days. She made him her person and she made it perfectly clear that she was his cat. Where X2 was, Squeekie was, usually on top of him, whichever way she could get there. X2 had pneumonia one winter and I have a picture of him in bed quoting, telephone to his ear, a blueprint spread out on top of the quilt and Squeekie right next to him with her head sticking out from under the covers.

One day I came home from work to find Squeekie up on the kitchen table squeaking piteously. She'd gotten up on the chair and then onto the table and, being blind, couldn't find her way back down. One thing about a blind cat, it won't spend much time on the kitchen counters. Squeekie had her own navigational system though, and it was pretty amazing to watch how she got around. She had very long whiskers and, once she became familiar with the house, you'd never have known she was blind. We'd have parties and she'd "circulate," managing to never get stepped on. Everyone loved Squeekie.

Squeekie used her whiskers to "feel" her way down the hall. She knew exactly how many openings there were between the kitchen and the bedroom, and exactly how many cat paces to take once she was in the bedroom before jumping up onto the bed. This all worked just fine until we decided to replace the carpet.

Squeekie knew that she had to pass the open bathroom door, the closed linen closet door, then turn left at the next open door, which was our bedroom. When we took up the old carpet, we took the door off the linen closet and poor Squeekie came cruising down the hall, past the open bathroom door, then came to the open linen closet door, thought it was the bedroom, made her left turn and crashed into the wall in the back of the closet.

She took this in stride, however, and adjusted her navigational plan accordingly, just in time for the new carpet to be installed and the linen closet door put back in place. Down the hall she went, past the now closed linen closet door, past the open bedroom door and, thinking it was the open linen closet (they can't fool me!), crashed into the wall at the end of the hall.

We were not cat abusers—please don't call the ASPCA.

Several weeks later, our new bedroom set was to be delivered, so we took the old bed out of the bedroom, leaving the mattresses on the floor to sleep on for a few days. Poor dear Squeekie, who had by now again adjusted her navigational system, or thought she had, comes down the hall, successfully arriving in the bedroom. She takes her required number of cat paces towards the bed and jumps up on what used to be three feet high, landing a bit hard on what is now only a foot high. No problem, just another minor adjustment to the plan.

We removed the mattresses entirely the day the new bedroom set was to come. Squeekie, now tuned into the new height, does her thing and lands on the floor. Undaunted, she takes another few paces forward and tries again, finally crashing into the bedroom wall.

You can't make this stuff up. The new bed arrives and here comes Squeekie, who has to have decided by now that we're nuts! She heads into the bedroom and, thinking there's nothing there, crashes into the new bed.

Squeekie had a bit of a problem with hairballs, so we had this gel stuff to give her. She would very cheerfully lick it off X2's fingers. When she needed medication in pill form, X2 would hold her in his lap facing him, put his hand around the back of her head, gently squeeze her cheeks to get her to open her mouth, look her in the eye and say, "open wide." After the pill was in her mouth, he'd stroke her throat and she'd swallow it and smile at him to boot. X2 could do anything with that cat. She trusted him completely.

They always knew it was Squeekie at the vet's, because she'd live up to her name from the minute we'd walk in the door.

When we'd go away on vacation, X2's secretary would come in to feed the "animals," which at that time consisted of Squeekie and X-number of fish. Squeekie got pretty lonely and missed us when we were away, so the secretary, being the trooper that she is, and in spite of her allergy to cats, would spend a few extra minutes with Squeekie before she left. Squeekie emphatically didn't want her to leave and would wrap her front paws around the secretary's legs to try to keep her there.

Dear Squeekie, who was ten years old when we got her, lived to be fifteen and then had a stroke. She was no longer able to walk straight, and her poor confused brain caused her to double back over on herself, almost like a backwards somersault. The vet said that she could possibly recover, so we waited a few days before having her put down. X2 fed her by hand and put her on a towel next to the bed, sleeping with one hand on her all night. Bless her little heart, she never had an accident, always made it to her litter box to the very end, although she could no longer clean herself afterwards. X2 would give her a bath every night that last few days and would brush her and love her up as he said his good-byes to her. She had a second stroke and we knew then that we would lose her.

Mike and Jason were with us the weekend before the dreaded appointment and they slept on the family room floor with her the last night. We were all heartbroken. X2 took her in and he held her in his arms as she went to sleep.

As I said earlier, X2 decided that the best way to survive the loss of Squeekie was to go get another cat. Mike and I named the new kitty Shai. Amy Grant's song "El Shaddai" was a favorite of ours at the time and Shai was sort of a contraction of Shaddai. Mike and I have always been on the same wavelength, in this kind of thing at least.

Shai really did love me and was my cat from day one. When I'd come home from work, she'd jump up onto my shoulder and purr in my ear. She'd startle friends who came to visit by greeting them this way, too. She was a "real" cat. She had the roam of the house, could jump up onto anything within reason, and spent quite a bit of time on the top of the refrigerator. Whereas Squeekie had been the more old-fashioned type of Siamese, softer-featured and chubbier, Shai was streamlined and somewhat sharp-featured.

She was also much more independent than Squeekie, but she knew to whom she belonged. When we moved to the new house, we thought it would be simpler to leave Shai at the old house while the movers were busy bringing the furniture in. I had gone ahead in my car and when the truck came up the drive, there was X2 was in his car behind it with Shai on his lap, her head peeking up over the steering wheel. She hadn't let him leave without her.

Step-Mike had a girlfriend at the time we had Shai. One night when she had come to our house to see him, step-Mike spent forty-five minutes "saying goodnight" to her in the driveway before she left. Unfortunately, he left the front door wide open the whole time. We had gone to bed and Shai, always tempted and taunted by the cats outside the window (they lived next door on the old farm), decided to venture out into the night.

I regularly trimmed her claws, so she was pretty defenseless out there. The next morning, I was still in bed when X2 came upstairs and said, "Your cat got out and she's in pretty bad shape." He'd opened the kitchen door to the deck and seen her out there. He didn't try to pick her up, just left the door open and came to get me. She came in and followed him upstairs and jumped up on the bed to be by me. This was a pretty amazing feat, because one of her hind legs was broken in five places.

Of course it was a holiday, the Fourth of July. These things always happen when the vet's office is closed, so he met us there. Shai had to have two pins in her leg and she had to be kept quiet for six weeks after she came home. I got a cage and kept her in it and took her out several times a day and just held her. It became quite a task after the first few weeks, because she still wanted to jump up on things and that was the one thing I could not let her do. It was a terrible experience for her and she was never quite the same after that. She was never again able to jump as high as she had before and, even after she recovered, she never again got up on top of the refrigerator or quite made it up onto my shoulder.

Several months after Shai recovered from the broken leg, X2 and I bought some tapestry-covered dining room chairs. X2 insisted that we get Shai's claws removed so that she would not tear up the chairs. She had never needed a scratching post and since I'd been cutting her claws all along, I didn't think we needed to do that, but the chairs had cost a small fortune, so I agreed.

On the appointed day, I dropped Shai off at the vet's on my way to work. I just blithely handed her over to the girl behind the counter and left for work. I never dreamed there would be a problem. I don't know what went wrong, but when I called to check on Shai, I was told that she was not coming out of the anesthesia well. I checked back later and was told that she had died. I sat at my desk and sobbed. I went over to the vet's to see her body and say good-bye to her. There was my beautiful kitty, but her eyes were dead. Shai had loved me with all her little kitty heart and I felt the loss of that love and devotion very deeply.

LIFE IS LIKE PITTSBURGH
Crissy Shreve

Life is a lot like Pittsburgh.
There's always a hill and the road is never straight.
You may be on top of a hill.
You may be climbing a hill.
You may be sliding down a hill—with or without brakes.
You may be in a tunnel under a hill.
You may be going around a hill.

If the road you're on goes straight for a minute, be grateful.
There's a curve just up ahead.
Watch out for the guy next to you.
He doesn't know where he's going, either.

Life is a lot like Pittsburgh.

CHAPTER SIX

STILL A KID

We'd heard from the older kids that we'd start having homework in third grade. We were all so pleased with that idea that we actually asked the teacher to give us homework the first night. Stupid kids.

For several years, Nana had been going blind, a complication of her diabetes. She'd also be sick from time to time, and she'd go stay at Ruth's so that Ruth could take care of her. Nana was in and out, and even if she wasn't at Ruth's, she was often sick at home. She no longer did much cooking or taking care of the house.

Nana did put my hair in a ponytail one time, though, which was nice. My mother always put my hair in what she called a horse's tail. I never saw anyone else with one, ever. Laura would gather the top part of my hair to one side, put it in a rubber band, and the thing would just hang down over the rest of my hair. It kept the hair out of my eyes, but I always hated it, and wanted to have a ponytail like the other girls had.

By this time I was regularly taking the streetcar downtown by myself to meet my mother after work. Once there, I'd cross the street with the light, then meet her at the tearoom on the second floor of the department store. We'd have something to eat, there or somewhere else, and then go back home together on the streetcar. We took the train home one time before passenger service was discontinued, then took the streetcar up the hill. Taking the train wasn't practical for my mother on an everyday basis; the station was "downstreet," whereas the streetcar stop was only a block from our house.

The school arranged for us all to go on a two-hour train trip a few months before passenger trains went out of service. My mother signed the permission slip and then changed her mind and decided I couldn't go. I told her that I'd need a note to the teacher that I'd be staying home that day, and she gave me one. I never turned it in; I went on the train trip. I admitted that to her decades later, and she said she'd known all along.

Although streetcar passes were available on a monthly basis for a set price and would have saved her some money, my mother seldom if ever bought one. She never wanted to part with the larger amount all at once, so she was always "digging around in the bottom of her purse" for change for streetcar fare. One time when I was in sixth or seventh grade, a boy from down the hill asked me to go skating with him. It was my first "date," and he said, "I'll pay your way." Since we'd agreed to meet at the skating rink, I was afraid that he'd not get there in time, so I borrowed my mother's carfare to pay my way in. She made it clear that it was all she had and wouldn't be able to go to work the next day if I didn't get it back. I didn't spend much time with the boy at the rink, he wasn't a very good skater, but I did make him give me the fifty cents.

I still remember the phone number we had at the house. At some point, it became a party line, probably to save money. Every time I'd pick up the phone to call someone, the neighbor lady was on the line talking in Yugoslavian. I was told to interrupt only if it was an emergency, so I didn't spend much time on the phone, plus I always figured she would be listening in.

Laura walked down the steps in our house quickly and affirmatively. It was always steps; you never heard the word stairs. Her high heels would go clop-clop-clop, at just the speed and rhythm you'd get if you said that out loud. One time there was something I needed to take upstairs, but wasn't going up right then, so I just stuck it to one side on the steps. My mother tripped on it and managed to "break her fall" by grabbing onto the railing. She was not pleased with me. She always worried about twisting her ankle, too, and with good reason. The alley was full of potholes and small pebbles, so it was an obstacle course for her, especially in those high heels. She'd walk with her head down, carefully picking her way through the pebbles. It's too bad someone didn't think of wearing gym shoes or something, anything better than high heels, and then changing shoes at work, as women do today. But back then, things like that "just weren't done."

Eventually I decided I'd had enough of sleeping with Laura, so I carried, well, probably dragged, a small bed down from the attic. It was the perfect size, and I set it up at the end of the upstairs hallway, outside my mother's room. There was a window, but no door. I was just fine there, but once I'd fall asleep, Laura would always carry me back to her bed. Then someone took that bed back up to the attic and so I decided I'd just sleep up there. It was freezing in the winter and blistering hot in the summer, but I didn't care. I wanted my own room. The attic was one big open finished but unheated room. There was a double bed up there, as well as the small bed. My mother quickly got tired of carrying me back down the stairs and, anyway, I was getting too big for her to carry. So I finally won that fight, and I slept up there until Nana died and I took over her bedroom.

We had cupboards. (Cupboard, by the way, is pronounced, correctly, "cubberd.") Most of the houses in our town were old and had pantries with built-in cupboards. There were very few cabinets to be found. There were, however, closets, but they too were called cupboards. When I lived there, I didn't know the difference, but once my horizons got expanded and modernized elsewhere, I always had to giggle whenever someone talked about putting their clothes in the cupboard. I'd picture them stuffing sweaters and underwear into the cupboard in the pantry.

The hardware store "up street" carried toys, and one summer day I shoplifted a cap gun. I knew I'd been spotted, so I quickly left the store and ran up the block and ditched the cap gun. The storeowner caught up with me and asked me if I'd taken something. I held out my hands to show him they were empty. He asked whether I had anything in my shorts, and I said no. That much, at least, was true, and he didn't risk touching me to make sure. But we both knew. Of course I retrieved the gun afterwards and cleverly returned to the store a few days later to buy caps for it.

Nana had a large round dining room table that sat twelve people. When my mother would try to catch me to spank me for doing something bad, I'd get behind that table and just keep moving around it so as to be on the opposite side. One time my mother thought she was smart, and she pushed the table towards me, blocking me into the corner. I thought I was smarter, though, and I stuck out my tongue at her. She still couldn't get to me. She usually gave up before I did and I seldom got spanked. I was perfectly capable of being a brat.

On summer evenings, I'd often ride my bike "up street." Laura found it handy to send me to the store, rather than having to go herself, and I'd spend the change on candy or ice cream. I was not amused, though, when she wanted me to buy her Kotex. The clerk in the store was a cute young guy, and I'd be embarrassed.

My bike had a light on it. I would walk it across the main road, then pedal up to the street above, which had a gentle grade that ran the three or so blocks, unlike the sidewalk along the main road, which was a steep climb both ways. This same street also paralleled the main road in the other direction and was again a long, gentle grade. I would get on my bike and ride all the way down it—no hands! It was a cobblestone street, narrow and lumpy, half taken up with parked cars, and when I drive it now, I shake my head in awe that I'd been able to do that. Of course, once I'd ridden down that street, I'd have to turn around and pedal my butt all the way back up. No picnic, that. As I pumped and sweated, I dreamed of a bike with a motor on it.

But I loved my bike. It was a 26-inch girl's model, so it took some growing into, but Laura didn't want me to get a smaller one, and she was right. I spent my summers on that bike. I even took it along when I'd go to Uncle Austin's, but I didn't take it to Ruth's. There was nowhere to ride it. It was all steep hills, and few of the kids there even had bikes.

We kids would decorate our bikes, particularly for the Fourth of July. We'd intertwine red, white, and blue bunting streamers in the spokes and have more flying off the backs of our seats and handlebars. We'd attach playing cards to the spokes with clothespins for sound effects. At least it *sounded* like a motorbike.

I was never afraid of the dark. I actually loved it and felt very grown up being out alone at night. On Halloween, I'd walk many blocks after school collecting for Unicef, and then, once it was dark, I'd repeat the same route for trick-or-treat. I always went by myself, and I'd be out until eleven o'clock at night, the only kid still on the street, and I never thought twice about it, often waking people who'd already gone to bed.

For a year or so, when Nana was away, I was sent next door to Scottie's house before and after school, and at lunchtime. I remember his mother telling him that he needed to *use* that tooth powder he'd insisted she buy. She always made her kids eat breakfast before they brushed their teeth or got dressed for school. Every day, Laura would make me a peanut butter and jelly sandwich, but I never ate it. Scottie's mother always gave me whatever they were having for lunch. Often it was pancakes with clear white corn syrup. I didn't say anything, but we at least used maple syrup at my house, although it was probably just maple-flavored corn syrup. Whichever, it tasted much better. I'd take the sandwich home to save for the next day, but my mother always threw it out and made me a new one.

Before the bank moved from town to the shopping center, my mother would give me a check for a dollar, made out to cash. I passed the bank on my way to school, and I'd go in, endorse the check and get my dollar. I'd buy candy at the drug store and take my stash to Scottie's after school. We'd be watching TV and I'd be eating my candy. I never shared it—but I think probably Scottie's mother didn't want him to have it, anyway. I probably would have done better myself without the candy. I had my fair share of cavities, and of course hated the dentist.

Summer vacation was nearly three months long. School let out by June 6th at the latest, and we never went back before Labor Day. The schools weren't air-conditioned, and it would have been too hot. We didn't have snow days, either. I don't ever remember school being closed for snow or cold. As I said, we walked to school, and we did so in the bitter cold and in eight inches of snow. The teachers managed to get there, too, and I never remember my mother staying home from work because of the weather.

The highlight of the year was the school picnic, which was held at the amusement park shortly before school let out for the summer. In those days, you bought and used tickets for admission to each ride. For some rides, you only needed one ticket, for others several. They sold tickets at local businesses in our town, and for weeks before the picnic, we'd all be saving our money to buy strips of ride tickets. The first trick was to have enough tickets to last all day. The second was not to lose them in the excitement of rushing from one ride to the next.

One year I had a silly round woven-straw purse that I thought would be perfect for keeping my money and my tickets safe. It had

70

a short strap sort of thing for a handle and I could just put it around my wrist and not have to hold on to it too tightly while I rode. It worked fine until I was on some ride that flew around in circles. Gotta love that centrifugal force. The purse succumbed to it and broke away, flying off the ride, while I was stuck spinning around with nothing but the strap around my wrist, terrified that I'd lost all my money and my tickets. Fortunately, once the ride had ended, I was able to find the purse before someone else did.

There were special streetcars and later buses that took us to the park. We'd leave around 9 A.M. and stay at the park until it closed at 10 P.M. I'd take the streetcar, ride the rides all day, and then my mother would show up after work, bringing new money for tickets, and we'd ride some more. Most people went as families and they'd spread their picnic goodies out on tables. The parents would visit or play bingo or Fascination[17], while the kids checked in and out between rides. I was safe enough on my own; I knew everyone there.

I loved Fascination and Skee Ball. It was tough trying to decide whether to spend my little bit of cash on games or to buy more ride tickets. I'd spend most of the day either on or in line for the roller coaster, but there was one thing I loved nearly as much, and that was the tractors. They were real miniature tractors, run with gasoline engines, and it was like driving a car, even though they didn't go very fast. There were boards on either side of the track that kept us from careening off the side of the hill or driving the tractor all the way home. I'm sure we all wanted to do just that. The amusement park was the best part of my childhood.

It was probably in fourth grade that I started having headaches every day after school. I never took anything for them for some reason—I just lay on the couch in the living room with my eyes closed, often for several hours. I don't know what caused those headaches, perhaps the stress of school. This went on for maybe a year or so and then stopped. I'm not sure I ever even told my mother about it.

---

[17] Fascination was a popular arcade game at that time, but I've not seen it in many years. You rolled balls across a glass tabletop and they'd drop through holes, landing below. The goal was to be the first to get five balls in a row. There was a room full of these tables. You can find out more on the Internet.

One of Laura's favorite remedies for just about anything was aspirin and baking soda. She'd dissolve both in water, the soda masking the taste of the aspirin. I loved baking soda water. One day after school, for no reason that I can think of, other than perhaps there wasn't much else in the house to eat, I decided to make myself a glass of baking soda water. Except that I grabbed the box of cornstarch instead. They both came in yellow boxes and I didn't read the label. I carefully measured some out and stirred it into my water. Yuck! Of course, not knowing what cornstarch actually was, I worried that I'd poisoned myself.

We must have studied European countries in school because I started sending away for travel brochures. Laura wouldn't allow me to get brochures from countries she didn't like. That meant that Italy, Germany, Austria and the Slavic countries were off-limits. I did get one from Austria and told her I'd thought it was Australia. She told me to throw it away, but of course I didn't. I had begun to recognize when what she told me to do made sense and when it didn't.

The new town swimming pool was to open the summer following fourth grade, and we were all thrilled. We ordered passes a month or so before school let out so that we'd be ready to go the first day of vacation. I took swimming lessons briefly that first summer, but I didn't like having to put my head in the water, so I never swam very well. Laura always swam with her head out of the water, too.

I had to hold my nose when I jumped in; I hated getting water up my nose. I was pleased when I discovered that it didn't happen when I'd dive in. I dove into the five-foot deep area and also learned to do flips off the side of the pool. I was afraid to dive or flip off the diving board, though. I did jump off the high dive, holding my nose, of course. I tried nose plugs, but they'd always get knocked off when I'd jump in.

That was also probably the year we Brownies "moved up" to the Girl Scouts. I had the green uniform with the sash for badges, which were actually patches. I didn't earn any badges, and, anyway, I didn't like the idea of having to sew them onto the sash. One of my classmates' mothers was the leader and we met at a local church. She had us making mosaics out of seeds glued to a piece of cardboard. That seemed boring and stupid to me, so I didn't last long in Girl Scouts.

My favorite TV show was "Rawhide." It was on Friday nights and was the official start of the weekend for me. I liked Saturday morning TV, too, but I was never much into cartoons, so I watched shows like "My Friend Flicka" and "Sky King,"[18] both ranch dramas.

My mother bought a brand-new 1957 Plymouth, the one with the fins in the back and the push-button transmission. She thought it was the most beautiful car ever produced and loved the automatic transmission. Laura was always into "beautiful" cars. We were out somewhere when we'd only had the car a day or two, and it wouldn't start. She was dumbfounded. She was trying to start it in (N)eutral. I suggested she try starting it in P(ark). It started right up. I was eight years old.

Aunt Ruth always hated the way my mother said beauty-full, but that's okay—my mother hated it when Aunt Ruth moved to Florida and started saying "arnge" instead of orange.

One early April day it got really warm out. We even hauled out the webbed chaise lounge and set it up in the yard to sun. The next morning, I wore my winter coat to school, as usual, but it was too warm, so at lunchtime I switched to my light raincoat. Of course it then decided to get cold in the afternoon and I nearly froze on the way home after school.

I wanted curly hair, so I sweet-talked my mother into getting me a perm. My hair was rather long and all the same length. Had they cut my hair properly, given me some layers, that perm might have had a chance, but my long, heavy hair mostly stayed straight. As a teenager, I did the curlers thing, and throughout my life I used curling irons, hot rollers, and had various perms. Perms were okay until they started growing out, but my hair grows fast and they never looked right after the first month or so.

Some time in my mid-fifties, when my hair started to turn seriously gray, it also got curly. Someone finally figured out that it should be cut in layers to make the most of the curls, so I have great hair now in my sixties. The best part is that it doesn't frizz. It just gets curlier the more humidity we have. It's quite wonderful after I work out—the more I sweat, the curlier it gets, and I usually look significantly better on the way home from the gym than I do on the way there with my terminal bed head.

---

[18]   More info on both of these shows can be found on the Internet.

REALITY
Crissy Shreve
1972
For the most beautiful man I ever met.

Soon I will be going back to reality.

So many miles.
I will not see the sky over your head,
Nor feel the rain that falls upon you,
Es macht nichts!

However many miles between us,
I must reach only into my pocket—or into my heart,
And I will return
To the beauty of that evening
When we danced and,
In your arms, if only for a moment,
Reality ceased to exist.

Chapter Seven

Transition

Fifth grade was a portal. Although I was still a year younger than the other girls in my class, I got pulled along with them into a whole new world. Suddenly clothes, music, boys, bras, sex, and periods became the subjects of interest.

A girl named Marcia, whom I'd known from church, moved into our neighborhood and joined my fifth grade class at school. Since I knew her already, we became friends by default. Her family dynamic gave me my first taste of a lot of things. I probably would have stayed a naïve child a few years longer had Marcia not come into the picture. With my being a year younger, this made for confusion mixed with enlightenment that I wasn't quite ready to navigate.

Marcia's parents built a brand new house down at the end of our block, and it was modern. There were cabinets in the kitchen, instead of cupboards. Being new, it was cleaner, in an overall sense. They were comparatively well-to-do and had nice things that they kept in logical places. If I'd felt like I had less and was less than other kids before, this increased those feelings significantly.

Marcia had several siblings, and I saw the workings of a larger and more normal family, particularly one with a father in residence. Her mom knew me from church too, and she sort of took me under her wing, so I spent a lot of time at their house. The mom spoke more openly to us girls about the things of womanhood than our own mothers did. Still, in those days, there was much we weren't told; it was a time of confusion, not only about the facts, but also about ourselves.

Marcia was much more sophisticated than the rest of us girls were, and she had the first boyfriend. His name was Tom. I don't know what she ever saw in him, to be honest, but apparently there was something. I did my fair share of daydreaming about boys, but I was mostly terrified of them.

Tom had an older brother named Tim. Tim liked to corner me on the landing at the bottom of the steps next to Ginger's garage. I never approached him; he sought me out for some reason. I was only nine; I didn't like him and felt terrorized by him. I don't think he "liked" me either; he was just being a bully. I ran into him fifty or so years later and called him a pervert, right in front of his wife. I suppose that wasn't very nice of me, but I was finally able to stick up for the little girl I'd been, who hadn't known how to do it at the time. Fair's fair.

Then there was this guy named Bill. He, too, was some years older than I, probably fifteen or sixteen. My mother hired him to whitewash the basement. He was there, so I hung out with him in the way I tended to do, as a lonely and curious little girl. Our garage hadn't been torn down yet, and was rather ramshackle, but I sort of liked it in there. One day when I was in the garage, Bill came in and asked me what I knew about sex. I said that my mother had told me a few things, and he wanted to know what she'd told me. It was an uncomfortable and embarrassing interaction, but he never tried to touch me. I was glad when he'd finished his work and didn't come around any more.

A man named Bob bought the lot next door to us, and that's when we found out that neither of our side lots actually belonged to us. In fact, our house encroached on Bob's property by an inch or so. In effect, he owned the shingles on that side of our house. There were a lot of raspberry bushes on that lot, and it was a challenge to beat the neighbors to them on summer mornings. When Bob cleared the lot, that was the end of the raspberries.

I, still that lonely and curious little girl, spent an entire year hanging out with Bob while he built his house. Except for the foundation, he did most of the work himself. I saw every wall he built and heard just about every nail he pounded. He even let me pound one every so often.

Then one day, when the house was nearly completed, we were in the lower level garage, and he tried to put his arms around me. That was the end of it for me. I never talked to him again, even though he and his wife moved in shortly thereafter. I suppose there must be something irresistible to men about prepubescent female bodies. I didn't have even the slightest concept of myself as a sex object. I couldn't figure out what it was all about. I was just a little kid in need of companionship and attention, not yet even really aware that I was a girl.

My cousin Johnny's family moved from North Carolina to Ohio in late 1957. Once Johnny lived closer, I'd see him more often at Aunt Ruth's on holidays. He was no longer all mine as he had been when we were little, though. Cousin John had an electric train. I couldn't compete with an electric train. John and Johnny would play for hours with that train, banning me from the room. I loved the train, too, and I was hurt and disappointed. Didn't they know that I was a little boy, too?

Ah, but it didn't end there. When John grew up and no longer lived at home, Aunt Ruth gave the train to his sister, my cousin Judy, for her girls. The girls never cared about the train, so when my boys came along, Judy was only too happy to pass it on to me. By then, though, the engine didn't work, and so the train just gathered dust in my basement.

Years later, when X2 and I built our house, I still had that train. I dusted it off, shined it up, and set it on a couple pieces of track curving around the mantel in our family room, where it happily pretended to chug around the corner. The first time John came to visit, he saw it, and wanted it back. I don't think so. I still have it and it's still chugging along on a shelf in my home today. The engine even works now, too, thanks to a friend whose motto is, "If I can't fix it, it's not broken."

But my days of being a "little boy" were coming to an end. I remember being in the bathtub and discovering my first straggly pubic hairs. I was embarrassed, and from that moment on, I never let my mother, or any other female, see me naked. I've never been comfortable being naked in front of women, probably because women are always critical of other women's bodies. Men just smile.

Another new house and another new girl, Nancy, came to our neighborhood. It was her mother who was constantly on our telephone party line. They had two Great Danes and a cat. I'd never had any pets other than Nana's canary Petey, so that, along with Nancy's family's speaking a foreign language, was more new territory for me.

Nana was completely blind by this time, so she didn't answer the door. I still had my room in the attic, too far up to hear someone knocking, so we kept the back door unlocked during the day, and my friends would just walk in and come upstairs looking for me.

Nancy's cat had kittens. When they were old enough to leave mama cat, Nancy brought one over to my house, came in as usual, snuck past Nana, and set this tiny black and white furry thing on my bed. Despite my mother's hatred of cats, he was there to stay, and I named him Trinket. He stayed hidden in my bedroom for a few days before I finally presented my mother with the facts: we had a cat, and that was that.

Laura hated the smell of cat food, so Trinket ate tuna, a can every day, and he supplemented that with whatever birds and mice he could catch. Despite his being a serious tomcat who spent most of his time outside, he was mine, and he loved me tenderly. He was always there when I'd go to bed, and he'd climb under the covers, leaving just his head sticking out, wrap his arms around my neck, purr, and chew on my hair. After I was asleep, he'd go downstairs, and my mother would let him out for the night. He'd always be back in the morning, though, and I'd wake up to his purring in my ear.

The path-street in front of our house connected with the big steps I took down to school. I would go that way whenever it wasn't too snowy or muddy. Trinket would accompany me as far as the steps, and then he'd head off into the woods. But when I came home at lunch and after school, there he'd be, waiting for me. He was a character. After I'd gone to school, my neighbor who lived down the street would walk her dog along the path. Trinket would join them as they passed our house, walk with them to the top of the steps and back, and then leave them once he got back to our house. Dear Trinket. He was a priceless gift.

A few years later, Nana died, and the house was sold. My mother and I moved to an apartment where pets were not allowed. I sadly left Trinket behind with the neighbor, knowing that he'd be happy there in his own element. I'd go see him from time to time. For decades, long after I'd grown up and moved away, I'd get Christmas cards from her, telling me that he was doing fine. I was astounded when she wrote to tell me that he'd finally died after thirty years. He was missing an ear and had only part of his nose left by then, but he'd been the king of the tomcats all his life. Must've been the tuna.

My class moved up to the chancel choir at church. We sat in our own area in the sanctuary, which I believe is called the transept. It had several rows of pews and was off to the side and towards the front, and there the pastor could keep an eye on us during the service. One time he actually stopped in the middle of his sermon to tell us to keep quiet. He preached standing in the actual chancel, but I guess calling us the transept choir wouldn't have sounded as nice.

Sixth grade was our final year in elementary school. We had become the big kids, at least for a year.

The new shopping center opened in the late 1950's, and many of the businesses in our small town moved there. One little independent grocery store remained, though, and they delivered, so my mother ordered her groceries from them for many years. The A&P where Dadum and I had shopped moved to the shopping center, and the "Five and Ten" closed.

A pair of enterprising brothers converted the old A&P into a roller skating rink. It was small, but great, and right there in town, so we could walk to it. Skating was one of the joys of my childhood. I had semi-precision skates and I became quite good. I taught myself how to turn around and skate backwards, practicing for hours on the linoleum floor in the hallway at home, where there were walls beside me to slow me down if I started to fall. We never did the backwards strut at that rink though. When I discovered it years later, I wished I still had that hallway to practice in. By then I couldn't do it without someone to hold on to for balance.

I was at the rink pretty much whenever it was open, and I got to be good friends with the owners. I kept my skates there, behind the skate rental counter, so I didn't have to lug them home with me, and I often helped to hand out rental skates to other kids. I'd even get in free once in a while when I didn't have fifty cents. One time, on my birthday, I saw one of the owners waving at me from the refreshment area. I thought he wanted me to come work for a bit, which I did from time to time. When I got there, he gave me a Coke and wished me a happy birthday over the loudspeaker. That was pretty special.

I was too young to be part of the in-crowd, though. They'd regularly go to the bigger skating rink a few miles out the road on days our rink was closed. I always wished one of the guys would ask me to skate. The best skater was a guy named Don. One time I guess I was the only girl available, and he invited me to skate a waltz. It was like a dream; he was so smooth, and for me it was like drifting on a cloud to organ music.

I later dated Gary, another of the really good skaters, but for some reason, we never went skating together. I never learned to skate or to dance with a partner. It might be just as well, I've never been much good at following, anyway.

When my mother's house burned many years later, we met with the town Fire Marshall. I didn't remember or recognize him, but he kept saying he knew me from somewhere. It turned out that he had been a guard at the skating rink. I hadn't really known him, but of course we saw each other several times a week. I was sad when he told me that Don and Gary had both died, and then this fellow, too, died a few years afterwards.

My friend Kris, the one my mother called Kristy, moved to an apartment above a drug store on the other side of town, but she still came to our school. I'd often go home with her after school, which made for a long walk home. There was a little bakery on the way, and they had just the best chocolate éclairs. The walk home was always much more enjoyable when I had a quarter to buy one.

One day Kris told me she suspected that her mom was pregnant—she'd found a skirt with a hole in the front while snooping in her mother's dresser drawer. In those days, that's how maternity clothes were made. Around this time, Marcia's mom also had another baby. Both Kris and Marcia moved away soon after that, so I never got involved with either baby.

In sixth grade, we were assigned to write and give an oral report on a country in Central or South America. It was usually late afternoon when someone would be called upon to give his or her report, but it was sporadic, so we never knew when it would happen. One girl had Nicaragua and she had a hard time saying it. "Nic-a-rag-a-rag-u-raw," she'd say, and we'd all laugh. I doubt she thought it was funny.

I don't remember what my country was. I never researched it, I never prepared my report, and I was perfectly willing to get a failing grade, but there was absolutely no way I was going to get up in front of the class and talk. The entire second semester, I lived in terror that I'd get called on. Amazingly, I never did, and I breathed a huge sigh of relief when the school year finally ended.

Our sixth grade teacher was also the principal of the school. She was a good teacher and I, like many others, would occasionally stop in to see her after we'd moved on to junior high. She told my mother that I'd make a good artist or librarian. Me? Never! Even my mother though she was nuts. There were several really good artists in my class. I was a relatively capable artist in some areas, but that's about all. I helped out after school with new books that came in for the library, pasting in pockets and making cards. It was certainly not my life's ambition. That library paste tasted pretty good, though.

There was a boy in our sixth grade class named Bob. He seemed to like me. He was a few years older than the rest of us—he had been held back a time or two—and he had bad teeth, but he was exceptionally good looking, anyway. He paid some attention to me, and I never quite knew what to do or what to say. He asked me for my school picture, and I said, "No, thanks." Duh!

One time when we were at the skating rink, I was sitting on the side and as he went skating by, I yelled, "Flunker" at him. Obviously my social skills were nonexistent. I had absolutely no clue what to do with boys. The background noise was naturally very loud, between the music and the kids shouting at each other. He and everyone else thought I'd dropped an F-bomb on him. Since I was too scared to talk to him to begin with, I didn't have a way of telling him what I'd really said, which was insulting enough, anyway. He no longer talked to me at school and then shortly thereafter his family moved away.

I was never scared walking up the steps through the woods at night after skating, which may just prove that I wasn't very smart, although it was certainly a gentler time then. I never saw any of Laura's "goofs" in the bushes, but there were a few who walked me home from the skating rink.

I did manage to have a couple of real boyfriends the summer between sixth and seventh grade. One was Jimmy. He lived even farther up the hill than I did, and he and another guy named Richie hung out with me and my friend Ginger. I think he did actually like me, but it probably didn't hurt that my mother always picked us up from the swimming pool on her way home from work. It was a long, hot walk after a day of swimming. One time we stopped for ice cream at the Dairy Queen and I gave Jimmy a lick of my cone. My mother was horrified. She wouldn't have "eaten off" someone else's food to save her life.

Laura took the four of us to see *South Pacific*. It continues to be one of my favorite movies of all time. I walked around singing "Bali Hai" for weeks. I was just old enough to appreciate the romance and the tragedy that was *South Pacific*. Jimmy traded me in for another girl shortly after that. She was actually someone I knew and liked quite well, and I don't think I fancied myself to be madly in love with Jimmy, so I wasn't overly heartbroken.

And anyway, a guy named Don, who had a twin brother Ron, quickly replaced Jimmy. Although they were identical, Don was just a bit cuter. He was sweet to me and I don't remember why, but it didn't last a long time.

Some of my girlfriends started getting their periods, or at least they said they did. It was a status thing, and I didn't have a prayer because, once again, I was a year behind in everything.

My mother, for no good reason, didn't allow me to go into the deep end of the swimming pool, let alone use the diving board. One night after work she picked me up in the car as usual, along with a bunch of my "friends." Right in front of them, my mother asked me, "Were you in the deep end of the pool?" Before I could formulate a good lie, several voices from the back seat piped up with, "Oh, yes, she was, and she went off the diving board, too."

Another time, a different set of traitors in the back seat, all girls, asked me, "When did you get your period?" Again, before I could come up with a lie, Laura said, *proudly*, "Oh, Crissie hasn't gotten her period yet." Thanks a lot. I felt betrayed, both by my "friends" and by my mother.

Famous Last Words

These are things I heard regularly from the people who said them. They are not necessarily original to that person, but I seldom if ever heard anyone else say them. Often they were specifically aimed at me.

"After me, you come first." My mother.

"You don't want to turn out like Crissy." Grandma Ruth to Jill.

"You're crazy. You think too much." X1 to me.

"You didn't ask." X1—his excuse for not telling me things.

"I don't want any trouble." X2 to me.

"Sassy." Nana. She'd also call me a "hoyden," but she used it to mean boisterous, in keeping with its meaning in her era.

"Wash your hands." Every woman in my family any time anyone walked into a kitchen.

"You catch more flies with honey than with vinegar." X2, to which I'd always reply, "That's predicated upon whether or not you want to catch flies."

"Be nice, Crissy." X2 to me.

"What's the big idea?" My mother when I'd do something wrong.

"Don't play your guitar around other people." My mother. Being able to play the guitar was the first thing I ever did that made me feel good about myself.

"I have to blow a fuse." Laura, just before passing gas.

"Must be the tight shoes." Right afterwards.

My mother actually had a great sense of humor, often in keeping with her general wackiness. She'd laugh like a hyena telling you about how one morning she had carefully measured a perfect teaspoonful of instant coffee and then sprinkled it on her oatmeal. It makes me sad that in the years I knew her, she seldom had much reason to laugh.

But that reminds me of the first time I saw the movie *Hitari*. I was on a date with some guy. He wasn't nearly as memorable as the hyena. When it came on the screen and started laughing, I started laughing with it. I heard myself sounding just like the hyena, and I was embarrassed, but I couldn't stop. I found it amazing then, and I still do, that I was the only one in the theater who caught the contagious laughter of the hyena. Everyone else, including my date, just sat there silently watching.

The same kind of thing happened during two other movies— *Romeo and Juliet* and *Elvira Madigan*, both of which had tragic endings. I sobbed uncontrollably, and when the lights came up, everyone else got up and left the theater, seemingly unaffected. I couldn't get up, and I sat there alone for another ten minutes crying. Many years later, though, at the end of *Schindler's List*, the theater lights remained dim for a while after the movie ended, and I wasn't the only one crying.

"Oops, stepped on a frog." My friend's husband Steve, right after passing gas.

When someone passes gas, my son Mike will say, "Sounds like that hurt," or, "Wow, that even made me feel better," although he actually borrowed the second one from X1.

"You have too much skin for your bones." My cousin Jill to Grandma Ruth, who was always a bit plump.

"Oh, just get tired of it." Laura again, when she didn't like what I was doing or when I'd be interested in something that didn't interest her.

"Eat every carrot and pea on your plate," my friend June's husband John would say. You might want to read this one out loud, make sure you catch it.

"Nothing is ever enough." For me, according to X2, to which I say, nothing was *never* enough.

"Some days you get the bear, and some days the bear gets you." A guy I dated when I was a teenager always said this. I still use it with some regularity.

"Have a blessed day." I think of him as the messenger at the gate. It was 6:30 in the morning and I was at the airport waiting to catch a flight to Nashville. The man was just there, for no apparent reason, other than to pass out blessings.

X2 and I were at a motor home rally and it was casino night. While we were in line for dinner, I noticed that the woman in front of me was carrying her casino chit—something she wouldn't need until after dinner. So I asked her why she had it. She looked down at it and said, "It was in my hand." What a great line, and one I've since found myself using more than I care to admit.

"I threw my dime in good faith." My cousin Judy as she pulled away from the tollbooth, having missed the coin basket.

"Oh." Also my cousin Judy, upon discovering a banana in her pocket. We'd just gotten home from the grocery store. She'd had too many things to carry and not enough hands, so she stuck a banana in the pocket of her jacket, fully intending to pay for it once she got to the checkout counter. And of course, she forgot all about it. Back home, she reached into her pocket for a tissue and there was the banana.

THE MAN I WOULD'VE CALLED DADDY
Crissy Shreve

The man I would've called Daddy
Said no when he heard about me
He already had a boy and a girl
Guess he thought he didn't need three
Well, maybe he just used my mother
Or maybe she used him
You sure wouldn't call me a love child
But maybe the child of a whim.

The man I could've called Daddy
I met quite by accident
I never dreamed that I'd found him
When into his arms I went
But there was something between us
Some tie I could never quite see
And though he belonged to those other kids
Somehow he belonged to me.

Those times when we'd laugh together
Were over before they could start
And the man I'd have loved to call Daddy
Tore a hole in a little girl's heart.

The man I should've called Daddy
Never knew he was precious to me
'Cause the way that he wanted to love me
Wasn't how a Daddy should be
And just like the letter I wrote him
The one I could never send
Walking away put a scar on my soul
That nothing could ever mend.

I don't know if he ever wonders
Whatever happened to me
If he does, Lord, just tell him don't worry
'Cause You've been my Daddy to me.

CHAPTER EIGHT

WALKING AWAY

A wise shrink once asked me whether I had any idea what it had cost me when I'd had to walk away from someone I loved. I've had to do it too many times throughout my life.

I hadn't had any idea. Once the concept hit my radar, I understood that it had taken a terrible toll on me. I'd had to harden my heart in order to be able to walk away. To allow my heart to be soft enough to feel such pain was more than I could bear. With each walk, my heart became harder, and it remained that way through much of my life.

If you will forgive a graphic concept, and even if you won't, have you ever noticed that the only functioning part of the body that was designed to face backwards is the behind? There's a reason for this. We're meant to leave the crap behind us. Crap biodegrades. It's not intended to be kept.

Life is full of what Dr. Henry Cloud calls necessary endings.[19] There are times when we have to walk away from someone in order to survive. There are people who just aren't going to be good to us, not ever, and it's not likely to change. We have to leave them behind so that we can move on, but no matter how justified we are in walking away, particularly if it's from someone we love or someone who should love us, it hurts.

I'm a big believer in "permission." Sometimes I need permission, or sometimes I find myself giving permission to friends, to make a hard choice. Permission is not something we easily give to ourselves. Cloud's book not only gives us permission to walk away, it tells us that we must in certain situations. Permission gets the job done, but the pain doesn't necessarily go away either quickly or easily.

---

[19]   NECESSARY ENDINGS, Henry Cloud, 2010, Harper Collins

Like most children, I didn't know how to grieve. I didn't know how to slog through my pain in a healthy way so that I could come out the other side of it and let it go. By the time I came to the place where I knew I had to do something about it, I was carrying a heavy suitcase full of crap.

I don't know who my father was. I never met my mother's husband. Several years before I was born, my mother lost a baby, a boy who lived less than a day. She never really recovered from it. My mother went off the deep end and the marriage came to an end.

That began a life of functional insanity in my mother. She was diagnosed as paranoid schizophrenic and was given shock treatments. Perhaps they helped, because she was highly functional in some ways, and yet she was completely helpless in others.

A few years after losing that baby, my mother got involved with another man and I, if she is to be believed, am his child. The family swears that her husband came back briefly at about the time I'd have been conceived and that I look just like him. Since I've only seen small black and white pictures of him, it's hard to tell.

I know so little of the husband that there's not much I can say about him, except that he was never in the picture. The family says they can't imagine his not claiming me had I been his child. I don't know whether he ever even knew about me.

I did meet the other man, though, and I got to know him rather well. It was by accident; he owned a record shop in the town where we lived and I went in there one day. We got to talking. I was about eleven years old. There was something special between the two of us, and I kept going back. I couldn't understand why, when I'd sometimes take friends along with me to visit him, he was different with them, and they never saw him as I saw him. It was as though he knew me, from the moment I walked into the store, and it is this that makes me believe that he probably was my real father, although I had no clue at the time.

I had just started getting into music, and I wanted a record of "The Lion Sleeps Tonight[20]." One night my mother and I went to his shop to buy it. I didn't understand the awkwardness between them. She told me later, on the way home, that she already knew him, but she didn't give me any details.

---

[20] "Lion Sleeps Tonight." The Tokens, 1961

He sold us the record. I'm not sure whether I wish he'd given it to me. I just think he could have. One time he did give me a cheap black glass ashtray. I kept it for many years, and then I sold it at a garage sale. Such a stupid useless gift; it never meant anything to me, even though it was the only thing he ever gave me.

He was funny. We laughed all the time. He had all sorts of zany things he'd say, like "That's the way the spheroid ricochets." There is a children's song that he misquoted, but I hadn't heard it before, so I didn't know the difference. He didn't sing it; he just said the words:

> "Peanuts on the railroad tracks,
> Their hearts were all a-flutter.
> Along came the choo-choo train,
> Toot toot! Peanut butter!"[21]

I thought it was the funniest thing I'd ever heard. I adored him. Had I been able to pick a man to be my daddy, it would have been he. Many years later, I wrote a song about him called "The Man I Would Have Called Daddy." You saw the words at the beginning of this chapter.

One day when I was visiting him, he said he had something to show me, and he asked me to go downstairs with him, to the basement of his shop. I was uncomfortable with the idea, but I went. I wasn't afraid of him. Once down there, it was quickly obvious that there was nothing to see, but he did put his arms around me. He didn't do anything more than that, and I don't know what his intentions were or what might have happened further, because I turned around and walked back upstairs and out the door. He didn't try to stop me.

I walked away.

I don't know whether he just wanted to hug his "daughter" or whether he had other ideas. I didn't tell my mother about it until decades later. When I did, she said it was no surprise.

According to my mother, when she discovered that she was pregnant with me, she went to this man and his mother, asking for help,

---

[21] The correct version, written by James Clarence Mangan: "A peanut sat on a railroad track, His heart was all a-flutter. The five-fifteen came rushing by— Toot toot! Peanut butter!"

but was turned away. He was married, of course, and had two other children. As far as I know, he never worked much, just lived on family money, and so, to some degree, I suppose it's possible that he would have been more responsive had he not been tied to his mother's purse strings. Either way, he was of no help to either my mother or to me.

In effect, two fathers abandoned me before I was even born. I was fortunate in my mid-forties to work with a guy shrink who said, simply, that he'd have been honored to be my dad. Such a small thing, and yet so healing.

Late one night, when I was thirteen or fourteen, I ran away. My mother and I may have been arguing about something, but I didn't really have a good reason to run away. I was just a troubled kid with a built-in desperation I didn't understand. Something was missing and I was looking for it.

By that time, my mother and I were living on the third floor of an apartment building. There was a flat roof outside our apartment that extended across the front of the building, covering the porches below. It had a railing and it served as our porch. I never used a key to get into the apartment; I'd just climb through the hallway window onto the porch, and then go through the French doors into our living room.

My bedroom faced the street and my window was several feet off to the side of the edge of the porch. I apparently thought I was indestructible. I climbed through my bedroom window, reached over to grasp the railing, and, three stories above the ground, climbed over onto the porch. Only God knows why I didn't fall those three stories to my death. He was clearly watching out for me. The building was old; the railing was rickety, and the ledge of the porch was unstable. I shudder now just to think of it.

Once I was out, the question became where to go, what to do. It was after midnight and it was cold out. I was wearing my winter coat. I started walking aimlessly and wound up at a local diner, about a mile away, that was open all night. I went in to get a cup of coffee to warm me up, still having no idea where I was headed, or, for that matter, why. There was a middle-aged man sitting at the counter, and we started talking. I don't remember much about that part of it, just that he somehow sensed that I was alone in the cold. He took me home to his house and to his wife. They gave me a warm bed to sleep in.

What can I say about that? How could that have been anything but God watching over me, even then, even when I had no idea Who He was or that He loved me? That man could have taken me anywhere; he could have raped or killed me. My mother didn't even know I was gone. Instead, God used him to rescue me from my own stupidity.

I slept very well. In the morning, after the man had left for work, his wife needed to go out, and she asked me to leave the house. I never saw him again, but I did run into the wife one time a few months later. I said, "Hi, remember me?" She replied, with some disdain, "Yes, I remember you," and didn't appear to be interested in further conversation, so that was that. I think the man's name was Ralph; I don't remember the wife's name. I hope that perhaps they will somehow get hold of this book and . . . know.

My mother didn't discover my absence until the next morning, at which point she called the police. I went home and there they were. I can't begin to imagine her terror. I am sorry about that.

As a result of this escapade, the "powers that were" wanted to put me in a reform school. My mother went to bat for me; she was not going to let them put me away. She had me hide in the women's bathroom on the 17th floor of a downtown office building so that I would be nearby if she was forced to bring me before the judge. She told me to stay there until she returned, and if she didn't return, I should not come home.

Apparently she made a good case on my behalf because she did come back for me and I didn't go to reform school. However, in the process, the judge had asked her about my father, and she'd had to tell them that her husband was not my father. She never told them the other man's name, but the judge insisted that she tell *me* who he was. On the way home in the cab, she told me about it, saying that I knew him, but that I needed to guess who he was. It didn't take me long to figure it out.

I never again saw the man I would have called Daddy. Years later, I was looking for an old record and ordered it from him by mail. By then I was married, so my name had changed, and I was living in a different state. I didn't tell him who I was, but I think he knew. He enclosed a rather weird post card in which he made several cryptic statements that wouldn't have made sense otherwise. He is no longer living.

MAUSOLEUM
Crissy Shreve

I live in a mausoleum
I am the deadest of the dead
Blessings turned to damnings
Icy fingers pointing
Staring
Screaming
You are not worthy
Of love
Of life
That
I am the exception
The one shunned of God
And most certainly of man

I walk among the dead
Alternately shouting
Live with me
Die with me
There are no takers
There is no rest
If hell is in this mausoleum
What hope can there be of eternity?[22]

---

22 One of the few ways I've ever had of dealing with my feelings has been through writing poetry. I thank God that His truth is so much bigger than my feelings at the time I wrote this. I thank God that I can look forward to eternity with Him.

CHAPTER NINE

WHO AM I?

Seventh grade. Kids from the three elementary schools converged in junior high. The eighth graders mocked us seventh graders a bit, but it wasn't nearly as bad as we'd been led to believe it would be. Older kids had also warned us that in junior high everyone would be expected to give a report on stage in front of the whole school. That thought really terrified me and hung over my head the whole two years I was there. I was, once again, prepared to flunk junior high, because I sure wasn't going to do that. As it turned out, no one ever had to do it.

Changing classes wasn't nearly as confusing as I'd feared it would be. We were split into two or three sections of seventh graders and each section had all the same classes, moving as a group from one room to the next.

The man who taught us math and science was a good teacher. I remember him saying, "Everything is made up of electricity; shocking, isn't it?" The social studies teacher liked to say "thusly" at the beginning of many of his sentences, and it always annoyed me. It's a nonexistent word; thus is an adverb on its own without the -ly. He was also perhaps the most arrogant person I've ever met. I saw him again some forty-five or so years later at a reunion and he hadn't changed one bit.

Our curriculum included Home Economics for the girls and Shop for the boys. Both these classes were held in the basement of the school. The Home Ec room had a sewing area and a full kitchen. We learned to use a sewing machine, which was a useful skill that I was glad to have in later years. Just knowing how to thread the stupid thing, and especially the bobbin, is three quarters of the battle. We hemmed tea towels and made aprons. Our cooking projects weren't very sophisticated, either. Girls who chose to continue taking Home Ec in high school got to make actual clothes and full meals. I didn't, so I didn't.

We were allowed to bring our lunch to school in junior high, and those of us who did would sit on benches in the basement hallway. I didn't bring lunch every day, only in nasty weather. Usually I walked all the way home, which was about twice as far as it had been from my elementary school, and yes, climbed those steps. I made myself American cheese and mayonnaise sandwiches nearly every day of junior high. That was what I wanted, for some reason. Hardly nutritious, but who knew anything back then? Certainly not I. Sometimes my mother would give me money to eat lunch at a small restaurant about a block from the school. That was a treat; the food was good.

I had a friend named Candy in seventh grade. If it were possible, she was even more messed up emotionally than I was. Candy, too, was growing up without a father. She hated her mother. At that point I didn't hate my mother yet, but I probably first picked up the notion from Candy.

I have always had a tendency to be loyal to my friends. Candy wanted to run away. We both started saving our money, such as we had any. I skipped eating lunch at the restaurant and saved that dollar or so. The plan was to go to Hawaii, which had just become a state. I don't know how we thought we'd get there, but we planned to live on the beach. We even went so far as to try to learn the language—well, we knew how to say "Aloha," anyway.

Candy and I went downtown one day for some reason and we met a couple of guys, men really, who were staying at a hotel. Coincidentally, Candy decided that same night that she had to run away right that minute, and she had some vague notion of going to find those men. I personally didn't have a need or a desire to run away, I just didn't want her going off on her own. It was that loyalty thing.

I'd found a wallet at the swimming pool the previous summer. I didn't steal it, but someone else had, and they'd taken out the money and ditched the wallet. There wasn't any identification in it, so I kept it. There was an initial on it—not mine, though. There were a lot of pictures of people in that wallet, a few I knew, most I didn't; they were all of older kids. I replaced them with pictures of my own.

We'd been skating, and when the rink closed that night, instead of going home, Candy and I started walking downtown. We didn't take the bus; either we had no money, which is most likely, or we didn't want to be seen. By this time, the streetcars had been replaced with buses, and the old streetcar right-of-way wasn't being used, so we walked several miles on that. Once we got to the end of it, though, we had to walk the rest of the way on a main street through a commercial area. Right past a police station.

This fat cop spotted us and chased us down the street. It was pretty late by then and we were tired, so I think we probably let him catch us. We ditched our purses so he wouldn't know who we were. That wallet was in my purse. I never got it back. I didn't miss it much, but I was sorry to lose the pictures I'd had in it.

Of course they figured out who we were pretty quickly. Both our mothers had called the police, so they figured we were together. A policeman from our town came to collect us and take us home. He dropped Candy off first. I was to remain in the car while he took her inside. Candy's house was on a steep hill and the front sidewalk was icy. The cop went down. It was pretty funny, and neither of us could stop laughing. He was not amused.

Then he took me home. Certainly my mother had been terrified that something bad had happened to me. I do remember telling her that I hadn't wanted to run away, I was just watching out for Candy. She suggested that perhaps a better choice would have been to bring Candy home with me. That had never crossed my mind. It probably should have.

Of course from that night on, Candy was no longer allowed to hang out with me. Go figure. I don't remember my mother putting any such restriction on me. And of course we both ignored that directive and remained friends until she moved away when we were in high school.

Uncle Austin came the next day and gave me a much-deserved lecture. Uncle Jimmy came, too. He drove all the way from Ohio. For some reason, I was more afraid of him, and I hid in the woods until he'd left.

As I look back at that some fifty-plus years later, I have to allow that they obviously did love me. I knew Uncle Austin did, even at that time. He tried, and he did spend a certain amount of time with me. Uncle Jimmy had always lived too far away, so I didn't see much of him. It's a shame, really—he was a funny guy and my cousins all knew that side of him, even if I didn't.

I continued to walk the ridge between being a kid and, well, no longer being a kid. Once again, my being a year younger than my friends made a difference. I was thrust into a world for which I wasn't ready. I wasn't a leader or a follower; I just sort of floated along, wherever the wind blew me.

I had no idea who I was, or where or even whether I fit in. I still turned cartwheels over the railing at the top of the steps, even as I stole my mother's cigarettes and tried them. One of my "friends" threatened to tell my mother that I'd been smoking, and told me that I had to go home and confess or she'd tell on me. So I did. I was really scared, but I didn't get punished in any memorable way. My mother wasn't strong enough to do anything with me other than to hope I'd survive being me.

Nana died in September that year. I inherited her bedroom, including the furniture, her transistor radio, a white cardigan sweater that I lost at the funeral home, and a wonderful onyx cocktail ring that I'd always loved. It had belonged to Nana's sister, my great aunt Ella.

Aunt Ella lived in California, so I never saw much of her, but she always sent me Christmas presents. The only one I remember was an umbrella. One time when she was in town, she took me to the amusement park. I don't know what she expected, but I was into boys by then and I went looking for some and riding the rides on my own. I didn't spend the day with her, only allowed her to take me and give me money for rides. She was disappointed, and I don't think I ever saw her again after that.

That year our team won the World Series, and at school we listened to the final game on the transistor radio that had been Nana's. My mother came home from work, picked me up, and we drove back downtown to see the celebration. People were throwing toilet paper like streamers from the top floors of office buildings, something you could still do in those days when the windows could actually be opened.

It was great to be able to move down from the too hot and too cold attic to Nana's bedroom. The spring after she died, I had a pet Chameleon. I kept a string tied around its neck like a collar and attached the other end to my shirt with a safety pin. Living jewelry. I even wore it to school.

Of course my mother hated the Chameleon. I'd pin it to my dresser scarf at night, so she had no reason to worry, but I'm sure she envisioned finding it in bed with her. One night after I'd fallen asleep, she threw the Chameleon out my bedroom window. She didn't admit what she'd done, but I figured it out. I ran downstairs and there it was, right under my window, and still alive. I have no idea what, or even whether, I fed it or how it got water, and I don't remember what finally did it in, but it may well have been starvation. My mother never suggested it might need food or water, and I'm sure she was thrilled at its demise.

Years later, when I was married to X2, I was checking a pair of his trousers before taking them to the cleaner's, and something fell out of a pocket. We were both ushers at church and it was standard procedure to pick up things we found on the floor after the service and stick them in our pockets, so I thought it was just a plastic toy some kid had lost. When I went to pick it up, it scuttled across the floor, scaring me half to death. It was a live chameleon! By the time I recovered, it had found an opening between the baseboards and disappeared, never to be seen again. Neither X2 nor I had any clue how it had gotten into his pocket. At least it hadn't found its way into our bed!

Speaking of finding things in bed, my son Jason told a story from when he rented a room in the basement of a house that was right next to a swamp. In the middle of the night, he felt something crawling up his leg. Thinking he was dreaming, he decided it felt quite nice. And then he woke up. It was one of those big five-inch long centipedes. As he put it, he squealed like a little girl.

Back to seventh grade, when I finally became aware of boys, I started daydreaming about them. The first was a really cute kid from church named Scott. I envisioned him running away from home for some reason, and my hiding him behind the fireplace in my bedroom.

Another was Dan who lived down the street from me. He didn't even know I existed and I never had any interaction with him. A shame, really, but at that point, I wouldn't have known what to do with him anyway.

Another, David, my favorite, was the most beautiful boy I ever saw. He'd been coming around the neighborhood for a while with his dad, selling produce out of the back of their truck. He was a very troubled kid and was even rumored to have spent some time in reform school. Nevertheless, I adored him and he was the object of many of my daydreams. I ran into David at a dance when I was in eighth grade and he wanted to walk me home. A daydream come true, except that when I called my mother to tell her not to pick me up after the dance, I made the mistake of telling her his name. He was Italian and she hated Italians, so she insisted on picking me up. That was the end of that dream.

One time I was visiting my friend Ginger, and we were going through her mother's dresser drawers. Ginger gave me one of her mother's bras. I actually wore it for a year or two. Can't you just imagine that poor woman wondering where her bra had gone? I suppose she decided that the washing machine must have eaten it.

Fast forward again to when I was married to X2. He announced one morning that the washing machine must have been eating his underpants because there were none in his drawer. It was his way of suggesting that it might be time for me to do the wash. Good wife that I was, I rushed right out and bought him ten new pairs of underpants.

AND GONE
Crissy Shreve

How hard I tried, how very many times I wept
Yet you remained so distant.
For all the time we spent, all the days so wasted
Is there no return of them—of at least a thought?

For that I would give so much, for anything
But such regret.
And yearning for something, short, but there to
remember
And gone as easily as the word good-bye

Chapter Ten

Bevy

In sixth grade, another girl I'd known from church came to our school, and we continued on together into junior high. Her name was Bevy.

We became best friends. She was beautiful and smart and tough. And she liked me. I never understood why. In my eyes, she was and had everything, whereas I was and had nothing. I didn't spend a lot of time at her house, but when I did, I saw what appeared to me to be comparative normalcy. Forty years later, I found out that, in reality, her home life was far from normal and that she, too, had felt inferior to everyone else because her dad was, in her words, the "town drunk." I don't know that we ever talked about these things at the time, though; we both just escaped from our respective houses as much as we could.

Despite it all, she was popular, and she somehow managed to fit in. Everyone loved Bevy. She was my ticket to the "in" crowd.

A boy from our class named Mike loved Bevy. She and I hung out with Mike and another boy named Billy. The whole town, or so it seemed, was watching the budding romance between Mike and Bevy. It was a big deal when they finally kissed in the tunnel on the roller coaster.

At the beginning of seventh grade, Bevy contracted TB. I was livid that my mother wouldn't allow me to visit her, but of course no one was allowed to visit, so I wouldn't have been let in even if I'd tried. The house was under county quarantine. There was some sort of intercom system between school and her house, so Bevy was still able to be part of the class. Mike carried the box from room to room and plugged her in. Every so often, a teacher would call on her and we'd hear her answer through the intercom. One time a teacher asked her something and she didn't respond. He said, "Guess she must be out making a sandwich."

Before Bevy returned to school that spring, I started hanging out with a girl named Linda. I don't know what was up with her, and fifty years later I still can't figure it out. She started telling me that Mike liked *me*. That made no sense to me. Why would any boy like me when he could have Bevy? Still, I was naïve and stupid and, well, flattered. I wouldn't have tried to get Mike away from Bevy for the world, but I got caught up in it nonetheless.

At this same time, many of the girls were wearing ribbons and little silver bells in their hair. Linda and I shoplifted some bells. Her father was a cop, though, and she was afraid that she'd get in trouble, so she spread it around that I had stolen the bells. This did not improve my standing in seventh grade society.

By the time Bevy came back to school, everyone hated me. I wrote derogatory things in chalk on the steps about the other girls, thinking that might get them mad at each other instead of at me. I cleverly wrote derogatory things about myself as well. No one saw me doing it, but somehow they knew I had. That didn't help the situation. I made a lot of trips to the steps with glasses of water during lunch hour to wash it all away, but with limited success.

At that time we still lived in the house and there was a side window I used to get in and out so that I wouldn't have to carry a key. All my friends knew about the window; most had used it themselves. One day after school, Bevy and another girl named Janet came after me. I saw that Bevy had her Girl Scout knife. I panicked. As they were coming through the window, I was running out the back door to my neighbor's house. Left to my own devices, I might have just let it go, but the neighbor told my mother and my mother called the police. In my terror and confusion, apparently I mentioned the knife.

Bevy was severely beaten by her father, and he took away the knife. When I saw her next at the skating rink, I tried to apologize and tell her that I'd never have tried to take Mike away from her. We were in the girls' bathroom, and she wouldn't even talk to me. She just gave me a dirty look and flounced out the door. Since we didn't talk about it, I never knew about the beating; for decades, I thought that she was just mad at me about Mike.

Terror became my new best friend. I was always afraid. Going to school was hell. And then I met Dana. She was a few years older than I. She was a serious reprobate, much more sophisticated and much more troubled than I was. She became my "bodyguard." No one messed with me after that. My whole world changed. I no longer got involved with anyone at school or any activities there other than classes. At that point, Dana was in high school, while I was still in junior high. Since my world no longer worked, I joined hers. It wasn't a good place for me, and if I'd been going down the tubes before, this was the express train.

I never realized that other kids actually had it worse than I did. Both Bevy and Dana did—much worse. I may have had no father, but I didn't have a father who beat me, and my mother, wacky as she was, was so much better than either of theirs was. The difference was that Bevy made lemonade and Dana made acid. Now I realize that I was probably better off not having had a father around. Since then I've heard so many horror stories from friends who grew up with drunken dads, abusive dads. I'm grateful my mother didn't remarry. Just my luck, I'd have gotten an abusive stepfather.

The old pastor at our church retired and we started confirmation classes with the new pastor. Between Bevy's no longer being my friend, and skipping school with Dana, I quit going to class. I won't say much more about Dana here. She'll be showing up a lot more as this story progresses.

There is one funny Dana story, though. Providing clothing for her or her siblings was not one of her parents' priorities. In those days, girls were not allowed to wear any kind of long pants to school, only skirts or dresses. One day Dana was wearing an old pair of underpants with worn out elastic. As she was walking down the hall, those underpants fell down. She blithely stepped right out of them and kept on walking.

Life went on with Dana and without Bevy. There were so many things I missed out on, things I chose not to do because I was afraid of being shunned by the "in" crowd. There were dancing lessons in eighth grade, which I attended a time or two, but no one wanted to dance with me. Later on, there were dances and teen nights at the swimming pool. To me, though, the greatest tragedy was finding out decades later that Bevy had been going alone to a local riding stable, where she cleaned stalls in exchange for riding privileges. I knew about the stable, but would never have thought to go there alone, and anyway, had I known she'd be there, I'd have run in the other direction.

But I wanted so badly to ride horses and it would have been the most wonderful thing for us to do together. Bevy hated going alone, too. We should have been best friends and "sisters" all our lives. We both missed out. We needed each other.

But God says, ". . . I will restore to you the years that the locust hath eaten . . ."[23] and He brought about an ending to this story that is nothing short of magnificent.

I had long been gone from our little town when someone decided to start having all-years high school reunions. Even those of us who'd not actually graduated there were welcome. The first time, before I even booked my flight, I carefully checked the list of those from our class who would be there, and Bevy wasn't on it. I felt safe to go. Yes, even forty years later, I was still afraid of being shunned.

They say you can't go home again, but they're wrong. I know because I did it.

I went to the reunion and all was well. Bevy wasn't there, and I enjoyed meeting up with people I'd not seen in so long. Amazingly enough, they either hadn't known all that much about me or they'd forgotten. They were actually happy to see me. Imagine that!

There was an icebreaker Friday night, and then the main banquet and dance Saturday night. After dinner Saturday, I was sitting in the hallway outside the banquet room. Suddenly Bevy appeared. She'd just stopped in to see who was there. All the old fears came bubbling up in me. I didn't know whether to hide or to run, so I just sat there, trying to disappear into the chair.

Bevy spotted me and screamed my name, ran over, and threw her arms around me. I was stunned. I started to cry. I was sobbing so hard I couldn't tell her why, and she thought I was nuts. Finally, I was able to gasp, "I missed you so much, and I didn't even know it until just this minute."

Since that night we've spent lots of time together, sorting through it all, trying to understand what happened and each other's

---

[23]   Joel 2:25 KJV

perspective at the time, and forgiving one another. The most significant statement was one Bevy made: *We were kids!*

It's a strong testimony to how the choices we make as kids can have a huge effect on our lives, how the pain of those years can color our thinking and get in our way for decades. I was still that kid forty years later. In our reconciliation, that shattered piece of me was finally able to grow up and heal.

God planned that reunion for us. And it turned out that we *are* sisters—sisters in the Lord. We have forever together.

APRIL SNOW
Crissy Shreve

April snow
Gently falling
Tiny shadows cast from a timid sun
Fall, yes fall
And polka-dot my world
The last hurrah of winter
On the run

CHAPTER ELEVEN

WOMANHOOD

I didn't have many clothes when I was in eighth grade. Aunt Ruth gave me a few cast-offs that had been my cousin Janice's. With Nana gone, my mother was suddenly responsible for all our expenses as well as those of the house. There wasn't enough to go around. She and Uncle Austin would have screaming battles when she'd beg him for money. He didn't want to give it to her, but he always did. Still, it wasn't nearly enough.

My mother was never any good with money. She'd buy an old car on credit, and it would run well enough for a month or two. Then it would break down. She'd take it in, but she couldn't afford the repairs, so she'd abandon the car at the service station. She'd still have to pay the loan on the car for the remaining months or years, even though she no longer had it. She did this more than once.

I met a girl who'd just moved into the area. She was from England and had a really cute older brother. I offered to pick her up the first day of school, walk with her, and show her around. What I really wanted was an "in" with her brother, although he never noticed me.

I had a pink skirt and a white long-sleeved shirt I'd gotten from Aunt Ruth. I carefully ironed them and hung them up to stay fresh. It was a pretty outfit. On the first day of school, I put it on and went down the hill to this girl's house. It took a while for someone to answer the door. It wasn't the first day of school; I was a day too early. I climbed back up the hill and went home. It was hot out, so my nice, fresh outfit wilted and didn't look nearly as nice the next day when it really was the first day of school.

I had started listening to popular music on the radio. Aunt Ruth made my cousin John give me a 45-rpm record called "School Days" by Chuck Berry. I didn't really like the song, but since it was one of the few records I owned, I played it over and over again.

When the popular girls at school would receive a compliment on their hair or clothing they would reply, "Oh, thank you." Obviously someone had taught them to do that. My tendency was to never believe anyone liked anything about me or, for that matter, liked me, and on the rare occasion I'd get a compliment, I'd belittle myself. This went on for many years until I finally figured out that those girls had had it right. Just graciously say, "Thank you." Even now, I think of them, two in particular, whenever I get a compliment. Both of them died young; one was murdered and the other died of cancer.

The desk where I sat in Language Arts was the homeroom desk of a seventh grade girl named Brenda. I have no idea how it started, but we'd leave each other notes in her desk. Neither of us had much of anything to talk about, so we'd just write page after page trying to persuade the other to write a long, long, long, long note. She and I never made any effort to see each other in person; we weren't even necessarily friends. For me, writing those notes was just something to pass the time in class. Interesting, though—some years later she wound up marrying my son Larry's father.

One morning I stopped at Marcia's house on the way to school. I was feeling a little weird, but had no idea what was going on. I had been wearing the same tattered dress to school every day all that year. Marcia's mother made me a skirt and top outfit out of a gorgeous muted red print fabric. That day I got my period for the first time. When I went back to Marcia's after school, there was my new outfit, and her mother was not at all surprised that I'd gotten my period. She'd suspected that it would happen that day.

Once I started hanging out with Dana, my escapades started in earnest. She was at the high school while I was still in junior high, so I was a child during the day while masquerading as a teenager at night. A walking dichotomy—passing notes in school like a little girl and out chasing men with Dana at night. I was two completely different people. I was neither of them.

Dana lived right at the edge of the next town over. We started going to dances there, and meeting older kids. I was still only twelve. I met a guy named Butch, who became my boyfriend for a time. His family was very poor and his clothes were patched, but he was sweet.

I also met a girl named Kathy, who lived near Butch, and she hung out with us too. At Christmas that year, Butch gave me a bracelet. I happened to be talking on the phone with Kathy the next day and she told me that someone had stolen the bracelet she'd bought for her mother. I put two and two together and described the bracelet I'd gotten from Butch. Same bracelet. I returned it to her and broke up with him.

I had a phone in my room, only because it had been my grandmother's room. One time when I was talking to Kathy, and we were giggling over something about men's anatomy, my mother was listening in on the downstairs extension. How annoying.

We did some crazy things. There was a bridge under which a storm sewer emptied out into the creek. The sewer ran for several blocks underneath a main street. It was about five feet in diameter; large enough to walk in, if one bent over and straddled the shallow stream of water running through it. So, walk it we did. We weren't brave enough to climb the ladders and lift the manhole covers (good thing), but we could hear the cars passing above us.

I turned thirteen in the middle of eighth grade.

Dana had a party at her house one night, and I met a really cute guy. He and I did some kissing behind the refrigerator. It was my first kiss. He was chewing spearmint gum and he was yummy. To this day, I love spearmint gum and it always reminds me of him. He was just visiting from somewhere else, though, and I didn't see him again.

Dana and I started picking up guys. They were always older guys with cars. One's name was Dave. He was twenty or so. I took him home to meet my mother. She was looking out the upstairs window and she wouldn't come downstairs to meet him. She didn't like his looks, said he had a "shrunken" chest. At this juncture, it might have been good for her to intervene and send him away, but instead she chose to stay upstairs and do nothing. Probably by this time she figured she'd lost control over me, and she may have been right, but I did bring him home, so maybe I was still looking for some kind of guidance from her.

Dave was also my first foray into sex. I kept saying no, and, in actuality, that probably would even have been okay with him, but not okay enough that he quit bugging me. I can't tell you why I gave in; I really don't know what I was thinking. I think I wasn't thinking. It may have just been curiosity. I was such a lost soul. I didn't have any sense of my own well-being or protection. However, when it came right down to it, he thought he'd done it, but he hadn't, although at that point, I didn't know the difference. The irony is that he accused me of not being a virgin because I didn't bleed. Well, I didn't know I was supposed to! And to top it off, I got trench mouth from kissing him, and I had to get shots in my gums from the dentist.

A few months later, I tried it again with someone else, with more "success." Neither of them stayed around after they got what they wanted. The second guy was quite a few years older than I was, too. I ran into him forty years later and discovered that I was still mad at him for leaving me. Plus, after forty years, I'd figured out that these older guys had had no business whatsoever with a thirteen-year-old girl, no matter how provocative she might have been. I'm not sure he even remembered me, but I didn't want to talk to him. I was embarrassed along with being angry. He saw how uptight I was, and he sat down beside me and started giving me a neck massage. It was so good that I nearly forgave him.

I had blond hair that summer after eighth grade. My neighbor downstairs, Louise, bleached my hair and gave me a perm. Dana kept telling me I was so pretty. I never felt pretty.

Dana and I picked up some guys named Richie and Joey. Joey was my first love. He was so, so cute. I adored him. I came out of school one day, and there he was, leaning against a wall across the street, waiting for me. He gave me what in those days was called a friendship ring, a somewhat wide silver band with a stamped pattern. One day we were walking in the park and I was so thrilled just to be with him. I was swinging my arm for some reason and the ring flew off. I couldn't find it. He broke up with me, saying it was because I'd lost the ring. I went back to that spot and spent hours searching through the grass for that ring. I never found it. And he was gone.

Joey and I didn't have sex. I never had sex with the guys I really loved. I suppose it was because they never pressured me. Even so, Joey didn't stay around, either. I walked around in a daze for weeks, brokenhearted and despondent.

Right at this time, we moved to the apartment. Uncle Austin bought Nana's house and paid his three siblings their shares, including my mother. Nana's will had provided for the grandchildren to receive

$200 each. Years later, after my mother's house burned, I was digging around in the mess looking for important things, and I found the paper she had signed for receipt of my money. I never saw a penny of it. If I had, I would have bought a TV for my room.

I did, however, have what I called an "air conditioner" in my room. It was actually a swamp cooler—a squirrel cage fan that you filled with water and the air came out, well, not cold, but cool enough. My mother had a fan in her window. It was hot up on the third floor of the apartment building.

It was only a month or so before the end of eighth grade, and the apartment was just around the corner from the school. Aunt Ruth borrowed a dress for me to wear for eighth grade graduation. It was quite beautiful. Dana wanted me to wear it to go looking for Joey. She was sure he'd be unable to resist me in that dress. I didn't do that, though; I was under strict orders not to damage the dress.

Right after graduation, I got really sick. I don't know what it was; I was simply down for the count, for at least a month. I would almost say it was mono, except that I didn't have the horrendous sore throat that comes with mono. My mother finally sent me to the doctor after about three weeks, and he gave me an antibiotic that made me better.

Joey briefly stopped by the apartment one day while I was sick. He wanted to go somewhere, do something, but I was too sick to move, much less go out with him. I was so disappointed and so, evidently, was he, because he never came back.

Joey was part of a "gang," which wasn't anywhere near as bad as gangs are today. They all wore black corduroy jackets with snaps on the front. I so wanted one of those jackets. A few years later, another guy who'd been part of this "gang," and who was just a friend, gave me his. It was bittersweet. I loved the jacket and often wore it, but it reminded me of Joey, which made me sad.

One Saturday Dana turned up at my house at 7 o'clock in the morning. My mother was still asleep, so she didn't know I'd left the apartment. We started walking to the town where Joey lived, but we didn't see anyone we knew, and we just kept walking. We finally wound up at a shopping center about seven miles from home. We didn't have any money, so all we could do was turn around and walk back. I'm fairly certain that Dana was looking to escape something that day, be it Saturday chores or punishment for something she'd done.

Her father beat her regularly. I always thought it was her father who was the mean one, but years later Dana's sister told me that no, it was their mother who insisted that he beat the kids. Often he'd hit the chair with the strap and tell them to scream. My mother got wind of the beatings and she actually went to Dana's father and told him that if he did it again, she was going to tell the police. I didn't remember this, but years later, Dana told me about it, saying that my mother had been her "hero."

Dana and I went to a dance that was held at the skating rink. I was too young, but I knew the rink owners well, and they let me in, anyway. I met a guy named Bill there. He was at least nineteen, out of school, and he had the best car. It was a 1956 fire-engine-red Oldsmobile we called "Big Red." I thought he was pretty neat at first, and I even told my mother that I, like her, was going to marry a Bill. He turned out to be a piece of work. He was a habitual liar. One time when I was going to break up with him, he told me he'd bought me a car. Right. What's a thirteen-year-old going to do with a car? It wasn't true anyway.

Circle pins were all the rage right at that time and I actually had one, which was unusual, because I seldom had anything that was popular. I loved it. It looked really great with the outfit Marcia's mother had made for me. Bill didn't like it; he said it was a "virgin pin." I never wore it again. I should have kept the pin and gotten rid of him.

Bill's grandmother had an apartment in a seedy part of town, but sometimes she wasn't there so we'd spend an evening listening to Marty Robbins on the record player there. One night as we were leaving to go home, someone on the street sucker-punched Bill. I went with him to the hospital.

Bill worked downtown at a record store and one day I went to meet him for lunch. He didn't have any money, so he "borrowed" five dollars from the cash register. We went to the lunch counter at the five-and-dime and I ordered a hot turkey sandwich. Bill didn't eat anything; he didn't have enough money for both of us. If I'd know that, I would have just gotten a soda or something.

I went to spend a week with Aunt Ruth that summer. Although she was completely against the idea, Bill came to pick me up. We just went out driving around in "Big Red," but, as usual, Bill didn't have any money, and we ran out of gas. Bill somehow sweet-talked the guy at a gas station to give him some gas, saying he'd pay him later. He then took me back to Aunt Ruth's. What I didn't know, and didn't learn until decades later, after he was long dead, was that my Uncle John had followed us that night. He'd wanted to protect me.

Despite my having left my cat Trinket behind because pets weren't allowed in the apartment, I adopted a cat that I found wandering around. I suspect she probably belonged to someone else, but I just figured she was a stray. I named her Thomasina, not a terribly creative name, since the movie of that name had come out around that time. Thomasina would come and go, and I didn't get terribly attached to her. Eventually she no longer came around. And I had become the "alley cat" myself by then.

I had a strong sense of desperation. I needed to have a boyfriend at all times. When one would be gone, I'd immediately start looking for another one. Whatever it took. It wasn't about sex, that much I know for sure. It was something deeper, perhaps a sense that I wasn't complete without a man. That was something I'd have gotten from my mother—she was always saying that she needed to "go look for a man." Of course, in my case, I really didn't need to look; they found me. I must have had "Will do anything for love" tattooed on my forehead. For the most part, the ones who found me weren't the ones I needed.

What's interesting, or perhaps tragic, is that there were a few nice guys from time to time, but for some reason, I quickly lost interest in them. Years later, a shrink told me that healthy people gravitate towards healthy people and that, if I wanted a healthy man in my life, I'd best get healthy.

Looking back at it, I see that that concept was at work in me, only turned around. I seemed to prefer unhealthy guys and of course they were drawn to me.

I suppose I was longing for my grandfather, coupled with a desire to replace Joey, or to replace the feelings I'd had when I was with him. For the short time we were together, I felt really good. He was so cute; if a guy that cute could like me, I must be likeable, maybe even lovable. I would pay any price, and I did, trying to feel that way again. There was an emptiness deep inside me that I didn't know how to fill.

One time my mother tried to discipline me for something and she actually managed to catch me. I grabbed her by the hair and bent her back over the TV. She never tried it again. I can make no excuse for this; it was just bad. I'd become so hardened and independent that I was incorrigible.

I was a mixed bag. Even though I desperately needed discipline and guidance, I'd been on my own, making my own decisions for so long, that I didn't know any other way. Those who were or considered themselves to be in authority over me didn't seem to me to be particularly concerned about my well-being, only their own needs or agendas.

I was unable to discern those times when someone actually did have my best interests in mind. I took on the same attitude about myself that I perceived others to have about me. If I was different, a misfit, I was going to make a science out of it. If I was a worry, I'd give them something to worry about. Someone had to take some kind of control, and I was the only one who was going to do it, even though I had absolutely no knowledge or resources that would lead me to do anything but dig myself deeper into the hole.

It's hard to climb a mountain when you're in a hole. It took me a few more years to even see the mountain, let alone decide that maybe I might want to climb. Meanwhile, my hole was getting deeper and deeper. I didn't know how to *stop digging!*

The definition of incorrigible is the inability to be corrected, improved, or reformed, and it's the right definition for who I was. The semantics of that definition, though, speak clearly to the solution. No, I couldn't *be* corrected, improved, or reformed, but I could correct, improve, and reform myself.

By God's good grace, the time did come when I saw that I needed to do that. It wasn't all at once. It was over the next fifty years, and it happened in stages. It's still happening.

THE RULER
Crissy Shreve
1963

Love, oh great ruler,
Get down from thy purple
And jewel-studded pedestal
Come down and share
Of thy wine, rich and red,
Like the blood we
Poor peasants that we are
Shed in thy name.

What, not for us
But for you, have we
That you drive us as slaves?
Withhold your whips!
They are torn and caked
With blood and mud
Like that on our hands
And how much on our souls?

Chapter Twelve

A Different World

Uncle Austin decided to send me to a private girls' boarding school about a hundred miles from home. I think it was a combination of his wanting to protect me from myself and his wanting me to be who he wanted me to be. Unfortunately, since I'd been running my own life for so many years at that point, I wasn't suddenly ready to trust anyone else to take over. It was already too late to protect me from myself. For better or worse, I was all I'd ever had.

Who did he want me to be? His heart was in the right place; I have no doubt of that. He was a stockbroker and was fairly well off, at least compared to the rest of my family. He lived well, and moved in better circles. Clearly he wanted more for me, too. I'm sure he hoped that by being exposed to a higher class of people, I would become one of them. Certainly I could have gotten a better education and gone on to college.

I didn't have the same aspirations for myself as Uncle Austin had for me, though. How could I? My feelings about myself and my experience of the world around me left little room for anything positive. I don't think I was trying to please him; that wouldn't have been on my radar. I just went because . . . well, it was there.

I suppose I saw it as an escape, too. There was nothing for me at the local high school. I had moved from being an outcast to being as intentionally removed as I could get from that crowd. The time away from Dana was probably a good thing, though. Who knows how much more trouble I might have gotten into?

The one thing that attracted me was that the boarding school offered riding. Horses could have become, even at that point, I think, my salvation. For whatever reason, Uncle Austin decided that I couldn't ride the first year. He spent all that money to send me there, and then denied me the one thing that would have made me happy, thrilled even, to be there.

Smoking was allowed, but only if one was sixteen or a senior. I was neither. Being able to smoke might have helped, but not being able to smoke, while others could, definitely put a damper on whatever enthusiasm I might have mustered.

Interestingly, the girls at the school were a mix of those who, like me, had been sent there to be "improved," and those who were "high class" and knew it. There were some very rich and classy girls there, girls who knew their place in the world and were sure they deserved it. I felt like a fraud. And guess which girls I gravitated towards.

Uncle Austin and I always had good conversations and laughed a lot. He seemed to think better of me than I actually was. I wish I'd agreed with him, or at least considered that I might have some potential. He didn't know how far off track I'd already gotten. On the drive to school, he said something to the effect that I should try to get along with the other girls. I remember telling him that they'd have to get along with me, my own self-fulfilling prophecy, typical of me. I was pretty sure I wouldn't fit in there any more than I'd fit in anywhere else, and my negative attitude assured it.

Before I left for school, Aunt Ruth took me shopping for clothes, on Austin's nickel. It's a good thing—left to my own devices, I'd have bought all the wrong things. Ruth, having sent two girls off to college, knew that you took winter clothes to school in the fall. I'd pictured lighter things, to be replaced with winter clothes at Thanksgiving.

Along with some really nice outfits, we bought a set of beautiful green towels. I wasn't allowed to take any of my new things home. First they went to Ruth's house, where I went to sew on name labels, but I didn't do a very good job of it. Then it all went to Austin's and got packed in a big steamer trunk. When I got to the school and opened the trunk, my beautiful green towels had been replaced with some ugly old towels of Audrey's.

I quickly lost a lot of my clothes. It had been my job to mark them. I was 13 years old. What did I know? I thought my clothes would just find their way back to me—after all, we put full laundry bags down the chute. Stupid. I'm sure the women who washed clothes for us loved finding unmarked things to take home to their daughters.

Socks and underwear were really a pain. I'd stuff a bunch of them together on a safety pin with a nametag attached.

I watched for weeks for my favorite blouse to come back with my clean laundry, but it never turned up. Near the end of the year, they had a "lost and found," but either my blouse had long before been taken, or someone beat me to it. It would have served us all a lot better to have the "lost and found" right away, after the first week, but I suppose that would have been too sensible. There was a coin laundry where we could wash our own clothes, but I didn't discover it until the middle of the year, and I never had any money, anyway.

We weren't allowed to wear jeans or any kind of pants. We wore skirts and blouses and sweaters to class, and on the weekends, we wore wool Bermuda shorts with knee socks. Weejuns, a brand of penny loafers, were a big deal. I did get a pair later in the year. I also got what we called a PGR—a pea green raincoat. It occurs to me now that, had I had my head on straight, I'd have worked harder at being whoever it was I was supposed to be, if only to keep getting nice clothes.

The family who owned the school lived in a house on the campus, as did most of the teachers. The owners thought themselves to be classy, and proved it by feeding their two miniature poodles from the table at mealtimes. We all ate in one huge dining room, alternating tables every week with a teacher at the head of each table. We rotated seats around the table every day. When you got to at a certain position at the table, you collected the trays of food from the kitchen and afterwards returned them with the dirty dishes.

The food was exceptional. Every Wednesday, we had something they called "hamwiches." Everyone loved them; we couldn't get enough of them. Heaping platters would arrive at the table and there'd never be any left. I've not tried to make them, but it's probably fairly simple. They were just crescent rolls, rolled up with a slice of ham and some cheddar cheese inside, and then baked.

My first roommate was assigned; her name was Heidi. She was very straight and naïve. We had a bathroom that connected with the room next door, so four of us shared it. There were no showers, only bathtubs. Within a few days of our arrival, one of the girls in the next room took a bath during her period and didn't clean out the tub afterwards, leaving a bloody mess behind her. It was reminiscent of sleeping with my mother, and I wasn't amused. I told the girl she needed to clean out the tub, and it was not well received. I quickly became anathema in our little suite.

This is something that's always puzzled me. Someone does something that's wrong or rude. I say it's not okay or ask them to stop, and I wind up being the bad guy. What's up with that?

Up until that point, I'd never met anyone who was Jewish. All I knew about Jews was my mother's hatred of them. I always found it a bit ironic that she hated Germans *and* Jews. I must've told the girls at school that my nickname was "Knish" because one girl asked me if I was Jewish, to which I replied, "Hell, no."

"Oh," she said, "I am." I'd only known "Knish" as a puppet on a children's TV show, and I had no idea of the Jewish origin of the word itself. I had to quickly develop a taste for crow. Fifty years later, as I write this, I want to wash my *own* mouth out with soap. Not, as you might at first suspect, for using the word hell. If someone were to ask me today if I were Jewish, my best answer would be, "Hell, *yes!*" Not in the traditional sense, but in a heart sense. My Jesus was a Jew and, because I am a Christian, He is my heritage.

After about a month, we were allowed to pick our own roommates. I wound up with a girl named Stevie, and moved upstairs to a hall that was mostly sophomores, with just a few of us overflow freshmen. Now I was two years younger than most of the people in my sphere. I was actually more in my element there, in one way, though. These girls were much worldlier than the freshman girls. I'd already had sex, as had many of them. But that didn't mean I was tough. I wasn't tough, and I definitely wasn't tough enough to know how to live with them.

We had group study hall in the chapel. All the freshmen had to go the first month until grades were established. If we had a B average or higher, we could study in our rooms. I kept my grades high enough that I only went back to study hall for one other month during the year. Study hall was horrid.

We weren't allowed to read fictional books during study time unless they'd been assigned in English class. One can only read those books so many times or, as in my case, if at all. We weren't allowed to write letters during study time either. Teachers (proctors) walked around watching what we were doing. There was nothing for it but to actually do our assignments. Unfortunately, that only took an hour or so, and we had one study hall during the day and another for two hours in the evening. It was hard to stay awake.

Studying in my room was much better. I'd hide a novel inside a textbook or write letters in my notebook so that I could quickly turn the page. On our floor, you could usually hear the housemother's heels clicking up the stairs. Sometimes she'd sneak up on me, though. I'd be sitting there, eyes glazed over, half asleep, and suddenly I'd look up and she'd be standing in my doorway.

We studied poetry in English class, so reading or writing poetry was acceptable study hall activity. That was actually a good thing for me. Writing poetry became a positive outlet for my feelings, and I was even fairly good at it, in terms of rhyming and cadence, if not content. I wrote a lot of poetry in study hall. The one at the beginning of this chapter is the first poem I ever wrote. I know it's awful.

Rooming with Stevie was not pleasant, and the two girls in the adjoining room were not easy to live with either. They were mean and they enjoyed being that way. They'd hide in their closet peering through the crack and waiting to see if someone would come in and grab an apple from the basket they left out in the open to tempt people. One day, having spied the basket, I walked in through their open door. My brain kicked in and I called out to them, asking if I could have an apple. I was quite shocked to hear a little voice answer me from the closet. It said no.

One day in study hall, a girl named Mary Anne cruised past me and somehow we connected. Her room was right across the hall from mine, and she wasn't getting along with her roommate, either. So across the hall I went. The best thing was that ours was a single room; we had our own bathroom. We got along well and stayed roommates for the rest of the year.

Mary Anne rode. One time, although it was strictly forbidden, she let me ride her horse. It was approaching dinnertime, and the horse knew it. He headed straight for the barn. The barn had one of those two-part doors and it was only open at the bottom, just high enough for the horse to get in. I didn't know how to stop him, so I just ducked and under we went. Since I didn't get knocked off, I rode all the way to his stall, where his dinner was waiting.

I was reminded of that years later when I was on Mackinac Island. You could rent horses there, and I watched in awe as some poor guy went galloping by, hollering, "Stop, horsey, stop, horsey." I am not making this up.

My dream was to ride bareback and barefoot, wearing rolled up jeans. It was a dream that never materialized. On that same trip to Mackinac, I saw a girl with long blond hair riding a beautiful palomino bareback on the beach. I stood there and cried. She got my dream.

The mail at school always arrived just before lunch—the highlight of the day. I got mail from a lot of people back home. Boyfriend Bill wrote regularly, as did Dana. One time she stuck a cigarette in the envelope. It seemed that her life goal was to get me in trouble. I don't know whether it was the process at the post office or whether someone censored our mail, but the cigarette arrived squashed and of no use to me. There was no place for me to smoke it, anyway.

I wrote a lot of letters, too. I have always been a writer in one form or another, and I just let it fly on paper. Bill suggested that I read what I'd written before sending it. It was a good suggestion, one that has since served me well, especially now with the advent of email.

On Saturdays, many of us would head into the local town to shop or just walk around. It was, if nothing else, an escape from campus. On one of those Saturdays, not long after I'd arrived at school, I was in town, going about my business, when I spotted "Big Red." Bill was cruising around looking for me. He wanted me to get in the car. I refused to do that; it would have meant immediate expulsion. I went back to school in the van and he followed. He had to check in, and we visited briefly in the parlor.

A week or so before Christmas break, I got a letter from "Joey," saying that he wanted to see me, and that he'd be at my house on New Year's Eve. Dana had written the letter, and I should have recognized her handwriting. Actually, I probably did, but I really wanted it to be from Joey. I sat home that New Year's Eve waiting for him, but of course he never showed up. I turned fourteen at midnight—alone.

That's when I should have dumped Dana. Instead, it gets worse. My roommate Mary Anne came home with me for part of Christmas break. Dana had somehow gotten hold of her mother's credit card, and she said that it had been given it to her to buy Christmas presents for her brothers and sisters. She swore she was allowed to use the card. I knew better, and made sure I didn't sign the charge slips, even though she tried very hard to get me to do it. Thank God I was smarter than that.

Dana loose with a credit card was an amazing thing. She never bought anything for herself, or for her siblings, for that matter, but she insisted on buying things for me. I got a sweater, and a black cigarette case with a matching lighter. Mary Anne also got a few things.

Dana knew how to get into the apartment thru the window, just as I did. After I'd gone back to boarding school, she came in and left all the receipts on my dresser. She wanted to nail me, and apparently told her mother that I'd been the one using the card. Her mother came to see my mother about it, but since I hadn't signed anything, my mother told her mother to stick it. I found all the receipts still lying on my dresser when I came home again for spring break.

At school, we could play either soccer or field hockey in the fall. I opted for field hockey. There was an on-campus store at which we could buy things we needed, such as school supplies and, in this case, a hockey stick and shin guards. The bill got sent to Uncle Austin. I liked that arrangement.

I also had a checking account. Can you imagine? Initially, Uncle Austin put fifty dollars into it. I spent most of that on my first trip to town and then wrote him a letter asking for more. He didn't agree that that was a good idea, so I was suddenly penniless. Occasionally he'd write me a letter and enclose a "five spot." His words.

Now, obviously I couldn't logically expect unlimited resources, but it didn't help me being penniless amongst all these rich girls who could and did buy anything they wanted. The lesson, meant probably to teach me to be a bit more responsible with money, actually taught me that I was, still, a poor relation and not really a part of the world into which I'd been thrust.

There was an indoor swimming pool at school, and swimming was a winter activity, so there we'd all be, shivering in our bathing suits, seeing snow on the trees outside. Once a week, a bunch of us would pile onto a bus and head to the bowling alley. One time, on the way back in the bus, a senior girl snidely announced that I'd had the lowest score that day.

Somehow I got ice skates. They were baby blue with gray fake fur around the top. There was a small pond on campus where we could skate. I was never very good at it, despite my being such a good roller skater. My ankles weren't strong, so I mostly just wobbled around. One Sunday the headmaster announced that he'd take those of us who were interested to the ice skating rink. Any chance to legitimately get off campus worked for me, so I went. I met a local girl named Jane. We stayed in contact and she came to visit me at home a year later.

One thing I really missed from home was the radio station I'd always listened to. I talked my mother into getting me what I hoped was a radio that would pick up that station, which was only about a hundred miles away. She tried, she really did, but the station wouldn't come in. There weren't any local stations that played popular music, but for some reason, I could get WOWO in Fort Wayne, Indiana, which was much farther away. Go figure. But the music was good enough and I listened illicitly to that radio every night with earphones, to help me go to sleep.

There was a student council made up primarily of upper classmen, if you can call girls classmen. Part of their job was to make unannounced room checks, looking for contraband. My radio was rather large and had a battery compartment big enough for four D batteries. I never kept batteries in it at school; I just plugged it in. It was a great hiding place for cigarettes. No one ever thought to open it up. My roommate's "big sister" called them "grettes" and would sometimes give us a couple, or I'd have some leftover from a trip home. We were allowed to smoke on the hired bus on vacations, so everyone lit up the second we drove off campus.

Still, there really was no good place to smoke at the school. The dormitory building was old and even I could see that it was a fire hazard. Nevertheless, I would open the window in our private bathroom, stick my head out, and sneak a smoke every so often. I had been introduced to spray deodorant, which coincidentally doubled as a great product for masking cigarette odor.

Then there was night walking. Lights out was at 11 PM. Wandering around the deserted halls at 3 AM was great fun. We never ran into anyone patrolling at that hour. Towards the end of the year, a new dormitory building was nearing completion and that was a great place to go in the middle of the night to have a cigarette. The best part was that the workers smoked there during the day, so we didn't even need to bring the spray deodorant.

I had a new partner in crime named Lynda, who'd come to the school late in the year. She was even more of a reprobate than I and we had some good times. She said that she was a "Bam" for a gang of boys she hung out with. It wasn't until some years later that I figured out what that actually meant. I'd just thought it was a cute word.

In the late spring, they imported some guys from a nearby boys' school and held a dance. When I'd been home on spring break, someone had taken me to buy a dress for the dance. It was a beautiful red dress with spaghetti straps and it required a strapless bra, something I'd never even known existed. I looked and felt gorgeous. We were assigned a partner and mine was a guy named Don. He was a real cutie and we hit it off very well. He, unfortunately, lived in another state, so there wasn't any way to see each other again, although we did write for a while. I still have his picture.

Very near the end of the year, when the weather was nice, another reprobate girl (whose name I don't remember) and I, went for a walk. We walked past the stables and up over the hill, through some woods, and found a road. We followed the road to a small town, where we immediately bought a pack of cigarettes. We met some local boys and went for a ride with them in their car. We never got caught, but one of those boys started calling me every day on the pay phone at school, and that raised some suspicion.

Meanwhile, my late night escapades with Lynda continued. The student council-*cum*-mafia girls found cigarettes during a check of her room. Lynda was suspended for the final two weeks of school. I was asked whether I, too, had been smoking. I was in the clear. I could easily have said no, but for some reason I was in my stupid loyalty mode. I never admitted to smoking, but I said some nonsense to the effect that if she was being sent home, I didn't want to stay. I got my wish and was also suspended for the last two weeks.

There was a little independent snack bar near the stables on campus. We could buy hot dogs or hamburgers there after school hours, and there was a pinball machine that was in constant use. We could cash checks there too. Knowing that I was going home, and fully aware that I had no money in my account, I cashed a check for twenty dollars. Someone then stole that money from my room, so I didn't even get to spend it. Meanwhile, Uncle Austin had been called, and he came to pick me up. He had to cover my bad check. He was not amused. Home I went.

Uncle Austin arranged for me to take my final exams at a private school near where he lived. I stayed at his house and while Audrey slept off her latest drunken stupor, I went through his drawers looking for money. I didn't find any. There were no guys driving around in cars where he lived, but I spent a lot of time at night walking around the area smoking and listening to my radio.

Once again, there I was, living two lives while living neither. Despite my quick return to my pre-private-school persona, I still thought I'd go back to the boarding school the next year. I looked forward to being able to ride horses. I, however, "wasn't invited" to return. Well, that's what I was told. It's possible that Uncle Austin decided that I wasn't such a good investment after all.

And then it was summer.

Aunt Ruth had moved to the city where fellow-reprobate Lynda lived, and my mother and I took the Greyhound bus to visit. While I was there, I called Lynda, but she wouldn't come to the phone. Talk about misplaced loyalty. On the way back home, I met some loser on the bus and sat in the back with him. My mother asked me, "Are you letting him kiss you?" I was.

I met and dated several guys that summer. One was Dave. He gave me his class ring, and then he didn't show up for a while. I saw him somewhere with some other girl, but that was okay, I was with another guy. He came by the next day and wanted his ring back. I told him I'd flushed it down the toilet. He whined that his mother would kill him, which I thought was a pretty good idea, but since I hadn't really flushed the ring, I finally gave it back. That was the end of Dave.

Meanwhile, Dana had a boyfriend named Eddie who started coming to see me. I should have known better, but I went out with him. Good old Dana went to the police and told them that he and I had been having sex. He was over eighteen and I was fourteen, which constituted statutory rape. Of course the police told me he'd admitted to it, and of course they told him I had. He got a bunch of guys to say they'd slept with me, which was ironic because I'd never even dated any of them. Eddie went to jail, although apparently not for very long.

I never found out what happened further, and I never saw him again except for one day, only a few weeks later, when he and a bunch of his friends sped past my house jeering and waving at me from a car I didn't recognize. I might, in fact, not even have noticed them, except that they were going up the hill. It was a one-way street going down.

I was sent to "JC Hotel," the juvenile court jail, and spent a week there. Upon arrival I was made to take a bath, with a matron watching. I did not like being naked in front of her. She wasn't unkind, though. She had a strong foreign accent and kept telling me things about the "gettels." At first I had no clue what she was saying, until I finally figured out that she meant the girls.

I met a girl there named Alicia, who coincidentally lived right around the corner from me, although I'd never met her before. She was only about twelve, and she was in for running away. I went to see her once we got out, and she told me to tell her mother that I, too, had been in for running away, but I told the truth, that it was for statutory rape. Her mother hated me and chased me down the street, telling me to stay away from her daughter. They were Hispanic, and I called the mother a stupid "Gringo"—what I meant to say was "Spic." That may have been why I opted to take Spanish in High School. If I'm going to hurl insults in another language, I may as well get it right. I was the stupid "Gringo."

I went out briefly with a cute young guy named Orville, whose last name was even worse. I just couldn't see any future in it—I didn't want to be Mrs. Orville Anybody. Then I dated Gary from the skating rink. My mother let us use her car. As I said earlier, he and I never skated together, which was a shame.

Meanwhile, I'd been flirting with the ice cream man all summer. His name was Jim and he looked a lot like Elvis Presley—very cute. He was from a well-to-do family and was only selling ice cream to earn college spending money. We started going out and one night when we were parking, we looked up to see a man looking in the window, watching us. Jim wanted to chase him but the man was gone before Jim could get his shoes on. That fall Jim went off to college. We wrote to each other, and his letters were all about his frat. He came to see me at Thanksgiving when he was home. Apparently all they did at his frat was drink beer, because he'd gotten quite chubby in just those few months. I no longer thought he was so cute.

INTERFERENCE

Uncle Austin and Aunt Ruth both wanted me to live according to standards that did not fit the reality of my life. Here is a story that tragically illustrates the consequences of expectation without engagement.

In the early 80's, my very dear friend June moved to a new town a few hours' drive away. I was very close to her and to her two daughters, who were then fourteen and sixteen. I went to visit them in their new home. While I was there, I met the younger daughter's friend, whom I'll call Barbara. Barbara was fourteen, an extremely disturbed young girl in a bad family situation. And she was pregnant.

She told me she planned to have an abortion. I talked to her about Jesus and I urged her not to terminate the pregnancy. Then I returned home, and although I prayed for her, I made no further effort to contact her.

A month or so later, I received a collect phone call from Barbara. She told me she was in California, on her way to a home for unwed mothers, where she would have the baby and give it up for adoption. She said she'd brought her "little dog" along, but that they wouldn't allow her to keep the dog at the home. She asked me to send her some money so that she could board the dog. Fool that I was, I wired her a hundred bucks.

Months later I learned that actually she had run off with some man, and that they'd used the money I sent to buy drugs. Barbara had the baby. He was born a vegetable, unable to function on any level. My money very likely bought the drugs that destroyed that unborn child.

Barbara and the baby moved in with her grandmother. Some thirty or so years later, she's still on welfare, and still taking care of this man-baby who's spent his entire life incoherent and on his back in a crib. For both of them, it has been virtually no life at all, certainly nothing even remotely resembling normalcy.

Would it have been better for her to have the abortion? On the surface, it might seem so, but I don't think so. What would have been better would have been for me to have taken her under my wing, brought her home with me, walked through the pregnancy with her, and helped her find the right agency to place the child for adoption. I could have done that.

Instead, I left a fourteen-year-old girl to figure it out for herself. Like I had been, she was pretty much on her own, without the guidance or resources to make good decisions. In her own way, she was trying to take care of herself, trying to meet needs I doubt she could have defined, let alone understood. I should have known.

Was she my responsibility? No, not initially perhaps, at least not until I opened my mouth. Certainly an argument could be made that I was in a position to see her pain and help her—that perhaps God had set me in place to be the only one who could. I wish I'd felt that nudge. I'm sure it was there.

We have influence over other people, often more than we'd ever imagine or expect. And with that influence comes responsibility. If I didn't want the responsibility, perhaps I would have done better to just keep quiet. At the very least, I wish I'd been more cautious, seeking to fully understand the situation, and considering the costs and ramifications.

Unbelievers cannot be held to God's standards, much as I might wish they could be. As a Christian, I have to be willing to allow people to choose not to do things God's way, even though I know God's way is always the best. Neither can I expect anyone else to adhere to my own personal beliefs or standards.

Instead, I need to teach those who are in my sphere of influence about God, about His love for them, and I need to demonstrate it! I need to allow the Holy Spirit to open their eyes to His ways. As Billy Graham said, "It's the Holy Spirit's job to convict, God's job to judge, and my job to love."

I need to take an honest look at myself in situations like this. Is it about them or is it about me? Am I trying to justify a choice I've made (self-affirmation), or am I trying to "save" someone else from making a choice I made (self-redemption)? Am I just acting out my need to fix, playing God, applying standards without grace?

Where was and where is God in this situation? I'm sure He was there and I'm sure that He is still intimately involved. He didn't send me there to influence Barbara, but to help her, to help Him help her, which I failed to do.

Influence without involvement is interference. Expectation without engagement is unfair, and can actually be interference with God's plan.

We are all put in place(s) where God wants to use us. I wish I'd been as good at being God's hands as I was at being His mouth. I don't take responsibility for Barbara's choices, but I have to take responsibility for my own. If nothing else, I have to learn from this experience, apply that learning and, in His strength and by His grace perhaps do better the next time. I need to pay better attention to those nudges!

PHANTOM ARMS
Crissy Shreve

Phantom arms, oh, I delighted,
In thy warmth, security,
In my dreams I was invited,
To embrace the all of thee.

Phantom arms, the truth belying,
Dreams are only fantasy,
In the light my hopes are taken,
Shaken by reality.

Phantom arms, thou didst deceive me,
Called unto me, bid me fall,
Never did those arms receive me,
Never there to catch at all.

Phantom arms, thou sought to break me,
Cling, then push, no clarity,
Soft when wanting still to take me,
Hard when thou were done with me.

Phantom arms, thou sought to bind me,
Chains of passion, bonds of fear,
All my dreams are far behind me,
All that I once held so dear.

Phantom arms that held my heart,
I once believed surrounded me,
Standing empty, holding nothing,
There is naught to hold of me.

Phantom arms, no trace of substance,
I can find no life in thee,
Void of all except resistance,
Seek to be the death of me.

Phantom arms, once so beloved,
Gently I must take from me,
Find that self not yet discovered,
Hiding there inside of me.

Phantom arms, thou ghosts of sadness,
Know that thou art but a ghoul,
Fold thyselves around thy master,
Thus wilt thou behold a fool.

Chapter Thirteen

And Back Again

Having not been invited to return to the boarding school, back I went to the local high school for my sophomore year. I still had plenty of nice clothes left over, so that wasn't much of a problem except that we were all expected to have white shorts for gym class. I actually had a pair of white shorts at first, but they split irredeemably after a few weeks. The gym teacher made a big deal out of my wearing my wool Bermuda shorts to gym glass, even threatening to have me suspended. My mother had no money to buy new white shorts, and how do you find white shorts in November, anyway? Welcome back.

My old boyfriend Eddie from Kindergarten reappeared after having been at the parochial school all the years in between. I had picked up a loopy sort of handwriting from the girls at the boarding school. Eddie liked it and copied it. I was still writing poetry, and he recopied some of my stuff and called it his own. Eddie fancied himself to be in love with me. We hung out at school all that year and into the next, but I never felt any romantic interest in him.

There was something different about Eddie, but I couldn't quite put my finger on it. I don't think he was really in love with me; it was more like he wanted to *be* me. After I left, we went in separate directions and lost touch. When we reconnected forty or so years later, I found out he was gay. I wasn't surprised.

I took biology in tenth grade. It wasn't my choice and I never did the assigned reading, so it should be no surprise that I didn't do well. On top of that, the teacher wanted us to dissect frogs and, lucky us, he knew of a nearby slough where he caught a slew of them. Pun intended. I was not about to slice up some poor frog. I kept mine for a while as a pet, but I don't remember what ever happened to it. Of course I flunked biology that semester and had to take it again the second semester. I managed to pass that time, albeit barely, but I still never cut up a frog. It must not have been frog season by then.

Laura had a hysterectomy that fall and had to be in the hospital for most of a week. I stayed at Dana's house. Of course we ditched school the whole time. Her parents both worked, so we just stayed home. We were afraid of being caught out walking the streets during school hours.

On that Friday, we noticed kids walking home much earlier than school normally let out. Kennedy had been shot. I remember thinking, well, nuts—had I known we'd get out early, I'd have gone to school that day. Shallow, self-centered teenager that I was, I didn't get caught up in the heartbreak of the death of our president, and I didn't even think to worry that our national security might be at risk. I did feel sad when they handed the folded flag to Jackie.

After my absence of most of a week, the school called my mother. She'd come home from the hospital by then, but I'd continued to stay at Dana's house. Laura wasn't fully recovered, but she took a bus and then walked a block or so to Dana's house to find out what I was up to and make me go home. That was unfair to her, but of course I wasn't thinking about anyone but myself. I wish I'd thought to go home and take care of her after her surgery, but that never even occurred to me.

At least it got me back to school. After ditching for so long, I knew I'd be in trouble, and as long as I stayed away, I could put off the consequences. Actually, I don't remember there being any consequences.

Dana pretty much never went back to school. She was kicked out twice from the high school, and after a few weeks at a different high school, she got kicked out of there, too. At that point, she quit school altogether.

One of Dana's favorite tricks was filling in my name and address on postage-paid offer cards she'd find in magazines. One time a salesman came to the apartment wanting to sell us a set of "Great Books."

I often stayed overnight at her house and one time, in the middle of the night, she woke me up telling me I'd torn up my pillow in my sleep and had been eating the feathers. I don't think so. But there were feathers all over the place and she had the vacuum cleaner handy.

Dana's younger sister Sue was in my class and we became good friends. She, Eddie, and I hung out at school, and Sue and I walked back to my apartment every day for lunch. Sue mostly went to school, while I continued to ditch regularly. I got very good at signing my mother's name to excuse forms.

Dana got involved with a guy named Frank and went to live with him. They had an old black car that she drove around. One time she let me drive it. I was still only fourteen. I'd never driven a car before, but it wasn't all that difficult. She taught me to take my foot off the accelerator when going around a curve and to pull forward far enough at a stop sign to be able to see when it was clear to go. A cop pulled right up behind us while I was driving, and I must've been doing well enough because he didn't take a second look at us.

Dana got pregnant and married Frank. They moved to a really weird subsidized apartment in the "projects." The ceilings were very low there, at most seven feet high. Once the baby was born, I no longer saw much of her. By then I think I'd finally figured out that she was not someone I could trust.

I'd been wearing the silver and onyx cocktail ring that had been Aunt Ella's and that I'd inherited by default when Nana died. I loved that ring and never took it off. One day when we were outside playing softball for gym class, I looked down and saw that the onyx was missing. There wasn't much future in trying to find a black onyx on a freshly blacktopped playground. I sadly put the ring away. I didn't know you could replace stones, and I didn't have any money to do it anyway, but I did have the onyx replaced some years later.

Money was always in short supply in my world. Being too young to get a job, there didn't seem to be a way to resolve this problem. One time I did a "Laura" and begged Uncle Austin for some money, telling him that I needed shampoo and a winter coat, both of which were true, and both of which I bought. The coat was beautiful—three-quarter length, and made of a suede-like fabric, with a fake fur lining and a hood.

It was in style, too. A number of other girls had similar coats. One day at lunchtime, as we were all on our way home from school, I was walking behind a girl from our class who had a coat much like mine. I don't remember having anything against this girl in particular, although I guess I was pretty mad at everyone in that school. She was just the person who happened to be in front of me, and her coat had a hood on it. I put the butt of my lit cigarette into her hood, right before we came to the corner where I'd turn right and she'd go straight. By God's good grace, the coat apparently didn't catch on fire and I never heard anything further about it, but it's a good bet that that butt burned a nasty hole in her hood.

It was a mean thing to do and, to this day, I don't know what got into me. I'm not going to even try to make an excuse—there wasn't any. It was just there in front of me. I didn't give a thought to potential consequences to her or to me. I suppose, though, that if someone needed an example of passive-aggressive behavior, this would certainly suffice.

Twenty years later, after I'd been long gone, I heard that my class had had a twenty-year reunion. I didn't graduate from that school, so I wouldn't have been invited anyway, but I contacted someone who'd helped plan the event. She sent me a booklet that had copies of yearbook pictures of those who attended, along with their addresses. As I paged through the booklet, I saw the picture of the girl with the coat, and it all came back to me. Oops. I immediately confessed my sin, but I knew that I had to do more than just that. I stuck a hundred-dollar bill in an envelope and mailed it to her. I included a brief note admitting that it had been I who'd done the deed, apologized and asked her forgiveness, and said that I hoped the money would bless her in some way. I signed my first name, but I didn't give her any further information. She died not long afterwards.

That same sophomore year I somehow reconnected with my old friend Kristy. She'd moved and was attending a different high school. I guess we'd stayed in touch to some degree, as I remember her telling me on the phone about going to a dance and dancing cheek-to-cheek. She was going with a guy named Ed, and they introduced me to Ed's friend Kirk. He and I dated for a while.

Meanwhile, a new family moved into one of the first-floor apartments in our building. The woman's name was Louise. She had two little girls and was expecting her third. We got to be friends and I babysat regularly. I learned how to change diapers and make bottles. When it was time for the new baby to be born, I was called downstairs in the middle of the night to take care of the girls while she and her husband went to the hospital.

One night when I had been babysitting, Louise and her husband came home and told me that they'd stopped for a hamburger at one of the local drive-in joints. They'd seen my boyfriend Kirk there in his car. Louise told me her husband's comment was, "There's your babysitter." At first they thought I was with him, but then saw that I wasn't. They didn't mention that he was with another girl, though, and for some reason, that didn't cross my mind. Years later, out of the blue, and when I hadn't thought about Kirk for a long time, it suddenly hit me that of course he had been with someone else.

Louise's husband had a motorcycle. He occasionally gave me a ride on it. I remember Louise cautioning me to wear socks so that I wouldn't burn my legs on the hot exhaust pipe. One night her husband invited me to go riding, but I rode with his friend. The husband picked up some other girl along the way. Louise had seen me sneaking out of the building wearing socks and she thought I'd gone out with her husband. That was a bit of a sticky situation, telling her that I was riding with the other guy without telling her that her husband also had someone with him.

A girl named Dee moved into a house around the corner. She was a senior and was finishing at her previous high school, despite now living outside of the district. She took public transportation to school every day. We became very good friends and she was a much better influence on me than Dana had been. Despite her being as poor as I was, she worked, went to school, and then went on to nursing school after graduation. I was still too young to work, which is unfortunate, but being around her gave me some sense of normalcy and possibility.

I turned fifteen in January and it turned into 1964.

One day when I was a sophomore, the very cute guy David I'd adored since the days of his coming around on the produce truck, was waiting for me outside after school one day. Apparently my reputation was already pretty bad; I can't imagine that he actually remembered me, although maybe from the dance when my mother wouldn't let him walk me home. We went parking, and then I never saw him again. I don't remember being particularly disturbed about it, though. He was someone to love in my dreams, but not in reality.

Not long afterwards, David, only sixteen, was killed in a car accident while coming back from an excursion to the next state where the drinking age was eighteen. A lot of kids had fake IDs. David died instantly and another boy died a week later. I ditched school to go to David's funeral, but I didn't actually go. It turned out that kids were excused from school and went, and I was afraid to go since I'd ditched. I'm not sure I'd have been able to handle it, anyway. I did go to the other boy's funeral, although I hadn't known him well.

Guys, and always having one around, continued to be my main focus. I noticed a new guy driving around town. His name was John, and he would be Larry's father. He was out of high school and working at the car wash. He wore black jeans and black t-shirts all the time. He had moved into the area from a small town about thirty miles away. He looked the part of a "bad boy," and of course that appealed to me.

Our relationship was fairly serious, well, as serious as it can be when one is just fifteen. I spent a good bit of time at his house. We all called his mother "Mommy." She spent the entire day in front of the television sipping beer with ice cubes. She thought it would be a good idea for me to iron his black jeans, and so I did. People didn't tend to have clothes dryers in those days, so the jeans had air-dried and were stiff and hard to iron. That was probably as good a reason as any not to marry him.

Still, John and I were pretty sure we'd get married. We even put a bunch of kitchen gadgets on layaway at a local store. When the time came for the school picnic, I really wanted to go, but neither of us had any money, so we canceled the layaway and took that money to use at the amusement park. John wasn't one for roller coasters, but he went on it one time with me. He was hanging on to the bar so hard I thought he'd break it. He was so terrified that we didn't even kiss in the tunnel. The rest of the day wasn't much fun with his being unwilling to go back on the roller coaster.

Around that same time, Dana concocted a story that her mother wanted to sell her 1956 Chevy for fifty dollars. John and I saved up the money and went to see about buying the car, but of course it was just another of Dana's lies. We were pretty disappointed.

Louise from the first floor had moved a few blocks away by then, but I continued to hang out with her and babysit regularly. Larry was conceived in her living room. When we knew I was pregnant, John went to live with his sister in another state. The idea was for him to work and get us a place there to live. Once he was gone, I quickly lost interest in him and in getting married. No one knew I was pregnant, and there were still plenty of guys around, so I just went on doing what I'd always done.

The summer ended and I went back to school as a junior.

HOMOSEXUALITY

It was kind of funny. After forty years, when I found out how to contact Eddie, my boyfriend from kindergarten and later friend in high school, I sent him an email saying that I'd like to reconnect, but that I would understand if he had a wife who wouldn't like that idea. The minute I'd hit "Send," it suddenly struck me: Oh! I bet he's gay. Sure enough. He wrote back saying that he was on a cruise acting as an escort for a woman friend, but that I probably wouldn't be surprised to hear that he had "grown up to be gay."

This was right when X2 trashed me for another woman after twenty-three years of marriage. Eddie, meanwhile, had been in an even longer monogamous relationship with his partner. There I was, struggling to survive betrayal by a supposedly godly husband, and being consoled by a gay guy who was in a committed relationship. Eddie was a good and supportive friend, *and he prayed for me every night for at least a year.*

This presented me with a bit of a conundrum. I had been quite sure that homosexuality was an abomination—end of discussion. And it's easy to end the discussion—until you find out that someone you love is gay. It was time to take a second look.

I hadn't had a lot of experience with gay people. I had one girlfriend who was gay, and in an effort to "agree to disagree," we decided that I didn't have to say it was okay and she didn't have to say it was a sin. Later on, my son's brother-in-law came to my son's wedding with his partner and they danced together and kissed, but aside from the shock of that to me and to my side of the family, the partner was actually a nice enough guy. Then I met Eddie's partner and adored him.

I don't know why some people are apparently wired up to be gay. It's nothing new. Homosexuality was practiced in Old Testament days, and was spoken of as an abomination to God. I took that stand for many years. Once Eddie turned up, and especially since he knows the Lord and was praying for me, I needed a change of heart in a hurry.

It's as simple as it can be. If Christ's blood is not sufficient for Eddie and others who are gay, it's not sufficient for me. God hates sin no matter whose it is or what it looks like. *And* God loves his children enough to have died to pay the price of our sin so that we won't have to.

This is the entire message of the Gospel. Not mine—God's.

I Thought Of You

Crissy Shreve

I thought of you again today
It's been a while (I've trained my thoughts)
And even longer since I've seen you.

Your face? It's faded now.
But, ah, the memory remains
Of feeling high
And not a part of anything at all.

That time was dear,
And no! I won't forsake the memory.
Yet, again, I must escape it;
My life is without you.

And even should we meet again one day
It couldn't be the same for you.
It was my dream.

But every so often I hear the words
That bring it back
And if I could just reach across the void
To touch you from time to time
I could hang on in the reality.

And so until I hear that song again,
Good-bye

CHAPTER FOURTEEN

WEIRD

Junior year, had I not been pregnant, had the potential for being a pretty good year for me. Dana was mostly out of the picture, and I was spending my time with Dee and Sue. I'd figured out that I was pregnant pretty quickly, but they were the only ones who knew.

My mother got herself a boyfriend. On the way home from work one night, she stopped for a cup of coffee at a place near the bus stop downtown and met him there. She brought him home and introduced him to me. His name was Richard, but I called him "Dickie Bird," and even she called him that when he wasn't around to hear. He was younger than my mother and, in my opinion, pretty much a loser.

I fell in love with a boy at school. He was only a year older than I, which was unusual for me. His name was Jack. He worked at the bowling alley and had a great car with a stick shift. Our apartment was on a hill, and he'd roll down that hill in low gear, the car growling all the way. It was fun at first, especially when I was in the car. Even when I wasn't with him, I always knew when he drove by.

Dee was dating a guy named Terry. One night when Jack, Dee, Terry, and I came into my apartment, my mother's door was closed. Since it was her habit to sleep in the evenings, it never occurred to me that she had company, and the four of us went about our business, which was usually Jack and me making out on the couch, while Dee and Terry took the window seat in the dining room.

Suddenly my mother comes out of the bedroom with Dickie Bird in tow. I was very embarrassed, and we all left immediately. I gave her a hard time about it afterwards, at which point she said the he'd not been able to "get it up," as if that made a difference, although knowing Dickie Bird, it was probably true. The irony, of course, is that there I was pregnant (Jack had no clue) and I was nailing her for having Dickie Bird in her room.

Another time, Jack and I were again on the couch while Dee and Terry were on the window seat. Both sets of us were lying down together and cuddling, but no one was having sex. My mother came out of her bedroom and said, "This isn't a flop house," even though Dickie Bird was known to regularly flop there. Her own irony.

I was madly in love with Jack. He was sweet and he was good to me. When I dropped and broke my big transistor radio, he bought me a new one for my birthday. He even took me to get my driver's permit.

That Christmas Eve, Jack and I went to midnight mass at a big Catholic church downtown. It was important to him, although it had no particular meaning for me, and he wanted me to kneel and do all the other things they did, like make the sign of the cross. I didn't mind doing these things, if only because he wanted me to, but I had never been to a Catholic mass before, and I didn't know what to do or when to do it, so I messed up a few times. He thought I was refusing to do it, and he got mad at me.

A few days later, still during Christmas break, Jane, the girl I'd met at the skating rink near the boarding school, came to visit, and brought her friend Carol along. I didn't know Jane very well; we'd written the occasional letter, but hadn't discussed our lives on any deep level. Carol was pretty straight, and she just stayed at the apartment most of the time, but Jane sure wasn't. She was barely there an hour when she told me all about some guy she'd been seeing at home.

Apparently they'd tried unsuccessfully to have sex and he couldn't make it happen. She stated the situation in rather vulgar terms (for those days), and to the effect that it was her fault. I was totally shocked and surprised—ironically so, considering my condition. It was then, in some sort of misguided commiseration, that I told her I was pregnant.

Jack arranged for his friend Mark to take Jane out. Apparently Jane told Mark that I was pregnant, and he told Jack. I think Jane had her eye on Jack. When he and I took Jane and Carol to the bus station to go back home, Jack said to her, "The *three* of us will come see you." Clearly he meant the two of us and the baby, even though he and I never discussed my being pregnant or his even knowing about it.

And then he just stopped coming around. I'd hear his car roaring down the hill, but he didn't stop. My heart was broken, and that was when I took the aspirin to try to manipulate him into coming back. He didn't come back, though. Jack and Mark had taken up with two girls who were, amazingly enough, even sluttier than I was.

After Jane and Carol went home, Jane's mother sent my mother a thank-you note. My mother sent Jane's mother a thank-you note for the thank-you note. I thought that was a bit weird.

I wrote to Jane, but my letter was returned unopened. Some things had happened while she was visiting me, things I never knew about at the time, although there was some talk on the grapevine about Mark and "some girl who was visiting me." Apparently she had gotten pregnant while she was there. No one directly involved ever told me anything about any of it, though; I just put the pieces together.

Looking back, I can see that Jane was as messed up as I was, perhaps even more. What was going on in her head? Her taking on as her own fault that her boyfriend couldn't perform, then finding out that I was pregnant, must have had a serious impact. Did it mean to her that I was "successful" and she wasn't? Did she think she had to compete with me, even to the degree of getting pregnant to prove that she could? Did she sabotage my relationship with Jack intentionally, by making sure he found out I was pregnant? I don't know the answers. I'll never know the answers, but I can certainly see how messed up we both were.

And then there was Dickie Bird—and this is really weird. For some reason, he wanted to take me out, and my mother went along with it. She apparently thought it was about his wanting to bond with me in some daughterly fashion. I went with him, although I can't imagine why; I really didn't like Dickie Bird at all.

He and I got on the bus and we went to the very street near Flo's where I'd be walking around pregnant a month or so later. He took me to a clothing boutique and ostensibly made arrangements for me to be able to buy any clothes that I wanted, and they should bill him for them. I didn't get anything that day, nor did I ever go back. Nothing would have fit me by that point, anyway. I was about four months pregnant by then, but it still wasn't obvious. Certainly old Dickie Bird had no clue.

141

From there, he took me to his house, where his mother had made dinner. He ate, and I may have eaten a bit, too, but I was annoyed with him because I knew that my mother was at home making dinner for us. He didn't come on to me overtly, probably because his mother was right there, but I got his drift. I wasn't even the slightest bit interested. We got back on the bus and went back to my apartment. I ate some of my mother's dinner, but he didn't; he was already full. I never told my mother what he'd been up to. I don't remember seeing much of him after that.

My time at the high school was quickly coming to an end. It was only a matter of weeks until my pregnancy would be impossible to hide. I started taking typing, and I was allowed to use the electric typewriter at school because we had one at home. Well, we had one sporadically; whenever my mother needed cash, she'd pawn the typewriter and then later bail it out. Of course she'd bought the typewriter on credit and was still making payments on it.

I also took Driver's Ed. Since I was one of the few participants that already had a permit, I got in a couple of sessions behind the wheel before I had to leave school. The car had a second brake on the passenger side of the car. The teacher obviously thought this would be useful for his own survival.

One day I was driving up a hill, and there was a delivery truck stopped on the side of the road, partially blocking my lane. I didn't slow, I didn't stop, I simply went around it. I had my eyes open; I could see that nothing was coming towards me. The teacher, who was of course on the other side of the car and couldn't see around the truck, knew no such thing, and he nearly had a stroke. But he didn't use the brake. I don't think he had time and he was clearly in shock. He yelled at me, said I should have slowed down, put on my turn signal, looked more carefully, that sort of thing. I didn't see what the big deal was; I'd handled it, at least in my opinion, quite competently.

And then it came out that I was pregnant, and I had to leave school, which wasn't a terrible tragedy to my way of thinking. I wasn't fond of school, anyway. I sat around all day watching TV and eating oranges for a month or so until it was time to go to Flo's.

Before I left, though, I somehow got word that "Mommy," mother of my baby's father, wanted to see me. It was my first foray into the world in maternity clothes. "Mommy" challenged whether John was really the father. She'd heard that I'd been seeing other guys, and of course she was right, I had, but only after he'd left and I was already pregnant. John knew it was his baby, and he paid for part of my sojourn at Flo's, although most likely at Uncle Austin's insistence.

My mother got a telephone at the apartment. We hadn't had one for a while, but of course she wanted to know when I went into labor, and she got herself to the hospital by the time Larry was born, even though it was the middle of the night.

I had a friend named Jimmy who wrote to me regularly while I was at Flo's. He helped me through it just by being my friend. Afterwards, when I was back home, Jimmy only came around one time. We went for a ride in his car. I was sitting on the console between the bucket seats, to be next to him. I was still recovering from the birth, and it was uncomfortable. He never said so, but he was dating someone else; I saw him with her somewhere a week or so later. It didn't matter; he'd been there when I needed him.

I finished my junior year that summer at a private school in the city. Uncle Austin paid for it. I took the bus there every day. There was no homework and it only lasted a few weeks.

I dated a guy named Glen for the rest of that summer. He was an engineer who had a job designing, if you can believe it, brassieres, although he always said "brazheers." I have a little trouble understanding why, in the first place, anyone would think a guy could design bras, and in the second place, a guy who can't even pronounce the word. Still, he was a nice guy. We'd drive around in his convertible with the air-conditioning running. He and I stayed in contact for a while after I left town.

And then I went to live with my cousin Judy.

REDEMPTION

So why, perhaps you wonder, did I get myself pregnant at age fifteen? Beats the heck out of me. I was looking for something, looking for love, like in the song, in all the wrong places. I looked to men. I was promiscuous before it became commonplace. My behavior was actually rather mild in comparison to what teens are getting into these days, but back then I was a mess. I traded sex for love, but all I ever got was screwed.

As I write this, I recognize, if not feel, the old guilt and shame that was attached to promiscuity in the early sixties. A lot of it was based on fear of pregnancy, and I believe that guilt and shame were tools used to keep girls in line. Just a few years later, with the advent of the pill and "free love," the whole picture changed and the rest of the world caught up with me. Still, what I was doing then wasn't good for me, and I think seeing that is more important than feeling guilt or shame.

John Ortberg did a message at my church called "Why Promiscuity?" He talked about God's design and intention for sex, that it was to be the deepest, most intimate connection between a man and woman, and that God intended it to be practiced within the safety of a committed marriage relationship. He said that sex is a sharing of the soul that, when done casually, shatters the soul.

As archaic as this idea may sound, I see the truth of it strongly in evidence in my life as a teenager and throughout the years since. There are parts of my soul scattered about in places I no longer even remember. I did a lot of walking away from my soul, leaving it behind me in bits and pieces.

I was in love with the illusion of love. That first poem, "The Ruler[24]," was all about that. Even today I find that my ability to relate to men in a healthy way is skewed. I still fall into the illusion too easily, still fall into those "Phantom Arms." I've finally figured out that that's not about the men; it's about *me*.

Back then, though, it was usually my boyfriends who walked away, and usually immediately after getting what they wanted. Probably largely from my mother, I'd picked up the idea that I needed a man to complete me. It wasn't until my mid-fifties that I understood that I *am* complete—in myself and in my Lord.

My early life seemed to revolve around either the pain of repeated abandonment or the pain of walking away. I carried my hard heart and my scars into my marriages and into the way I did life. Walking away was always a matter of choice: should I get my heart broken by trying

---

[24] At the beginning of Chapter Twelve

to stay in it, or should I break my own heart by walking away? As Tim Timmons said, "If your horse is dead, get off." I did that, but then I hopped right on the next horse to come along.

If I seem to be belaboring the concept of walking away, there's a reason. I spent my life holding inside me the pain of having walked away from people I should have been able to love and trust. If I was to get on with life, I had to let go. The trouble is, I was never able to consciously mourn the losses. The pain was too deep. I wasn't sure I'd be able to stop crying if I ever got started. Call it denial if you insist. By the time Larry was born, I was a master at walking away.

First there was Nana, my grandmother. I didn't feel any love from her; when I recall her face, she's always wearing a scowl. Of course, now I know that that scowl wasn't necessarily directed at me, or surely not always. I'd have been scowling too were I in her shoes. But a little kid doesn't have the resources to know what's going on. She only feels the scorn and sees herself as the object of that scorn.

My earliest memory (I was very young, not yet three) was of walking down the stairs one morning and, about halfway down, becoming "cognizant," for the first time, of the world around me. I don't know who had dressed me or anything else that had transpired upstairs. I only knew, halfway down those stairs, that my grandmother was my enemy. I don't know that the word enemy actually entered my mind, just the concept and the knowledge. From that moment on, I regarded her as my enemy. That was my core experience of walking away from someone I should have been able to love and trust.

It is instinctual for young children to believe that their parents or caretakers love them, and that they are safe. They don't have the feelings to know how to feel, let alone what to do, when that's not the case. All of my life I have had a hard time believing anyone could love me, that I might be loveable. This was where it started.

As an adult, I recognize that, like all parents, my grandmother did the best she could. I have forgiven her, for my own sake and for the sake of healing. I wish I'd known to do so years earlier. Still, I have to work at believing it when someone actually does love me.

Then there was Dadum. My beloved grandfather was the only "father" I ever knew. He loved me like crazy and he was the only one, most particularly the only man, in my world, whose love I could actually feel. He'd get up in the morning and make himself three or four slices of bacon. About the time they were nicely crisp, I'd show up in the kitchen, and he'd give me his bacon, gladly, then make himself some more. Sometimes I'd eat that, too. I wasn't bratty with him. I responded to his love because I could feel it and believe it.

And then, when I was seven, my Dadum died. I still needed him. No one ever took his place. I said good-by to that love when I walked away from his grave. I had to; it was gone. Still, I spent the rest of my life trying to get someone to love me as Dadum had. It wasn't until a few years ago that I finally understood that only God could love me that well, and that He does.

The family talks of my mother as a young woman—beautiful, creative, fun. I never knew her that way. All of that got lost in her illness. Still, she had a young child to raise—me—and she managed to work her entire life. She was very good at shorthand and typing and actually had some good jobs, although they never paid much. I always had a roof over my head and enough to eat, but not much more than that.

My mother lived with insanity and depression most of her life. It wasn't easy for her, by any means. She was very smart and she said some of the wisest things I've ever heard, and most of the craziest. She had some extremely wacky ideas. Much of my growing up happened between trying to figure out when to take her seriously and when to run the other way. As a result, I more or less had to raise myself, without any of the things I needed to do so.

My cousin John tells a story of how, when he was a kid, some of his buddies tied him to a tree and lit a fire under him. He talks about how his mother didn't come to his rescue and how scared he was. He felt his mother had betrayed him. I don't argue that, but when he told me this story, I realized that, in my case, it was my mother who lit the fire. Figuratively, of course, but that's the difference. In effect, I had to walk away from her, too, in order to find sanity.

I always had an underlying fear of my own potential for insanity. I've finally come to see that, if I were going to go off the deep end, I'd have done so long ago. Or, perhaps I did, and I'm the only one who doesn't know it.

I was afraid of my grandmother and afraid of my mother—for very different reasons, but afraid nevertheless. Yet, by the grace of God, I look forward to seeing them both in heaven, where they will be healed, where *I* will be healed, and where we all will enjoy for eternity the special relationships we were meant to have.

Then I had to walk away from "The Man I Would Have Called Daddy." There were others, too, less significant, but still losses, and my heart grew harder each time.

Walking away from Larry, my baby, was the hardest of all. That hard heart enabled me to do so, I suppose, but by that time I had pretty much determined that there was nothing and no one of any value that I would be allowed to keep.

Finally, when I went to live with my cousin Judy, I left behind everything and everyone I'd known. For the first time, though, even though I'd walked away, I walked toward something, something new and positive.

At the end of my marriage, actually about a month after our divorce, I was in X2's office with him, and suddenly it was over. It had been over for him for some time, but it wasn't over for me until it was over. At that moment, I walked away from him, out of his office, and never looked back. I'd already walked away from the home I'd loved, and from the motorhome, both of which were a big part of what defined me. I walked away from my whole life in that moment, from all it had been for the past twenty-five or so years. However, I didn't walk away from myself that time. I left a lot in the ashes, but not everything. By God's good grace, this time there was enough of me to go on.

Of course I recognize that, to a great degree, life just is that way, and that everyone suffers losses. I don't see myself as a victim; this is not a pity party. It's just my story.

And it's a story of redemption. See, when years later, Larry came back into my life, God redeemed not only the loss and the years of missing him, but all the other losses of all the years too. He healed those I'd chosen and those that just happened on their own. He healed my shattered soul, and He added peace about my son Jason's death. I finally wept out all the old, stagnant pollution of pain and breathed in the fresh air of joy.

In this He set me free—as only God can do.

THE MOUNTAINTOP
Crissy Shreve

Come with Me,
Said the Lord.
I want to show you the mountaintop.

I'm not asking you to fly.
I know your wings have been broken
And your spirit is weak within you.

But I am He,
I am the Lord.
And I live on the mountaintop.

It's your home too.
It's where your spirit was born to live.
Let Me show you.

I will lift you there.
Come be with me,
And find your life again.

CHAPTER FIFTEEN

SENIORITY

As I've said, you can't climb a mountain when you're stuck in a hole. Even though I was still deep in the hole, at Judy's I could start to see the mountain rising above me, inviting me to climb. I was able to stop digging even deeper and over time I started scrabbling my way up out of the hole.

Judy would've taken baby Larry, but no one had told her I'd had him until after he'd been born and placed for adoption. So she got me instead. Apparently, she understood that it would be difficult for me to return to school and invited me come live with her.

Going to live with Judy was my new beginning, and a time of many firsts. Perhaps the most remarkable was that, from that time on, although there were more losses, there were also gains. Some of them were physical, many of them were emotional, and I began a process of healing. With each gain, I got a bit closer to the top of the hole. It took some years, but I finally reached even ground and was ready to begin my climb.

I took my first airplane flight. I wore a beautiful new brown tweed suit on the plane, with matching brown suede shoes and purse. I looked and felt classy. You still got dressed up for things in those days. My mother had given me a credit card and sent me out for clothes. Unfortunately, I accidentally left the card at a store, so my shopping spree got cut short. Still, I got plenty.

At the airport, my mother, in typically Laura fashion, wrote out the check to Trans Continental Airlines, which is what it had been called in her day, instead of TWA. They made her rewrite the check. Poor Laura—the world had a way of moving ahead without her. And I was on my way to join it.

When I landed, Judy and the whole gang were there waiting for me at the airport. I instantly became part of a real family. I met my three little cousins, Jill, Janice, and Sarah. As soon as we got home, Judy's husband Al offered me a drink—a cocktail! I was always allowed to drink at Judy's if I wanted to, which I didn't particularly. My friends would come over and bring beer and we'd all drink some. No one ever got drunk or drove when they shouldn't. It was a safe place. The effect for me was that because drinking wasn't forbidden, it wasn't desirable or tempting, and so I didn't do much of it at all. I didn't really like alcohol anyway, and I still don't.

From one day to the next, I was no longer enmeshed in the loser status I'd always known. It took me a while to grab onto that concept, but grab on I did, and it made all the difference. It bears repeating—Judy saved my life. She was my biggest fan. I don't know whether she'd just never known many losers and didn't recognize me as the fraud I was, or whether she saw some potential in me that I hadn't yet discovered. She thought I was great. I wasn't probably all that great, but having her think so was huge. No one had ever thought I was great before. Somehow it made me want to be as great as she thought I was. Over time, Judy's belief in me became the foundation for my own.

It was different. Where before there had been expectation without engagement or resources, now I had engagement and resources without any particular expectation. In that, I began to expect more of myself. And the crazy thing is, somewhere inside me, like in everyone, there was and is the potential for greatness. Judy looked beneath my surface and found me hiding inside.

I'd actually met Jill when she was a baby, but I'd not met Jan or Sarah. I had carried a picture of Jill around in my wallet, so proud of my beautiful little cousin. She was seven when I arrived, and she was extremely intelligent. She'd tell you something and then add, "If you'd like to know." I was sixteen and self-centered. I wasn't always kind to Jill. I'm sad about that.

Judy tells a story about Jill playing outside with a little friend and running inside shouting, "Mom, we saw something on the sidewalk; we think it's a creep." Can you guess what it was?[25]

---

[25] You figured out that what Jill saw on the sidewalk was a caterpillar, didn't you?

Janice was four, a little blond bombshell who'd strut down the sidewalk wearing little high heels. I loved choosing clothes for her. I guess I finally grew into dolls.

Sarah was two and snuggly. She had long, light brown, loosely curly hair. And she had her very own knock-knock joke:

"Knock-knock."
"Who's there?"
"Sarah"
"Sarah who?"
"Sarah baby in the house?"

Sarah called hamburgers "hangerburs." So of course we *all* called them that. One time I was at a drive-in burger joint with some of my friends, and I ordered a hangerbur. I wasn't even embarrassed—it was that good to feel like I belonged and was part of a family. We always used Sarah's word basghetti too.

Perhaps the best Sarah-ism was when she asked her mom for a "chee." She just wanted one piece. Makes sense to me. Recently I tried to send someone a kudo, but apparently there is no such thing as a kudo, at least according to trusty Mr. Spell-checker. So I sent two. I'm easy. And not long ago I read something some journalist had written about John McCain's being able to well understand our troops because he himself had once been a troop.

Judy originally tried to enroll me at the high school right up the street, only to discover that due to zoning, I had to go to a different one two towns away. It was a brand-new school, very modern, very huge. I rode the school bus every day—another first.

I discovered "greasers" there. A girl at Flo's had talked about the greasers where she lived, but I didn't know what they were. I found myself being one—sort of. Greaser girls wore black stockings and black shoes with heels. Their clothes were often black, too, topped with long leather coats called Cabrettas. I never had one of those, though. Some of the greaser girls wore nicer outfits. I was a classy greaser, I guess. I had nice clothes, but since I smoked, I mostly hung out with the greasers. The other alternative was to be a "collegiate" or "rah-rah," and I neither dressed like nor wanted to be one of them.

Ironically, though, I had always taken college-prep classes. The boarding school had been geared towards grooming students for college. It never occurred to me to do anything other than to continue along the same track. So, as a senior, I took Spanish 4 and Senior English, but I needed two sophomore classes in order to graduate. One was Geometry. The other was a combination of Physics and Chemistry, both of which were far outside my sphere of comprehension. And Gym.

I despised Gym. Mostly, it was because we were supposed to shower after class, which I never did. Since I had stretch marks from having been pregnant, I lived in terror that someone would see them and know. I had a partner in crime, though. The girl who had the locker next to mine had hair on her chest (although she probably didn't know I'd seen it), and she wasn't about to get naked either. We'd both change as quickly as we could and sneak out of the locker room.

It was also my first experience with staying at school all day and having lunch in a cafeteria. It was remarkable in that it was all so . . . normal. It was another world, and it was a good one, and I was part of it. Knowing that I only had one year left of school was good, too, as was seeing that there was potential for a decent life after I got out of school. I'd never felt hope for any sort of future back home. I couldn't see out of the hole.

I was nearly seventeen by the time I landed at Judy's, and shortly after my arrival, Al took me to get my driver's license. I passed on the first try. I never even got another learner's permit. Shortly before I got my license, though, Al was out of town, and Judy had a panic attack in the middle of the night. She called for help, and an ambulance came and took her over to the hospital where she worked as a microbiologist. I stayed home with the girls.

An hour or two later, Judy called, wanting me to come pick her up in the car. I didn't have a license yet, but she said to just do it. It wasn't far, it was the middle of the night and no one would be on the road, and she was embarrassed to take a cab because she was in her nightgown. So, good soldier that I am, I got in the car and drove over there. I left the girls sleeping. When I got to the hospital, I wanted Judy to drive, but she said no, I'd gotten there, so I may as well drive home. I did and it was fine.

I got my first job at a now long-defunct local department store. We lived two blocks from one of the first all-under-one-roof shopping malls, so I could walk to work if I needed to, although I usually either took Judy's car or someone drove me. I made a whopping $1.25 an hour and thought I was rich. After school I'd start at five and work till nine, plus some Saturdays and Sundays. That was a first for me, too, stores being open on Sunday.

Five o'clock was the dinner hour, so there wasn't much going on for the first couple of hours the night I started my job. I was in the glove department and there wasn't anything to do. I was bored and thinking about the hours stretching ahead of me. Then it got busy, and all of a sudden it was quitting time. It was a valuable lesson for me—if one has to work, it's better to be busy. A few days later, I got my permanent placement in the children's clothing department. The counters all had drawers underneath where additional items were kept, and I saw mouse droppings in the baby blanket drawers. I never told anyone, but now you know.

I was still a reprobate at heart. It being convenient that I worked in the children's department, I stole an outfit for one of the girls, put it in a store bag and carried it out on my break. I removed my nametag so that I'd just look like any other shopper. There were lockers in the mall, and for a quarter I stashed my booty and retrieved it later. When the store closed at night, employees had to leave by one exit so that the store detectives could spot-check us for stolen goods. A girl I recognized from school worked in the lingerie department and she got caught stealing stockings—she'd hidden them between pages of her school notebook. I was smarter than that. I'd have probably made a good store detective, had I thought of it.

I was also the live-in babysitter. Judy often worked weekends at the hospital and I'd be in charge at home. Al would be home on the weekends too, but he'd be in and out doing his own things, so my being there got him out of babysitting. One time I had Sarah in the tub, and I got distracted by something and forgot about her. I'd left the bathroom door closed to keep it warm in there. All of a sudden I remembered Sarah in the tub, and I didn't hear any splashing, so I panicked. I charged, or tried to charge, through the door, only to slam into Al's knee. He was sitting on the toilet. He was not amused.

Al had a company car, and Judy drove an Olds station wagon, which is the car I drove most of the time. Being able to drive, and actually having access to a car, really broadened my horizons. For a while, there was even an extra car around—Al's father had lent them his old pink Lincoln before they got the station wagon. It must've originally been a Mary Kay car. I loved that crazy Lincoln. I could be entertained just sitting in the driver's seat playing with the seat buttons. Up, down, slant, forward, backward—unlimited options. Unfortunately, Al's father took his car back, which was a real shame; I would have loved to keep it.

The first night I had my license, I got in the pink Lincoln with some friends and took the expressway into the city. That was when I discovered that I'd sometimes need to change lanes. I got to hear a great variety of horns, all of which were directed at me. I was pretty undaunted in those days. One time I was going too fast and needed to turn right into the street behind the shopping mall. I didn't hit the brake, just made the turn, and nearly flipped the car. Another learning experience.

Judy and Al also had an old Jag that mostly lived in the garage, but it would get hauled out, decorated, and driven through the neighborhood for Fourth of July parades. I never drove it; it was a stick shift and I wasn't good at that then.

I had study hall last period at school, which was convenient on the rare occasion when I deigned to actually do some homework. If I had math or some written assignment, I'd usually do that, but I seldom cracked a book, and certainly never carried one home. I've never been able to retain what I read, even though my comprehension is fine. I just don't remember any of it. So, of course, study hall became naptime. It would usually be okay; whatever teacher was on study hall duty didn't care, but one time I was rudely awakened and told to go stand in the hall. My locker was right outside the classroom, and I just leaned up against it and went back to sleep.

A girl named Sue, who lived only a block or so from me, and whom I recognized from the school bus, had the locker next to mine. I don't know why she was in the hall—she shouldn't have been, but she was—and she asked me whether I had a car. As it happened, I did have the car that day, and I now wonder why I didn't just take it and go home instead of continuing my nap standing up.

I said, "Yes," and she asked if I'd take her into the city. She, too, had come to the school as a senior, and had previously lived in the city, some twenty or so miles away. I agreed, having no clue about rush hour and how long it would take. This was long before the advent of cell phones, and I didn't think to call Judy and tell her I wouldn't be home on time, or for that matter, to ask permission. Sue and I drove into the city and didn't get back until after seven. Judy was worried, of course, but she was even more worried about me than she was about the car. Imagine that!

Sue and I are still best friends these many years later. One of the benefits of a lifelong friend is being able to talk about things without having to explain a lot of history.

I didn't get into all that much trouble though, generally. I had too many good things to do—I was in a good place, and I was mostly smart enough to know it. One time I was sitting in the living room with my friend Diane who, to digress a bit, introduced me to my first Italian beef sandwich. I'm still friends with any Italian beef sandwich that crosses my path, but I long ago lost touch with Diane.

Anyway, Diane, too, was a transplant from the city. Her parents had died and she was living with her sister around the corner from us, but she'd quit school. She hated the suburbs and said so, to which I replied that I hated it there, too, which really wasn't true. Judy heard and said, "Really?" I realized immediately that I didn't hate it, and I admitted it. I'd just been so used to being in places I hated, that I momentarily fell back into that thinking. The truth was that for the first time in my life I did like where I was. I still hated school, of course, but that wasn't going to change no matter where I lived, and it wasn't going to last much longer anyway.

Judy played guitar and she showed me a few chords. I was off and running. I spent hours in the bedroom, teaching myself to play Peter, Paul, and Mary, and Joan Baez songs. It was exactly what I needed. I started out on Al's guitar, which had steel strings, so I developed some serious calluses on my left hand.

That Christmas, under the tree, there was a magnificent brand new Arne acoustic guitar with nylon strings. It was for me. It was not only the perfect guitar, it was the gift that no other will ever surpass. It represented someone knowing me, loving me, and wanting good things for me. After nearly fifty years, it is still my treasure.

I had a stool I'd sit on to play. I got pretty good at it, and I'd strum random chords and ad-lib songs, trying to impress my friends. Sometimes I even did. One night I came home from work to find Al's father sitting on my stool. He looked up and asked, "Am I usurping your throne?" I never did like that man.

I continued playing guitar for many years. More than once, a medical technician who was trying to stick my finger for a blood sample asked me whether I played guitar. They'd typically start with my left hand because I was right-handed, and those calluses stymied them every time.

Judy was a good cook, and an inventive one. One time she had some cream of shrimp dip left over from a party. She decided it was too good to waste and served it to us on rice for dinner. She cleverly named it "leftover cream of shrimp dip," and it became a family favorite.

Another time, though, Judy made some cranberry bread. It happened to be time for a trip to the grocery store, so there wasn't much else to eat in the house. And I was hungry. It also happened that Judy had inadvertently put in double the cranberries the recipe called for. The minute that bread came out of the oven, there I was, plate in hand, and I gobbled down several pieces while they were still hot. I lost it shortly afterwards. It was years before I could even think about cranberry bread again without turning green.

I got revenge for the cranberry bread, but not intentionally. I was just stupid sometimes. The whole family had to go somewhere for a week or so, and I stayed at home alone. Judy charged me with watering her plants. I did a great job. So great, in fact, that I even watered the dried flowers that were in a wooden vase on the buffet. That water spot is still there on the buffet to this day.

I had a friend named Mary whom I met at work. She went to the school up the street and had an entirely different set of friends. Even so, she and I became close friends and she was much a part of my life for the next few years. I didn't get involved in her circle though; our friendship was mostly just the two of us. My social life was more with Sue and Diane.

Sue and I met some brothers named Guy and Scott, and then we met some of their friends, and then some of their friends, creating an ever-widening circle. I dated Guy and Sue took up with his friend

Tim, whom she later married. Then we met Larry M., who also played guitar. He, Tim and I decided to start a group. We spent a lot of time in Judy's living room and, once the weather warmed up, out on the covered patio, strumming and singing.

I messed up big time. Larry M. asked me out, and I said I'd go. Then Guy called and asked me out for the same night. I called Larry M. back and said I was sick, and then went out with Guy. As Guy and I were waiting at a red light, there was Larry M. in the car next to us, out delivering a pizza. He'd decided that since I couldn't go out, he might as well go to work.

He was naturally not pleased and, although we stayed friends and continued playing guitar together, he never again asked me out. I'm sure he figured I wasn't to be trusted, and he wasn't about to take another chance on me. So of course I decided that I was madly in love with him. Diane and I even played with the Ouija board, hoping it would say he'd change his mind. It didn't, and neither did he.

One night when the whole gang was at the house, I was feeling sorry for myself over Larry M. and I drank a bit too much beer. I fell forward onto my face on the living room carpet, which was quite well padded. I actually did it on purpose, and I caught myself with my hands. I was just trying to be cute, but everyone thought I'd genuinely passed out. I hadn't, but I was several sheets to the wind, and the floor felt just fine to me, so I just went to sleep right where I was. My friends unhooked my bra (they really did), covered me, and went home.

I woke up a few hours later, needing to throw up. I made it to the bathroom, but not to the toilet. I threw up all over the bathroom rug. Thinking that Judy would kill me for the mess sobered me right up, and she found me there trying to clean it up at 3 A.M.—with the vacuum cleaner. Dear Judy just shook her head, put the rug in the washing machine, and went back to bed.

One morning around 6 o'clock, a tornado came through the area. Judy said it sounded like a freight train coming down the street. She and Al and all three girls were stationed next to the bed where I was sleeping, ready to jump into the open crawl space trap door, which was right there in the closet. They figured that if we needed to get down into the crawl space, they'd just pull me in, so they didn't bother to wake me up. The tornado bent the trees in the back yard down to the ground and ripped the roofs off several apartment buildings in the next block. I finally woke up and looked out the window to see trees all over the place and wondered what had happened.

Since I'd missed the school bus in all the chaos, I took the car and started driving to school. About halfway there, I saw all the school buses heading back towards home. There was no power at the school and we all got the day off. Tornadoes can be useful.

A few weeks before graduation, Sue went out with Larry M. I was really mad at her and we didn't talk at graduation, nor did I invite her to my party. Fortunately, their thing was short-lived or I doubt we'd be the good friends we still are today.

My Spanish teacher was the one who handed me my diploma, and he did it with a wry grin. He and I both knew that I didn't deserve to pass Spanish, but only he knew whether or not he'd taken pity on me. When we walked, we didn't know for sure that we'd been graduated— we picked up our real diplomas after the ceremony. You can imagine my relief when I found one with my name on it.

All we had done in fourth year Spanish was read novels, except that I didn't read them. My history of not doing homework had caught up with me and I really didn't understand much Spanish. Typically, the first year of a language is all about vocabulary and the second is about grammar. In my case, I'd learned the grammar at the boarding school, so my second year back at the local high school was a repeat. I could conjugate a verb quite handily, except that I didn't know many verbs. My third year, we published a newspaper in Spanish and all I did was create the crossword puzzle. My having had four different Spanish teachers, each of whom spoke a different dialect, further complicated things, all with the result that I was severely deficient in the language.

Of course having taken four years of Spanish, I had to marry a German—two of them, in fact. Many years later, when X2, my second native-born German husband, and I were in Spain, he always knew what I was trying to say because I'd start a sentence in Spanish and wind up ending it in German. I did find Spain to be much less complicated than Germany, though. The only problem I had was finding the right word for bathrooms. It turned out to be *los servicios*.

There are two things I make sure I know when visiting a foreign country. The first is the numbers and the money system, and the second is to know how to ask where the bathroom is. On that trip to

Spain, I figured out that, in any town, there is bound to be a hotel and most hotels have bathrooms off the lobby somewhere. You just walk in and look for it. Not quite as foolproof is going into a restaurant. In Spain, we did that, ordered coffee so that we'd be "legitimate" bathroom users, only to find out, after having drunk our coffee, that the bathrooms were out of order. The coffee didn't improve the situation.

After graduation, Sue and I would both turn up at parties the gang would have and we eventually went back to being friends. Another set of brothers we knew threw parties when their parents went out of town, which was fairly often. These were all-weekend bashes that began on Friday night and ended up with breakfast and cleanup on Sunday morning. We played pimp guts, a poker game, and everyone drank a lot. I never stayed overnight, but most people did. I usually didn't have any money, so I'd borrow a dollar from someone to get into the game, then win, return their dollar, and usually go home with an extra ten bucks or so in my pocket.

And then I got a real job.

CHRISTMAS VISION

I was up early one Christmas morning when I was in my mid-forties. Everyone else in the house was still asleep and I was sitting on a stool at the kitchen counter, enjoying a cup of coffee and some temporary peace and quiet. Once the caffeine kicked in, I remembered that it was Christmas, and I said, "Lord, it's Your birthday. Is there anything you'd like me to give You, or is there something You'd like to tell me today?"

His response was immediate. He said, "Crissy, there in the living room is a beautiful Christmas tree, as tall as the ceiling, and decorated all in gold. Underneath it are many presents, all beautifully wrapped and they are all for you. In fact, everything you need is under that tree and it is all from Me. The problem is that you always look at the to/from tags. And if the tag doesn't say that it is from X2 (my husband at the time), you don't even bother opening the present. Because of that, you are missing out on all the gifts I give you through other people."

Since then, I have tried consciously to receive the gifts of my children, my grandchildren and my friends, as well as the love with which God has given them. They are great and many, and yes, they are enough.

A Sort Of Funeral

Crissy Shreve

How can there be sadness upon a death
Where there was no life, no connection?
Like someone you never met, never touched,
Never knew, dying in Toledo, Ohio.

Funerals are for the survivor.

So for years we took up space,
And never even called it love.
I feel a need to justify my lack of sadness,
My great relief,
To calm my guilt.

And as I stand among the left-behind,
I feel a sense of something barely missed,
Like had I known in the dark that it was there,
I might have reached for it.
And yet I thought I did.

I need a sort of funeral.
A gathering of loved ones to celebrate release,
I need my people near to fill the voids.
Oh, no, not the voids of now, but of a thousand years.

And so 'tis not for lost love I weep,
But for all the years' pretending.

Chapter Sixteen

Independence

Only a month or so before the end of my senior year, I somehow hit the radar of the teacher who ran a program for kids living in unusual circumstances. Apparently, because I lived with relatives instead of parents, I qualified. I knew there were special classes for kids who'd previously quit school and returned, because some of the guys in our group of friends were in that program. They only attended school for part of the day, and then went to work. Had I know about this program earlier, I could have taken fewer classes and worked more. I hadn't even needed the Spanish to graduate.

One day I got summoned to see the teacher, Mr. T. I don't know how he found out about me, but he asked me what I'd like to do career wise and offered to help. At that time, I aspired to be a flight attendant, but I was only seventeen and couldn't apply until I turned eighteen. He said he could help with that when the time came, and then he suggested I work for him within the program until it did. So after graduation, I once again got on a school bus every day and went to work helping set up another new high school that was to open the following fall.

I only lasted a week or so. I was still only making the minimum $1.25 an hour there too, and the work was so boring I don't even remember exactly what I did. I started looking at want ads in the newspaper to see what else might be out there and discovered that there were much more lucrative jobs available. The downside was that, if I got another job, I'd be out of the program.

Judy's husband Al was a salesman for a large industrial chemical company, and he told me they were looking for someone for customer service. Not being at all above nepotism, I applied and I got the job.

The next problem became how to get me to work every day. I could ride in with Al when he was going to the office, and I could use his car when he was out of town, but it wasn't the optimal arrangement. I needed independent transportation. I had my eye on a Volkswagen beetle, but Uncle Austin was still mad at me for having a baby, so he wouldn't bite, and no one else could afford to front me the money.

One of the best "firsts" about living with Judy was that a problem was seen as something to be solved, unlike back at home where, when something stopped working, the TV for instance, you simply went without it.

Judy placed an ad in the local paper looking for someone who lived near us and who drove to the area where I worked, about fifteen miles away. It worked like a charm. In only a few days, a young woman named Darlene answered the ad. The beauty of it was that she started earlier than I did, and got off later, plus my office was beyond hers. So every day, she'd pick me up, she'd drive to her office, then she'd get out, and I'd take the car the rest of the way. This gave me a car at lunchtime, too. It was a pretty sweet deal for the fifteen bucks a week I gave her for gas.

My job was to be in Central Order Processing (COP), but first I was trained in the entire shipping process. I filed and called trucks and generally learned the products and how it all functioned. Finally, the girl whose job I was to take over, taught me about the process of taking orders, and I got my own desk.

I spent my day on the phone taking orders. I got to be good buddies with many of the customers and the people in the home office. I even went to a customer's wedding, just to meet him and others from that company. Meeting someone face-to-face with whom I'd had only a telephone relationship was always a revelation. They were *never* the way I'd pictured them, and often I didn't like them as much in person. (Conversely, years later when I was doing genealogy, I had a lot of email "disagreements" with a cousin and didn't like him much, but when I met him at a reunion, I found him to be delightful in person. Go figure.)

Some of the customers had great names. First there was Mrs. Legree, who had to have been Simon's wife. She was very unpleasant and I was even warned about her. Another was Mr. Sippy, and I'll let you think about what his wife's name was. Then there was Miss Peehow. The trick was not to snicker when they'd call and say who they were.

The greatest name story is about a girl who was filling in for the regular secretary one time in the leather department. Everyone loved our customer Mr. Hale. Apparently he was flirting with her on the phone and got her so flustered that, at the end of the conversation, she said, "Thank you very Hale, Mr. Much."

It happened to me, too. There were two young guys who regularly flirted with me, but they didn't know about each other, so they didn't always think to identify themselves at the beginning of a call. They just assumed I'd know who they were, which I did—I just didn't always know *which* of them it was. So one day one of them called and started right in with our normal repartee. He had me all flustered, and when we finally needed to get down to business, I said, "Are you who I think I am?" He didn't catch what I'd said, but I did, and I was laughing too hard to explain why I was laughing.

We had a lot of fun at work. Each department had its own secretary, plus there was a typing pool, along with those of us in COP. I discovered that there was a lot more nepotism going on—a bunch of the girls were each other's cousins or friends. Al called them the Polish Mafia. I learned a few Polish phrases, and we used our Polish names for fun at lunch or after work. I was Krisha. There was, of course, the typical bickering and gossiping in the office, but I got along with most of them well enough.

There were two of us on the central order desks, and the only real trouble I ever had was with the girls who worked right next to me, supposedly doing the same job. One left and was replaced by another. There was something about that other desk; I don't know what it was. Maybe it was about me. The customers asked for me, so I got all the calls and all the work, even though the first incoming call was supposed to be routed to the other desk. Instead of being useful and helping, they'd just sit there.

Those of us in the Polish Mafia (I was an honorary member) weren't at all above picking on people, though, and we weren't kind about it. One girl who was an object of our derision worked at the switchboard. She was very skinny, and we called her Tweety Bird. She wasn't terribly bright. One time when the district manager called in to the office, she answered with the name of her previous company. The district manager apologized for dialing a wrong number, hung up, and called back. I will never understand why they gave Tweety Bird my job when I left. I heard that a customer ordered 5,000 gallons of product, but she sent him 5 gallons. He had to shut down his production line for several days until the material could get there.

Another one we picked on spent the entire morning flirting with the truck dispatchers she called for pickup. We might have left her to it had she not been so loud and boisterous about it. We had a phrase in Polish—"*Gadu gadu ja sie smieje*," which means something to the effect of "talk, talk, and self-laugh. " When she'd be at it on the phone, someone would always say "*Gadu gadu*," and the rest of us would laugh. She never had a clue what we were saying or even that we were talking about her.

From time to time someone would come up to me while I was talking on the phone and try to tell me something. This was extremely annoying in that I'd not hear what they said *or* what the customer was saying on the phone. I've always said that it would be great if all the idiots in the world would just disappear—except that I'd probably disappear right with the rest of them.

No one ever told me about wisdom teeth. One of mine decided to emerge and to emerge sideways, cutting into my cheek. It needed to go. A buddy at work came to my rescue by telling me about a dentist who used nitrous oxide. Nitrous oxide is a wondrous thing. I had it a number of times and every experience, at least in that office, was identical. Every single time, my first thought would be that it was a good thing I wasn't out driving a car. The dentist would put the mask on my face and then go do something else for a while, so that the gas could take effect. Then when he'd come back into the room, he'd always say, "Put some of this in your scuba tank." And I'd always laugh and snort.

When it was time for him to pull my wisdom tooth, he fiddled around in my mouth for a minute and then asked if I was ready. "Okay," I mumbled. He held it up and showed it to me. It was already out!

My broadening cultural experience continued at work. There were a number of Jewish people who worked there and lived nearby. I'd drive one girl home at lunchtime in exchange for a bagel with lox and cream cheese. I'm not sure what I thought or expected, but I remember being a bit surprised to find that her house was pretty much like any other house.

A girl named Chris and I got to be buddies. She was Assyrian, and she belly danced, although I never got to see her do it. She and I often went out to lunch together, usually to a favorite place just down the street that served great mushroom cheeseburgers. Right behind the restaurant there was a *Yeshiva*, a Hebrew school. We'd see the boys outside in their *yarmulkes*, and we'd laugh and call them the "little Heebies." One time an older Jewish woman came along with us to lunch. Chris didn't know she was Jewish, and started in on the "Heebies," while I was giving serious thought to crawling under the table. Poor Chris wound up eating a mushroom *crow*burger that day.

I often went shopping with another Jewish girl named Mary. This was right at the time when panty hose came on the scene and made mini-skirts possible. Mary always wore the latest fad clothes, including very short skirts, so she was a good clothing advisor. She also talked in something of a monotone. She never seemed to get either excited or upset about anything. One day a bunch of us were at a restaurant, and I ordered a baked potato. The waitress asked whether I wanted butter or sour cream. I said I'd like both. The waitress said she'd have to charge me an extra nickel for both. Without thinking, I muttered something about "cheap Jews." Mary didn't bat an eyelash; she just calmly pointed out that it was a Greek restaurant.

Darlene and I talked about all sorts of things while driving to and from work. One day she told me about a cute guy to whom she'd been engaged for a while. She thought I ought to meet him. She was still part of a bowling league with him, so I went along one night. He and I started dating, and a year or so later, he became X1, my first husband. When people would ask how we'd met, I always said that my cousin Judy had advertised for him in the newspaper. I'd have never met him had Darlene not answered that ad.

X1 had a white Plymouth Barracuda. After we'd been dating a while, I started using his car. He lived between home and work, so I'd take his car home with me at night and pick him up again the next morning. He had a hard time waking up, so his mother was always pleased when I'd arrive to cajole him out of bed.

I started eating dinner there regularly; it made sense since I was dropping him off anyway, and we'd usually go out afterwards. They spoke German to each other and English to me. One time, X1's mother called her husband to dinner, hollering, "Werner," although in their dialect it sounded like "vennay." I thought it meant 'c'mon," because to me it sounded like the Spanish word *venir*.

When X1 came to pick me up for our first date, I'd told him how to get to Judy's, and said that I'd pull the Jag out of the garage to help him find the house. I forgot to do that, and when he finally turned up, he told me he'd been driving around the neighborhood looking for the "Yaguar." X1 didn't always know how to pronounce words in English. The funniest was Pericles. He called him "Prickless." I'm not making this up.

Along the same lines, one time X1's aunt was writing a letter to her sister in New Jersey, but she wrote New Yersey. Since the J is pronounced Y in German, apparently she decided that it was New Yersey and wrote it that way in English.

One night as X1 was dropping me off after a date, we had a fight in the driveway. He was so mad at me that he jumped into his car, slammed it into reverse, and backed smack into the trashcans that were neatly lined up at the curb for pickup the next morning. Garbage was scattered all over the street, and he had to pick it all up. He didn't think it was funny, but of course I did. Judy finally suggested I ought to help him.

Occasionally, I'd still use Al's car. One morning it was snowing like the dickens, and several inches fell while I was on my way to work. I needed to make a right turn. I dutifully turned the wheel, but the car had a different idea and just kept going, sliding straight ahead. I was still a fairly new driver, and I got a good lesson in inertia and slippery roads. That snow kept falling all day long and they let us out of work early, but it was already too late. I barely made it the few miles to X1's house, where I spent the night. X1 somehow made it home too, but his dad, who worked in the city, didn't. He walked home the next day—about fifteen miles.

Later that same year, during the summer, I again had Al's car. I'd dropped him off at the airport and was driving to work from there. I knew the way, but there was road construction, and the sign for the street where I needed to turn had been taken down. I was waiting at a red light, facing north, and looking to my right for the sign. The sun was coming up in the east and it was in my eyes. In front of me was a pickup truck with several long pieces of black iron pipe sticking out the back. There was a red flag on the back of the pipe, but it was up high, above my line of vision, especially since I had the visor down. As I was trying to see where I was to turn, I didn't realize that I didn't have my foot securely on the brake, and that I was creeping slowly forward.

Crunch! I ran into those pipes. Immediately afterwards, the light changed, and the pickup truck started to move forward. The driver hadn't noticed that I'd hit him. One piece of pipe was embedded in the roof of the car, just above the windshield and, when he moved, it stayed stuck there. He only figured out what had happened when he heard his end of the pipe hit the pavement. Clank! I watched that pipe slide off the truck and cringed as I envisioned myself getting impaled. Fortunately, that didn't happen and I'm still here to tell the story.

Poor Judy had to take the car to get three estimates for the repair. There she was, with this car that had about a three-inch round hole in the front of the roof, plus a windshield that was cracked from top to bottom. It was pretty strange. At every place, they asked her, "Lady, how'd you ever do *that*?" And every time, she'd say, "You don't think *I* did that, do you?"

At some point, X1 and I got engaged.

Judy and the family went on vacation, once again leaving me alone in the house. X1 and I concocted a story for his mother about how we were going to South Bend to see my Aunt Jane, and he stayed with me at the house for the weekend. I still had to hide him from the neighbors. We stashed his car a block away at an apartment complex. X1 lay in the back seat of Al's car while I drove into the garage, and then I hit the button to close the garage door. I thought I was pretty clever. And it worked really well—until it was time to smuggle him back out.

There he was, lying across the back seat again. I backed out of the garage, hit the button to close the garage door, and headed out. The street abruptly turned left and I took the turn a little too fast. Meanwhile, the back car door wasn't closed tightly. It came open, and X1 started to fly out of the car, so I slammed on the brake. He flew into the back of the front seat instead and landed on the floor. Of course the neighbors saw it all.

When we went to retrieve X1's car, the owners of the apartment complex where we'd left it were just about to have it towed away. He married me anyway. I suppose it could be argued that he suffered something of a head injury in that incident.

Oh, and I don't have an Aunt Jane in South Bend or anywhere else. Years later, X1's mother told me she'd known all along what we were up to. Of course she did.

The following Christmas, X1 and I drove to see my mother. She never liked him, because he was German. We also met up with my friend Dee, who was very excited that I was engaged. The minute we saw each other, I whispered to her, "Doesn't he look like Jack?" while she grabbed my hand, wanting to see my ring. We were so young, and so into the wrong things.

Dee was staying at her dad's, so we went there to see her. It was an older area where the traffic lights were on the far side of the intersection. X1, used to lights being on the near side, stopped for a red light—right in the middle of the intersection. He hated my hometown from that day on.

DIFFERENCES

Although I didn't inherit my mother's hatred, it influenced me, and it took me some years and some exposure to people who are different than I am to begin to intentionally challenge her messages when they played in my head.

When X2 and I were in the process of divorcing, I lived in an apartment for just a few months while I looked for a place to buy. There was subsidized housing across the street, and every ethnicity you can think of was represented in that neighborhood. I'd come from an all-white, fairly well-to-do neighborhood, and had been a sheltered suburban housewife all my adult life. But the world had changed over those years while I wasn't looking. There were all kinds of people I'd never been around before.

There was a playground right behind my apartment. During the day, I'd see kids of all colors and nationalities playing together. I was impressed. The kids were utterly unaware of their differences. I learned from them. I saw that they had parents who worked and had nice cars and cared about raising their kids. At night, though, some really big guys would be in the park shooting hoops, so I stayed inside.

I didn't feel dislike, and certainly not hatred for these people at all. What I did feel was culture shock. I was completely out of my element and living alone for the first time in my life. I simply didn't know whether or not I was safe.

One day I was out walking my Chihuahuas, and two young black guys, maybe sixteen or seventeen, were coming towards me on the sidewalk. They were beautiful boys, both wearing do-rags on their heads. As they got closer, I had a decision to make. Who did I want to be? Did I want to be afraid; did I want to just ignore them and walk past them with my eyes averted? I decided that that was exactly who I didn't want to be, and so I smiled at them and said hi.

These two young men smiled back and talked to me and schmoozed with my dogs for nearly half an hour. I enjoyed them immensely and it was a delightful experience. I'm so glad I didn't miss it.

Recently, a choir from the inner city came to my church to lead worship. They were a mixed group—White, Black, Hispanic, and Oriental. Not only was this a slice of heaven, but it was heaven as it should be and as it *will* be—brothers and sisters of all colors and tongues, worshipping our God together. I cried a bit. God lives in the praises of His people and He was surely there with us that day.

I think I've always tended to gravitate naturally towards people who are different. These experiences just made me more comfortable doing it. I've always felt different, so in effect, I am one of them.

I think of the two girls I met while smoking outside a hotel, and I think of some of the upright, uptight, good Christians I know who, dear as they may be, would never have thought to "associate" with those girls. The one girl had those *big* holes in her ears; the other had several colors of hair, none of which were colors God assigned to hair. I had a great time talking to them.

I think of the cute little teenager with the amazing Mohawk who was hanging out with a bunch of other young guys by the church doors one day as I was leaving. He was adorable. I walked up to him and said, "Hey, I really like your hair." He even let me touch it. I wanted to take him home with me.

I think of the girl in church who was enthusiastically clapping out of rhythm and singing too loudly, and out of tune. She appeared to have Cerebral Palsy. I was beginning to be annoyed by the disturbance she was making when God said, "Look at her. She's praising Me with all her heart. Her out-of-rhythm, off-key praise is beautiful to My ears. Some day she'll be whole and perfect in your eyes, but she's already whole and perfect in Mine." Her parents were working very hard to control her. I went over to the mom and told her what God had told me. She was very touched. *I* was very touched.

I never know who God's going to put in my path. My job is to not pass them by. And every single time I engage, I'm the one who gets blessed!

"And for our inheritance, give us the lost.[26]"

---

[26] Song lyrics, Kevin Prosch, Vinyard.

WHEN I LEAVE YOU
Crissy Shreve

When I leave you, it will be
Because you reached for the blanket
Instead of for me.

CHAPTER SEVENTEEN

MARRIAGE

X1 and I got married in July of 1967. In order to get a marriage license, his mother had had to sign for him, since he was only nineteen. I, at eighteen, could sign for myself.

Dee, Mary, and X1's sister stood up for me. I made Mary maid of honor because she was local and would be around to help put the wedding together and to throw me a shower. Dee was not happy; she really wanted to be my maid of honor and would have been had she not lived so far away.

Al walked me down the aisle. Uncle Austin drove my mother out for the wedding. I hadn't officially invited her and I wasn't sure I even wanted her there, considering her dislike of X1, but she behaved herself.

We held the reception in Judy's back yard. The weather cooperated, and it was delightful. X1's brother drank too much and passed out on the front lawn, but otherwise everything went smoothly, at least until honeymoon time. X1 and I drove to a resort about an hour away. I'd made a reservation, but we got there late and they hadn't held the room, so we had to go looking for a motel at midnight. We were tired and that was not pleasant.

After a day or two at that resort, X1 decided he wanted to go fishing, so we drove to another area. I'd never been fishing before. We didn't catch anything, and I didn't see much point in it.

We came home and moved into our first apartment. I was into green, preferably olive green. Everything I bought for that first apartment was some shade of green. I loved looking at my olive green pots and pans, even though I had no clue how to cook.

I'd somehow acquired a huge 5-foot-tall pink teddy bear. Judy was very pleased to get it out of her house when I moved to the apartment. Of course it had to sleep in our bed; it was too big to fit anywhere else, and it wasn't green, so it certainly couldn't be in the living room. X1 was not amused. He was the one who'd insisted on a king-sized bed, so there was plenty of room. I don't know what the problem was.

Our apartment was on the second floor, and the bathroom window faced the parking lot and the ten-story hospital across the street. The window had frosted glass in it and, although we had a plastic window curtain, we never thought to actually close it when showering. We cleverly assumed that the frosted window was there for a reason.

After we'd lived there for some months, I happened to come home one night in the dark, and as I drove into the parking lot, I looked up and saw X1 in the shower, as clear as day from the waist up. Not a huge deal, but how many times had *I* been in that shower at night, in full view of the parking lot and all the hospital windows across the street? I was an exhibitionist unaware. Hmmm. I wonder why no one ever told me. Someone probably got rich selling binoculars over at the hospital.

Not long after we were married, we had a small car accident. We weren't hurt and there wasn't much damage to the car. When we took it in for repair, we saw a great yellow Barracuda convertible in the show room. The top was down, and I sat in it, pushing buttons and turning knobs. When I hit the windshield washer control, I squirted myself in the face. My having "cristened" it, of course we had to buy the car.

The next summer, we took our first real vacation. We headed east to Cape Cod, stopping along the way to visit friends and family. On the Cape, we saw a small motorboat that was for sale and decided to buy it. Then we had to get insurance so that we could drag it home. The nearest agent was in Worcester, Massachusetts.

Now, I grew up in a family that regularly used Worcestershire Sauce. I *knew* how to say "wister-shur." I didn't, however, connect the dots. There we were in Worcester, Massachusetts, looking for Worcester Road. There weren't any signs. We stopped at a drug store to ask directions. It was, not surprisingly, the Worcester Pharmacy. I walked boldly up to the pharmacist and asked him how to find

"Wor-chester" Road. He suggested that perhaps I wanted "Wister" Road and, oh, by the way, I was on it.

The best part of the story, though, is that, years later, when X2 and I were on vacation in Ft. Lauderdale, I met that same pharmacist. We had a great laugh together.

The boat's steering wheel, typically, was on the right. Neither X1 nor I had ever even been in a motorboat, let alone driven one. Our first time out, I was at the wheel and I figured that, if the steering wheel in a car is on the left and you pass other cars on the right, apparently you were supposed to pass other boats on the left. The first boat to approach us just didn't know what to do with me trying to go to his left. I nearly ran right into him.

Backing into the water with a trailer behind me was a challenge, and it was my job, because X1 had to get the boat off and back onto the trailer. I got good at backing up over time, but I'd have loved to be a fly on the windshield watching that first day out. Fortunately, thinking bass-ackwards comes naturally to me. Whatever you typically do is exactly the opposite of what you have to do when backing up a trailer.

X1 nearly cut off his hand on a grinder at work. He was in severe pain for some weeks. Fortunately, we found a good surgeon who was able to restore the nerve damage so that he was able to use it. It being summer, and despite his being temporarily one-handed, we took the boat out. Getting it in and out of the water suddenly became my job too.

The one good thing about the arm injury was that it helped save X1 from the draft, which was still in place in those days. Everyone our age was terrified at the threat of Viet Nam. By the time he had healed sufficiently to be considered fit to go, there was a final draft lottery by birth date, and X1's number came up very close to last. We were in the clear, which was good, because by then I was expecting Mike.

My friend Mary's parents were Susan and Robert. They were a lot of fun. Susan wanted a new refrigerator, specifically a side-by-side refrigerator. Robert didn't want to spend the money and said he thought their old refrigerator was just fine. Susan didn't argue with him. She just went out and bought a bunch of one-pound packages of hamburger and stuffed them all into the freezer. Poor Robert opened the freezer after dinner to get his ice cream and all the then-frozen hamburger packages fell on his feet. Susan got her new refrigerator.

One day X1 and I went out for lunch with Mary and her husband Scott. X1 was allergic to several foods, including mayonnaise. He ordered a BLT, not expecting it to have mayonnaise on it. When the sandwich arrived, he sent it back, asking for one with no mayo. The cook just scraped off the mayo and sent it back to him. This not being acceptable, he sent it back again. The waitress was very apologetic and promised that if the sandwich was wrong again, lunch would be free.

Meanwhile, the rest of us were eating, and I was watching to see what would happen next. Sure enough, the cook put another club sandwich up on the pick-up shelf, this one without mayonnaise, but a different waitress grabbed it for her customer, and her customer's sandwich with mayo came our way. By that time, the rest of us were finished eating. Poor X1 gave up and never did get any lunch, but the rest of us ate for free.

While I was pregnant with Mike, my friend Dee from back home decided to get married. She was again disappointed because I didn't want to be her matron of honor. I not only lived too far away to be of much use in that role, but I couldn't see myself all dressed up as a bridesmaid in a maternity gown. I did go to the wedding, though.

It was February and it had snowed quite a bit there. I stayed with Uncle Austin and borrowed his car to drive to the wedding. The church was on the top of a hill. I drove up a long street to get to the top of that hill, and then made a 360-degree turn onto another street to get to the church. The parking lot was down the hill below the church, with access from a side street. When it was time to leave, I got into Uncle Austin's car and pulled out of the parking lot onto the side street. It was icy and steep.

After sliding sideways down the hill for nearly a block, somehow managing to not hit anything, I figured that attempting to go back up was probably futile. So, I headed down instead and wound up on the lower street that would take me home. A quick right turn and I was on my way. A great shortcut I'll remember the next time.

X1 wanted to invite a friend and his wife to dinner. I wasn't much of a cook, but I made an effort to make a nice dinner for them. I'd met the wife briefly, but I didn't really know her. The meal wasn't gourmet, but it wasn't awful, either. Nevertheless, the wife proceeded to criticize the food and to contradict everything I said the entire evening. I am neither making this up nor exaggerating. Her behavior was obnoxious. To top it off, she informed me that she never invited people to dinner.

Someone had given us a set of wooden salad bowls as a wedding gift. Once this couple had left, I started to complain about how rudely she'd treated me. X1 made the mistake of sticking up for her. Bad move. I was drying the dishes and I had one of the wooden salad bowls in my hand. I was so mad at her, then at him for taking her side, that I threw the bowl at him. He blithely lifted his elbow to deflect the blow and the salad bowl shattered. I vowed at that moment to have nothing further to do with that woman.

Another year passed, and it was again vacation time. And X1 again wanted to go fishing. We got in the car and started driving north, ending up in Canada at a resort fifty or so miles from anything even remotely (if you'll pardon the pun) resembling civilization. We rented a cabin and unloaded the car just as it was getting dark. X1 wanted to get right to all those fish with his name on them, so pole in hand, he headed off to the dock. The minute the sun went down, the mosquitoes descended on me in the cabin. Not just a few, hordes of them. The screens in the windows didn't slow them down even a little. I couldn't slap them away fast enough, and I got scared.

I ran down to the lodge and pounded on the door. The resort owner sold me some mosquito coils. I took them back to the cabin and lit a few. They burned slowly and put an incense-like smoke into the air. The next morning, I swept up an inch of dead mosquitoes that covered the entire floor.

Meanwhile, X1 didn't last long at the dock. He heard something scream and thought it was some sort of wildcat, so he headed back to the cabin. Clever man—by that time, I had the mosquitoes under control.

We had rented a rowboat with a small motor, and at dawn the next morning we set out onto the lake to fish. We'd been told to cross the lake to the other side, where some white birch trees had fallen into the water along the shore. The water was crystal-clear and only a few feet deep, and we could see the bottom through the trees. We hooked minnows by the tail and just lowered them into the water between the branches.

We were able to watch exactly what was happening below the surface, something unusual for lake fishing. I watched my minnow flitting around, and then I watched as a huge Northern Pike quietly came out from between the fallen trees. That Pike just hung there, not moving, with only his mouth working, eyeballing my minnow, for probably ten minutes, while I was trying not to wet my pants in anticipation.

I've always said that there's only one reason to go fishing, and that's to catch fish. If it's not exciting, why bother? Well, *this* was exciting. I could hardly stand it, waiting for that Pike to bite. Finally, slowly and smoothly, he just moved in and . . . *chomp*!

This was only my second time fishing and I knew nothing about things like setting my hook. I got so excited when that fish hit that I jerked my pole, and in the process, jerked the minnow right out of his mouth. X1, obviously operating on the principle that all's fair in love and war and fishing, had his minnow waiting on the other side of the boat.

Mr. Pike, now seriously thinking breakfast, headed right over to it and once again went *chomp*! X1 had him, but the fish ran under the boat and snapped the line. At that point, there was nothing to do but get that fish.

We headed back to shore, hopped in the car, and drove fifteen miles down the gravel road to the nearest store. We bought heavier test line and returned to try again. By that time, though, I was exhausted, and I decided to take a nap in the cabin, leaving Mr. Pike to X1. An hour or so later, I woke up to find him standing in the doorway holding up that fish. And it *was* our fish; it still had X1's first hook and minnow in its mouth. That guy was huge, too, at least two feet long.

Not being a cook or a fisherperson, I had no clue how to get the fish safely home. We got some ice and packed him in a cooler, but by the time we got home, I was afraid to cook him. We gave him to X1's aunt, who pickled him, and I was told he tasted quite good.

Had I known then how good Northern Pike tastes, I might have tried harder. I wish I'd known then the secret I learned years later from friends in Arkansas on how to transport fish. You cut them up, put the separate pieces in water-filled Baggies, freeze them, then wrap them in layers of newspaper and put them in a cooler. They'll remain frozen for several days that way.

There was a tiny, but tall, island in the middle of the lake. Fish don't tend to bite in the afternoon, so we just went cruising. We tied up the boat and climbed up the rocks to the top of the little island. Although I suppose someone with binoculars could have seen us, there was no one around for miles. If I had it to do over again, I'd go skinny-dipping.

So there we were up on top of this island, and X1 had to . . . go. Since no one had thought to bring toilet paper along, he just took off his underpants and used them. I imagine they're probably still there. And, already having his pants off, he figured we ought to take advantage of the situation. I'm certain that that's where my son Mike was conceived.

Mike was due to be born in May, and I continued to work until February. I refused to have morning sickness, and I mostly felt fine aside from some occasional heartburn and general bitchiness.

We bought our first house and moved in. There were lots of kids in the neighborhood, and they loved X1. They'd come to the door after dinner asking if Mr. D. could come out and play, which he usually did.

The bathroom door in the house was eccentric. Sometimes it would get stuck and you couldn't get it open. This, of course, always happened when you were inside the bathroom. One day a few weeks before Mike was born, I was alone in the house, and I went in to take a shower. Since the bathroom was right next to the bedroom, I didn't take any clothes with me. The door stuck and I couldn't get out. There I was, buck-naked, huge belly, trying to decide whether I could climb through the window and, even if I could, how I'd get back into the locked house. What a sight that would have been. Fortunately, I was finally able to get the door open. The only redeeming factor in the whole thing was that, being pregnant, at least I was in the bathroom if I needed to "go."

The neighbor women took me under their wings. Right across the street lived Gladys. She was particularly fond of me. Of course I always jokingly called her "Glad-ass." She always corrected me, saying that no, she was "Happy Bottom."

On the day Mike was born, I started feeling weird in the morning, and then had light contractions all day. It was a beautiful, sunny day to be born. The neighbors and I sat out front all day, timing my contractions. I finally called X1 around 3PM. He drove home with all the car windows open and the radio blaring, and when he got there, he couldn't remember driving home. We headed for the hospital and Mike was born three hours later. He was two weeks early. He didn't waste any time in the hospital, and he's not slowed down since.

Once I was in a room, I noticed what felt to me like a huge chunk of foam rubber lying on top of my belly. I asked the nurse what it was, and she said it *was* my belly—I was still numb from the anesthetic.

Everything I'd read said that I should buy nursing bras in my regular size. They were wrong. Judy came to visit me at the hospital, asking if there was anything I needed. Well, I needed nursing bras. I had no clue what size to get; I just knew they had to be *big*, so I sent her out for some in size 38E. The saleswoman just looked at Judy, who's never been busty, and said, "Lady, you're dreaming."

All the way up until he was born, Mike had been Jennifer, at least in my mind. I hadn't thought much about a boy's name, so X1 picked the name Michael.

I was pretty mad at X1's mother for moving back to Germany right after I got pregnant with Mike. I suspect she saw herself taking care of any potential babies we might have, while I'd go back to work. And that's exactly what would have happened. Either way, I sure could have used having her around those first few months. Instead, I was on my own. My mother was far away and would not have been of much help, anyway. X1's aunt came the day I came home from the hospital, but that was the only time. She showed me how to swaddle Mike, who was already making sure we clearly understood that sleep wasn't on his agenda.

I'd be sitting in the chair in the living room in the middle of the night, desperately needing sleep myself, and he'd nurse a bit, and then doze. When I tried to put him in his crib, he'd wake up. I was afraid to take him into bed with me, so I'd sit there in that chair thinking, twenty more years, twenty more years.

To be fair, he probably wasn't getting enough milk to be satisfied. No one taught me about breastfeeding—things like latching on or pumping. I had no effective way to measure how much he'd taken, either. After a few weeks, I finally switched him to a bottle and formula, and then he started sleeping through the night.

Of course, using bottles created a whole new set of problems. Very few people had dishwashers in those days, so bottles and nipples were sterilized by boiling. But if he was willing to sleep, I was willing to boil. One time, for some reason, I had just one nipple to boil. I stuck it in a small pan, put it on the stove, and promptly forgot about it. You have no idea, or maybe you do, what burning silicone smells like. It's not pretty. It permeated the house. Even worse were the little black foosies that wafted through the air and landed all over the kitchen. For months afterward, I was finding silicone foosies in places I didn't even know I had.

OK, I hear you—what are foosies? First, you've got to say it with the oo sound as in book. There is no correct spelling; it isn't a real word.

Remember the Polish mafia? One of those girls, whose name was Kathy, or Kasha in Polish, came up with it. She'd be heard to say, "Crap! I've got foosies in my coffee again!" She was talking about coffee grounds, which did turn up in the coffee at work entirely too regularly. I always thought it was a great word and I've used it ever since, for little bits of anything that don't belong where they are.

My neighbor Gladys adored Mike and she came over every day to check in, mostly with him. Her husband was a produce manager at a local grocery store. One day she ran giggling across the street to tell me a joke. Gladys was not one to ever use gutter language or talk about things like sex, and that made it even funnier. She giggled and blushed her way through the joke, then quickly scurried back across the street.

Let's see if I can tell you Gladys's joke without being too raunchy about it.

There's this produce manager, see? He's just gotten in a huge shipment of cabbage, and he wants to sell it quickly, so he stacks it all into a neat pyramid. Just about the time he's finished and is standing back to admire his work, a little old lady comes toddling around the corner, pushing her shopping cart. She walks right over to his pyramid of cabbage and pulls out a head from near the bottom. Naturally, the whole pile comes tumbling down.

"Madam," smiles the produce manager, "may I help you?"

"I'm looking for broccoli," she replies.

"I'm very sorry," he says, "but we're out of broccoli."

So she toddles off towards the cereal aisle, and he proceeds to rebuild his cabbage pyramid. Once again, when he's just about done, there she comes, and she again pulls a head from the bottom, causing it all to tumble down.

The produce manager grits his teeth and again says, "Madam, may I help you?" They repeat the whole previous conversation, with her again telling him she's looking for broccoli. There being none this time either, she again toddles off.

The third time, he's ready for her. He hides behind the bananas and, sure enough, he sees her coming. Just as she's about to grab a head of cabbage, he grabs her hand and asks one more time, "Madam, may I help you?"

"I'm looking for broccoli," she says.

"Madam," he asks, "Do you know how to spell the horse in horseradish?"

"Of course," she says. "H-O-R-S-E."

"And how do you spell the egg in eggplant?"

"E-G-G."

Then he asks her, "How do you spell the 'f—' in broccoli?"

She stands up straight, tosses her head, and says imperiously, "There is no 'f—' in broccoli."

To which he replies, "Lady, that's what I've been trying to tell you."

No one was dropping f-bombs in those days, although today they permeate many conversations, especially among young people. That made Gladys's dropping one even funnier. There were a lot more jokes going around back then, too, and I knew some great ones. I've always appreciated clever humor, and I love to tell stories, so the more convoluted a joke, the better I like it.

I am not particularly offended by f-bombs. An f-bomb has no power. Instead, I get offended when people use the name of my Lord Jesus Christ inappropriately, whether it's as a blatant cuss word or a simple "OMG!" There is power in the name of Jesus. The Bible teaches that we are to pray in His name. It astounds me that the same people who cringe at an f-bomb think nothing of using God's name in nasty ways.

The night I became a Christian, I was driving home, thinking about it all and wondering how my life would change. Instantly I knew that I would never again use Christ's name inappropriately, often adding a middle initial. Ever since then, I cringe when I hear it. That was my first clue that He'd actually come into my heart, that it was real, that *He* is real. Now, when I hear it used in a way that dishonors Him, I say in my heart, "Hallowed be Thy name, Lord."

I recently suggested to my granddaughter, who shouts "OMG!" regularly and enthusiastically, that she think about how that might make God feel. It's interesting how just a suggestion brings awareness. She now says gosh with some regularity.

AWARENESS

About ten years ago, my daughter-in-law was kind enough to bestow upon me the Fed-Ex jinx. She said that from that moment on, every time I'd be out in the car I'd see a Fed-Ex truck. Sure enough, and often I even see several of them.

More recently, a similar concept has come into my life. My granddaughter introduced me to a game where, every time you see a yellow car, you holler, "Bingo!" It has to be a regular passenger vehicle, not a business truck or a taxi or school bus.

Being the grandmother in the equation, and since I'm usually busy talking when we're in the car, I can get away with pointing frantically mid-sentence and saying, "Ab, ab, ab," until I remember what I'm supposed to say. I think I've got it down to a science now, though. I've been practicing.

It's amazing how many yellow cars I see when I'm out driving by myself, and every time I do, I dutifully shout, "Bingo!" Just the other day, between the bank and home, which is all of about ten blocks, I saw four of them.

One very good thing about yellow cars, especially the bright school bus-colored ones, is that you can't miss them. They stick out like a sore thumb. I have on more than one occasion nearly pulled out in front of a road-colored car because it blended in with the pavement and I didn't see it coming.

So now, having read this, you too will start noticing Fed-Ex trucks and yellow cars. You won't be able to help yourself. I've given you the jinx.

No, I've not really given you a jinx. Fed-Ex trucks and yellow cars are everywhere. What I've given you is awareness. Awareness is a funny thing—once you have it, it's hard to get rid of it. You can ignore the Fed-Ex trucks and the yellow cars, and you may not shout, "Bingo!" but you will notice them. An awareness of road-colored cars might be useful, though.

You're welcome.

I can cheerfully admit that I've done some time in therapy. It's not the people who are in therapy who are crazy; it's the people who aren't and should be. One of the best lessons I learned in therapy was that awareness is the key to the solution of any problem. Once we become aware of doing something, even if we choose to do nothing about it, we can no longer just go on blindly doing it. If we're smart, we eventually come to a place where we realize that we don't *have* to do something just because it's what we've always done.

That might even be a good moment to shout, "Bingo!"

So I've been writing my life story—you know this, you're reading it. Running through the whole thing is the thread of God's involvement, His closeness to me. In some cases, the awareness is hindsight, but as the story evolves, it becomes more and more real-time awareness.

He's been particularly faithful of late in this regard and has shown me His remarkable sense of humor (or is it irony?). He seems to delight in putting people in my life who annoy me. It should come as no shock that they display the very behaviors that are most annoying about me.

I also have to admit, albeit somewhat less cheerfully, that I have little patience with these people who are so like me. But I suppose it's a good thing. Gaining awareness through their behavior causes me to have to take a hard look and confront those very traits in myself. But only if I'm smart.

A good friend of mine, having read one of my chapters, commented that she found it remarkable that I am so aware of God's involvement in my life. I think she may have hit on something. I *want* that awareness. It all comes down to paying attention. I've been extremely fortunate on a number of occasions over the years that I was paying attention when God nudged me in some way. More than just a few times, lives were spared as a result—some very close to me, others strangers.

I know that there were also times when I wasn't paying attention, and I wonder what might have been different, better, had I been. I'll probably never know.

ROCKY HORSE COWBOY
Crissy Shreve
For Mike

Go to sleep now, my rocky horse cowboy,
Close those eyes and dream of the day,
When you will grow up and ride a real pony,
Sit in the saddle and sleep in the hay.

Little boys grow up and I will remember,
When years have gone by and you have gone too,
How much I loved you, my rocky horse cowboy,
Sleep now, my darling, your dreams will come true.

CHAPTER EIGHTEEN

MIKE

I'd found a rocking horse at a garage sale, and it grazed peacefully in the living room, waiting for Mike to grow big enough to climb on and ride. It inspired a lullaby. While he was still too little, I'd sit in the chair giving him his bottle, and I'd sing "Rocky Horse Cowboy." When he got old enough, he practically wore out the grass—um, carpet—galloping that pony across fields only he could see. Mike has always taken life at a gallop.

Life in the neighborhood went on. In those days the local butchers' union had a rule that meat could not be sold after 6PM weekdays, after noon on Saturdays, or at all on Sundays, even though the grocery store was open and everything else was available. I had no car during the day, and X1 didn't get home until after 6. He also worked Saturdays. There was never a time when I could get to the grocery store to buy meat. It was a dilemma.

Occasionally I'd bundle up Mike and drive X1 to work so that I could have the car. It was a two-hour hike round trip, though, and then I'd have to do it all over again when it came time to go back and pick him up. There were no car seats like we have now. I'd just hook the baby carrier into the seat belt, but the arrangement was flimsy at best. I was never comfortable driving any distance with the baby in the car. Mike wasn't fond of the idea either, so I'd be trying to drive with a screaming baby all the way. Mike in the grocery store was no picnic either.

We couldn't afford a second car. A few days after we moved into the house, we discovered that we'd have to cough up an additional chunk of money to pay for street improvements. The assessment was not made official until the day after we moved in. If we had closed on the house just a few days later, the sellers would have had to pay for it. We were young and naïve, and excited about the house. The sellers and the realtor knew about the street assessment, though, and they saw us coming. We had a second mortgage before we'd made even one payment on our first mortgage. There went any dream we may have had of air-conditioning or a second car, and certainly any thought of decorating

I struggled with being stuck at home, in a hot house I couldn't fix up, with a new baby who wouldn't sleep, and with no relief in sight. There was no one who would babysit during the day, not that I could have gone anywhere since I didn't have a car. My wings were severely clipped.

The only thing that would keep Mike happy was his swing. He lived in that swing for most of the first year of his life. I lived in five-minute increments between rewinds. X1 wasn't much help, even when he was home. He adored Mike and was good at playing with him, but he never got up with him during the night, and he'd never get anywhere near a dirty diaper. One Sunday I went out for a few hours and left the baby at home with his dad. I came home to find Mike in the swing, covered in poop from neck to toes, with a huge smile on his face. I was not amused. If I'd never come home that day, Mike would still be in that diaper.

At least there were several girls in the neighborhood who were good evening babysitters. There was a lot of competition for them, though, so if we wanted to go out at night, we had to book them early and pay them well.

One night we came home and couldn't find the babysitter. We heard a voice calling from the bathroom, "I'm in here." She had gotten stuck in the bathroom. After that, I guess we must have somehow gotten the door fixed.

I did manage to get out one night a week. I still bowled on a team with the girls I'd worked with. We started around 9 P.M., so I had time to put Mike to bed and get there after X1 got home from work.

Louise, my neighbor next door, had a baby girl named Amy, two months after Mike was born. Mike and Amy were inseparable by default for the first four years of their lives.

We all decided to have a neighborhood garage sale. It was my first and I was very excited. We did it at my house because I had a double garage facing the street. One of the neighbors had sold a basket, and another neighbor, Clara, remembered a basket she could sell, so she ran home to get it. She didn't price it, though, just stuck it on the table and left again for some reason. Of course the next customer who came along wanted the basket and asked the price. I said ten cents. It sounded reasonable to me. Clara came back and was dismayed—she'd wanted a quarter. I gave her the fifteen cents difference. Those were the days.

In July, two months after Mike was born, X1 and I took a trip to see my friend Mary and her husband Scott. It was about a three-hour drive. We packed Mike into a flimsy car bed in the back seat and took off. It was beastly hot, and the car had no air-conditioning. Poor Mike roasted in the car bed, but it was too hot to hold him, and we were all miserable.

Once I quit working, I pretty much stopped wearing shoes. Mary and Scott lived in a trailer and their driveway was gravel. When we got there, I went to put on some shoes so that I could walk on the driveway. Except that I hadn't brought any shoes. Mary and I headed out to the shoe store and I bought a pair of what we'd now call "strappy" shoes. The straps had cheap metal rivets wherever they intersected, and the rivets cut holes in the tops of my feet. The store had by then closed for the night, and it wasn't open the following day, a Sunday, and so I couldn't return them there. We were scheduled to leave Sunday anyway.

When we got back home, I returned the shoes to another branch of the same store. The manager was not happy, but he took them back. He told me that he didn't get credit for the sale, but he'd have to take the loss. I didn't allow that to be my problem. He suggested I not patronize his store in the future, to which I gladly agreed. That kind of thing wouldn't happen today. Meanwhile, the "great American shoe store" is no more.[27] I can't imagine why.

Louise and her husband taught X1 and me to play Bridge. Well, I guess I should say they *tried* to teach us to play. Bridge has rules for bidding. Neither X1 nor I were much for going by the rules. I was a natural reprobate, so I was the perfect partner for X1. He played a German card game called Skat. It's a bit like Bridge, a bit like pinochle, and infinitely more complicated and strategic than either.

---

[27]   The "Great American Shoe Store" closed its doors in 1998.

His incredible card sense and Skat strategy gave him the ability to manipulate the playing of the hand in a way that made us hard to beat.

We developed a seat-of-the-pants bidding style that worked better than Hoyle. The trick was for us to get the bid and for X1 to play the hand. I'd bid my best suit, and if X1 had coverage in the other suits, he'd go straight to three no trump, which was game. And he'd make it most of the time. When we started playing in the neighborhood Bridge club, we wound up in first place several years running. No one ever knew what we were doing, and neither did we—we just knew it worked.

We went to Louise's house a time or two in the evening to play. I'd call her house, she'd answer, and we'd leave the phones off the hook so that we could hear Mike if he cried. We invented our own baby monitor. I wish I'd thought to patent the concept. Their house was right next door and it was early fall, not yet cold out, so when I was the dummy, which was most of the time, I'd quick run outside and listen at Mike's open window to see if I could hear anything. Still, I didn't like the arrangement, and we soon stopped doing it.

A month or so later, our furnace motor caught fire in the middle of the night. There was a lot of smoke in the house, and X1 ran downstairs and pulled out the motor. I shudder to think what would have happened had we been next door when that motor decided to burn up. *Thank You, Lord.* This was before I was a believer. God was watching out for me, and especially for Mike, before I ever knew it.

I did, by the way, also learn to play Skat. I doubt that there are many American women who can play it, and I may have the dubious distinction of being the only American woman ever to have played it in Germany, in a tavern, with German men. All bidding and conversation is conducted in German. I have a Skat game on my computer that I still play regularly.

I bought a puppy at a garage sale for eight bucks. She was a sweet little thing, a shepherd/lab mix. We named her Sheppie. She lived in the kitchen and never wandered into other parts of the house. Sheppie was never aggressive. One time some friends were going to come over. They'd never been to our house before. We were going to be out somewhere ourselves, and were due home about the time they were to arrive, but since they had a new baby, we wanted them to be able to get in, even if we weren't back yet. We left a door unlocked and in they came. Sheppie never said a word. I didn't even think about the dog when we made the arrangement.

When Mike was a year and a half old, he and I went to Germany to visit X1's parents and meet other family who lived there. It was the first time I'd ever been to a foreign country, other than that fishing trip to Canada.

We flew overnight, and of course Mike never slept on the plane. The "knock-out drops" his pediatrician had prescribed for him just revved his engine, and he found running up and down the aisle much preferable to the constraints of the seat belt. Passengers behind and in front of us helped by stopping him from going too far, which he thought was a pretty neat game. By the time we arrived in Frankfurt the next morning, I was a basket case.

I have been to Germany many times since that first trip, but never as a tourist. I have always been a "non-German-speaking native," if that makes any sense. I've stayed with family or friends there, seeing and knowing the people themselves and their way of living. Although there were side trips, most of my time was spent in the homes and the small towns where these people lived. My observations are from that perspective, which is very different from that of a tourist.

On the way from the airport to X1's parents' house early on the morning we arrived, I got my first taste of how utterly different the culture can be in another country. Frankfurt is a big city with lots of tall apartment buildings, and I saw something hanging out of just about every window. It was the same with every house we passed as we left the city. German women hang their bed quilts out the window in the morning to air. It was no surprise, then, to find them hanging out the windows at X1's parents' house when we got there.

They don't use central heating systems in Germany. Each room has its own radiator, and a room is not heated unless it is in use. Because of that, one keeps all the doors closed, all the time. Of course I was always leaving doors open behind me, and of course X1's mother Mama was always right behind me closing them. The same thing was true in reverse—whenever I had a bunch of Germans visiting my house, I'd often find one of them waiting outside an empty bathroom because the person ahead of them had closed the door.

The upside of the radiator system is that there is always plenty of hot water. That is unless you live in an apartment, as did X1's aunt,

Tante Elli. In her bathroom and in the kitchen, there were small pay-per-use water heaters above the sinks and tub. For 25 *Pfennig* (about the size of a quarter) you could get enough hot water to wash the dishes. For two quarters, you could get just about enough for a bath.

They worship water in Germany. To be fair, water is expensive there, and the Germans are nothing if not *über* frugal. Even more expensive, someone told me, is sewer usage. For that reason, very few people even have showers. They take baths, using a hand-held shower minimally for rinsing their hair.

I was shocked the first time I watched someone in Germany wash dishes. They use a brush to scrub them in one small pan of soapy water, and then put the dishes in the rack without rinsing them. I thought it was just that one first person, but no, they all do it. They always dry the dishes. Apparently to their way of thinking, this takes off the soap, but I don't buy it. I quickly discovered that, when in Germany, I could get out of ever washing dishes—I'd just insist on running the water to rinse them.

I've always said that if there's a hard way to do something, the Germans will do it that way, whereas here in the U.S. it's the exact opposite. We look for the easiest way to do things. I know only one person in Germany who actually owns a dishwasher, and very few who own clothes dryers. Electricity is also very expensive there.

Ironically, Germans are serious gardeners. I say ironic because, if you have a garden, you need to water it. I have a theory. At least in north Germany, it rains all the time. When it's not raining, the air is misty with evaporation. It would seem that the rain dare not go elsewhere—like to France or Denmark. No, it needs to come down, water the gardens, then go straight back up, make some nice clouds and come right back down. It must be true, because that's exactly what happens. It's the ultimate in water conservation, with magnificent gardens as a fringe benefit.

You'd think, with all that rain, there'd be a lot of mosquitoes. Amazingly, there aren't, at least not in any of the areas in West Germany where I've been. There are, however, flies, and they are nasty. No one has window screens in Germany. They have those heavy white rolling shutters. There are little holes in the shutters to let in the air and the flies. You can't be in a room at night with a light on. The flies will find you. There are sheer floor-to-ceiling curtains, but the flies are smart enough to get around them. There were lots of mosquitoes in Dresden, in the former east zone, though, and there, at least in the hotel where I stayed, we had window screens.

Apparently the tap water in Germany is not pure. Germans only drink beverages that come out of bottles, except for tea or coffee, which require boiled water. You can't get a glass of plain tap water or an ice cube to save your life, neither in anyone's home nor in a restaurant. The weirdest thing is seeing a bottle of Coke with the name *Limonade*. *Limonade* refers to pretty much any carbonated drink. And it's *all* carbonated. Not being a fan of carbonated anything, I tend to be stuck with fruit juice in Germany. I was so pleased to discover a cold can of iced tea for sale at a rest stop on the *Autobahn*. I bought one and took a big gulp—you guessed it—carbonated. They also offer a carbonated iced coffee. I can only scratch my head.

I love German ingenuity—the toilet is the best example. There is nothing about a German toilet that makes any sense whatsoever. First of all, inside there's a platform with only a small water reservoir at the front. You do your thing and your thing sits there high and dry and reeking. I won't even begin to speculate why that would be desirable. And then, when you flush, you don't get much water. Instead, beside each toilet is a toilet brush, and you are expected to clean the toilet when you're done.

When you're out and about, it costs ten *Pfennig* to use a public toilet. In some places, there is a woman attendant in the washroom, and she expects a tip. I find that preferable, though, because she cleans the toilets after they are used. The coin-access toilets are usually pretty nasty.

After I'd been going to Germany for many years, and had been complaining those same many years about the toilets, a friend of mine finally came up with an explanation. If you can believe it, she said that when Germans come to the U.S., they hate our toilets because when they do their thing, the water splashes up and hits them in the butt. I'm not making this up and, astoundingly, neither was she. I dunno.

Just recently, I replaced a toilet in my house with a taller "comfort height" model. While I stood in the toilet aisle in the home improvement store trying to decide which brand to buy, I noticed a group of people who also appeared to be studying the toilets. Thinking they were store employees, I asked them which toilet I should get. It turned out that they were all representatives of a certain toilet manufacturer, one that is quite popular here, although German in origin. They of course highly recommended their brand, and so I bought it.

Well! Prior to having that toilet installed, I hadn't had any experience with "water saver" toilets. The one I bought wouldn't flush worth crap, if you'll pardon the pun. Suddenly I discovered that I was using the toilet brush almost as often as I was using the toilet.

After a while, I'd had it with that toilet. I called the manufacturer and they sent me a refund voucher that I took to the store to replace it. Here's where it gets stupid—well, here's where *I* got stupid. I foolishly felt some obligation to buy the same brand again. So I got a second one that was even worse than the first, if that's possible.

And here's the great irony: the stupid thing *splashed* when I'd flush it—all over me, all over the seat, and onto the floor, but there *still* wasn't enough water to get the job done. I'd have to flush at least twice, sometimes three times, and then again after using the brush. Yep, lots of water saved in that process. It's now been replaced with an "American" brand that, ironically, uses even less water and actually manages to get the job done on the first try. I donated the other two to Habitat for Humanity.

While in Germany that first time, I met X1's *Tante* (Aunt) Anni. She was huge; so big that when she visited the U.S., she had to buy two plane seats. Someone had told me that she was "funny," and I thought they meant weird. They actually meant funny. I didn't know enough of the language then to know one way or the other, but I was learning a few words here and there. One time she said to me, in German, "You smoke too much," to which I promptly replied, also in German, "You eat too much."

Tante Elli, who lived in the apartment with the pay-per-use water heaters, had a baby boy named Ralf, who was Mike's age. We'd go out walking together after naptime. Despite my virtually nonexistent German, we managed to have a lot of conversations. She was a sweetheart, and she taught me a lot. One day she asked me how long Mike had napped. I told her "*zwei Uhr*" meaning two hours. *Uhr*, in German, means and sounds a bit like hour, so I thought it would be the same word, just as it is in English. *Uhr* means the hour on the clock, not a period of time. Two hours is "*zwei Stunden*." We went round and round, with her trying to pantomime the difference for me, until I finally believed her.

X1's parents lived on top of a steep hill, and everything else was down the hill. Mama, X1's mother, would send me to the bakery for *"Ein kleines Michbrot und sechs kleine brötchen."* That means one small loaf of mixed-grain bread and six small rolls. I'd head down the hill practicing that phrase. It all made sense to me except for the *kleine and kleines.* It was that pesky *der, die, das* thing, something I still don't have a good handle on. After thirty-plus years of regularly going to Germany, there's a lot I still don't have a good handle on. I now, however, speak a reasonable what I call "survival" German, which I can even say in German: *Überlebens Deutsch.*

I had to laugh when I saw a rerun of "Dallas" on TV. There was old J.R. in his cowboy hat and bushy eyebrows speaking German. I didn't understand a word he said. I've also always found it a bit humbling to hear little kids three and four years old speaking German so much better than I do—and worse, they can't understand me when I try to talk to them.

I took a side trip to meet up with a friend in Munich. My German at that point was largely nonexistent, but I'd mastered one or two stock phrases like *Guten Tag,* which means "good day" or "hello." In smaller towns in central Germany, like where X1's parents live, you greet anyone you pass going down the sidewalk and everyone when you enter a shop. It reminds me of the movie where Crocodile walks down the street in New York City saying "G'day," to everyone he passes.

I got on the train in Darmstadt, and by the time I got to Munich, I'd had to replace half of my limited vocabulary. In the south, instead of *Guten Tag,* they say, *"Grüß Gott,"* which means "God greets." That's actually a nice concept, albeit difficult to translate sensibly. A cute young guy on the train asked me where the dining car was, but of course I didn't understand him correctly. I only picked up on the word meaning food and thought he wanted me to go eat lunch with him. I had to do some serious back-pedaling once he figured it out and explained it to me in English. We did wind up going for coffee later, though, and I picked up a few useful tips from him.

Another thing that was interesting in Munich was that they'd seat you with other people in a restaurant. My friend in Munich and

195

I went out to dinner. There were long trestle tables with benches, and we were placed wherever there was space. Later on, we went to a nightclub, and although there was no one else in the place, the next couple that came in was seated with us at our table for four.

I was taken to a billiard parlor in Munich where they played real billiards—not pool—no holes in the table. There were only three balls, and you had to hit two of them with the cue ball on each shot. Great game. At one point a young German fellow came up to me and asked me something, to which I replied, *"Ich weiß nicht,"* which means, "I don't know." The guy laughed at me—he thought I didn't know the answer to whatever he'd asked me, but I had no clue what he'd asked. He just thought I was stupid.

A main attraction in Munich is the *Englisher Garten.* Nude sunbathing is allowed in certain areas of the park, and on warm days, many people spend their lunch hours doing just that. Remarkable, at least to me, was that the nude sunbathers were not Mr. and Mrs. Atlas. They were ordinary people of all ages and sizes, most of whom I didn't think ought to be displaying their bodies publicly. Ick! Sex and nudity, however, are viewed very differently in Europe. It's just not a big deal to them.

While in Munich, I stayed in a hotel owned by another friend. Every morning I'd head down for breakfast, where the waitress, who was also a foreigner and whose German was nearly as limited as mine, would ask whether I'd like *ein drei-Minuten Ei*, a three-minute (soft-boiled) egg. Breakfast in Germany is always a good thing. A typical German *Hausfrau* will run to the bakery every morning for fresh *Brötchen* (rolls). They're great. To go with them is an assortment of cold cuts and cheeses and various kinds of *Liverwurst.* And the coffee is the best!

My first day in Munich, I was on my own and I ventured alone into the main part of the city. This required a ride on the *Straßenbahn,* or trolley. It ran conveniently down the center of the street on which the hotel was located. How hard could it be? After a short tutorial on the workings of the transit system, I was ready to go. A few details had been overlooked, though. I crossed the street and waited at the stop, and within a few minutes, along came a trolley. It had two cars. I hopped onto the first car and saw nothing but passengers. The

196

conductor, who took your money, was in the second car. OK, fine. So I hopped back off and the stupid thing took off without me.

I waited again, and when the next trolley appeared, I got on the second car. Sure enough, there was the conductor. I gave him my money and got my ticket. I started back to find a seat, only to hear a loud, '*Hallo!*' I'd forgotten to get my change.

The ride itself was uneventful, except that I noticed that the addresses on the two sides of the street were very strange. Here our numbers are within the same range on any given block. There, although even numbers were on one side and odd numbers on the other, they were not in range. The effect was that you'd have number 621 on one side of the street and number 12 on the other. If there was a stretch where there was no building, they just used the next number, no matter how far apart.

Once in the city, I cruised around the various stores and tried to figure out what size I wore. That accomplished, I bought a beautiful suede mini-skirt. I did pay attention to where I was in conjunction with the trolley stop, though. When it was time to head back to the hotel, I found it without difficulty. Now a seasoned traveler, I was ready, and I cleverly hopped on the second car. Oops. No conductor—no one to take my money. The cars heading out of town were reversed. Of course they were. And of course I got back off and the stupid thing took off without me again.

Undaunted, I once again waited and got on the first car of the next trolley. I carefully paid exactly the right amount so that I'd not forget my change, and I proceeded towards the seats. And once again came that loud "*Hallo!*" I'd forgotten my ticket.

Luckily I'd at least noted the weird street number system on the way in, and so I managed to get off at the right stop. The hotel was on the left, and if I'd been looking only at the numbers on the right side of the street, I'd still be on it waiting to get to number 621.

Back at the hotel, I was told that most people riding the trolleys have passes, and that the conductorless car was where they rode. Usually no one checks for passes, so many young people *schwartz*, which is the German word for black, and means riding without paying. *Now* you tell me.

Although Mike was only a year and a half old when we went to Germany, X1's mother Mama thought he needed potty training. She had a thing that looked like a large orange dog food bowl, and every morning after breakfast, she'd make him sit on it. She had kids' books written in German for him to look at, and it didn't matter at all that he held them upside-down. I brought that potty back home with me and put it away until it was really time to train him. When Mike was finally ready, his dad just took him into the bathroom and showed him how to "make bubbles." We gave the bowl to the dog.

Mama would routinely sweep the sidewalks in front of her house every Saturday afternoon in preparation for Sunday. People would go out walking or visiting on Sundays, and those sidewalks had better be spotless. There is a lot of living to impress the neighbors in Germany. X2, also born and raised in Germany, told a story about how one night he'd been out very late drinking and wanted to sleep late the next morning. His mother came into the room at 7 A.M. and pulled up all the shades. She didn't want the neighbors to think anyone was still sleeping.

I had taken a picture of X1 along to show his mother. Mama's comment was that if he showed up there with hair that long, she wouldn't let him in the house. She cried when we arrived and cried when we left, but she called Mike a "bad little boy" the whole time we were there. I have never understood the way these people think. I am so glad I live in the United States, although the first question most people I met in Germany would ask was, "Isn't it better here?"

The flight home was completely different than the flight over. Mike had come down with intestinal flu the day before we were to leave. He was sick on the plane the whole way home, alternately throwing up and having diarrhea. He willingly stayed on my lap the whole flight, which was actually easier for me than trying to keep him from running up and down the aisle. The poor woman sitting next to us on the plane was very gracious about it. He nailed her a time or two.

I was using cloth diapers in those days, although I would have used disposables, had they been available in Germany. By the time we landed, I had a bag full of extremely nasty diapers.

Meanwhile, all the relatives in Germany had shown up the night before we left with "just a few little things," presents I was supposed to take to X1's aunt and her family in the U.S. I was not amused. I had too much baggage of my own, plus a sick baby. I sure didn't need the excess, but they insisted. I wound up with an extra suitcase full of their stuff. When we landed, my main suitcase was one of the first to turn up in baggage claim, but the one with the presents took an extra fifteen minutes, just enough time for the lines for customs to have gone from being empty to very long.

When I finally got my turn at the customs checkpoint, I was no longer a nice person. I handed the clerk the bag of nasty diapers. She reached right in and was aptly rewarded. If I hadn't been so livid at the whole scenario, I would have laughed. She waved me through without risking a look through the rest of my bags.

That wasn't the end of it, either. There was a major construction project going on at the airport, and when I finally came out, I was expecting X1 to be there waiting to take something, *anything*, out of my hands. Instead, I had to climb on a bus with my sick baby, my several suitcases, and my very weary body, and ride to another location where X1 was waiting.

After I'd been back home for a week or two, X1 and I went out to eat at a local restaurant. Not long into the meal, I started feeling nauseated. I went to the bathroom, which was small, and the air was oppressive. I didn't actually get sick, but that was only because I refuse to get sick unless it's absolutely necessary. I got my coat and waited for them in the car. After that, the same thing would happen whenever I'd go into a restaurant. In some places, I'd only need to walk in the door and my throat would start to close up. I thought I was just nuts, but ten years later I found out that restaurants had finally stopped using Sulfites as preservatives, due to complaints from people with allergies. That's when I learned what had been happening to me, and I was once again able to eat in restaurants.

That summer we left Mike next door with Louise and went to the boondocks of Minnesota for a week with Sue and Tim. We hauled Tim's dad's boat up there for him. Tim and X1 took turns driving. At one point, X1 was driving merrily along, telling himself jokes he'd never heard before, and then laughing at them. Sue, Tim, and I were all dozing, and largely ignoring him. X1 started into a joke about Laurel and Hardy pedaling up a hill on a tandem bicycle. When they finally get to the top, Ollie says to Stan, "Good thing I pumped so hard, or we'd never have made it," to which Stanley replies, "Yes, and it's a good thing I kept my foot on the brake, or else we'd have rolled back down." We all woke up laughing.

That was a great trip. We did a lot of good fishing. I even broke the record for catching the largest Crappie to date in Itasca County, Minnesota. That was, of course, purely by accident. I had no clue what I was fishing for—I was just happy when something turned up on the end of my line.

Sue and I did a lot of pan fishing, basically sitting in a boat and dangling bait. One of the boats we used was aluminum with solid seats that had holes at the bottom to let water run through. Just as we were about to get into that boat, we noticed that there was a snake in the bottom, peering out from one of the holes. The guys dutifully removed the snake for us.

I was at the tiller. About halfway across the lake, Sue said to me, "Don't look down, but there's a snake between your feet." I didn't look down. I calmly said, "Hang on," gunned the engine, turned the handle, executed a very dandy U-turn, and zoomed back to shore. I drove that boat straight up onto the beach, and Sue and I kept moving right on out of it. I think they call that inertia.

There were actually several snakes still in the boat. The snake that had been removed was the mother. They were probably harmless snakes, but water moccasins are known to be in that area, so we weren't taking any chances on whether or not those babies had teeth.

Then one evening, Sue and I again decided to do some pan fishing. We went out just a little way onto the lake and dropped bait. Fortunately, we were using leaders, because the fish started hitting, hard and fast. Sue's comment when she caught the first one was, "It's a freaking catfish," never mind that she didn't say freaking. Actually, they were bullheads, big black things, and we caught a bucketful, never touching them, each time disconnecting the leader and attaching a new one.

I had gotten good at cleaning fish by that point, but I wasn't about to touch a bullhead. Bullheads have stingers. You don't scale bullheads; they don't have scales, they just have skin. You take a board, you drive a nail into it through the fish's head, you cut the skin around the neck, and you pry the skin off with pliers. Then you cut off the head and gut the fish. I don't remember them being tasty enough to warrant all that work.

The very best fishing, though, was at a tiny lake called Mosmo. We drove there shortly before dark with several rowboats, and then we carried the boats about half a mile to the lake. We had three people to a boat; one person rowed very quietly, just enough to keep us moving around. The other two fished. We used plugs—big minnow-shaped plastic things with hooks all over them—nasty things, actually. The trick was to not hook yourself or your clothing or whatever else was within reach. We cast towards the lily pads. If we didn't have a large-mouth bass on the hook by the time the plug hit the water, we reeled back in and cast again. We hauled dinner for a month out of that lake in just an hour.

Around that time, Judy and Al inherited a baby grand piano from someone, and they gave me their old upright piano. I put it in my living room and started to teach myself to play. I wasn't at all good at it, but I loved it.

Then we decided to get new carpet in the living room. Since we'd have to move the piano somewhere to get it out of the way, I had the bright idea to move it to the basement and leave it down there. We gathered Al, X1's Uncle Fritz, and Steve from next door. They started moving the piano down the stairs. It went about halfway down and then got stuck on the stairway ceiling. It was not going any farther. Meanwhile, Uncle Fritz was down the stairs alone, beneath the piano. There being no other way out of the basement for him since he was too big to fit through the windows, and the guys above had nothing to grab onto to pull, poor Uncle Fritz pushed that piano back up the stairs by himself. Al, grandmaster of tongue-in-cheek humor, quipped, "It's always easier to measure a stairway with a piano than with a yardstick."

I should have put the piano back in the living room, but no, I wanted it in the basement. X1 took it apart and carried it down in pieces. He couldn't get it back together in such a way as to be playable, though, so it just sat in the basement gathering dust. We left it there when we sold the house, and it's probably still there.

FROM THE ANALS
MIKE STORIES

I suppose most families have annals of some sort, be they immortalized in writing or by word-of-mouth. Step-Mike came up with the word Anals for ours and it just . . . fits. Recently I was telling a very smart friend about the Anals. She's always using words I don't know. She said, without a blink, "Oh, isn't that the British pronunciation?" (Actually, it's not, but so what?)

Not everyone who gets mentioned in the Anals is necessarily part of our clan, but their antics or statements have had an effect on some or all of us to the degree that they are worthy of inclusion.

I'll start with some stories on Mike:

Mike likes to say that there are three kinds of drivers in the world: Those who can't drive, those who shouldn't drive, and him.

He also says that whenever anyone asks him why he works with toddlers, he tells them it's because he can pass gas at will and no one ever blames him. They just do a diaper check.

One time when I was out to dinner with Mike, the waiter took his order first, then turned to me and said, "And for the lady?" Mike said, "That's no lady, that's my mother." To be fair, I think it's a line from some movie.

I didn't kill him. It took me a year or so, but I got even instead. We were sitting in the food court at church, surrounded by many others at tables, and I inadvertently passed gas. I immediately turned to look at Mike—as did everyone around us.

When Mike was maybe 10, they installed a big double-track wooden roller coaster at our local amusement park. Of course, advertising was rampant and so was Mike's mouth. He just couldn't wait to get on it and he wouldn't shut up. We heard about little else for weeks beforehand and all the way there in the car. We waited in line for the requisite hour and a half, with Mike babbling excitedly the entire time, and finally, just as we were about to get on, he chickened out.

Now that might have been okay, except that he was my partner and I didn't want to have to deal with finding someone else. So, good mother that I am, I made him get on. All the way up the first hill, and you know how slowly those wooden roller coasters go up, he was in sheer terror. What he didn't know, and what I had forgotten, is that a wooden roller coaster is actually quite slow going down as well. Halfway down the first hill, Mike was shouting, "This is great! I love it!" I'm sure he continues to appreciate my having made him get on.

When X1 and Mike joined Indian Guides, they had to have Indian names and the son got to pick the names. Mike decided that he would be "Shining Son" and that X1 would be "Blowing Wind." I should not have to explain that further.

After seeing a corvette drive through a red light in front of traffic, Mike said, "That's right sir, blow off that red light. It was only a suggestion."

When Mike was in 7th grade, he told me that some of the boys at school were using a word and he didn't know what it meant. The word was orgy, except that they were pronouncing it with a hard g as in good.

I'd regularly take Mike to the shopping mall with me when he was two and three years old. He loved to run around the store like a wild man, hiding and darting between clothing items on the racks. One day inspiration struck. I had him stand at the check-out counter, asking him to hold onto it so that it would be there when it was time to pay for my purchases. Amazing. It worked like a charm. He was so proud of himself.

THE CAROUSEL
Crissy Shreve

God was for me, I guess,
A bit like the golden ring
On the carousel . . .
I was going 'round and 'round.
I didn't even notice Him.

Then something sparkled
In the corner of my sight
And I saw Him standing there.

Yet I feared falling
From the safety of my pony,
Not believing myself good enough
To reach Him,
Thought that by holding on
I could continue in my dizzy weakness
To survive.

Then someone else
Grabbed the Golden Ring and,
Calling back to me
Saw my circles going nowhere,
Saw my pain,
And cried, "Try Him!"
And in that precious moment I believed.

As I approached the Golden Ring
I closed my eyes
And reached for Him.
Now I watch the sad, the lonely,
Clinging to their ponies,
Passing Him by,
Frantically holding on to their weaknesses,
And I too call back.

But not all hear.

CHAPTER NINETEEN

TESTIMONY

I wish I had made note of the date I became a Christian. It was in the summer, probably of 1973. I'm not terribly good at dates for some reason. I can tell you who I was with and what I was doing when a song was popular, but I seldom know what year it was. I have seven grandkids. Whenever I see them, the first thing I do is ask them, "What's your name, how old are you, and what grade are you in?" They laugh and tell me. The problem is that between times I see them, they get older and move up a grade. I usually remember their names, though.

My first Sunday school memory is from when I was real little—two or three years old. We had been standing up singing, "Jesus Loves Me," and when we finished, the teacher said to me, "Don't sit down." I didn't listen. I landed on the floor. The little saint next to me had pulled my chair away.

When I was six and my cousin John was twelve, we were baptized together at the mainline denominational church (MLD) my grandparents and I attended. There was no intention in it for either John or me; it was just what the family wanted us to do. No one explained what it meant, at least not to me.

Throughout my elementary school years, I continued to attend Sunday school and church regularly. I went by myself. My grandfather had died and my grandmother didn't drive. My mother wouldn't go.

In seventh grade, I started confirmation classes, but I quit after a short time, for several reasons. I'd had the problems with Bevy, and she was in that class. I was also starting to get into trouble, like ditching school, so going to classes at church seemed silly to me. The excuse I used, though, and it was a fairly valid excuse, was that we were being taught the difference between the different branches of that church. I didn't know what I needed, but I knew I didn't need to know that.

What I needed, desperately, was to know that God loved me and had died for me. I needed to know that I was okay, and that someone, even the Creator of the universe, could love me. Apparently the pastor didn't know either. Surely had he understood it for himself, he'd have told us.

I stopped going to church altogether.

When X1 and I got married, I wanted to have the ceremony in the same kind of MLD church, simply because that was the church with which I was familiar. We took classes—dry church history that we sat through for an hour once a week for six weeks. There was nothing about how to navigate marriage, and once again, there was no mention of Jesus having died for us. It was all about becoming members of the church, which we did. But we did not become Christians.

Once we were married, I tried to go to church with some regularity. X1 didn't bother. I didn't know what God wanted from me. I remember being in the car early one Sunday morning, on my way to church, alone, and actually having that thought. I don't think there was ever a time that I didn't believe God existed. I just had no clue what He had to do with me.

I know several lifelong MLD church attenders who managed to "get it," at least on some level—through osmosis, I guess. Maybe I just wasn't paying attention or maybe I needed to read between the lines. I can state unequivocally, though, that the main truth of the Gospel— that Jesus had died for me personally—was never directly stated to me at any church, my own or any other I visited when I was young.

The church where X1 and I were married was the church my friend Mary and her family attended. One Sunday the pastor announced that Sunday school teachers were needed. Mary and I decided to do that. She, however, was in nursing school in the city and didn't often make it home on the weekends, so it was mostly my job. I taught Kindergarten-age kids. It wasn't difficult; the material was simple. If there was preparation involved, I didn't do it, just flew by the seat of my pants at class time. I do remember getting a bunch of presents from the kids at Christmas. That was cool, especially since I hadn't expected it.

It was ironic, though, perhaps even tragic. There I was, not knowing God at all, yet trying to teach little kids about Him. I was a fraud.

Early one morning when Mike was only a few days old, he was miraculously sleeping. I gratefully fell into my own bed, exhausted. It was about 7:30, and X1 had already left for work. I had just drifted off to sleep when the doorbell rang. Standing there was a pastor from a local MLD church telling me that he was in the neighborhood and just couldn't resist stopping by to welcome me to the area and invite me to his church.

I was not amused. I was not awake. I was not nice.

He quickly found out just how not amused, not awake, and not nice I was. He should have known better than to show up at that hour, even to visit someone who didn't have a new baby. I told him that with such an insensitive idiot for a pastor, I'd most assuredly never set foot in his church, and I slammed the door in his face.

It occurs to me to wonder, these forty-some years later, whether that man really was who he claimed to be. It could have just been a ruse to get into my house. Either way, I'm sure glad I was not nice.

We had baby Mike christened at our MLD church, and my friend Mary and her husband were sponsors. It was just what you did. It had no meaning to me then, either.

When Mike was a few years old, probably the summer of 1973, our neighbor Kathy told Louise and me that she was going to go to a meeting on "tongues." I had no idea what that was, but she described it as the ability to speak in languages you've not learned. You can imagine how my ears perked up. I went to that meeting, hoping I'd wake up the next morning able to speak fluent German. Honest!

The meeting was held at someone's house, and there I met a man named Ed Smith[28], along with a woman whose name I don't remember. They told me about Jesus—that He'd died for *me* personally and that He loved me and wanted me to know Him. Wow!

---

[28] I haven't been able to find Ed Smith again. I'm using his full name in the hope that this book might find its way to him and that he would know. Riches in heaven, Ed.

Since I'd grown up in church, I knew all the "stuff." I'd memorized the books of the Bible, heard all the stories. I could recite the 23rd Psalm. All those years, it had been like hearing a joke where someone forgets the punch line. I'd been taught in a general sense, everything except the pivotal piece—that Jesus had pictured my face as He hung on the cross, and that my sin could be erased. I didn't have to "measure up" after all. Christ had done it for me.

Everything they told me fit with what I'd learned. It was the same God, not some cult or religion. It was the rest of the story. They gave me the punch line.

God opened my ears and my heart to hear. Ed and the woman laid hands on me, and I asked Jesus to be my Savior. To be perfectly honest, I figured that if it wasn't true, I had nothing to lose. But if it was true, it was *everything.* Either something would happen or nothing would happen.

Now, of course I didn't become fluent in German overnight. I didn't get the biblical gift of tongues, either. I've never even especially sought it, and I don't think it was God's intention for me. His intention was to find me there and to adopt me into His family, and to love me and bless me far beyond anything I could ever have hoped for or imagined.

Not long afterwards, I got a letter from my cousin John, the one with whom I'd been baptized when we were kids. He, too, had become a Christian. Years after that baptism, both of us came to know Jesus as our Lord right around the same time, even though we were miles apart. We had been sanctified in that baptism—set apart. God knew what He was doing, even though we didn't, our families didn't, and the church apparently didn't, either.

I joined a Navigators Bible study. I stopped going to the MLD church; there was no longer anything there for me. Then, through one of the woman in that group, I found out about the church I've attended ever since.

One day I got a phone call from the pastor of my old MLD church. He wondered why I hadn't taken communion in some time. I told him I was now attending a different church. He recognized the name and he said, "Oh, well, we're not in the entertainment business." I said neither was my church and that, oh, by the way, I had become a born-again Christian. I told him that Jesus was now my Savior, and that I needed to be in a church where I could learn and grow and be with like-minded believers.

He actually stated that he sort of knew what I was talking about, but that he couldn't teach like that at the MLD church because he'd get fired. I am not making this up. I *wish* I were making it up!

One night we had a worship concert at my current church, led by Darlene Zschech, a worship leader from Australia. It was wonderful, and I felt God's presence surrounding me, as I never had before. I didn't want to go home. I just wanted to stay there forever and sing His praises. That's when I knew. This little reprobate kid, who's never felt like she fit in anywhere and wasn't sure she'd fit in in heaven, will not only fit in, because of Who He is, but will have forever, *forever*, to sit at His feet and pour out her love.

I hadn't been so sure I'd even like heaven. I've never been particularly impressed with "good" people. I wasn't sure I wanted to be one, even if it was Jesus who made me that way, even if it probably wasn't going to happen until I got to heaven. But that night, that concert . . . it was a slice of heaven for me to taste. Oh, how I'm gonna love heaven!

When I was married to X2, we attended a wedding in Germany, in the German version of the MLD church. The building was 400 years old and quite magnificent. The church ceremony was held in the afternoon, after the morning civil wedding. I don't really know why they bothered with the church. God's name was only mentioned once, and that was in a hymn.

If the church is not about God, what good is it? The unfortunate thing is that the church can too easily be the evil one's greatest weapon. If it's not going to teach the truth, if it's not going to proclaim the Gospel, what is it going to do? It can only lead people away from God. This is the very work of the evil one. Of course there are plenty of churches that know this and teach the Bible. I'm talking about churches that hide God's truth under layers of religion.

Religion is all about what one supposedly has to do to gain eternal life. Christianity is all about what Jesus has done to make eternal life available to anyone who depends solely on Him. I can always tell when someone doesn't understand this because they call me "religious."

Religion, with its rules and rituals, is not the route to eternity with God. Even good behavior is not the route to eternity with God. Jesus is the only route to eternity with God.

This is the truth of the Bible.

Sometimes, people put faces on God that don't belong to Him. It might be the face of an abusive father, and that makes it hard for them to perceive God as a loving father. It might be a member of the clergy or it might be the Bible-thumping neighbor next door who mistreated or abused. We all know that many atrocities have been done supposedly in the name of God—the Crusades or the Holocaust, for example. God did not do these things. People did. Hurt, broken, stupid, misguided, even evil, people did these things.

Albert Camus said, "I would rather live my life as if there is a God and die to find out there isn't, than to live as if there isn't, and die to find out there is." This is wisdom, and this, although I hadn't seen this quote at the time, is precisely what initially led me to try Jesus. I use the word try intentionally. How many times have we all tried something, only to be disappointed—all those products or self-help concepts that make big promises they can't keep? Imagine my delight to discover that God is very real and that He keeps his promises. Life still disappoints me on a regular basis. God has never disappointed me.

You couldn't convince me that God isn't real or that He isn't all He says He is in the Bible. I've seen too much.

This is not to say that I moved into Wonderland and life became "happily ever after." I am not Alice, and God isn't Santa Claus, to mix metaphors. I don't always get what I ask for. Often it's a good thing I don't get what I ask for. I've learned that what I really want, what I always want, or at least want to want, is what God wants. His will is perfect, and that is what I pray for, in all instances. God doesn't make mistakes. He knows exactly what He's doing and He's trustworthy. I'm the one who makes mistakes.

God wants nothing more than to be invited into our hearts, our lives, and our world. He wants us to want what He wants and He wants to give it to us. Next time you're thinking about how messed up our world is, or how messed up *we* are, maybe take a moment to think about how God feels, and how much better it could be if we'd try doing things His way.

Perhaps the most well-known Bible verse is John 3:16. "For God so loved the world that he gave his one and only Son, that whoever believes in him shall not perish but have eternal life." Verse 17 goes on to say, "For God did not send his Son into the world to condemn the world, but to save the world through Him." It's this second part that's the really crucial information.

So many people think that God sits up on some cloud wielding a celestial sledgehammer and that He can't wait to bash them over the head with it. It's a lie. Many people have turned from God because they don't think they can live up to His standards. That's the truth; they can't. Neither can I. It doesn't matter. He loves us.

If anyone ever deserved to be hit over the head with a sledgehammer, certainly I do. It's a funny thing, though; He never did that. Oh, I've taken some lumps, usually the consequence of my own foolishness. I've landed on my butt from just living in this world, too, as we all have. Every time, He has gone through it with me, reminding me of His love, and picking me back up so that I could get on with it.

I haven't been easy to put up with. Imagine God trying to put up with me. Imagine my coming to understand that *God loves me*! Even before I met Him, acknowledged Him as Lord, He loved me. He loved me when I was "good" and when I was "bad."

It's so simple. I am a sinner. He died for me—not because I deserved it, but because I *needed* it. He never condemned me. Instead He saved me. One of the most beautiful verses in the Bible says, "But God demonstrates His own love toward us, in that while we were yet sinners, Christ died for us."[29]

Imagine God trying to put up with you. It's the most amazing thing. He loves you every bit as much as He loves me. Isn't that something?

There is nothing either you or I can ever do to make Him love us; there is nothing either you or I can ever do to make Him stop loving us.

So, what are you going to do about it? When I die, I'm going to be with Him. Are you coming too? Heaven won't be quite as good without you.

---

[29] Romans 5:7-10 NASB

UNITY IN THE CHURCH

I think the unity we're finally beginning to see between Christian denominations may be about Jesus showing us that He will soon return. I hope he waits a while—think about how embarrassed we'll be when He finds us separated into sects and denominations fighting against each other instead of loving each other as brothers and sisters in Christ. I'm not talking about religions as a whole—not every religion is Christ-centered—but within the Christian community there is still an awful lot of division that simply should not be there!

It's nothing new. Paul confronted the Christians in Corinth on this issue.[30] Jesus Himself prayed for unity among believers, wanting us to enjoy and to be an example of the oneness He enjoys with God His Father.[31] We're supposed to love one another, for heaven's sake! Literally.[32]

Doctrinal differences are not the same as different worship styles. If the doctrine is biblically sound, we don't need to be squabbling over worship styles. God gave us variety in worship styles and He probably

---

[30] 1 Corinthians 1:10 I appeal to you, brothers, in the name of our Lord Jesus Christ, that all of you agree with one another so that there may be no divisions among you and that you may be perfectly united in mind and thought. NIV

[31] John 17:21–23 And the glory which Thou hast given Me I have given to them; that they may be one, just as We are one; I in them, and Thou in Me, that they may be perfected in unity, that the world may know that Thou didst send Me, and didst love them, even as Thou didst love Me. NASB

[32] Colossians 3:12–15 And so, as those who have been chosen of God, holy and beloved, put on a heart of compassion, kindness, humility, gentleness and patience; bearing with one another, and forgiving each other, whoever has a complaint against anyone; just as the Lord forgave you, so also should you. And beyond all these things put on love, which is the perfect bond of unity. NASB

enjoys the differences. I think even God gets bored with the same old thing. He gave us all kinds of gifts and He meant for us to use them.[33]

In 2001, the Lutheran and Episcopalian churches voted to recognize each other as Christian organizations. That is, I suppose, a good thing, but isn't it astounding that, prior to that, they apparently didn't recognize each other?

This, I believe, is one reason mainline denominational churches have too often failed to bring the message of salvation in Christ alone to their members. With their focus on secondary doctrines, and disagreements over worship styles, they can too easily lead people away from Christ—and Christians away from each other.

I've talked about my own early church experience. They thought I needed to know the difference between the synods of the Lutheran church—more division, even within the denomination itself. What I needed to hear, and didn't, was that Jesus died *for me*.

I ran into an article in *Guideposts*, written by a man who nearly lost his faith.[34] He wrote, "As a young boy my faith in God seemed so natural. It was a simple comfort, unquestioning and personal. But once I went to school and was forced to sit through daily chapel services with prayers in Latin and people droning on, I thought that I had got the whole faith deal wrong. Maybe God wasn't intimate and personal but was tedious, judgmental, boring and irrelevant. The natural, instinctive faith I had known was tossed out with this newly-found delusion that because I was growing up, it was time to 'believe' like a grownup." When his godfather died, he needed that remembered comfort and prayed, "God, if you're like you were when I used to know you, will you be that again? Comfort me."

Jesus is quoted in three of the four Gospels, "Truly I say to you, whoever does not receive the kingdom of God like a child shall not enter it at all."[35] God is not the least bit tedious, judgmental, boring or irrelevant. It is people who seem to need to make Him that way. The

---

[33] Ephesians 4:11–13 And He gave some as apostles, and some as prophets, and some as evangelists, and some as pastors and teachers, 12 for the equipping of the saints for the work of service, to the building up of the body of Christ; 13 until we all attain to the unity of the faith, and of the knowledge of the Son of God, to a mature man, to the measure of the stature which belongs to the fullness of Christ. NASB

[34] "Survival Secrets," Bear Grylls, Guideposts, June 2012.

[35] Mark 10:15 NASB, Matthew 18:3, Luke 18:17

tragedy is that, in turning from the fake religion-god taught in too many churches, people turn from the real God of the Bible.

I received an email forward from a female Episcopalian priest. The email contained statements that just weren't biblical, such as "all roads lead to God." I asked her why, especially since she was a priest, she would send out something so unbiblical as this. Her response was that in her church they didn't focus as much on Jesus as much as we do at mine. Really?

If Christian churches are not about Christ, what are they about?

For some weeks I regularly attended a little country Baptist church in Georgia. I was well loved there, received and treated warmly, even as a Yankee, although I was quick to assure them that I was not a "damn Yankee." I had every intention of going back home.

Still, several comments that were made to me caught my attention and have stuck in my mind. Near the end of my stay, I attended a Thanksgiving feast at this Baptist church. Let me tell you, these people know how to eat! I've never seen so much food in one place in my life. In fact, I kidded the pastor that he cooked almost as well as he preached.

Before leaving, I spent a few moments with the ladies from the Sunday School class I had visited. As we exchanged good-byes, one of them mentioned that it was unusual to meet a Yankee who was friendly. It occurred to me just how often we tend to put labels on people and how we then proceed to judge them by our experience of other people upon whom we've hung the same label. This woman never got past her preconceived notion of me. Friendly or otherwise, to her I was still a Yankee. And in hanging that particular label on me, she limited her ability to see me or know who I really was—her sister in Christ.

The week before, in that Sunday School class, the subject of Bill Clinton came up. It was shortly after he had been reelected, and it was clear that these women had some concern about his presidency. I mentioned that a pastor I know had been regularly counseling with Bill Clinton, at Bill Clinton's request, and that it seemed to me that God had his hand on Bill Clinton, and in the process, on our country.

The same lady who was surprised to meet a friendly Yankee asked me, "Is he a Baptist?" I said, "I don't know, but I think he might be a Christian." "Oh," she said, "I guess that's what counts."

The preacher did a great job the few times I heard him speak. In one of his sermons, however, he was discussing the Southern Baptist way of thinking and suggested that if one did not agree with it, one ought to find another church, one which would be perhaps more in sync with a person's own beliefs. The Gospel as presented in his sermons and in his church as a whole was right on, and I had no argument whatsoever with the doctrinal teachings. If anything, I'd think he'd want to encourage people to stay and hear what the Bible says. A person's following his own beliefs is exactly what gets him in trouble.

There is also a large population of black people in that part of Georgia. During my stay, I heard a number of disparaging jokes and malicious comments aimed at black people, often from the mouths of Sunday Christians. I'd always been as quick as the next guy to tell an ethnic or racial joke, but after that, whenever I tried to tell one, I felt very uncomfortable. I was strongly convicted of my own tendency to sin in this regard.

Later, as I was confessing this, I was reminded that all God's people matter to Him and that I break His heart when I diminish any of them with my jokes. Not to mention that I might meet them one day in heaven. Frankly, I hate the thought of all the people I'm going to have to apologize to there.

X2 had an amazing healing experience with a doctor who was a charismatic[36] Christian. After returning home from a trip to Florida where he'd drunk a can of soda purchased from a street vendor, he started having stomach problems. We went to see this doctor the day before X2 was to leave on an extended ministry trip. He was feeling so sick that he was seriously considering cancelling the trip.

There's no question that God was in it. The doctor told X2 that there was nothing wrong with him, and that it was an attack of the evil one, meant to keep him from ministry. The doctor and I laid hands on X2, and the pain not only subsided, but it never returned.

God does not need my hands or anyone else's hands to heal, but He will do His will when we ask Him to, which was clearly the case in this instance.

---

[36] Charismatic Christianity (also known as Spirit-filled Christianity) is an umbrella term that describes a form of Christianity that emphasizes the work of the Holy Spirit, spiritual gifts and modern day miracles.

Afterwards, this doctor tried very hard to tell us that if our church, or more specifically our pastor, were "Spirit filled," just imagine what God could do. It was ironic because God is so clearly using our church to make a huge impact locally and all over the world.

The Bible speaks of the gift of tongues in First Corinthians. There is a difference in the interpretation of this gift between evangelical and charismatic Christians. The charismatic perspective is that speaking in tongues is the sign of being "Spirit-filled." And it is a sign, but it's not the only sign. You can be *sure* that not speaking in tongues raises no question of salvation. Jesus said, ". . . no one comes to the Father but through Me." He didn't add "and tongues." When one accepts Jesus Christ as his or her own personal Savior, he or she is indwelled by the Holy Spirit.

I know people whose claim to being able to speak in tongues I've found questionable because of their personal credibility. I know others whose credibility has led me to believe that God does give certain individuals the gift of praising Him in a special language. It's because God *wants* them to. But not all of us; He wants some of us to "stay sober" and do the work of His kingdom.[37]

It hurts God's heart to see such disunity among believers. My church holds an annual leadership conference that is attended by thousands of pastors from many different denominations. Joining with them in praise, in unity, is for me a highlight of the conference. Another little slice of heaven, where we will all be united in Christ.

Why not start now?

---

[37] See 2 Timothy 4:5 and 1 Peter 4:7-11

THE PARADOX

Crissy Shreve
To my son Mike, 1990

I love I hate to see the paradox;
My strengths are yours,
And in them we are weak.
Like the words to the song I didn't hear you sing:
"Me here at last on the ground, you in mid-air."[38]

I've thought of buying you a fire truck, but know,
The past is gone, however present it may seem.
I cannot bring it back. Not for you. Not for me.

I wonder.
If I bought the fire truck, would I see?
I cannot redo my childhood. I cannot redo yours.
Some things can't be fixed.
I wasn't there for you. I know that.
I wasn't there for me.

I hear you shouting,
"Don't ask me to be there
For you."
I hear you. I understand.
I've made the same shout and I have the same reason.
I too have nothing to give.
The same nothing I gave to you.

What's next?
Do you pretend or finally give up trying?
Does it really matter how you feel when nothing works?
Why feel? It only hurts without result,
And you are left alone inside the pain.

Somewhere deep inside I feel the sadness.
I've talked it down; I've smoked it down.
How hard the pain of searching for a mother's love in strangers.

It's enough to make you cry.

---

[38] From "Send in the Clowns," a song written by Stephen Sondheim for the 1973 musical "A Little Night Music."

Chapter Twenty

New Wings

I finally got a car. We traded in the yellow Barracuda for an Opel, and X1 got himself a clunker to drive to work. Having wheels again was like sprouting a new pair of wings.

I've always said that just about the time you can't bear the thought of another minute of trying to keep up with a two-year-old, the two-year-old turns three. Oh, the relief! In those days, you could still toss a three-year-old out the door at 8 A.M. and tell him to come home when the streetlights come on.

When Mike was still two, X1 and I went on another vacation, and that time we left Mike with Judy for a week. She took him to the swimming pool every day. He hadn't yet learned to swim, but he wasn't satisfied with the baby pool; he wanted to go in the big pool. He'd run towards it, and Judy couldn't keep up with him. The lifeguards kept yelling at her to stop him from running. She told them that *they* should try catching him. When I got home, she told me that if he'd been her kid, she'd have just let him jump into the big pool. I wish she had; the next summer, when I took him for swimming lessons, he was afraid of the water.

One night, again when Mike was still two, we had a babysitter, and the babysitter got sick. She dutifully put Mike to bed and then she fell asleep. The next day, the neighbors reported spotting him heading down the sidewalk in his blanket-sleeper. He'd climbed out of his crib. Of course they took him back home.

My neighbor Louise and I would regularly walk to the "Little Store," about six blocks away, with Mike and Amy. One day, the summer they had both just turned two, they had been playing in the sandbox, but suddenly they were missing. Neither Louise nor I knew where they were. After some frantic searching of houses and yards, we jumped in the car to look further afield. There they were, a block down the street, holding hands and heading for the "Little Store." They clearly knew the way, but fortunately they hadn't yet crossed any streets. They freely admitted where they'd been headed—they were going to buy candy. The fact that they didn't have any money didn't matter to them one bit.

The irony of this is that Mike knew the way to the store, but once he learned to read, he'd always be in the back seat of the car with his head in a comic book, never paying any attention to where we were going or how we got there. Into his forties, he's still asking me how to get places. I finally bought him a GPS.

My mother came to visit. For some reason, when my mother was around, weird things happened. She and I were sitting in the kitchen talking, while Mike was playing in his room. I realized that it was too quiet, which generally meant that Mike was up to no good. I was on my way to investigate when I heard him yell.

He had one of those push-toys that I always called a "bubble gum machine." When pushed or pulled, multi-colored balls would bounce around inside the clear plastic bulb at the end of the stick. Mike had hit his bedroom window with the thing and it had made a small hole in the center with long, sharp jagged pieces hanging from the top.

Mike, who couldn't reach high enough to pull out those long, sharp, jagged pieces, perchance to have them fall down and cut his throat, had cleverly pulled his little stool over to the window so that he *could* reach them. The only reason he was yelling was because he got his finger stuck between the pieces. Not a scratch on him, of course; the kid lived a charmed life, and there he was, standing on his little stool, mad as can be, just because he was stuck.

Typical of me, I handled it calmly, carefully pulling his finger out from between shards of glass, and then afterwards having a major meltdown.

The next day, my mother was scheduled to fly home, and when it was time to take her to the airport, I couldn't find my car keys. I did not want her to miss that flight! I searched for my keys all over the house. At the last possible minute, I remembered that, earlier in the morning, out of the corner of my eye, I'd vaguely noticed Mike putting something into the garbage under the kitchen sink. Sure enough, there were my car keys. Apparently he didn't want Grandma to leave.

One summer day, Louise and I, and another neighbor who had a little boy, took the kids to a lake where there was a beach and a picnic area. Because the water was dark, you couldn't see the bottom, and we were very careful to hang on to the kids. Mike was at the picnic table eating lunch with the rest of the crew, and I went out wading alone in the water. It wasn't terribly deep, just above my knees. I bumped into something, reached down, and hauled out a tiny girl, maybe two, certainly no more than three.

The little girl wasn't pleased with me and her mother wasn't even particularly grateful. But I'd been wading right there for a while, and I'd not seen this child enter the water. I have no idea how long she'd been under. She wasn't sputtering or doing anything that would indicate that she'd been drowning. She was just . . . there. It was strange. I don't know what would have happened if I hadn't happened to bump into her, but I'm convinced that I was in that exact spot for a reason and that it was no accident.

Mike started watching *Sesame Street* when he was two. It was one of few things that would hold his attention. I'd doze on the couch with one hand on him while he watched; I wasn't taking any chances that he'd wander off somewhere.

He was reading fairly well by the time he was three, and he loved the J. C. Penney Christmas Wish Book. He'd spend hours perusing the toy section. Spider Man was his hero, and the catalog offered a Spider Man costume, which Mike desperately wanted for Halloween. I heard little from him for weeks other than that I had to be sure to order that Spider Man costume and I should not forget to order the utitily belt (sold separately).

Reread that last sentence and note the spelling of utility.

Mike didn't know the word utility; he misread it and said utitily. Of course that became another family catchword. I now have a closet in my house duly labeled the "utitily closet."

Mike also loved the TV show *Emergency*, except that he pronounced it with a hard g as in good.

I wish I had been smarter when Mike was little. He had a ton of toys with little pieces, things like Legos. And, being just a little kid, he had no concept of neatness or how to pick up his toys. He'd scatter things all over his room, and it was overwhelming even to me. Had I been smart, I'd have packed his toys into small containers and stored them out of his reach, giving him only a few things at a time, so that his scattering would be limited to what he might have been capable of picking up.

I spent as much time threatening him about what would happen if he didn't pick up his toys as I did picking them up myself when it was time to run the vacuum cleaner. I'd tell him that either he did it, or I would do it, but that if I did it, it would be with a big, black garbage bag in hand.

One day I did just that. One of the things I put into the bag was his favorite red fire truck. I didn't throw it away; I just hid it for a time, and then gave it back to him. Twenty years later, that fire truck came up in a conversation Mike and I had. That's what my poem "The Paradox" is all about.

A good full-circle story: many years later, when Mike grew up, he became an administrator at a daycare center. One day there was a little boy who'd scattered toys all over the place and the teacher couldn't get him to clean up the mess. Mike got involved and helped the kid first pick up only the blocks, and then the Legos and so on, until the job was done. He helped the boy find a way to navigate an overwhelming task.

Mike's ability to connect with the little boy inside him is something I admire and love about him. It's a big part of what makes him good at his job. I have a *Calvin & Hobbes* comic strip delivered every morning to my computer via email. I enjoy Calvin's imagination and antics, and I marvel at Bill Watterson's ability to think like a precocious six-year-old. I love it when guys I know allow the little boy inside to come out and play. He's always in there waiting. But I really, really love it when Calvin's parents outsmart him.

X1's brother lived with us for a year or so and he gave me $40 a week, a small fortune at that time. X1 let me keep that money for myself, which, coupled with finally having a car and with Mike no longer being a baby, set me back on my feet. I bought some things I'd not have been able to get otherwise, like my banjo, and I put Mike in preschool three days a week, which gave me time for my own pursuits.

I'd had my eye on a Yamaha 12-string guitar. There was one in a local store, but I didn't want that particular one—it was a bit too stiff for me. My plan was to have them bring in another one for me to try, but I hadn't yet accumulated enough money to pay for it. Sadly, the stiff one appeared under the Christmas tree. X1 had heard me talk about it, so he'd gone to that store and bought it for me. What was a truly wonderful and thoughtful gift backfired. I couldn't play that guitar—my hands weren't strong enough. I later found out that the neck was irreparably bowed, so the guitar had been flawed to begin with. I suspect the people at the store knew it and saw X1 coming.

I was young; I didn't know how to handle it. I should have tried to return it, but I didn't know enough in those days to consider that they might take it back. X1 liked deals and on some level I think I feared that he'd probably gotten it at a closeout rate. If that was true, then it would have hurt him if I found out. I just figured that we were stuck with it. I didn't play it, which I'm sure X1 noticed and didn't know what to think. I never said anything, and he never asked. It was just sad.

Some years later, when we were visiting Judy, Al showed me the Yamaha twelve-string he'd just bought for himself. It was exactly what I'd wanted and was so much easier for me to play. This made me even sadder.

More years passed, and that twelve-string lived in its case, forgotten. I'd married X2 by then, and some young people from Germany were visiting us. Their plan was to go to California and do street ministry, but they needed a guitar. I brought out the twelve-string and one young man was strong enough to play it. I was thrilled to give it to him.

This is one of my favorite stories of God keeping his promise that He will "work all things together for good . . ."[39] And, after all those years, now that there was a happy ending, I was finally able to tell X1 what had happened.

The same Christmas I got the twelve-string, X1 and I got a card from the couple we'd had to dinner, the one where the wife had criticized and contradicted everything I said or did. I had intentionally avoided any further contact with her. In the card, the wife had written, "It would be nice to hear from you." I was fully prepared to ignore it and her. X1, however, insisted we invite them to the New Year's Eve party we were planning.

---

[39] Romans 8:28

They came, and she behaved better than I expected her to. It would have been difficult for her to do otherwise; I was surrounded by my friends and she was odd man out. I played guitar and sang for everyone at the party, and she was apparently impressed.

Not long afterwards, she got together a group of German guys who could play Skat, and they started a Thursday night game, alternating houses. X1 and her husband played regularly, and they would be at either her house or mine twice a month. This meant that either she or I had a built-in babysitter on those nights, so she suggested that we hang out together. She bought a guitar and I helped her learn to play.

I can't say that we became fast friends, but we were close acquaintances. After several months of Thursday nights, I finally told her how I'd felt about that first night they came to dinner and how I was still mad at her about the broken salad bowl.

The next time I saw her, she had a present for me—a lovely new set of wooden salad bowls that were actually much nicer than the ones I'd had.

REMEMBERING A FRIEND

In the early seventies, I met a woman named June. She was quite a character. I was subbing for one of Judy's Bridge groups, as was June. Not being much of a Bridge player, June just occupied a seat, bid as best she could, and then sat out while her partner played the hand. She and I started talking, and it didn't take long for us to discover that we both played guitar.

June tended to collect young friends, usually guitar players or people who liked to write songs. One time she and I and a teenage boy she knew did an "after room," which was held following the annual play at her church. They'd set up schoolrooms as mini-nightclubs and they'd get a temporary liquor license for the nights of the play. People would wander from one room to the next to listen to the "entertainment." I still have my third of the single dollar bill we received as a tip and tore up to share.

We all played guitar. I did most of the singing and they sang along. June was famous for sort of "humming" her way to a note. I can actually "hear" her doing it as I write this. And I smile. She was unique and very special.

June took guitar lessons and spent a lot of time practicing, but she had more passion than natural talent. I have her mandolin; it is one of my most treasured possessions because it helps me to remember the time we spent together learning to play the mandolin and the banjo.

I joined a women's singing group at the local YMCA. I played guitar and only sang on pieces where no guitar accompaniment was needed. I dragged June along—any excuse to play the guitar was okay with her. We wore hot pink double-knit pants suits with colorful scarves.

June and I talked about sex, or rather I guess I did. I will always remember her telling me that, when I got older, I would get "sprinkled." She actually used that word. What she meant was that women often get more sexually responsive in later years, sometimes even in conjunction with menopause. She was a wise woman.

But she wasn't much of a housekeeper. I was still in the stage of needing everything to be perfect in my house in those days (I've since wised up a bit), and I'd sometimes allude to the dirtiness of her house. It was from June that I first heard the phrase, "I am not in this world to live up to your expectations." It was her way of telling me to chill out and back off.

Even then though, I realized that there wasn't a thing I'd have changed about June. She was "real," which was a fairly new concept in those days. June never put on an air in her life. She didn't need to. She gave who she was to others and it was a gift. She had a plaque in her kitchen that read, "Nothing is ever my fault." That too was June, from a tongue-in-cheek perspective. She just didn't worry about stuff like whose fault things were.

When I had my hysterectomy, June and her daughter Mary took care of my baby Jason for several weeks while I recuperated. Mike flew to Germany to visit his grandparents.

June smoked Carltons. They had some sort of a filter with holes in it, and one had to really suck to get any smoke out of them. They tasted lousy, too. I could never figure out why she liked them. Every year, she'd quit smoking for the month of February, because it was the shortest month. I'd pick her up to go somewhere, and she'd get in the car and immediately say, "Hurry and light up." Then she'd inhale my smoke with a big whistley ooooph (well, how would you spell it?) I can still hear it. And what a smile she'd have when she got that whiff.

Even while still living near me, June was having occasional minor blackouts where she'd forget small periods of time. Later, after they'd moved away, she had a blackout that lasted several weeks. No one could figure out what was going on, but it turned out that something was slowly leaking in her brain. The day she finally had her stroke, she had a horrendous headache and her husband took her to a local hospital, but apparently they didn't have the right doctors or equipment to take care of her. By the time he got her to another hospital, it was too late. We lost her a few days later.

June's daughter Mary had put her through some difficult times, and June would tell her that "she'd get hers" when she had her own kids. I've heard Mary admit to the truth of that on more than one occasion.

June always knew what mattered, and she took the time for the important things. It's one of many things I learned from her.

I miss her.

LITTLE DOG

Crissy Shreve

Little dog,
You've seen more winters than springs
And yet I'll shove your stuffing back in
And mend your seams just one more time.

Little dog,
You've been there to comfort
When I've been too busy or caught up in myself;
You've meant a lot.

Little dog,
Is not mending tears and broken hearts
What a mother does,
And loving, being there?

Little dog,
I could have thrown you away

Except
I couldn't.

Chapter Twenty-One

Moving Up

X1's business was doing well, and I got pregnant with Jason. We found a bigger house.

While preparing for the move, X1 did too much lifting of things that were too awkward and heavy for one person. After closing on the house, we went out to breakfast with the realtor. When X1 went to lift a forkful of scrambled eggs into his mouth, he keeled over onto the floor, instead. There we were with a new baby on the way and a new mortgage. It was scary. Fortunately, he'd only slightly fractured a rib while moving moving things, and lifting the fork finished the job. It was painful, but soon mended.

X1's friend from work and his wife helped us move. Being newly pregnant, I didn't want to risk carrying things, so I was the director. Unfortunately, the friend's wife was also newly pregnant, which we didn't know. She did lift and carry a lot of things. Her baby was born with a heart problem, possibly as a result, and he died of that heart problem, at age 33, shortly after my son Jason died.

Upon arrival at the new house, Sheppie the dog headed directly to the kitchen and moved right in. X1's brother came to live with us again too, and his clothes all smelled like the laundry products that Mama had used in Germany. Some time later, after he'd moved out, their sister came from Germany to visit. Sheppie, who'd never met her before, greeted her like a long-lost friend. Apparently she smelled just like her brother.

One day that summer, Mike was out playing, and he hollered in through the front door, "Look, Mom." I went out and he was standing there with both hands fisted. He opened them to show me a wasp in each hand. They didn't even fly away. I took one look, screamed, and headed back into the house. I couldn't imagine that those wasps were happy, and I wasn't about to find out. Amazingly, Mike didn't get stung. Now that he's grown up, Mike is terrified of all bees, thanks to being stung in the forehead some time after the wasp incident.

The time for Jason's arrival was getting closer, and since Mike had been born two weeks early, I had X1's mother, Mama, come from Germany two weeks before Jason's due date. She walked into the house, took one look at me, and pronounced that it would be four more weeks before I delivered, and that it was a boy.

I still say she jinxed me. Up until then, I'd been determined to have a girl. Her name was to be Shelby (just as Mike had been Jennifer until he was born). I didn't even have a boy's name picked out. Four weeks later, I borrowed the name Jason from my roommate in the hospital. I cried when he was born, and then I decided that I would just love Jason more than I'd ever love a girl, and I did.

It's probably just as well I didn't have girls. God knew what He was doing. Girls are squealy. I would not have been good with squealy.

Mama and I had four weeks to kill before Jason finally showed up. She cleaned the house from top to bottom, and then cleaned it again. That month was actually a nice break for me, not to mention that she made us some great dinners. She also taught me how to prepare several of her best recipes.

We spent a lot of time talking, and she told me her life story. She lived through WWII in Germany, and when it was over, she walked over a thousand miles finding and reuniting her family members. How I wish I'd thought to have a tape recorder running. She did make me a tape a few years later, but she didn't go nearly into the detail she had at my kitchen table as we waited for Jason. I'd hoped to write her story, but she'd skipped too many of the most interesting parts, and I couldn't remember them on my own.

So much has been written about what happened to the Jews and other minority groups in the war, but I'd never seen much about how it was for the German women and children. One story I do remember was that Mama and her sisters blackened their teeth to appear undesirable to enemy soldiers. Still, a Russian soldier raped Mama's sister right in front of her.

Meanwhile, and with impeccable timing, my driver's license came up for renewal. So at 9 ½ months pregnant, I squeezed into the Opel and, with Mama (who couldn't drive), headed for the closest facility, which, in those days, was about thirty miles away. I even studied for the written test, but when I handed it in, the guy behind the counter didn't even look at it. He just said, "Everyone passes today."

"Oh, no," I said, "I studied and I want you to check my answers." I got them all right. I couldn't, however, get any of the examiners to go out with me for a road test. Chickens.

Patty, who was about nineteen, lived next door with her family, and she and I got to be friends. She had a dog named Lance. He and Sheppie were buddies. When Sheppie went into heat, Lance wanted to be even more than a buddy. One of the funniest things I've ever seen was Mama, broom in hand, chasing Lance away and screeching at him in German.

I had bought Mike a toy ditch digger that he wanted, and while I was in the hospital after Jason was born, I had Mama give it to him, "just because."

Mama was there for two more weeks after Jason was born. When he'd only been home a few days, he got constipated. I didn't know what to do. Mama calmly put him on a towel on the kitchen table, cut a tiny chunk of Ivory soap, and stuck it just a wee bit into his rectum. It worked quite well—Jason was no longer constipated.

Patty from next door often babysat for me, and she would also drop in to visit regularly. Jason had a "Johnny-Jump-Up," and he spent much of his time hanging in the doorway between the kitchen and the dining room. Sheppie the dog knew Patty well, but one time when Jason was hanging there in his doorway, Patty started playing with him, making googly noises and wiggling her fingers at him. Jason was giggling and loving it, but Sheppie growled at Patty. It was one of very few times Sheppie ever showed aggression. She wasn't taking any chances with her baby Jason.

I joined the PTA—it was actually the year before Mike started school, but it was a good way to meet other mothers in the area. I was put in charge of Cultural Arts and I had a small budget. I invited various people to come to the school and do assemblies. A local pet shop brought a number of small animals, including a snapping turtle. I held my first snake, a beautiful king snake. It wasn't at all slimy or disgusting, as I'd imagined a snake would be. My attitude toward snakes changed from one of terror to one of fascination. Still, I'm not going to get up close and personal with any snake unless I know for sure what kind it is and whether or not it's poisonous.

A well-known local TV weatherman came. Everyone watched this guy, so the kids knew who he was. I was surprised that he was a lot cuter in person than he was on TV, and much taller. Best of all, because I was his main contact at the school, I got to talk (okay, flirt) with him one-on-one.

Another time, a chalk artist came, and he told stories to music, illustrating them as he spoke. It was a great act, but he had insisted on being allowed to eat lunch in the teachers' lounge with the teachers. He didn't say why. It turned out that he wanted to sell his pictures to the teachers. I thought that was inappropriate. He'd been paid to come, and he'd not been up front about it with me. The teachers didn't seem to mind; they even bought things, and so did I, but I still thought it was inappropriate.

I met my friend Jeanne at PTA. She was a poet and lots of fun. She and I went out to a local bar one night, just to get out of the house and to spend some time together. The guys in the bar couldn't imagine that we might not want their attention and they kept approaching us. It was annoying. Both of us were in our mid-twenties, but because we were married with kids, we must have been feeling "old." Jeanne commented, "Isn't it comforting to know that we're still attractive to jerks?"

On Jason's first birthday, it was bitterly cold outside. I put him in the car and we went to the bakery to get him a cake. I picked one out and had them write "Happy Birthday Jason" on it. In those days, I wrote checks for everything, and seldom carried cash. When it was time to pay for the cake, the cashier pointed to a sign that was on the counter, but hidden behind something else, so I hadn't seen it. The sign said that they didn't take checks.

Apparently, there had been a number of occasions where people had given them bad checks. I pointed out that, although that might be true, I wasn't one of those people, and I didn't think I should be penalized for what someone else had done. Nevertheless, they would not take my check. I should have told them what they could do with their cake, I suppose, but I felt obligated to take it since I'd had it personalized. So I went back out into the cold with my one-year-old baby and walked over to the bank to cash a check, then returned and paid for the cake. That was the first of many experiences I've had, I'm sure we've all had, of being penalized for the acts of others. It's always been one of my major peeves.

My little blue Opel, Elsie (LC for "little car"), was a good girl. She'd slide around a bit on ice, but she was fairly high off the ground, and if I'd just take my foot off the brake and not hit the accelerator, she'd idle over deep snow quite handily.

One morning that same bitter cold winter, poor Elsie didn't want to start. X1 opened the hood and did something to get her going for me, and successfully, but when he'd finished, he slammed her hood shut. The hood was frozen, so the brackets that held it snapped loose and it would no longer close. I took Elsie to a local garage for repair, and they welded the hood back onto the brackets. The welding burned right through, resulting in black marks on the hood. Elsie had freckles from then on.

I caught the flu one day that winter, too. It had snowed—a lot—and it was cold ourside. I drove Mike to school in the morning, leaving Jason in his crib, then hurried back home and spent the rest of the day on the floor, curled up around the toilet. I'd left the front door unlocked so that Mike could get in. I was in no condition to go pick him up.

Some time during the morning, my friend Kathy stopped by and stuck her head in the door. I hollered down that I was sick, to stay away from me, but to *please* change Jason's diaper and give him a bottle. Dear Jason, he stayed in his crib all day and never once cried. She took care of him and then went on her way, but she still wound up with the flu a few days later. Ironically, it was her abusive husband who always said, "No good deed goes unpunished."

Meanwhile, Judy and Al and gang cleverly picked that same day to come through en route from New Jersey to their new home in Minnesota. I suggested they not sleep at my house due to my flu. They didn't care; they stayed anyway. Turns out no one got sick except Sarah, and then not until they were in Minnesota. The snow and cold were terrible, and yet they still left the next morning. I guess they figured that if they were going to live in Minnesota, they might as well get used to snow and cold.

My friend Kathy finally decided to leave her abusive husband. She hid at my house for a week or so, and in the middle of the night I found her peering out the living room window. She was watching a "detective van" that was parked in front of my house. There was a van, all right, and the motor was running. It was just my friend Patty from next door and her boyfriend, doing whatever they did in that van all night.

The following summer, we hired a friend to paint the exterior of our house. He happened to be Black. His name was Sylvester. He and Mike struck up a fun friendship, and Mike spent that week or so watching him and talking to him. Sylvester would be up on a ladder, and he'd holler *down* to Mike, "Hello up there," and Mike would holler *up*, "Hello down there." Then they'd both giggle at their own cleverness.

Our house was on a quiet cul-de-sac, and in the year we'd lived there, I'd never seen a police car on our street. That is, until we decided to have a black man paint our house. The second day Sylvester was there, a squad car cruised by. Very slowly. Several days later, Sylvester stopped by to finish some touch-up work on the garage door. He'd brought his brother along. Suddenly there were two policemen at my door—they had had a report that "the coloreds" were breaking into my garage. In broad daylight on a Saturday afternoon? I don't think so. If two white guys had actually been breaking in, no one would have even noticed. Only a month or so later, a cross was burned on the lawn of a black couple who'd moved into a house in our town. Thankfully, things have changed since then.

Before I found my new church, I was still somewhat involved at the MLD church. I played guitar and led worship at Vacation Bible School. I remember one time asking the kids to belt out "Jesus Loves Me," and they did, but the pastor wasn't pleased. He thought it should be sung quietly, with reverence. He might have been right. I hadn't thought about that; I just wanted to get the kids to sing.

I somehow wound up being in charge of the talent show one time at that church. Rehearsal was on a Friday night, and I'd spent that afternoon out sunning in the back yard with Patty. She'd brought over a joint, and I'd taken a few hits. I didn't like it much, and I think it was laced with something else. I got very hungry and inhaled a peach yogurt. I don't know if it was the pot or too much sun or the yogurt, but I got sick. I didn't throw up, but I had the dry heaves. Jason was napping, so I climbed into bed and passed out for an hour or two. I was worried because I had the sound equipment for the talent show and they were depending on me to run the rehearsal. Amazingly, I got up and went and I was just fine.

I suspect that God had His hand in that. Of course He did. I can see it now, but looking back at that time and those activities in the MLD church, I realize that I never connected that church with God or with being a Christian.

In my new church, I was able to actually experience God in a church setting. I sometimes wonder whether I mightn't have been able to bring Jesus back with me to the MLD church. Perhaps, but being such a new Christian, I wouldn't have known how to do that, and having had the pastor tell me he'd be fired if he taught the things I'd learned, I saw it as a dead end.

My cousin Johnny and his wife lived nearby for a while, and one time they came to dinner for my birthday. To be fair, my birthday is on New Year's Day, so I've always had to compete with football. I usually lose. I spent the day alone in the kitchen cooking them dinner, while they and X1 watched football on TV downstairs. The three of them graciously deigned to come up to eat at half time, gulped their food and rushed back downstairs for the second half of the game. I then cleaned up—alone. Some birthday.

My friend Kathy had a baby grand piano and she played quite well. I wanted one, too. I missed the old upright that I'd played briefly at the other house and I knew that if I had a piano, I'd play it. I started perusing the want ads for a baby grand. Someone had told me about a great piano tech named Jan, and I had her meet me and do an appraisal on the first piano I looked at. She said that I'd picked the perfect example and proceeded to show me everything that could possibly be wrong with a piano. Obviously, I didn't buy that one.

I looked at several others then finally found a magnificent Schiller baby grand that had been built in Ottawa, Illinois in the 1930's. The piano had belonged to a woman who'd died, and her son just wanted it gone. It had been in the house for decades and never moved. I had come armed with flashlight and screwdriver, and I did my own appraisal. Jan had taught me that a cracked soundboard wasn't that big a deal on a grand, but that the pin block had to be in great shape. It was.

I sweet-talked X1 out of a couple hundred more dollars than he'd agreed to, and bought it. When Jan first saw it, she was thrilled with it and amazed that I'd managed to find such a great piano on my own.

The reason I loved the piano so much when I played it at the man's house, and also at first at home, was that it was a perfectly even half-step low. It sounded great. After allowing it to acclimate to my house for six weeks, it was time for a first tuning. Jan dutifully tuned it to a normal A440 pitch. Suddenly it didn't sound right to me any more. I'd been playing it regularly and the things I'd played were now in a different key—the right key, but they sounded all wrong to my ear. I got used to the proper tuning, but it took me a while. The piano truly was and still is magnificent. Everyone loves my piano. I could not have made a better choice.

I spent my afternoons playing while Jason napped. He must have liked the music because he never cried when he woke up. I wanted to play "Malagueña," but I couldn't read music, so I wrote in all the notes and memorized it one measure at a time. It took me a month or two, but I could play the whole thing.

Then I started taking piano lessons, and I made the mistake of wanting to show off for the teacher. I played "Malagueña." She told me I was doing it all wrong, that the beginning should be staccato. Oh! That's what all those little dots over the notes mean? I'd been doing it with the pedal for so long I couldn't seem to change it. I got frustrated and stopped playing it altogether. That was stupid.

One good thing was that the teacher gave me music to play that I'd never heard before. That forced me to actually read the music and figure out the rhythm. I came to realize that I was never going to be a good sight-reader, though; by the time I could actually play something, I'd memorized it. I could understand the written music intellectually, but I couldn't look up at it and play. I had to look down at the keys.

Patty and I both regularly let the dogs, Sheppie and Lance, go out to potty. They stayed around, but they'd wander over to the next yard, on the other side of Patty's house. New people had moved in there, and at Christmas time, the man came to my door to warn me not to put lights on my bushes. I told him I was unlikely to put lights on my bushes, that I thought it was tacky. He then proceeded to tell me that he had put lights on his bushes and vandals had broken all the bulbs. Oops.

These people were seriously nuts. That summer, when Mike and their little girl were about five, I got a call from the woman telling me that Mike had twisted their daughter's "boobies." That's Mike for you.

Right about that same time, my phone started ringing, and when I'd answer, whoever was on the other end would just hang up. This went on several times a day for months. Then one day, inspiration struck. I realized that it only happened when Sheppie was out. So, I asked Patty whether they, too, were getting hang-up phone calls. They sure were, and they had no clue who it was, either.

Then I knew. It was the crazy neighbor lady. She had an unlisted phone number, but that didn't stop me, and it only slowed me down a little. Never one to be daunted by minor details, and being on the PTA board, I just went to the school and looked up the child's emergency card.

I didn't have to wait long. Next time the dog was out, sure enough, the phone rang and the caller hung up. I dialed the neighbor's number right back and hung up when she answered.

It never happened again.

And we continued to let the dogs out.

X1 and I found an interesting older house that was for sale. We put in an offer contingent on the sale of our house. The owners of the older house showed up one day to look at ours, not knowing it was ours. They really loved it, but they couldn't afford what we were asking. Had we only known, we might have been able to work out something without realtors involved.

Ultimately, our house didn't sell, and theirs did, so that was the end of that. We had put a stipulation into the contract with our realtor that we were only interested in that one house so that if we couldn't get it, we would be out of the contract to sell. Immediately upon cancelling that contract, other realtors started calling constantly and showing up at my door.

I got pretty tired of explaining that we were no longer interested in selling our house. That was long before the days of Caller I.D., and maybe even before answering machines, because I remember always having to answer the phone in case it was someone I actually wanted to talk to.

One realtor, a man, was particularly persistent. He just wouldn't go away. He'd call several times a day or show up at my door. He was the only other person beside Patty at whom Sheppie ever growled. I'd never gotten his name because I didn't give him, or any of them, that much attention. He was some sort of psycho, I guess. He kept harassing me for weeks. One day, when he called, I'd finally had enough. I called him an extremely vulgar name with an even more vulgar adjective.

A few days after that, I got a package in the mail. In it was a tube of . . . well, not nice stuff . . . and a threatening note. I filed a police report, but since I didn't know who he was, there was nothing much they could do. I was a bit scared, though. I didn't know what he might do next. Fortunately, we had a trip to Germany scheduled, and we took off for four weeks. I never heard from the man again.

When we were in Germany, X1's parents figured we'd get bored just sitting around in the small town where they lived, so they booked a week's vacation in an even smaller and even more boring town in Bavaria. To Germans, *spatzieren gehen* (going walking) is a vacation, and any place you can do it is good. Jason stayed with *Tante* Elli, and Mike came along with us.

X1 and I took several bus excursions from there, one of which was through Austria, over the Brenner Pass on the old road, and into Italy. We went under the *Europabrücke*, a bridge that was until 2004 the highest bridge in Europe. Seen from below, it is terrifying.

The old road went over the Alps at some really high elevations. Cows grazed on the mountainside. I don't know how they kept their footing—the mountainside was just short of vertical, and from the bus window, you could look straight down some three thousand feet. At one point, the bus stopped, and a cow came right up to our window. Of course the cows all wore cowbells.

The bus would make the occasional stop for potty breaks. The toilets were filthy and disgusting, but you still had to pay the requisite ten *Pffenig* to use them. There were a lot of tour buses on that route and few available stops. There would be twenty or thirty women in line for each toilet, and they would hold the door open for the next person in line. That was safer than opening the door of an unoccupied stall. You never knew what you'd find, but it wouldn't be pleasant.

We finally got to a town in northern Italy, right at lunchtime. I discovered, to my surprise, that everyone still spoke German there. And typical of European tourist spots, the waiters recognized the nationalities of the tourists and addressed them in their own language. We were hungry and we got something to eat, then set off to explore the town for the hour or two we had before the bus would leave again.

I'm not a tourist. I'm a shopper. Again, typically of Europe, the shops were all closed after lunch and scheduled to reopen at exactly the time we'd have to board the bus. The only one open was a souvenir shop and even I didn't want a cowbell. The worst part was that we'd exchanged money—not much, really, twenty dollars would get you thousands of *lire*. There I was with about twenty thousand *lire* left over after buying lunch, but with no place to spend it. I was not happy. It was probably a beautiful and interesting little town, but I was too annoyed to notice. I don't even remember the name of it.

We did stop briefly in another small town on they way back, though. I was on a mission to find something on which to spend those leftover *lire*, and I had about half an hour in which to accomplish it. In a tiny music store, I found a bowl mandolin, including a carrying case, for fifteen thousand *lire*. I bought it and carefully carried it all the way back to the U.S. The first time I tried to tune it, the whole top cracked, but I kept it as a wall-hanger for years, just so I could tell people I'd paid fifteen thousand for it.

Another jaunt we took on that trip was up an alp via a cog railway called the *Bayerische Zugspitzebahn*. It started out in Garmisch-Partenkirchen and traveled for forty minutes up and through the mountains to Germany's highest point, the *Zugspitze*. The only other option was a ten-minute ride on a cable car that hung high over the valley on what looked to me like a very thin strand of wire. It was suggested that we take it back down, but I wasn't about to get on that thing. I was too young to die.

Back home again, Elsie the car and I drove to a town about fifteen miles from home, returning late at night. All the way home, I noticed someone following me. There was no attempt to stop me or communicate with me, but I knew I was being followed. There were only the two of us on the road the whole way. When I drove into my driveway, the guy was still on my tail. I opened the garage door with the remote and shut it immediately behind me. He took off then. Scary stuff.

When Mike was in kindergarten, he'd routinely show up at about quarter after twelve for lunch, allowing for time to stop and investigate the myriad delights that five-year-old boys can find on the way home from school. One spring day I was outside in the yard, and I suddenly realized that it was nearing 12:30 and he hadn't yet materialized. And somehow I knew I had to go find him.

For some reason, I had my car keys in my hand, so I jumped into the car, no shoes, no purse, and sped around the block to look for him. As I approached a 4-way stop sign, I saw that he was almost at the intersection where he'd have to cross. I stopped, then crossed the intersection and pulled over to the curb so that he could get in the car.

Just then, a car full of teenagers from the high school came speeding down the street, blew the stop sign and sped through the intersection—right where my son would have been crossing. Mike would have been in the middle of the intersection had I not been there at that exact moment.

I don't know exactly what the message was or why I happened to be listening, but God spoke to my heart that day and I heard. When Mike was nineteen and in college, he renewed his relationship with the Lord. In telling me about it, he said he'd been praying about some needed car repairs, and at the end of his prayer, the words that came to him were, "Thanks, I love You." Sounds just right to me. Yes, Lord, thanks. I love you too.

Remembering this story some 40 years later, shortly after my son Jason died, I realized that God knew then what was going to happen, and He spared me the loss of both sons.

My Gunny Sack

Although I don't have a lot of major regrets, these are things I wish I could do over, or do differently, or just do . . .

My son Mike singing *Send in the Clowns*, and I'd be there to hear him. When X2 and I were first together, we'd planned a trip to Florida and right before we were to leave, I was told that Mike would be singing in a show at school. I went to Florida and missed it. At least I have a picture a friend took of him sitting on a stool, clown hat on his head, and microphone in his hand.

My son Jason as a baby, so I could hold him more than I did. His death at age 33 made this even truer. At least we did a lot of hugging when he was alive.

A few days with my grandfather Dadum, just to get some of that love again.

The day Jason cried when I had to leave him at daycare.

Another chance to just gaze at Klaus, who was the most gorgeous guy I've ever met.

My circle pin. I wish I hadn't listened to the yahoo who told me that it was a "virgin" pin, and that I'd not stopped wearing it.

A horse. I think having a horse, or at least having an opportunity to ride regularly, would have made a huge difference in my life. I've heard it said that adolescent girls who get into horses don't get into boys as early as others do. I don't know whether or not that's true, but I wish I'd been able to test it out.

School. I think I wish I'd been more interested in school, both academically and socially. I definitely wish the things that interfered wouldn't have, or that I'd been able to rise above them.

My semi-precision roller skates and a fellow named Gary who was a great skater and whom I dated after my skating days. We never went skating together. I later bought a pair of full precision skates, but never used them much.

A dance floor and guy I dated named Glen who was known to be a really good dancer. We never went dancing, mostly because I was too young to go to the clubs where he went to dance. We never danced together anywhere, not even at home.

Mike's red fire truck. I wish I'd known what an impact my taking it away from him would have.

My cousin Jill at age 7. I wish I'd been kinder to her. I wish I'd been her friend and her advocate, rather than just another of her detractors. By the time I was ready to be different with her, it was too late. The old patterns were too ingrained in both of us.

I wish I hadn't lost the friendship ring my first love, Joey, gave me. I'd like to know whether my losing it was just an excuse for him to break up with me.

My second great love, Jack, whom I dated when I was pregnant with baby Larry. Jack just stopped showing up and, although I didn't expect anything from him, I would like to have closure.

My third great love, Larry M., and the night he saw me out with someone else. I'd like to find out whether I really had feelings for him or whether they just "developed" when he no longer trusted me.

X2 totally in love with me again. The first time he told me he loved me, he said he was totally in love with me. I think it was actually true—for a time.

I wish I hadn't smoked through my pregnancies. They didn't know then what they know now—that the addiction passes on to the child.

My best friends from my home town. Long ago, I added them to this list, wishing I could see them again. Thanks to the Internet, I have since reconnected with all but one, and it's been great.

The number one item on this list for decades was my son Larry. Having him back in my life makes up for many of the rest of these things.

At some point I added a guy I dated named Kirk, and I wrote "just so I wouldn't dump him for Larry's father." Now that Larry's been restored to me, I realize that had I stayed with Kirk, there would be no Larry. So, I take that one back.

10,000 YEARS

These are some of the things I look forward to doing when I get to heaven. When I was in Branson, Missouri, I heard Roy Clark playing "Malagueña" on the guitar. I remember thinking that I could listen to him play that song for 10,000 years. That was when I started this list.

A visiting pastor, who talked about the table for eight he envisioned hosting in heaven, gave one of the most poignant messages I ever heard. He told us about each of the individuals he was looking forward to seeing again. He even included his beloved childhood dog.

My son Mike has a list of questions he wants to ask God. Some people might say that once we're in heaven, none of it will matter any more. That may be true or it may not. To my way of thinking, the very delight of heaven will be having enough time and energy for all the people I love, along with healing for all the relationships with people I didn't love, or didn't love well. The only thing that matters is that they show up.

There are things I missed the first time around, and which can only happen now in heaven. I sure hope Mike won't be too embarrassed to reprise "Send in the Clowns" for me, although maybe not for 10,000 years.

I've spent a number of years doing genealogy, most particularly around one ancestor, Hans Peter. I can't wait to meet my ancestors and find out about their lives in their times.

Reuniting with the pets I've lost. I can just see myself surrounded by cats and dogs and one very crazy mynah bird. Perhaps even my chameleon will be there. Surely there will be safety pins in heaven, so that I can attach him to my shirt. Or maybe I won't need to.

I can't wait to ride that beautiful palomino bareback on heaven's beach.

My friend June needed surgery one time, and she asked the doctor whether she'd be able to sing after the surgery. He replied, "Sure." "Oh, good," she said, "because I sure can't sing now." June's already there singing. I, too, will be singing, and I'll be part of a great chorus praising God. Maybe I'll try soprano for a while, and then see if I can do the "lovely contralto" voice my family says my grandmother had. I never heard her sing. I can't wait to hear her sing in heaven—and to hear her laugh, too.

I will watch a heavenly video of the first 45 years of my son Larry's life.

I will be able to speak German fluently, in fact any language, if I want to.

One time when I was sitting up in the balcony at church, I noticed movement below—it was a woman sitting near the front, facing the congregation, and waving her hands about. Those facing her were doing the same. They were all praising God in sign language! I thought that was pretty neat, and then it struck me—God could hear them. I'll be able to hear them too, and I will share their joy.

One day I saw a really neat BMW Z3, a silver convertible. And as I walked toward it oohing and aahing, I noticed a man in a wheelchair, sitting alone nearby. I smiled at him and said, "Great car, huh?" He agreed as best he could. You see, he had cerebral palsy, or something like that. He wasn't able to move his arms or his legs or his head other than in a spastic, uncontrolled way. Yet he smiled as best he could, and said, "Fast car."

His speech was virtually impossible to understand. I asked his name, and though he tried very hard, and several times, I could not catch it. I said, "I'm so sorry, I just can't understand you," and he replied, "That's OK." He was clearly intelligent, yet he was bound to his chair, unable to use his body in any functional sense, unable to voice his thoughts. How I would have loved to hear what he had to say. How he would have loved, I'm sure, to be able to say it. The agony, the frustration he must feel every day, locked inside a prison more anguishing than I could ever imagine.

I prayed silently: I come to You, Lord, knowing you share my sadness; indeed you grieve so much more deeply than I. I don't have any answers; I have no idea how to pray for this wounded child of yours who has touched my heart so deeply. Yet I have hope. Because of Who You are, he and I *will* have that long talk in heaven. And I have comfort. Whatever the seeming hells of this life, it is short. Thank You, Lord, that he will have all eternity to say all the things he has to say, on that day when you draw him home into your arms. Thank You too, Lord, that I will be there to listen.

I pray that meanwhile, he would know Your love and your presence in his life, and that he will know that his whole and healed forever is yet to come.

As I left Lauren, whose name I found out later, I said, "Someday you and I are going to have a long conversation in heaven." He agreed heartily and with some excitement. That much of each other we could understand and share.

Afterthought: since I wrote this some years ago, my memory has . . . well, deteriorated. I did not even remember this encounter until I ran into what I'd written about it. Good thing my computer has a memory! But what strikes me today is that, regardless of whether I remembered Lauren while I'm still here, I *will* remember him when next we meet.

That which we bind on earth will be bound in heaven.[40]

---

[40] Matthew 18:18

FUNNY MAN IN SAN FRANCISCO

Crissy Shreve

He was a funny man.
He was black with dirty white pants,
And a plaid shirt.
All colors . . .
The absence of color?

And he talked to himself,
And to us to himself,
And he smoked butts from the ashtrays,
And snatched the food from leftover plates.

The cable car was stuck at the end of the line,
At Powell and Market.
And if we hadn't stopped for coffee and egg rolls,
We would have missed him.

Chapter Twenty-Two

Back To Work

Around this time, I started having severe female problems. My blood count was dangerously low. I was wearing diapers to bed at night, and this was before they made adult diapers, so I had to jury-rig some of Jason's leftover disposables. It was time to do something about it.

In the hospital hallway, the night before my hysterectomy, I met a woman named Judy, who was there for a D and C, a comparatively minor procedure. She was terrified and was amazed that I seemed so at peace while facing a hysterectomy. I was able to tell her that I felt safe in God's hands. Then it was time to kiss our husbands goodnight, see them onto the elevator and return to our rooms for pre-surgical procedures. So, we had no chance to talk further, but we quickly exchanged phone numbers.

Alone in my room, despite my absolute faith that God was with me, the panic set in and I felt very alone and afraid. I reached out my hand in the darkness and asked Jesus to come hold my hand. He did, and He stayed close during the surgery and throughout my recovery.

I've thought of that moment so often since then. It was the first time I intentionally asked God to be with me. It was the first time since I'd become a believer that I was facing something I knew I couldn't handle on my own. I know that God's always with me, even when I don't think to ask Him to be. But when I do reach out to Him, He comes even closer and He gives me an extra measure of peace. Now I try to remember to tell Him regularly that I need Him, because I know He likes hearing it. And because I know I do.

Before my surgery, I had people telling me that I would still be a "woman" and that my husband would still find me attractive, that sort of thing. I kept telling them that that stuff didn't matter to me, I was only worried about *pain*. I even told my doctor that I didn't want to wake up hurting, and that it was a good bet I'd survive, so if I did wake up hurting, sooner or later I'd find him and shoot him. He laughed. I didn't.

When I woke up, there was a moment or two of what felt like rawness in the incision, so I rang for the nurse, got drugs, and never felt a thing after that. I didn't have to shoot the doctor.

I was standing in line at the bank a few days before my hysterectomy and there was a woman in the line next to me who looked familiar. She noticed me looking at her, smiled, and reminded me that I knew her from my pediatrician's office. She said it happened to her all the time—people knew they knew her, but couldn't place her out of context. I mentioned that I was going in for a hysterectomy. She said, "Drink water, it's a great healer." She told me to start as soon as I could after surgery, even just sucking on ice. Thanks to that little gem of wisdom, I had a remarkable recovery.

A day or two before I was scheduled to go into the hospital, X1's uncle dropped off his daughter, who was the same age as Mike, for me to babysit while he and X1 went out for a beer. I could barely move, and I was really weak, so surely what I needed was another kid to worry about.

A month or so later, Judy, the woman I'd met in the hospital, called me. It was her turn to have a hysterectomy, and she was even more afraid than she'd been when I'd first met her. I was able to admit to her how scared I'd been when the lights were out, and how I'd asked Jesus to take my hand. I suggested she do the same. It was a new concept for her because she was Jewish. I also told her to drink water!

Her surgery went well and after her recovery, we got together. She told me that her husband was a closet alcoholic and that she was attending Al-Anon meetings. She was discovering a relationship with God and learning to put her trust in Him.

At some point, though, Judy and I had some sort of misunderstanding and we were angry at each other for a while. When we finally talked about it, I apologized, fully expecting an apology in return. I didn't get one. Instead, at the end of that conversation, she said, "I love you, Cris." It was a beautiful gift, so much better than an apology could ever have been.

My friend Jeanne moved to the San Francisco area. The summer after she left, X1's sister decided she wanted to go to California—and she wanted me to go with her. X1 couldn't very well argue, since it was his sister, so she came from Germany and off we went. We stayed a few days with Jeanne while we were there.

When we had landed in L.A., I saw my first palm tree. It wasn't the happiest palm tree, growing right there outside the terminal, but being my first, I had to hug it. That was the beginning of my tradition of hugging the first palm tree I'd see on any later trips I took.

One day we were in downtown San Francisco, about to board the cable car to Fisherman's Wharf, but the cable car had broken down. We decided to get something to eat at a restaurant right there while we waited. There was a man in the restaurant; I suspect he was homeless and hung out there all the time. I don't know why he made such an impression on me, but I wanted to remember him, so I wrote a poem about him. I can still picture him flitting about that restaurant talking to himself and being . . . well, crazy.

I had hired a woman to come in every day to take care of Mike and Jason. She nearly quit because X1 wasn't being terribly responsible about coming home at a reasonable time. One night his Skat buddies came to play and sat there waiting for an hour, while he didn't show up. Mike wasn't terribly nice to her, either.

X1 and I started having serious problems and were heading toward divorce.

My cousin Jill, who by then had started being called Julie, got married in central Pennsylvania, and I drove there on my own with Mike and Jason, a two-day trip. X1 flew back and forth because he couldn't take the time away from his business to drive us. Jason came down with chicken pox the night before the wedding. My cousin Jan's husband Raphael stayed with him and their son during the wedding and reception. A babysitter had been hired, but she'd not had chicken pox, so we couldn't use her.

At the reception, Uncle Austin's wife kept telling me how handsome my husband was. I kept telling her it didn't matter how handsome he was—he didn't love me any more.

When the wedding was over, I had to get back to my mother's with Jason because I didn't think I should stay in any motels with his having the pox. From there, I had to get back home before Mike came down with them. I had taken X1's car, a big old dark green Ford. It broke down while I was at my mother's, so I had to wait a few days for it to be repaired. Although that narrowed my window for getting home, it was a blessing that the car broke down there and not out on the road somewhere. God again.

My cousin John and his wife hadn't made it to the wedding in time, but they caught up with me at my mother's, and then they followed me home and stayed a few days. Their daughter led Mike to the Lord.

X1 got a bit too friendly with a girl at work. He had the hots for her and he wanted me to be friends with her. (Why do guys *do* that?) One day he went downtown to meet up with this girl for an assignation. Now, guys lie about these things, so I don't know all the details, but X1 turned up with the clap (gonorrhea). He came home in misery in the middle of the day, and of course it had to be a Wednesday. In those days, all the doctors' offices were closed on Wednesdays. So we drove to the only VD clinic we found open. It was in a really nasty neighborhood in the city, some twenty miles away. I was tested, too, and we were both given two huge white horse tablets, and shots as well. They insisted on having the names of our "correspondents" to notify. X1 had to name the girl. I had no one to name.

I threatened him on the way to the clinic, that if he didn't tell me the whole truth and nothing but the truth, my next stop would be at a divorce attorney's office. He said that he'd gone to the city to meet up with the girl, but he'd met a prostitute on the street and had some fun with her before meeting up with the girl.

I was pretty messed up about the whole thing. I talked to a friend about it, and she suggested I see a pastor she knew and had worked with. I went regularly for a few months and even had some hypnosis. I never believed I was actually hypnotized, but perhaps.

Things deteriorated quickly after that. I totally forgot about our eleventh anniversary. I'd spent the day hanging out with a friend, and she was still there when X1 came home. He had brought roses for me. Having forgotten it was our anniversary, I thought the roses meant that he must want to work on our relationship. He was mad that my friend was there, and he went straight upstairs to bed. After she left, I remembered that it was our anniversary. That was all the roses were about, a perfunctory memento. That was pretty much the end.

WHEN ROSES FAIL
Crissy Shreve

Lord,
I see the beautiful yellow roses You created,
And yet, the one who gave them,
Gave them not in love.

Did he think they were expected?
Is there nothing more than tradition?
They only serve to mark
The anniversary of the end.

Still,
They proclaim that all beauty is not lost.
Your love will sustain when roses fail.

I started job hunting. X1 had never wanted me to work once we had kids. I found a great job as a buyer for an HVAC firm. I got lucky. We'd just had some work done at the house, so when the boss asked whether I knew what HVAC stood for, I did. Then he asked me whether I could spell the word *duct*. I could. He also gave me one of the best pieces of advice I've ever received: "Don't be afraid to make mistakes—if you never make any mistakes, you're not doing anything."

I was hired as an assistant to the buyer. The poor guy was very unorganized and had papers all over his desk, in several overflowing stack units, and tacked all over the wall. He never knew what to do next. He'd regularly go get a cup of coffee, then come back to our office, take one look at his desk, throw his hands up in despair, and go back out for more coffee. I, meanwhile, being organized by nature, had one pile I worked from, and I managed to get things done. Within two months, the buyer was let go and his job was mine. I don't flatter myself that I was so great; I was simply doing the job when he wasn't, plus they could pay me a lot less and not have to pay him at all.

I was very sad, though. He'd been good to me. He and I were both tearful. The irony was that, not only had he wanted to hire me, but he also had something of a crush on me, which I only knew because he started dressing better than he had before I started. I wasn't interested in him, though.

Jason went to day care. In those days, working people didn't have the parenting options they enjoy today. I was expected to be at work. Jason was sick one morning, and I frantically called around looking for someone to take care of him because they wouldn't let him come sick to day care. Fortunately, I found someone—a woman in my church small group.

Jason was mostly happy at day care, but I remember one day he cried and cried when I had to leave and get to work. I can still see his little tearful face.

I gave up piano lessons once I starting working. I had no time to practice. X1 moved out, and I had the house and the kids to take care of when I wasn't working. The house was too big and we put it up for sale with a realtor friend. A woman who was renting a house across the street, and with whom I'd had something of a casual friendship, yelled at me when she saw the sign, saying, "You *knew* I was looking for a house!" Actually, I hadn't known. Since X1 hadn't yet signed the contract with the realtor, I cancelled it, in order to sell by owner to the lady across the street. She worked at a title company, and she thought she knew it all.

She and her husband tried to get me down from my asking price, which I'd already lowered because there would be no realtor fees. I wouldn't budge and they finally agreed to my price and signed the offer. Thirty-one days later, she called me and said she was backing out of the deal because she couldn't get financing. I said, no, she wasn't, it was too late to back out. She'd passed her thirty days to cancel, and I was about to make an offer on a smaller house. She said I'd better not make the offer. I again stuck to my guns and she in fact got a mortgage, although I doubt it was at desirable terms. She was so mad at me, but I'd wasted a month of market time and she'd treated me like I was stupid. I guess she didn't know it all, after all.

I bought and moved into my little house. Looking back, I can see that it was one of the few times in my life when I was truly happy, truly at peace, living in that house with my kids and my job and my dog and no man.

I was regularly attending my church and taking the kids to Sunday school there. X1 was quite certain that the church was at fault for destroying our marriage. That was not the case. I was at fault. He was as fault. We were never really right for each other. I can't say that I wish we'd never married, though. That would mean that I wouldn't have had my sons, and that's unthinkable.

Mike, at age ten, fell in love with the play *Annie*. Mary Kay Lombardi played Annie when we saw it the first time. Mike wrote to her and even received a reply, which made him really want to be in that play. We heard that they were holding auditions in the city (some twenty-five miles away) for a further run. There weren't any boy parts, but that didn't matter to Mike; he wanted to play Annie. We had a record album from the Broadway version, and we listened to it constantly. Mike knew the words to every song and he could sing them, on key.

My favorite song from the play was "Little Girls," sung by Miss Hannigan, the mean matron at the orphanage. One line goes, "If I wring little necks, surely I will get an acquittal." Mike was sure that the word was *appointal*. It didn't matter that there is no such word. It took me a month to convince him that the correct word was *acquittal*.

There was no way he was going to get the part of Annie, and even if it had been possible, there was no way I was going to drive to the city with him every night for rehearsals after working all day. I had to find a way to talk him out of the idea. Finally, I happened to mention that he'd have to dance. Oh. That took care of it; he no longer wanted to audition. Phew!

We did see the play three more times though.

When we were out in the car, Mike would be in the back seat with his nose in a comic book. Jason, on the other hand, always watched where we were going. I had a babysitter named Shawn, and both my boys loved him. He'd put Jason in front of him on the banana seat of his bike and they'd ride to the park, about four blocks away.

Now, we'd just moved to the neighborhood, and I didn't even know there *was* a park over there. Further, the route to the park went around several corners and then down a sidewalk that ran between two houses in the middle of a block. I didn't know that sidewalk was there, either. One night I stuck Jason on the banana seat of my bike, and as we rode down the street, he turned the handlebars to the left and then to the right until we wound up at that park. He was only three, and he hadn't yet learned to ride a bike himself, but not only did he know the way, he turned the handlebars just right. We didn't even land in the bushes.

My friend Jeanne had told me that when she'd turned thirty, she'd decided that her thirties were going to be the best decade in her life. I thought that was a good idea, so I decided the same and turned thirty.

I was still navigating the X1 thing—did I want to try and salvage the marriage or didn't I? I went to visit him one night at his apartment. It was winter, and I left my wet boots in the hallway outside his door. When I was ready to go home, my boots were gone—someone had taken them. X1 lent me a pair of his shoes to get me through the snow to my car, and I drove home in my socks.

Over the previous several years, I'd become friends with the guy who played Skat with X1 and who was married to the salad bowl woman. He'd regularly call me in the afternoon on Skat day and we'd talk. One night, when he'd come to play, he and I went out for coffee instead. He, too, was having problems in his marriage. We talked a lot about both our situations. Then X1 and I split up, and I no longer had any contact with this guy for a while.

Some time in the spring, after X1 and I had been separated for six months or so, the Skat guy ran through my mind, and I wondered how he was doing. I called him up and asked whether things in his marriage were still the same. He said they were—they had separate bedrooms and were each living their own lives and were both dating.

I asked, "Well, would it interest you to know that X1 and I are separated?" It did, and we began to date. He and I eventually got married, so I will start calling him X2 at this point, rather than the Skat guy.

On our first date, we went out for dinner and I had trouble eating. I still had my problem with restaurants and sulfites. I'd ordered a really nice steak. X2 said, "You don't have to eat it." That was the first of several times I remember him making a remark that made me feel accepted and understood. Still, I had the steak wrapped, took it home, and I ate every bite of it.

He had a huge black Lincoln Mark V. We both loved going for long rides and just being together. I was always the navigator and as we'd approach an intersection, I'd say, "Turn left up there." X2, who couldn't see very far, would say, "How do you know?"

"I see the sign."

"What sign?"

It became an oft-repeated joke between us. This was at the time when CB radios were hot, and X2, being the gadget guy he is, of course had one. One time as we were out riding around, he was talking to some guy on the CB and the guy asked for his "handle," as they did in CB language. The guy misunderstood X2's handle and said, "Who? Mr. Magoo?" X2 was Magoo to me from that day on. I like having my own names for people, and of course his vision problem sealed the deal.

One day we wound up in a small tourist town. We had lunch, and then we walked around looking into the shops. It was chilly out, and I was cold, but the sweater I was wearing had no pockets. He had his hands in his coat pockets, so I stuck my hand in his pocket to get warm. I found his hand. It was nice and warm, and a good fit. For years, when I told that story, I ended it by saying that he never let go. Sadly, he did, but it was twenty-five years later.

As I write this, I'm reminded of a time just recently, when a guy friend of mine and I were at church together. We were all asked to grab the hand of the person next to us during prayer. This was several years after X2 and I divorced. Holding my friend's hand, I was aware that it wasn't a good fit. I don't think that it was because it wasn't X2's hand; I was pretty well over him by then. It just didn't feel right.

Once I started seeing X2, X1 wanted me back. I was aware that my seeing someone else, particularly someone he knew, had spurred this new interest. He'd pretty much let me know, both during the marriage and at the end, that he didn't want me. I didn't particularly want him, either, but it was hard to determine whether that was just it, or whether my having a new love interest was more . . . interesting.

As a Christian, I thought maybe I should stay with X1 and work things out, as opposed to having X2 on a silver platter. So I told X2 I was going to try to stay with X1, and X2 allowed that that was the right thing to do, even though he wasn't at all happy about it.

Except that I couldn't do it. X1 and I even had a few sessions with a pastor, but my heart wasn't in it. It was too late. He and I and the kids drove up to Minnesota for Easter. All the way up in the car, I was thinking about X2 and wanting to be with him.

When I got back home, I called X2 at work and told him I couldn't do it. His secretary's comment was, "Oh, good, he's been such a bear." Shortly after that, we met for lunch at a park near where I worked, and sitting together on a picnic table, he said to me, "I'm totally in love with you." It was a good thing, because I was totally in love with him.

X2 took a trip to Germany for three weeks to visit his mother. I was an empty shell the whole time he was gone. I learned a Chopin etude on the piano, one that I thought of as "our song." I wrote a whole lot of poetry. I painted my bedroom and wallpapered my bathroom. And of course I went to work. Keeping busy helped a bit, but I felt utterly empty. It was like when my mother went away overnight those times when I was a little girl.

I had a problem with my car while he was gone, so I borrowed the Mark V. I had my own office at work. It was upstairs in the front of the building, and I'd park that car right under my window so that I could look out and see it and feel close to him.

I had become neurotically dependent on X2. This was not a good thing, although I didn't realize it at the time. I didn't see how damaging it was, or that it was a continuation of my childhood feelings of neediness and fear of abandonment. The irony is that I'd been so happy and at peace on my own before he came into the equation. I lost all that, and so quickly. Suddenly there was no more me, or, better put, no more me without him.

We listened to a Roger Whittaker tape all the time in the car. One of the songs had a line, "The first time that we said hello began our last good-bye." I would get weepy whenever I heard those words. I couldn't bear the thought of it, even as, at the same time, I was telling myself that it couldn't happen to us. We were solid. And we were solid, or at least as solid as two wounded people can be. Of that I am certain, even as I am now equally certain that we both, each in our own way and in our own neediness, started chipping away at that solidity. Roger Whittaker was right.

As a Christian, I knew that I needed to be with someone who understood and believed as I did. I invited X2 to church and asked that he attend six times. If, after that, he hated it, we would reevaluate. My church is large and modern, and in those days, met in a movie theater. It usually took the first several times just to get past the differences from traditional churches, such as the music and the theater-style seating. By the third visit, some of the novelty should have worn off, and a person might actually start to hear what's being taught. By the sixth time, X2 started to enjoy going and, about a year afterwards, he accepted Christ as his Savior.

I got sucked into the notion of romantic love being dependable. It's not. Real love has staying power—power to stay in it and weather the storms together. I always told X2 that instead of standing on opposite sides of the ring fighting against each other, we needed to be on the same side, fighting against whatever problem we faced. Neither of us listened to me.

I remember a guy we knew telling his wife that he was not her enemy. Romantic love, without real love, sooner or later becomes adversarial. Those things X2 and I most loved about each other, and those things we overlooked in the heat of infatuation, became the things we hated most about each other.

One time early in our relationship, X2 and I were out walking with another couple. X2 and I were holding hands. The other woman was walking alone ahead of us, and her husband was trailing behind. I remember thinking how sad it was that they weren't holding hands. Well. They're still together. X2 and I are not. To be honest, I wish they had been holding hands *and* were still together. I wish *we* had been holding hands and were still together. I'm not willing to believe that it can only be one way or the other. I wish they had retained whatever first love they'd had. I wish we'd had staying power.

One observation I can make, though, is that their walking separately was an indication of their ability to be independent of each other. It was customary at many weddings for the bride and groom to light a unity candle, signifying two becoming one. They would then blow out their individual candles. At one wedding I attended, I noted that the couple did not blow out their individual candles. When I asked them afterwards why they hadn't, I was told that they felt it was important to maintain their own individual identities *and* be united as one. A subtle, but huge difference I didn't recognize then. X2 and I blew out our candles.

I needed to understand that I was whole and complete in myself *and* utterly dependent, but on my Lord. It took me thirty more years to finally figure that out. Being dependent on any person is not God's design for me, for anyone. Being dependent on Him is.

People die. They betray us and abandon us and abuse us. They can't help it. As Will Bowen said, "Hurt people hurt people." God never does.

A Hard Lesson

I made a big mistake—two, actually. X2 and I were involved sexually from the beginning. Then, to make matters worse, we started living together. You ask, "What's the big deal? Everyone lives together these days." It wasn't a big deal—unless we wanted God to bless us.

We started out in sin. It was primarily my sin; X2 wasn't at that point answerable to God since he wasn't yet a believer. I fell back into my old pattern of trading sex for love. I knew perfectly well that that wasn't what God wanted for me. I didn't turn my back on God, but I avoided Him to enough of a degree to keep me from feeling completely overwhelmed with guilt.

Here's the thing: when I chose to do things my way instead of God's way, I chose the consequences. God wasn't obligated to bless our relationship, or later, our marriage. Now, of course God's never obligated to do anything. But He does make promises, and He keeps them. He blesses those who do things His way. So, from that perspective, I could not expect Him to bless my marriage.

That's not to say that we weren't blessed at all during those years. We were, and often mightily. But our relationship and then our marriage lacked the kind of foundation that would stand. Just as the Bible says in Psalms 127 that, "Unless the LORD builds the house, they labor in vain who build it," so it is with anything else we do.

How could we build a marriage on a foundation of sin and expect it to stand?

As my cousin John likes to say, and as I've learned the hard way over the years, "When God and I disagree on something, He's always right and I'm always wrong." There is still a bit of a dichotomy to it, though. God's been putting up with us sinners for eons. He loves us and He takes care of us, even uses us, despite our waywardness. If you have a Bible, read 2nd Samuel chapter 11. It's the perfect example.

We come to God one time, through Jesus Christ. Then we spend the rest of our lives coming *back* to God. There's no one I know, and no one you know, who's ever gotten everything right on his or her own. The thing I find most remarkable about the story in 2nd Samuel is that David was restored to relationship with God, even after committing adultery and murder. We mess up, we admit that we've messed up, and we find God waiting to embrace us again. He was there all the time; it was I who left his arms for a while.

I'm not talking about rules—keeping them or breaking them. I'm talking about God's *way*, about how he designed things, how he wired us up, and how he intended it all to work.

Ask a dog to recite, "Friends, Romans, countrymen, lend me your ears . . ." The dog is not going to do it. He isn't wired up to do it—he can't talk. He wasn't intended to do it. We, on the other hand, were wired up by God to follow his intention for his children. Anything we do outside of His intention is counterintuitive and counterproductive.

We were not designed for casual sex.

God's way of doing things is always intended for our good. Always. And God's way always makes sense. I find it ludicrous when someone blames God for things that happen to them. Whatever it is, the blame can always be traced back to some choice that was made outside of God's intention.

God's intention for me, and His desire for X2 and me was that we love and honor Him above all things and choose to do things His way. We did exactly the opposite. We did things our way. It's no surprise that it didn't work.

Still, although I eventually lost X2 and my marriage, I never lost my Lord, even for one second.

Lost

Crissy Shreve

Why do I feel so lost at midnight,
Knowing you'll return?
And yet I face another night alone.

It gets to me!
I'm clinging to you like a fool,
And yet I can't pretend . . .

That I don't cry,
And blow a kiss to your disappearing tail lights.
You're gone so fast.

And suddenly I'm alone again,
Where once you filled my emptiness.
With love.

In the silence I cry out,
How can you be so strong?
And then I see . . .

That to cling to you is poison,
In the well of love,
And if I drop my bucket in too deep . . .

Love will die.

CHAPTER TWENTY-THREE

PROPOSAL

Hindsight, they say, is always twenty-twenty. I see a lot of things today that I didn't see at the time. Still, the trouble with second-guessing is that we can never know how things might have gone had we done it differently. I'm not trying to justify things; I'm not sure that I even can, but I can try to explain them.

When I went to live with X2, I left my boys with their dad on a trial basis, pending our divorce and final custody decisions. There were a lot of reasons why their staying with their dad seemed like a good idea.

I wasn't cut out to be a mother. I hated having my wings clipped. I hated having to put myself aside to take care of little people who were completely dependent on me. It took everything I had just to take care of *me*. No one else had ever much taken care of me, and that hadn't changed. I had this idea that, if I was the only one who was going to take care of me, then everyone else in the world ought to have to take care of themselves, too. If that sounds self-centered, it was. I was.

The first three years of Mike's life were hard on me. He was a difficult baby. There was no money. X1 wasn't particularly helpful. He was the one who'd wanted kids. I often said that he wanted the great American dream: the house, the car, the 2.3 kids—and someone to take care of it all for him. And I did take care of it all for him. He worked hard and was actually a good provider, but there was no relationship between us.

I did all the things I was supposed to do. I cleaned the house, I cut the grass, and I made the dinner. I didn't have much of anything left afterwards, but it all got done. This was not only expected of me, I was expected to like it. I know there are women out there who are fulfilled by doing these things. I wasn't one of them. I just got emptied out of what little there was of me to begin with.

As my grandmother had for me, I did the basics for my kids. They were fed and watered and dressed. I never played with them much—I didn't know how to play with little kids. When Mike wanted to play Hide and Seek, he'd always want to be the one to hide. This worked for me. I'd tell him I'd count to a thousand and I'd be saying, "1-2-3," as he disappeared up the stairs. Half an hour later, I'd find him sound asleep in his closet. It would have been silly to wake him.

I craved sleep, I craved quiet, I craved "me" time. I felt as though I didn't exist. There was no escape. I needed adult interaction. I needed a husband. I was lonely and depressed and damned mad about it all. Whatever it was I needed—and I'm not sure I knew then or even know now what that was—it wasn't there.

X1 and I had often said that, were we to split up, he'd keep the kids. When we finally did split up, he didn't seem to mind that I'd be gone, but he couldn't live without the kids. He needed them. He didn't need me, outside of my taking care of it all for him. I realize now that I wanted revenge. I wanted X1 to have to take care of it all for himself. I wanted him to lose me. I resented his loving the kids and not loving me. The sad thing is that, yes, I got my revenge, but it was my kids who paid for it.

I wanted a real husband. Actually, what I wanted was a mommy and a daddy for myself. I wanted someone to take care of *me*, something I'd been searching for all my life, whether I knew it or not at the time. I finally found, or thought I'd found, my daddy in X2. It felt like it for a time, but of course my idea of a daddy was so skewed that I was easily fooled. Had I looked more closely at X2's parenting of his own boys, I'd have quickly seen that he wasn't qualified to be my daddy, either.

Of course he was never supposed to be my daddy. He was never supposed to fill my emptiness. He was never supposed to make me happy. That was my job, but I was too sick and too needy to see it, and I certainly had no idea how to do it.

To further confuse things, for a while X2 and I thought we'd have all four boys, my two and his two. His ex was also entertaining the idea of leaving her boys with him. Once she found out that it was I he was with, she changed her mind. She quickly remarried and took her boys to live out of state. I didn't think it was fair to X2 to have to raise my boys if he couldn't have, could barely even see, his own. Another reason.

But I'm being honest here, so I will admit that probably the biggest reason was that I needed X2 all to myself. I might have resented my kids if they'd been with us and he'd paid any attention to them. As second-guessing goes, I can't be sure that would have worked any better, and it might have been worse for all of us.

There was one good thing about it, though. My kids were with us most weekends and all summer long. I was basically happier myself, so it was easier for me to be happy with them. They were older by then, too, so they were able to entertain themselves and weren't utterly dependent on me for everything. In that, I had the best time with them. X1 had all the responsibility, while I had all the fun. As revenge goes, it was pretty perfect. Like in most cases of divorce, though, it was far from perfect for Mike and Jason.

Mike, who was eleven, was all for staying with his dad. Even then, he recognized that his dad needed him, and he more or less became the father in the equation, not only to his dad, but also to Jason. Jason, who was much younger, just went along with it all, even though in reality he felt abandoned by me. As time went on, he felt abandoned by his dad and ultimately by Mike, too, when Mike went off to college

If I had known then what I know now, I might have done things differently. I'm just not sure exactly how, or what might have worked better. I don't think there was any perfect solution.

When we finally divorced, I gave X1 full custody of the boys. I felt that if he had the responsibility, he ought to have the control. I trusted his love for them. I didn't feel as though I was abandoning them, only that they would be with their dad. Joint custody was not an option in those days. Had it been, it would have been a much better option, easily seen on hindsight.

After the final divorce hearing, X1 and I went out to breakfast together. I bought. He was happy with the arrangement, and his attorney even said to me that I had a lot of class.

It didn't all go downhill after that, but too much of it did. X1 did the best he could.

I lived with X2 for a year and a half before we got married. I've read that Edith Galt, second wife of President Woodrow Wilson, purportedly said, "When Woodrow proposed to me, I was so surprised that I nearly fell out of bed."[41] They married in 1915. I doubt she meant it literally.

One Sunday, our pastor gave a message about sexual purity in which he challenged anyone who was living together to stop it. I could tell that X2 had something rolling around in his head for the rest of the day. He later said that he was quite sure the pastor had been looking right at him. That night, as we were lying in bed, X2 turned to me and set some rules. The first was that there would be no screwing around and no divorce. Then, he said that I didn't have to have dinner ready when he got home, and he didn't have to be home in time for dinner. He'd eaten a lot of cold food served by an angry wife in his first marriage. Finally, his third rule was that he could regularly visit his mother in Germany.

I could agree to all of that. Apparently, though, the rules only applied to me, because twenty-five years later, it was he who screwed around and wanted a divorce. For me, even the thought of being unfaithful to him could make me cry.

Then he proposed. It wasn't the first proposal made in bed and probably not the last. I asked him, "Are you sure?" I was a bit concerned that he felt coerced by the message that morning. He said he was sure.

We got married in May. X2 wanted a "romantic" wedding. He checked with our church, but they could offer only the main auditorium or a room with folding chairs. Neither was particularly romantic. The church also required some serious pre-marital counseling, which X2 didn't want to do. I'm sure they'd have required us to stop living together until we were married. They would have been right.

Instead, we found a simple, old, country church just down the road. We went in to see the pastor, and after about five minutes, he said that we were so well suited that he would be happy to marry us. Then we started interviewing him. We wanted to know whether he himself was a believer and whether Christ was proclaimed there as Lord. Looking back on that now, I shudder at what a couple of hypocrites we were. We were living outside of God's way, even as we

---

[41]   http://www.jumbojoke.com/presidential_quotes.html

were insisting on a.Christ-centered church. I can imagine that God shuddered, too.

One day I was wandering around a small local shopping mall, and I found a little kiosk flower shop there. The owner's name was Marie, and she became one of my best friends. Ours being a second marriage, I wanted to keep things simple, so I had her supply me with three white roses to carry, and matching boutonnieres for the guys. I spent a whole eighteen dollars on my wedding flowers, and she even delivered them to the church.

I got a lovely dress from a local boutique. X2's boys already had light blue suits, which went well with the blue interior of the church, so we bought Mike and Jason similar suits. X2's sons were his best men and stood with him in front, while mine were my boys of honor and they both escorted me down the aisle. We all got married.

I was absolutely ecstatic—so happy I was practically hysterical. I couldn't stop laughing—I laughed all the way down the aisle, and when I got to the altar, I had to pull myself together. The only other time I've felt that degree of elation was when my son Larry came back into my life.

It was a beautiful, simple service. The church had provided a soloist, and while those attending enjoyed her wonderful rendition of "The Lord's Prayer," X2 and I knelt before the altar and confessed our sin in living together.

We didn't hire a professional photographer; half of the people who came to our wedding had cameras, and they all took pictures and gave us copies. We posed with the four boys in front of the altar, and to their later dismay, that picture shows Mike and Jason holding hands.

We took the out-of-town guests out to eat at a restaurant, and then we had a party at the house. Someone had decorated the garage door and the mailbox, and one of the neighbors ran over to congratulate us, saying she'd not known we weren't already married. I happened to mention this to one of the wedding guests, a friend from church. Apparently I was a bit flippant, saying something to the effect that I didn't much care what the neighbors thought. My friend took offense at that and didn't stay very long. She avoided me for years after that and finally confronted me about it. She felt that I had disrespected God and that I *should* have cared what the neighbors thought. She was right too.

Once we were married, it was a lot easier for me to be at church. Still, during the continuation of the marriage, I was not a fully devoted follower of Christ. I talked the talk, as one friend said, but I didn't walk the walk. God stayed close to me, though.

The day after our wedding, X2 and I were having a picnic in bed. It was one of our favorite things to do. We'd bought our favorite goodies, like shrimp and chocolate, and we spread them out on a tray on the bed between us. Unknown to X2, he had some sort of allergy to mint. He ate an Andes candy—chocolate over a mint filling—and the mint closed up his throat, trapping the chocolate. He was getting absolutely no air. There he was, buck naked, on his hands and knees on the bed, rocking back and forth to try and dislodge the chocolate from his throat. It didn't work; neither did my pounding him on the back.

Posters showing the Heimlich maneuver had just started being displayed in restaurants at that time. I'd never looked closely at one. I'd just barely spotted them out of the corner of my eye, only enough to sort of know the maneuver existed. When, after a minute or so, X2 was still obviously getting no air, I screamed, "Jesus, help me!" He brought those posters to my mind and placed my arms around X2 and He did a Heimlich. I didn't do it. Jesus did.

Once X2 got his first breath of air, I lost it. I cried uncontrollably, and then I started laughing hysterically. X2 had to hold and console me for half an hour.

I got into a disagreement with the boss at the HVAC place. They had billed a customer for a bunch of air-conditioning units that hadn't actually been installed, assuming that they must have been. Those units had been on back order for months, and I'd been calling every day, to no avail. Meanwhile, I'd try to talk to the boss about it, but he'd be on the phone and I'd stand in the hallway, unacknowledged, waiting for him to finish. After five or ten minutes, I'd give up and go back up to my office because I had other work to do. I got called on the carpet, not because we still didn't have the units, but because I'd not told him. I was livid, and I quit. It was actually just as well; I was living much farther away by then, and it was a long drive every day, especially in the winter.

I got a job at a much smaller HVAC company, just a few blocks from our house. It was a totally different environment—a "one-girl" office—and much less stressful. I didn't need insurance, so I just worked by the hour, often leaving early when things were slow.

One morning when I arrived at work, I found a computer on my desk. I didn't know a thing about computers. We had an accountant, the boss's cousin. They both wanted me to do the accounting so that the cousin could just oversee and do the tax returns. It was an early Apple computer, and they bought a canned accounting program, and then jury-rigged the process to get around its limitations and make it work for us.

I took two accounting courses at a local junior college. The first week there were about thirty people in the class, most of whom were kids just out of high school. There were also a few others who, like myself, were older, and were there because of their jobs. The kids dropped like flies. By the third week, there were only seven or eight of us left. The kids didn't have a clue—they'd never heard of things like accounts receivable or accounts payable. Not knowing what these things were made it hard for them to learn how to account for them.

For me, it was great. I don't retain what I read, but for this class, I'd read the chapter to get the drift, and then I'd immediately do about four hours of practice exercises. It was hands-on and I nailed it. Of course, my having office experience helped; I knew what accounts payable and receivable were. I aced the course both sessions. I even have the highest college grade point average in my family—a 4.0—for my two little courses.

I didn't have my own office at this new company, but I had my own bathroom, since I was the only female there. I'd occasionally clean the office, and I kept the vacuum cleaner in my bathroom. The boss had brought in some things he'd gotten when his father died, things his wife understandably didn't want at the house. One was a large framed picture that he didn't bother to hang, so it just stood against the wall for months.

One day as I was vacuuming, I moved the picture to clean underneath it. There was the biggest, blackest, ugliest spider I'd ever seen. I didn't want to squish it on the carpet, so I just swept it up in the vacuum cleaner. It was an old canister-type vacuum cleaner with a long metal hose. Every time I'd go to the bathroom, I'd look at it and wonder whether that spider was going to crawl back out. It took him a while, but sure enough, a week later, he appeared on the concrete bathroom floor. I stepped on him. I still feel a bit bad about it.

We would regularly sub-contract for various services that fell outside the scope of HVAC. One day the boss was reading through a proposal for some roofing work. It read, "All roofing derbis will be removed from the job site." He scratched his head, looked up at me and asked, "What the hell is derbis?" It even took me a minute to untangle that typo, but ever since, I've used the word *derbis* regularly. It's always good for a laugh.

I traded in dear old Elsie and her freckles for a Mazda RX-7 with a 5-speed stick shift. I'd had a bit of experience driving a stick, but I was far from proficient. After a week or so, since I hadn't stripped the gears or blown the clutch, I thought I might try downshifting. So, as I approached a red light, still going maybe 40 MPH, I threw the car into second gear and nearly threw myself through the windshield. Oh— you're supposed to goose it first?

Grandma (my aunt) Ruth would come to stay with us for a week or so from time to time. She was in her eighties. One night, X2 served her some vanilla ice cream and he put some chocolate liqueur on it for her. We were about to leave the house to go for a walk; good thing we didn't. She started choking, and I did my second Heimlich. It did the trick, but Judy thinks I fractured her back doing it. Could be, but Grandma Ruth went on living until her mid-nineties.

After a couple of years at the small HVAC company, I left and started my own business in my home. Basically, I provided office services for small contractors who didn't need a full-time office or secretary. The only thing I didn't offer was answering service. This saved my clients overhead and expenses for office employees, and since I'd only work about ten hours per week for each of them, I could charge a hefty hourly rate. I could write off my office and other expenses, and the best part was that I could work any time of the day I wanted, even in my jammies.

It was a pretty sweet arrangement. I handled their insurance, did their payroll and union reports, and anything else these guys had no clue about or didn't want to bother with. I even had a joint checking account with one guy, and I paid his personal bills. He would have let me sign his corporate checks as well, but I said no, not unless I was a corporate officer, which I didn't want to be.

Around this time, X1 had some problems and I didn't feel he was able to care properly for Mike and Jason. I filed a lawsuit to regain custody of my boys. It didn't work out—apparently courts are more concerned with upholding their own earlier rulings than they are about the welfare of children. The irony, of course, is that I'd chosen to give custody to X1 in the first place; it was never the court's idea.

Mike was very much into Star Wars, and he'd left his At-At, a large toy warrior space ship that looked kind of like a dinosaur with long legs, at my house. When I realized that the two of them would not be living with me after all, I was very sad, and I wrote a poem about it.

GRAY THEY STAND

Crissy Shreve

Gray they stand on my linoleum
Ready to attack,
No enemy in sight—
But, oh, how they make me know my lack.
It won't be right
Till my sweet boys are back.

I'd planned a great addition to our house, but just as we were about to go out for bids, we noticed a "For Sale" sign in front of a house two blocks from where we lived. The sign said that the lot was five acres. We couldn't imagine how they could be hiding that much property right there in the middle of tract house suburbia, but sure enough, it was in a small, unincorporated area. The front yard was a full acre, and the house sat on the next acre back. Behind that there were three more acres of trees, or perhaps more accurately, jungle. The story went that the old Swede who'd built the house would plant a tree every time his wife got on his nerves. Apparently she did a lot of that.

X2 loved the property and I saw potential in the house. "I can fix it," I said.

The house had been built in the early nineteen-fifties, and everything in it was original. Unfortunately, little of it was in good condition. There were pink and yellow glass tiles that were falling off the kitchen and bathroom walls, and, if you can believe it, the bathroom ceiling. There was a built-in spice rack with a flour sifter in the kitchen. It was like nothing we'd ever seen before. The spice rack held large and small glass drawers and bottles made in Sweden. It was really neat, and it was the only thing I salvaged and incorporated into the new kitchen. I was even able to find some additional glass inserts on the Internet.

A few pieces of furniture had been left in the house, one of which was a small wooden kitchen table and a couple of chairs. I spent the next month or so sitting at that table redesigning the layout of the house, including three additions. One squared off the very strange triangular front entry, another extended out the recessed dining room, and the third was a huge two levels at the back of the house. This took us from two bedrooms to five, one of which was right next to the new entry, and I used it as my office.

It took a full year to finish, but it turned out really well. Wanting something different and unusual, X2 had picked up a catalog of fireplaces in Germany, and we incorporated one of those designs into the lower level family room. An old Russian guy turned up one day to build that fireplace. He had all sorts of ideas, like I should use wood where I wanted ceramic tile. He really wanted to do it his way. I sat on a milk crate arguing with him for an hour, then I finally got smart and told him that he could do whatever he wanted to do, but that before I wrote a check, that fireplace was going to look exactly like the print and the picture. Sure enough, it did.

There are two things I won't hear from men who do work for me. The first is, "Lady, that's the way we always do it," and the second is, "It's easier that way." Men never fail to think I couldn't possibly know what I'm talking about.

One time I was at the hardware store looking around for a somewhat unusual item I already owned, but needed another. I wish I could remember what it was. To be fair, it wasn't something most people have or know about. The "helpful hardware man" asked whether he could help me. I told him what I was looking for. He said, "Lady, there is no such thing." I thanked him sweetly, and then proceeded to find the item myself. Of course I had to go back and show it to him.

The original fireplace in the living room was two-sided and quite delightful, but it was an ugly brick, and it came straight down to the floor. We redid the mantel and added a brick ledge around the bottom. Then the whole thing had to be painted. I bought primer and spent nearly eight hours brushing it on. Those old bricks sucked that primer right in, but the two finish coats of gloss paint went on quickly and smoothly. It was beautiful and unique when it was done.

While the rehab of the house was in the works, I'd be there every day, watching everything that was happening, and being a general pain in the neck. I'm good at that, and it was the only way to get things done the way I wanted them. I finally convinced the workers that it was cheaper for them to do it my way the first time, rather than rip it out and do it again. The construction company's superintendent and I seldom saw eye to eye, and we got into it one day. I only have so much patience for fools, so I walked away. I later heard the guys joking that he'd kicked me off the job. Right. He was fired from the company not long afterwards.

One very hot summer day, I walked in the front door to see the head carpenter running out the back door in his underwear. He'd been cutting off his jeans, and I showed up just as he was finishing. It was quite funny watching his tighty-whitey-clad butt disappearing through the door. He didn't want me to see it, even though he apparently wasn't so concerned about the neighbors.

I've not had good luck with cabinetmakers over the years. Two died, another took forever to get the job done, and another just quit building cabinets altogether. What's a woman to do?

The first one was a friend's brother. He'd just moved back into the area from out of state, and he needed a place to live. We needed cabinets. He moved in, but before he could start building the cabinets, he had two heart attacks, the second fatal. We'd tried hard to talk to him about God, but he wasn't interested. His comment to us the night before his final surgery was, "Murphy will be with me." I guess he was right.

There were quite a few feral cats at the old farm next door, and when this guy lived at the house, he'd feed them. He was utterly shocked when he tried to pet one of them and it bit him.

FROM THE ANALS
A FUNNY GUY

X2 really was a funny guy. One time he got distracted and tried to light a cigarette without having first taken one out of the pack, and said, "I nearly lit my nose." Another time he was trying to enter the bank, and he applied the right amount of pull needed to open the door, but it was locked. His comment was, "I nearly tore off my hand." It wasn't just what he did that was funny, but what he said about it.

X2 was quite the able gardener, and he made a number of beautiful flower gardens around the house. One time he couldn't identify a particular plant, but he watered and fertilized it with all due tenderness until it finally grew to several feet high, without producing anything of any value. It was finally determined to be a weed. X2 yanked it with somewhat less tenderness and a few choice words.

X2's English was wonderful and his accent virtually non-existent, despite his having come to the United States at age nineteen with no knowledge of English whatsoever. He did still have a few quirks I called his "style," such as "making" an oil change or a driver's license, eating at restaurongs (sic), and saying "with other words" instead of "in other words." He never used a turn signal—he always "put his indicator out."

Not so obvious—in fact, had he not told me, I would never have known—he did math in his head in German. It makes perfect sense; that was the language in which he'd learned it. I am fairly proficient in counting and understanding numbers in German, but I can't imagine trying to use it to add a column of numbers. I suppose I could do it, but it would take me two weeks.

He dreamed bilingually too, and I could often tell when he was dreaming in German. One night during a nightmare he started talking in his sleep, crying, *"Hilfe, hilfe!"*[42] I of course had to poke him and say, "Can I *hilfe* you?"

---

[42]   Of course *hilfe* is the German word for "help."

When I was having back problems, X2 had a dream that he was wearing a white suit and Fella the dog was jumping up on him with muddy paws. X2 gave Fella a swift knee to the chest to ward him off, but of course it wasn't Fella in the bed, it was I, and he kneed me right in the sorest part of my back. I don't know what language that dream was in, but you can be quite sure what I had to say about it was in "French!"

We were disagreeing on something one day and I was being my usual argumentative self. X2 said to me, "Crissy, *must* you be so vituperative?" I'd never even heard the word! I had to go look it up! He'd pick up new words from *Reader's Digest,* and although I'd know most of them, he'd get me from time to time.

X2 had a colonoscopy. The doctor removed several polyps from his intestine. Afterwards, he was discussing it on the phone with his son (step-Mike), who is a doctor. X2 asked what would happen if the polyps came back and step-Mike replied that they would have to repeat the procedure. X2 said, "You mean they'd have to go through all that crap all over again?" Then he giggled and added, "Literally."

"T—(his first ex) sucks pickles," said X2 one day while we were eating at Burger King. The kids and I had been busy making up phrases for combinations of letters on the license plates in the parking lot. X2 had not been participating up to that point, but he just couldn't resist when he saw "TSP" on one of the license plates. Mike and I still regularly use the phrase "sucks pickles" long after X2's departure from the scene.

One day X2 and I stopped in to see my friend Louise who had a particularly dour boyfriend at the time. As we were about to leave, the guy asked X2 what kind of gas mileage he was getting on the Lincoln. X2 said, "Well, it's not too bad, but I do have to shut off the car when I get gas so that the pump can keep up." I laughed all the way home, but neither Louise or the boyfriend even cracked a smile.

Animals, children, and females of all ages always loved X2. He was famous for smiling at the homely woman in the tollbooth and asking how she was doing. I stopped being jealous after the first few times he did this. He just liked to make someone's day. He'd also been known on a number of occasions to be the only person around who could hold a baby and it would go to sleep. He was just snuggly, I guess, like a big teddy bear. One time an elder at our church named

Betty shook X2's hand and said, "Oh, I just love those great big warm paws." Yeah, so did I.

Animals came to X2. When we were in line waiting for a ferry out in the Seattle area, a crow came and sat on the side-view mirror of the car and ate grapes out of his hand. A burro stuck its head in the car window near Yellowstone Park and gave him a kiss on the cheek. I'm not making that up; I have a picture. He's had chipmunks and pigeons sitting on his knee and eating out of his hand. I also have a picture of him trying to tempt a goose, but geese are stupid—or perhaps smart? X2 was holding out apiece of food and saying, "Come to Papa." The goose didn't buy it—one of few times X2 was rejected.

Possums are definitely stupid, and near-sighted to boot. One night, just at dusk, X2 was wandering around in our back woods and he heard a rustle in the bushes. He stopped to see what it was and a possum walked right over his foot and then proceeded to walk, not climb, up a tree. Another time, we saw a young possum up in the crook of a tree branch, and I'd swear he was smiling down at us.

On vacation in Florida, we had been across the waterway for dinner and were coming back over the bridge. Next to our hotel was the Bonnet Estate, which is owned by the city of Fort Lauderdale. The lady who owned it had deeded it to the city with the understanding that she could spend winters there as long as she lived. It was closed to the public during the time she was there, and the beach in front of the estate even had signs saying "Private Beach." The city of Fort Lauderdale must've thought they'd gotten a good deal, but we were told that she was 105 years old in 1995 (she died in 1997) and was still going strong. Meanwhile, the city maintained the property. Such a deal!

Anyway, there are lots of monkeys living on the Bonnet estate and they play on the wall between that property and the hotel. You can usually see them around four o'clock in the afternoon if you're sitting by the pool. I had only seen the monkeys once at that point and as we crossed the bridge, I saw lots of small animals to the north of the hotel, in the Hugh Birch Park, which had also been a private estate deeded to the city. I thought it was some of the monkeys from the Bonnet estate, so I said we should go see them.

We went across the street and into the parking area and saw a lady feeding Oreo cookies to a hundred raccoons. She was ready to leave (escape) and so she handed her last few Oreos to me. I suddenly had all one hundred raccoons at my feet, and since I'm not fond of raccoons, I handed the cookies to X2 who then had them all around his feet and up his jeans leg to his waist. Not all one hundred, but three or four of them. Of course they ate the cookies out of his hand.

We didn't have any more food, so we went back to our hotel. The next night, just before dark, X2 asked, "It is time to go feed our raccoons?" We stopped at the 7-Eleven, bought a loaf of bread, and headed over to the park.

X2 was once again knee-deep, literally, in raccoons, when I happened to notice a very big sign: "PLEASE DON'T FEED THE RACCOONS." Smaller print pointed out that raccoons are wild animals and could be rabid or have other diseases, and were known to bite. It also said that, if fed, the raccoons would lose their natural fear of humans and their ability to forage for their own food. We decided it was best not to continue, so X2 closed up the bag of bread and we headed off.

The raccoons were following us, so we didn't cross the street, but went down the block instead, trailing raccoons. Most of them gave it up after we'd gone about half a block, but one little guy really wanted that bread, so he grabbed onto X2's pant leg with his teeth and hung on. After dragging the raccoon for several steps, X2 finally got the message and dropped the bag of bread.

X2 hated crows, though, and from time to time he would find a dead one in our back jungle. He'd happily bury it, telling me that there'd been another "crow funeral."

I still hated raccoons, so of course we had plenty of them around. They'd been invading our attic for several years. We had a company come in to set baited traps (tuna fish or liverwurst worked best) on the roof to catch them—at 125 bucks a pop. We probably relieved our town of most of its raccoon population over a three-year period. One time I asked the guy who set up the traps what they did with the raccoons they caught. He told me that they "dropped them off" in a forest preserve about 20 miles north of us. "Right," said X2, when I told him that, "and I bet I know right where they drop off the raccoons they catch up there. Now that's job security."

The raccoons chewed through the exterior soffit on our house and settled happily into the attic. Raccoons will return to the place they were born to bear their young, so this became a recurring problem. After several episodes, and while the last batch was still in residence, X2 went up on the roof to check out the soffit. He had his *face* right next to the hole they'd made, with Mama raccoon and several babies inside chattering angrily at him. I stood on the ground below telling God that I wasn't sure whether I'd rather X2'd not get bitten in the face or not get attacked and fall off the roof. After that, however, Mama raccoon decided to move out and X2 patched the hole.

Unfortunately, the raccoons had been in the area of the attic that was right above my office. X2 went off to Europe, and the *fleas*, no longer having the raccoons to attack, decided to seek out human prey. Fleas, it turns out (I did get a good education through all this), pick on *one* person in a household and leave the rest alone. Now, had X2 been there, they'd have picked him, but since he wasn't, they were stuck with me. I finally got that problem solved with the help of Mr. Friendly Exterminator and a can of flea killer. But there's more.

The following fall, Mike and I (ironically) had just come home from the flea market. It was cold out, and pouring rain, and we were warming up in the kitchen with a cup of coffee. X2 was of course away again. (I called him that guy that lived in Europe but came around every so often and masqueraded as my husband).

Mike and I heard this very big bang in the garage. We went out to investigate, and saw that a big chunk of the ceiling drywall was hanging down, as if it were hinged, right above the sink. All the insulation from above and buckets of rain were pouring into the sink. It was the first cold spell of the season and the raccoons had been trying to get in. They'd gnawed a new hole in the roof, but at least this time they didn't get into the attic. I do get lucky every once in a while.

X2 always had his own unique but effective way of dealing with bad situations. His office at work was right next to the loading dock, separated only by a concrete block wall. The trash dumpsters were kept next to that wall on the dock side, and the garbage truck would back up to the door. The garbage man would make a lot of noise getting the dumpster emptied into his truck. X2 would be on the phone with a customer, or trying to concentrate on quoting while this was going on, and it got to be a bit annoying. One day when the garbage man was there, X2 walked out to the dock and handed him a twenty-dollar bill saying, "I just wanted to thank you for being so quiet when you pick up the garbage. I guess you must know that I'm sitting right on the other side of the wall." The garbage man was quiet from that day on.

X2 did that number on me, too. One day he told me how much he appreciated my buttoning the top button on his shirts when I hung them up after washing. I guess the collar area gets less wrinkled while hanging if the top button is buttoned. I started doing that, and I'm sure I'd never done it before.

When we were in Houston for one of step-Mike's many graduations, we were running a bit late getting out of the hotel. X2 was anal about being on time. Our room was on the 9th floor. We got into the elevator and X2 pushed the button for the 1st floor. The elevator decided to stop at the 6th floor, although no one got in. Apparently someone had pushed the button and then changed his mind.

X2 flew out the 6th floor door, which instantly closed behind him. There was no time for me to say or do anything, he was just *gone*— the ultimate disappearing act. Of course, the thing stopped again one floor down and there I was, all alone in the elevator, laughing hysterically. People got on, and I couldn't stop laughing long enough to tell them why.

Meanwhile, X2 was still up on the 6th floor. He hit the down button, the elevator came, he got on, and it went all the way *up* to the 12th floor before heading back down. I stood in the lobby watching the arrow . . . still laughing.

X2 had a marvelous sense of humor and was a master of the quick comeback. My cousin and her family came to see us in Naples (Florida). Her son Drew was cruising around on his roller blades, showing off. He asked X2, "Can you do this?" and then immediately fell smack on his butt. X2, without even cracking a smile, said, "Yep, *that* I can do."

One morning X2 walked into the bathroom where the light was much brighter than in the bedroom. He looked down at his socks and saw that one was black and the other navy blue. Having pointed that out, he giggled and said, "And I've got another pair in the drawer just like them."

As I write this, I have a horrendous cold. As X2 would say, "Anybody want to buy a nose? Slightly used, but it runs good."

My cousin and her two kids, Steph and Drew, lived with us for a while. Drew was just a baby, but Steph, age four, was the entertainment most days. She and X2 were a thing. If he was sitting, she was on his lap. One time they were eating lunch out on the deck and just as X2 was trying to put a pickle in his mouth, Steph, who was always talking and usually with her hands, reached out in some exuberant gesture and knocked the pickle out of his hand. It flew across the deck. This would not have been particularly funny except that she looked at him and asked, "Why did you throw your pickle over there?"

So then she decided to "help" X2 clean up. She proceeded to put the four-inch lid from the pickles (maybe X2 ought to just give up pickles?) "on" the mayonnaise jar which just happened to have a five-inch opening. While X2 was busy fishing the pickle lid out of the mayonnaise, which in itself was a messy proposition, Steph knocked over his orange juice.

Steph was a bit hyper. One time when she was bouncing off the walls, her mom brought her to me saying, "You'd better take this kid or else I'm going to kill her," then headed back downstairs. This was one of the times God helped me know what to do. Steph was out of control, screaming and crying and flailing her arms, and for no apparent reason. I sat down on the kitchen floor with her, put her on my lap in front of me and wrapped my arms tightly around her, and just held on. It took some time, maybe fifteen minutes or so, but she finally settled down and fell asleep.

Afterwards, I wondered why holding her like that had helped. I think I understand—something inside of her was making her feel like she was going to burst out of her skin. She was just little, five or so, and whatever it was, she couldn't contain it on her own. By holding her, I must have contained it for her.

Looking back at my own childhood, as well as to the time when my son Mike was little, I see that both of us were probably hyper to a degree. Nobody knew how to deal with me, and I didn't know how to deal with Mike. I understand now that it's not a matter of a child's being bratty. It's a matter of parents or caregivers not understanding what's going on. Of course much more is known today about hyperactivity than when I was a kid, or when Mike was.

Steph was ultimately diagnosed with A.D.D. and Ritalin was prescribed for her. Although it helped her immensely, and she was much easier to deal with, she became almost zombie-like, or at least it seemed that way to me. I missed her exuberance.

My favorite of many delightful memories of Steph is the time she came to me saying, "Aunt Crissy, can I see your biggamajigga?" I had to have her show me what she meant. Bet you can't figure it out either.[43]

The sweetest thing X2 ever said was one day when we were out driving around together and the weather was dark and dreary. He said, "No problem—we'll make sunshine in our hearts."

Lest I paint too pretty a picture of X2, he did have some quirks. He had an employee who would steal tools and then try to sell them back to him. X2 told me about this, and guess what I said. What would *you* have said? X2 got furious with *me* for suggesting he fire this guy!

Some time after that, a neighbor told X2 about a small company in our town that was going under. The owner was looking for someone to bail it out. X2 invested a healthy chunk of money in this company and installed me in the office to take over the finances. It didn't take me long to see that the previous owner had been milking the company to death, using company credit cards to buy things for his wife, like a coat, etc. I told the owner that that would need to stop, that we weren't looking to underwrite his personal lifestyle. The owner complained to X2. And guess what? Once again, X2 was furious with *me*.

X2 had his own reasons in both cases, but I can't begin to understand them, so I won't even try to explain them. I do know that he seemed unable to confront anyone except me. For a while, I thought that was a good thing—that I was someone, perhaps the only one, he trusted enough to get angry with, without fear of being abandoned. Ultimately, though, I think that these situations and others like it led to his hating me. He mostly wanted me to understand, I think, regardless of whether or not I did.

---

[43]   It was my magnifying glass.

WHILE YOU ARE AWAY

Crissy Shreve

The trouble is,
That while you are away
I need you here
To soothe my sadness
That you are away.

If only I could tell you
In the time we are together
All the things I tell you
When you're only in my mind.

CHAPTER TWENTY-FOUR

REHABBING

I continued to work on the house, a never-ending project, but I liked it that way. I didn't want to try to do everything at once; the doing of it was the fun of it. One of my greatest pleasures was to design a space and watch it turn out exactly as I'd pictured it.

One of the guys I worked for gave me a wonderful old pedestal barber's sink and a claw-foot bathtub. Shortly afterwards, we happened to travel to Sacramento, California, home of Mac the Antique Plumber. I bought a great old forties-style toilet there, similar to those we'd seen at Hearst Castle, and had it shipped home. I replaced the pink and yellow glass tile with simple square white tile halfway up the walls. The whole bathroom was white, and I had no preconceived notion for a color or pattern for finishing it.

I told the woman at the wallpaper store that I needed something wonderful and dramatic for an all-white old-fashioned bathroom. Just that morning, she'd spotted something in a new book that she thought I'd like. It was a fairly wide swan border on dark green with black accents. Perfect.

I put the swan border just above the tile over dark green paper. It was striking. One visiting friend spent an inordinately long time in there, and finally emerged saying that she never wanted to leave—she wanted to live in that bathroom. She'd sleep in the tub.

When step-Mike brought Martha home to meet us for the first time, she and I instantly bonded, and the two of us were determined that it would be a permanent arrangement. It took step-Mike a few years to catch on, but when he finally proposed to her, he did it one morning right there in that green bathroom while they were brushing their teeth. I believe his exact words were, "So, you think we should get married?" Well, at least the bathroom was romantic.

We occasionally had problems with kids in our back woods. Before we bought the property, no one had paid much attention to their playing there, but we were concerned about liability. We didn't want some kid falling out of a tree and hurting himself. Signs did no good.

One time we found a brand-new tent from K-Mart, all set up and complete with an air mattress and a tube of KY Jelly. Some enterprising young stud had plans. He'd cleverly left the receipt in the tent, so we packed it all up and returned it to K-Mart. A few days later, we noticed a clearly disappointed kid snooping around and looking in our garage. He didn't have the guts to admit what he was looking for, and we didn't enlighten him.

At one point there was a small fire back in our woods, but we didn't see it, just heard from the neighbors that the fire department had been back there. They didn't come to talk to us; apparently they didn't know we owned the property. Some interesting tall spiky weeds sprouted up from the blackened soil, and we collected some and put them in a vase. We saw something similar when we visited Mount St. Helens in Oregon, about ten years after one of its eruptions. The trees had been mown down by lava, all in one direction, sort of like fallen matchstick dominoes. It was surreal. The unusual foliage that grew in the midst of the devastation really impressed us. Dead as the area was, new life was appearing, and some of it was actually quite beautiful.

Another time, we caught a kid trying to cut down one of our nicer trees with a hatchet. We asked him why he'd want to do that. He didn't know. We confiscated the hatchet and told him that, if he wanted it back, his parents would have to come and ask us for it.

We bought a lawn tractor that just happened to be black with red striping. We figured that X2's black car, appropriately named "Mark," and my red "Mazda" must have procreated, so we named the tractor "Mazdark." The kids loved driving the tractor and especially learning to back it up with the trailer cart attached.

We then acquired an old yellow full-sized tractor that only had one headlight, so of course it had to be named "Pididdle." When Jason was about twelve, we put him to work removing a bush. He dug and dug, but those roots just weren't going to come out. Finally, he hopped on Pididdle, attached a chain, and pulled them. We watched him driving by with the roots in the bucket, and the biggest grin on his face. A job well done.

We took a trip to Arizona and we went spelunking. It was a real cave, not one with lights, sidewalks and a guided tour. Being somewhat claustrophobic, I wasn't sure how I'd do in a cave, but I was pleasantly surprised and I loved it. We went with people who were experienced spelunkers and knew the cave well. It wasn't terribly big, but it had all the right elements. We entered at ground level by slithering on our bellies through a horizontal open slice between some rocks. If you didn't know the cave was there, you'd never have noticed it. It was actually very comfortable inside. There was plenty of good air and it was neither too cold nor too hot. The ground was cool and silty.

We slithered another ten feet or so after entering, then the passage widened enough for us to crawl. There was one place where we had to sit, slide down a bit, turn around, and then slide down some more. In another area, we had to chimney down a narrow vertical space. None of it was extreme. There was a notebook and pen in a plastic gallon milk jug inside the cave, and it was exciting to add our names to the list of visitors. When we came to the main grotto, we all sat down and turned off our headlamps. We'd never really seen dark before. It was the utter absence of light.

I turned forty and became a grandmother; well, technically I was a grandfather's wife, but it was all the same to me. Oma has always been my favorite name.

I was becoming increasingly aware that something was missing—in me. I couldn't say what was missing; whatever it was simply wasn't there. I started seeing a therapist who worked in the field of Bioenergetics—bodywork. I am convinced that God led me to this type of therapy because it is designed to get through one's experiential barriers and in touch with feelings that hide unrecognized in the body. It's as if there's a wall between the head and the heart. You just can't get to the heart via the head.

I had missed something in my very early life, but because it was during my pre-conscious infant time, I couldn't be consciously in touch with exactly what it was. I can only assume that it was a combination of my mother's absence during my first several months of life and my grandmother Nana's disconnected parenting. By that I mean that she was there but she wasn't. I suspect that that's the root cause of my lifelong feeling of loneliness, even, or perhaps even more, when I've got people around me.

I crave deep connection, but of course I gravitate towards people, especially men, who aren't capable of deep connection. In its absence, I've always found it easier to be alone than to be ignored.

My task in therapy became to re-parent myself. Until I was able to learn how to do that, the therapist acted as my "good enough" mother. She even held me and fed me a bottle.

I also discovered that it was okay for me to take care of myself; in fact it was crucial that I do it. When I'd be at the dentist getting fluoride treatments, for example, it was okay to say I was going to sit up so that the liquid wouldn't be choking me and running down my chin.

My therapist said, "If you don't take care of yourself, who will? If you only take care of yourself, what good are you?" She said it was like being on an airplane, where they tell you to put the oxygen mask on yourself first, before you put one on someone else. Such a simple concept. I've never liked having to take care of anyone else. It's always taken all I had just to survive. I discovered that taking care of myself well was different than mere survival.

What changed the most was that my understanding went from "I am the screwed up result of all my life experiences (sins I committed and those committed against me)" to "I am the product of my life experiences and God has brought me through all of it. In the process, He's built me up to be uniquely who I am, and He has a place and a purpose for me."

The therapist pointed out one time that I never complained about X2. I didn't. I can't decide, even now, whether I was in denial or whether I truly was happy with him, at least at that time. As I look back at poetry and other things I wrote, I think some of both is true. Even truer, though, is that I wasn't happy with myself.

After a year or so, this particular therapist left the country and I started with another who, although she didn't do exactly the same kind of work, was still very much a part of my re-parenting process. One day she suggested that I "go find my baby." She didn't say much more than that, didn't try to explain or set any rules to the idea. It was one of the best things I've ever experienced. I didn't even ask questions; I just headed out to the toy store and found "Shelby," a beautiful baby doll. I knew her the minute I saw her on the shelf. She became baby "me."

It was interesting to see others in the waiting room or in therapy groups carrying their babies. One woman had a Raggedy Ann doll, clearly representative of how she felt about herself. Everyone's work is different. When I found Shelby, I was focusing on who I "should" have been, not who I had been. The genius of it was that by picking our own babies, we instinctively picked the work we needed to do.

Shelby was, for several years, a huge part of my life. I'd always take her along when we traveled, and I'd carry her with me; I wouldn't stick her in a suitcase. It took me a while to be comfortable with that—at first I worried that people on the airplane would think I was nuts. Then I decided that it didn't matter, they could think what they wanted. One time I saw a middle-aged man carrying a bag with a large stuffed toy alligator in it and I didn't think he was nuts. I just figured he was taking a gift to a grandchild.

X2 got used to Shelby and he even interacted with her on some level. When we were in the motor home, she rode on my lap and I'd point out horses and sheep as we'd pass. Sometimes he would, too. We traveled through the Chattanooga area with some regularity, over Monteagle Mountain, which is pretty scary, and I'd reassure her (and myself) that we were safe going down that steep grade. Shelby's favorite place was Nickajack Lake, which came up shortly after we were down the mountain.

Of course this was all projected, but it was fun watching myself do the things with her that I'd have liked when I was little, and speaking to my own fears through her. Shelby was a little healer in God's hands.

I also had some back problems for several years when I was in my forties. My first shrink had a cheap couch in her living room. I sank practically to the floor when I sat on it. At our first session, I spent nearly an hour on, or perhaps I should say *in*, that couch. Then on the way home, I stopped to visit some friends, and there I sat on a very hard wooden chair. While on that hard chair, my back started hurting, and it was bad. It was all I could do to get up.

My Uncle Austin had a phrase he always used about someone being stupid. He'd say, "Stupid—you know—bent way over like this."

That was exactly how I was—I couldn't stand up straight, and I drove home in agony. I was pretty much incapacitated for several days, and when I was on the phone telling a friend about it, she suggested her chiropractor, who happens to look just like Elizabeth Taylor. Over the next several years, I got to know Dr. Liz quite well and we became friends. X2 and I even went to her wedding. She took good care of my back.

On one of our trips to Arkansas, I noticed that our friend Bea had a really great heating pad. After we returned home, I got one just like it, and the next time I had a back episode, I tried it out—for about three hours. It just felt so good! It was not a good plan, though. All that time on the heating pad turned my muscles to mush. The next morning, I could not get out of bed.

I had X2 call the paramedics, who dutifully turned up and hauled me off to the hospital on a stretcher. It was my first (and so far only) ride in an ambulance. An interesting twist was that the paramedics asked me how I had fallen down the stairs, insinuating that X2 had pushed me. I had to laugh. X2 was the last guy who'd have been likely to be physically abusive.

I spent a night in the hospital and then was released with muscle relaxants and instructions to visit a sports doctor for therapy. There I was given exercises to do to strengthen my abdominal muscles (which support the back). That doctor told me that when the body learns to depend on chiropractic adjustments, it becomes less able to naturally adjust itself.

Maybe, but after a few days, when my back wasn't getting any better, I crawled into Dr. Liz's office, and after being adjusted, walked back out. For a quick fix, nothing could beat Doctor Liz.

A few months later, I visited a local health club, and I told the trainer there that I was a bit fearful of working out because of my bad back. He said there was an exercise that, if I'd do it every morning before I got out of bed, I'd never have back problems again. I said, "Show me."

He had me lie down on the floor on a mat and do a "pelvic tilt." I'm not going to explain it in detail because I can't do so in a way that will clearly communicate how it's done, and I don't want to cause anyone to hurt themselves. I will say, though, that I have shown this exercise to a number of people in the years since and those who have listened to me have had great results, as did I. He was right—I've never had a back problem since. By the way, if you do know how to do this, please lie flat, no pillow under your head!

Dr. Liz took a cruise to Alaska, which included a train ride into the interior. She brought back a book that had a picture of a gorgeous brown Kodiak bear. That bear looked just like X2. I recently met a guy at church who lived in Kodiak when he was in the service. He told me that he had always carried a gun there. Apparently Kodiak bears will eat anything they can catch.

When I was on a group trail ride in Wyoming, we spotted a baby bear. He was adorable. I wanted to get off my horse and go hug him. The leader had another and more intelligent idea, though. He had us all turn our horses around and go in the other direction. Where there is a baby bear, there will be a mama bear not far away, and she's not going to respond well to anyone hugging her baby. Bears may look like they're very gentle and snuggly, but they'll cheerfully tear you to shreds.

To digress slightly, I had a neighbor once who never used the word *bear* alone in a sentence, but always said, "Bears that eat people." According to Wikipedia, bears will eat people, but only if absolutely necessary—we don't taste that good to them. But that reminds me of something along the same lines that I've always used to kid kids about alligators. You don't have to be afraid an alligator will eat you. You won't taste good to him—he'll just bite off your foot and then spit it back out.

So I was in a shop somewhere, and they had a huge brown teddy bear for sale. To give you an idea of the size of this thing, its body was as large as the burliest man you've ever seen, but with much shorter arms and legs. And it looked just like the picture of the Kodiak bear in Dr. Liz's book. Of course I had to buy the silly thing. And of course his name had to be Cody. We already know I like big teddy bears. At least this one wasn't pink.

The dilemma was where to put it. It was too big for our bed, even if I had wanted to evict X2. I found the perfect spot. When we built the house, we put in a bidet and a double-size whirlpool bathtub. We thought we'd use the tub regularly and never use the bidet, but it turned out the other way around. So there sat this huge tub with no one enjoying it.

Cody fit perfectly. People always wanted a tour of our house, and I quickly learned to take a camera along as I showed them around. Invariably they would climb into the tub with Cody and invariably they'd need to have their picture taken with him.

The people in the shop where I bought Cody were quite fond of him and they even made me promise to be good to him. I guess I'm not the only crazy person on the planet. I assured them that I'd love him and take good care of him. On the way home in the car, I had him in the passenger seat, and everyone I passed waved to him and laughed.

I broke my promise, though. When I moved out of the house, I had no place for Cody, either in my apartment or in my first little house. So I left him in the bathtub, and I don't know where he is now. He may still be there. I hope someone is loving him.

Recently I heard a great talk given by Dr. Henry Cloud. It was about happy people, and the first point he made was that happy people are connected. To illustrate his point, he told of a study[44] done with monkeys where, during times of stress, a monkey would be measurably calmer once another monkey was put into his cage. The catch-question from that talk was, "Who's your monkey?"

I don't have a monkey. I'm still single and I've been heard to say that if I ever make any noises about a potential X3, someone should shoot me. And a recent just-for-a-lark foray into the realm of Internet dating pretty much affirmed it. The one guy I really liked turned out to be a registered sex offender. Nope, single's good. I'll tell you more about that later.

But after hearing that message, I briefly pondered the question again and thought about how it's not a monkey I'd want, it's a teddy bear—a big, warm, snuggly human teddy bear. But no. My last teddy bear tore me to shreds.

From time to time, we had young women from Germany stay with us, wanting to work on their English. They acted as my personal assistants in exchange for room and board, and I called them my "gophers," which of course they hated. They would often stay at the house when we were away. One of my "gophers," Ulrike, was with us

---

[44] John Ortberg also mentions this study in his book THE ME I WANT TO BE. It was done by Dr. Harry Harlow. You can find several of his videos on YouTube.

for six months. She was tall, over six feet, and after she'd been there a week, I could no longer find anything in my kitchen cabinets. She'd put everything up high, at her eye level.

Her boyfriend came from Germany and joined us for her last week or two, and we took them on a trip to Florida. She eagerly anticipated his arrival and counted down the days. She'd get annoyed that he didn't write to her often enough, and she called him *Blötman*, which would translate to something like "dumb guy." I put a note on the refrigerator showing the date that he was to arrive, but I spelled it as it sounded to me—Blurtman. She was afraid he'd see it and know what she'd been calling him, until she saw that I'd spelled it as I had. Then she decided it was okay—he'd never even notice it, let alone know what it meant. *Blötman* lived up to his name. His most famous comment was, "Hey, look, they have McDonald's here in America, too!"

En route to Florida, at their insistence, we stopped and visited Ruby Falls, near Chattanooga. X2 and I had passed those signs regularly for years and never stopped. As tourist traps go, it is actually quite wonderful. We took an old rickety elevator way down into the mountain, and then we walked half a mile farther into the cave. The walkway was dimly lit, and at the end we stopped and waited in the dark. Then they turned on the light, and there before us was a beautiful waterfall, deep inside the mountain. Recently I went back there with my son Mike and my granddaughter. This time we were able to walk behind the falls.

One Friday-after-Thanksgiving evening, X2 took Grandma Ruth, my mother, Judy and me for a ride to look at Christmas lights. Out of the blue, my mother piped up with, "A few weeks ago, I had French-fried brains." We all cracked up. X2 nearly drove off the road. My mother was not so amused. Sadly, no description could have fit her better.

My bird-phobic friend Marie and I are a pair of neurotics—put us together and it can get pretty funny. One time we were waiting at a red light. Ahead of us was an overhead trestle we'd have to drive under, and on which two trains were passing each other. When the light changed, Marie floored it and we flew through that underpass. I said, "Oh, good, I didn't want to be under that trestle for long with those two trains on it." She said, "Oh, no, that wasn't it, there were *birds* under there."

Marie lived in an older house that had wood siding. One time she heard something tapping on the wall. Her husband climbed out on the roof over their front porch to investigate and quickly identified the source of the noise. And there was Marie, in panic, with her head sticking out the window and screaming for all the neighbors to hear, "How big *is* that pecker?"

Another time, she and I passed a "Deer Crossing" sign on the road. Marie asked me how the deer knew to cross right there.

As I keep saying, you can't make these things up.

X2 and I took his mother on a trip to Hawaii. Kauai had just been devastated by tornadoes, so we stayed on Maui and the big island of Hawaii. We took helicopter rides on both, taking private tours instead of going with a group. It was pricey, but well worth it.

The first time, I wasn't sure about the helicopter, but I figured I'd know by the time we were fifty feet off the ground whether I'd be okay or not. I sat in the back while X2 sat up front with the pilot. We all wore earphones; it was too loud to hear anything over the roar of the engine. Even in the back seat, it was like being a bird, flying free.

When you're in Hawaii, you are on a volcano. We flew over the Haleakala crater on Maui and then around the perimeter and into the interior. We chased wild goats and pigs. There was a time when you could hire a helicopter to take you deep into the interior to a secluded waterfall and drop you off for a few hours. Apparently that is no longer allowed. That would have been the perfect thing to do.

On Maui, we stayed in Kehei, a more residential town than touristy Lahaina. The temperature stayed between seventy-five and eighty-five all day and all night. The air was amazing—fresh and sweet. Every morning, right outside our rented condo, I'd pick a flower for my hair.

We drove to Hana along a narrow, winding road that hugged the coast, stopping along the way to explore the rain forest. We climbed up to a waterfall and grotto. There were other people there so we couldn't strip and skinny-dip. We hadn't brought suits. Too bad.

Standing in the rain forest, surrounded by lush greenery, I felt God's presence deeply, and I experienced one of what I call my divine moments—a moment when I would not want to be anywhere else, doing anything else, with anyone else.

We rode in a van up to the top of Haleakala at sunrise, but the sun didn't make much of an appearance that particular day. Armed with rain jackets and gloves, we got on bikes and headed downhill. Those bikes were rather primitive, but they had the one component that really mattered: good brakes.

We started out above the clouds and most of the riders, including X1, took off flying. There were no guardrails—the road was narrow and switchback, with big tour buses coming up the other side. I got a little dizzy and got back into the van for a bit. I was afraid I'd either fly off the side of the mountain or run splat into a bus. Once below the clouds, I got back on the bike and went on down from there. It was delightful.

We then spent a few days on the big island of Hawaii, which did not impress me. There wasn't much to do there if you weren't into nightlife. We did take another helicopter ride, though. This time, as a seasoned rider, I took the front seat. We even had the option of going "doors-off," but it was too drizzly. Next time.

X2 persuaded his mother to go along on this ride—big mistake. She spent the entire time in the back seat throwing up, and he spent the entire time handing her one airsickness bag after another. Thanks to that roaring engine, I was blissfully unaware.

Along the coast there was a tall waterfall, and we flew right up to it, just above the water, then slowly rose up in front of it to the top. We flew over an area where lava had taken out the road. It wasn't pretty. We discovered that "black sand" is actually a mixture of lava and sand. I didn't find it particularly attractive.

I did fall in love with Maui, though, and I wanted to go live there. My scheme was to pack up my computer, rent a place for a year, and write. I saw no reason to go indoors at all; just eat, sleep, write, and live on a lanai. X2 didn't like the idea of living there; he was afraid he'd get island fever. I will allow that it's a long ways from . . . well, anywhere, but I was pretty sure that living out in the air would solve that problem. X2 allowed as how he'd come visit me from time to time.

I started making serious plans for my Hawaiian sabbatical, but I didn't get very far. X2 and I started out on a road trip to New England. He needed to stop to see a customer in Detroit on the way, so he suggested we swing by a place in Holland, Michigan, to see what motor homes might be available.

We never made it to New England. We bought a gorgeous six-year-old Blue Bird motor home instead. And I never made it back to Hawaii.

I'm guessing that it shocked X2 that I could consider living apart from him. It certainly wasn't like me, but Hawaii had made that big an impression. The motor home was just as good, though, with the added appeal that it was something we could enjoy together.

X2 decided to semi-retire so that we could travel in the motor home. It didn't take long, though, for him to panic. Part of it was about not going to work every day, something he'd done all his life, and typically of men, was the thing that most defined him. I suspect another part was that it occurred to him that he'd be spending a lot more time with me. He got heavily involved at our church, which took care of the "going to work" aspect.

We still did a lot of traveling in the motorhome, though, and we attended rallies in different parts of the country. Most of the people we met were quite a bit older than we were. We got a healthy dose of senior citizen humor.

Step-Mike, our self-proclaimed "commodian," called our motor home the "COW"—Condo On Wheels. Not a bad description. As I said to someone one time, "We go away in our motor home so that we can have ourselves all to each other." It just came out that way.

A few years earlier, before we bought the motorhome, we were on our way to Florida, and just before the last exit in Georgia, we passed a big, white Winnebago towing a Volkswagen. In the back window of the VW was a sign: "Please be patient—I'm pushing as fast as I can." We pulled off at that exit to get something to eat and everyone in the restaurant who'd passed it was still laughing.

We loved the concept, and when we bought our motor home, I immediately ordered license plates for our tow Jeep that said, "IM PUSHN." There's only so much you can do with seven letters. The second after I'd stuck the plate application in the mailbox, it struck me that it might be misconstrued. Whoever approves vanity plates (probably some computer) didn't have a problem with it, though, and the plates showed up in the mail a week or so later.

Sure enough, on our first trip out with those plates, we passed half a mobile home going down the highway. Behind it was an escort vehicle, driven by a blond. The blond got on the CB and said to the semi driver, "Did you see that license plate? Talk about advertising." She thought we were pushing drugs. The driver replied, "Think, Blondie." It took her a minute, but finally we heard, "Ha, ha, ha."

I'm not going to start telling you a bunch of blond jokes, but there is one that's noteworthy. My gorgeous and very intelligent goddaughter Erica is a blond. One time her mom started to tell her a blond joke. Erica interrupted her, saying, "Please don't tell me blond jokes. I don't get them."

Another thing I learned in therapy was to distinguish what's about me and what isn't. Applying that simple concept gives me clarity. When we first picked up the motor home, we drove a hundred miles or so north to a small campground run by some other Blue Bird owners who knew how things worked. Neither of us having any experience with any of it, they could help if we got overwhelmed with all the bells and whistles. We stayed there for a few days, and we were parked next to a couple in a travel trailer with their two kids. Delightful people. They were there with another couple who had a pop-up trailer. We all spent time together around the campfire at night.

When we were getting ready to leave, I went to the couple in the travel trailer to say goodbye. I would have gone to the pop-up couple as well, but the woman beat me to it, telling me that I was a snob and that I thought I was too good to say goodbye to her. That wasn't true at all; I'd simply not gotten there yet. It was about her, about her own feelings of inferiority and jealousy. She tried to make it about me, but it wasn't, and my being able to see that helped me to respond kindly to her, rather than defensively. This was when I first realized how damaging competition can be, whichever side of it one is on.

Competition, or at least negative competition can be deadly. When I was still married to X1, a young wife and mother in my first home, I lived in a neighborhood where everyone knew everyone else's business. Competition and comparison were the guiding lights. I felt as though everyone else's husband made more money than mine, that everyone was better educated, better dressed, skinnier than I, all of that stuff. I compared myself with my neighbors and wound up hating myself and hating them. It wasn't until I'd moved out of that neighborhood to another, where people weren't peering out from behind their curtains all the time, that I realized how harmful that environment had been.

Of course it wasn't about the environment at all. It was about my own feelings about myself. After the campground incident, I made a decision to simply not compete—with anyone, for anything, ever. And I've pretty much stuck with it. The pain of negative competition, in either direction, just isn't worth it. The other person can have it, whatever it is, with my blessing.

Once I married X2, who made much more money than any of my old neighbors did, I discovered that although having money certainly made life easier, it didn't make me happier. What I needed could not be bought, nor could it be manipulated. I needed to feel loved, and being married to a rich man didn't seem to make a difference. Still, it's just as easy to fall in love with a rich man as with a poor one. I've said that for years. More recently, I added, especially if he's going to trash you for someone else anyway.

With our motor home being an older model, there was the occasional glitch. The inverter[45] misbehaved one night and made the clock on the coffee maker run backwards so that it brewed the coffee at 2 AM. It was quite cold by the time I got up. That pesky inverter then proceeded to fry my curling iron.

This happened on the way to our first motorhome rally. We'd picked up three other Blue Bird coaches on the road. These people insisted on spending the night in the parking lot of an outlet mall, all to save the $17.00 it would have cost to stay at a campground. We had an eventful night, serenaded by "road music."

Around 2AM, I was still awake thanks to all the trucks passing by with their jake brakes kicking in at that very spot. Suddenly I heard an even louder noise—something between a dive-bomber and a giant bumblebee—and it was right outside our bedroom window. I looked out and saw headlights heading straight towards me. I was just about to shove X2 out of the bed and onto the floor, thinking we were about to get rammed, when the thing made a 90-degree turn—about 2 feet from the side of our coach. It was a vacuum truck, cleaning the

[45] If you don't know what an inverter is or how it works, you'll have to do your own research. I can't explain it.

parking lot. After that, I was so emotionally wiped out, I actually went to sleep—to wake, of course, to the above-mentioned cold coffee.

But, we still had our $17.00.

The generator in the old coach worked, but it was loud and stinky. When we turned it on at that first rally, our neighbors in their newer coaches were quick to offer power from their generators via extension cord. Later, in our new all-electric coach, the inverters would kick in if there was a power outage, and if that failed, the (nice, quiet) generator would come on automatically. Most RV refrigerators have a propane option, but ours was a household model that only ran on electricity. Nevertheless, Blue Bird, always true to RVIA standards, had put the requisite sticker on the refrigerator door that tells you what to do "if you smell gas." X2 read that sticker, giggled and said, "If you smell gas, Crissy farted."

One time when we were at the factory waiting for some repairs on the motor home to be completed, we parked the Jeep in front of the service building, a place where we normally just left the keys in the ignition. We finished our business inside, got back in the Jeep, and X2 reached to start the engine . . . oops, no keys in the ignition. "Oh," he said, "Someone took my keys." Then he fished around and said, "And they put them right here in my pocket."

YELLOW STUFF

Let me tell you how my mind works (and how I make coffee). As I was doing one of my many "final" read-throughs of all of this, I decided I needed another cup of coffee. I ground the beans and put the freshly ground coffee into the filter thingy on top of my mug, then ran boiling water over it from my handy under-sink water heater. Most motor homes come equipped with these wonderful little water heaters and now I can't imagine living without one at home. It's nearly as fast as instant coffee, but it's the real deal, freshly brewed coffee from freshly ground beans. Yum.

As I was shaking and opening my two packets of sweetener, I was thinking about what I'd written, and at the same time, the lyrics from a song I'd heard on the radio were running through my mind. So of course I emptied the sweetener packets into the used coffee filter instead of into my coffee. I'm just not good at multi-tasking.

I've used various kinds of artificial sweeteners most of my life. Partly because they have few or no calories, but also because sugar doesn't dissolve well. Plus, I need way too much sugar to get things as sweet as I like them. For a while, I used a liquid saccharine that worked very well in iced tea. Eventually though, I somehow figured out that that was what was making my face break out, plus I heard that saccharine caused cancer in laboratory rats. About that time, the blue stuff came along, and I used it for many years, with no problems, although I've talked to other people who've had serious problems with it. So, when the yellow stuff came along, I was only too happy to make the switch.

Since I like things sweet, I was using a lot of the yellow stuff, buying it in huge boxes at Sam's Club. Over the years I used it, my legs became increasingly weak and painful, but I had no reason to connect that with the yellow stuff. And then God intervened.

My friend Sue, who eats only "real" food, is, as she puts it, a racetrack shopper. She buys only things found in the perimeter areas of the grocery store such as produce and dairy products, and little or nothing from the interior canned goods aisles. She wouldn't sip anything containing an artificial sweetener with a ten-foot straw.

God's got a great sense of humor, or perhaps it's irony, but He does know how to get my attention. Sue was living on the 6th floor of a condo building and as she rode down in the elevator one day, a woman she'd never met before started a quick conversation with her. The woman told my friend Sue that her doctor had told her that if she wanted her legs to stop hurting, she needed to stop using the yellow stuff. That message, delivered to her by a stranger in the space of a six-story elevator ride, was meant for me!

Sue immediately emailed me this interesting piece of information and I decided to test it out. By this time, my legs were so bad that I was practically crawling up the stairs, hauling myself up by the railing. I gave up the yellow stuff and within two weeks, my legs were back to normal.

THE SMILE
Crissy Shreve

The frost is alight with sunshine;
It was cold in the night.
The air sparkles.
Dew on the leaves reflects Your smile.
I can't help but give You one of my own,
Creator of it all.

CHAPTER TWENTY-FIVE

PICKLE SOUP

X2 and I frequented a local Polish restaurant and we got to know the owner and her daughter quite well. They served the best pickle soup![46] One night the daughter approached our table and stuck a puppy in my lap. I didn't want a puppy, but she said that this one had been abandoned on the street, and if I didn't take him, she'd have to give him to a shelter, perchance to be put down. I gave in.

I took the little guy home and named him Fella. The next day I took him to the vet and he was given shots, including one for worms. The vet said, "Whatever happens, don't call me." Shortly after we arrived home, Fella presented me with what looked like a large pile of spaghetti. Nasty. Then I understood.

Of course Fella's favorite place was my lap, and he spent as much time there as he could. This was fine for the first week or so. Then I got the call that my mother's house had burned, and I had to go take care of her and that whole mess.

My mother had taken advantage of a county deal to put storm windows on senior citizens' houses for free. The contractor had left an exterior spotlight hanging by the old fabric electrical cord about a foot down the outside wall. It had hung that way for a year or two, open to the elements, and one day it decided to short out. My mother was sitting about five feet from this wire burning inside the wall all afternoon and she didn't even smell it. But the neighbors all smelled it—they just couldn't figure out where the smell was coming from. Finally the flames started, and my mother ran outside.

---

[46]   If you've never eaten pickle soup (it's actually cream of pickle soup), you simply must. There are recipes on the Internet.

Interestingly, due to the construction of the house, which was built in the early 1900s, it didn't burn down. Only a few areas actually burned. Most of the damage was to the contents, and that was largely caused by smoke and water. Still, the damage was greater than a reasonable cost to repair it, so the insurance company paid out the value of the house.

That was a good thing, except that then we had to figure out what to do with the remains. It couldn't just be permanently left as it was. We got bids on having it torn down, but that cost would have eaten through most of the insurance money. We decided to list the house for sale for the value of the lot. Some guy bought it, restored the house, and then sold it at a healthy profit. He actually did some things that I'd envisioned for years. It would have been a great project for me had I not lived five hundred miles away and had my mother and a new puppy to contend with.

I was gone for a week and by the time I got back, Fella had doubled in size. He no longer fit in my lap. Any progress I'd made towards training him had gone south, and since I'd brought my mother back with me, the dog got completely lost in the shuffle. He never quite learned the difference between grass and carpet.

Fella was much happier as an outdoor dog anyway, so we put a dog door in the garage and strung an airplane cable run for him from there to the barn. He tore that down within a day or two, so we built a kennel. That was too confining, so we got an electric dog fence. That worked just fine, and he spent most of his days cheerfully running in circles around the trees, nose in the air, looking up at the squirrels that taunted him from above.

One day, Fella caught a mother possum that had wandered into his territory. I thought he'd killed her—Mama appeared to be dead, but her tiny baby was still hanging on to her as best he could. I dragged Fella into the kennel and then got the snow shovel under Mama. Baby fell off, but climbed right back up onto the shovel next to her. Still thinking she was dead, I carried her on the shovel and disposed of her in the weed garden. About an hour later, I checked back and they were both gone. Sure enough, Mama had been "playing dead."[47]

Just because I know you're wondering, the weed garden was what had been our vegetable garden until we started traveling and were no longer around to tend it. Living in that well-tilled and fertilized black soil made the weeds quite happy and profuse. Apparently the toads liked it too. When X2 was busy digging with a spade in the weed garden one day, he sliced a little black toad right in half. He looked down and said, "Sorry, Froggie."

One time when we were off in the motor home, I called home to check in, and our "gopher" of the moment told me that Fella had caught a skunk. We thought it was rather clever of us to be away when that happened. The "gopher" had had to bury the skunk and wash Fella.

We'd take Fella out walking in the large field behind our house from time to time. We'd let him loose to run, but he didn't always want to come back. A friend had told me that if your dog won't come back, lie down on the ground. I did that, and Fella came running to me full speed, plowing right into my head. It felt like I'd been hit by a bowling ball. But it worked.

When we travelled and didn't have a "gopher' at the house, Fella would be home alone, with only someone coming to feed him once a day. He did just fine though, until one day a neighbor spotted him out "loose" and called the police. The stupid cop pulled poor Fella through the electric fence. Once he'd done that, Fella, who was not as stupid as the cop, escaped. He was a nice dog and he didn't even bite the cop. They caught Fella again later and put him in the pound. We arrived home that day, and when they called me to bail him out, I asked what it would cost for them to keep him.

Same price, so I left him there. I was sad about it, but the reality was that we were going to be away more than we'd be at home, and I'd been pet rescue to Fella for six years. I prayed someone would take him, and I hope someone did and loved him well.

---

[47] According to various Internet sites, possums do not "play" dead at all; a possum goes into shock when threatened, much like a person who has fainted. They're slow moving and can't outrun a predator, so the hope is that the predator will lose interest in dead prey, although this doesn't always work. I guess if I were going to be eaten alive, I'd just as soon be unconscious.

Back to when my mother's house burned. Laura had always been something of a hoarder in her own peculiar way. She would put things in plastic grocery bags, with no rhyme or reason, and then scatter the bags all over the house. A bag might contain an empty cigarette pack, a loose paper clip, a nickel, and one or two unpaid bills, complete with envelopes and junk enclosures. It was a dilemma when I was there sorting through the wet and the smoke-damaged debris (derbis, of course) to salvage what I could. I couldn't just assume that these bags were trash. I found important items in some of them.

There were also piles of things in the house that she'd ordered from various catalogs, often still in the packages, never opened and never used. She'd never return anything—it just got added to a pile. She'd run up huge credit card bills, finally accumulating a debt of over twenty thousand dollars, on an income of about seven hundred dollars a month. Laura invented the concept of, "Can I pay my Visa with my Master Card?" long before someone made a joke out of it.

Apparently the answer is yes—she was doing just that. A year or two before the house burned, she'd called me in a panic. They'd threatened to take her house, and she begged me to bail her out, saying, "I have money in a Visa account, but they won't let me have it." I advised her to file bankruptcy, which she did. All of this baggage came along with my mother when I brought her back with me.

She had the insurance money from the house, and the plan was to get her a condo near me, although I'd have to kick in some money towards it. But until we could find a place, she lived with me and it did not work well. Her life was out of control and I went into control freak mode. I had her best interests at heart, but I was also trying to survive her.

She was eating way too much, and as a result, spent an inordinate amount of time on the toilet. One time I noticed her sneaking downstairs for no apparent reason. She was on her way to the lower level bathroom. Since she'd always used the bathroom near her bedroom on the main level, I asked her why she had gone downstairs. She'd clogged the toilet. When I went in, plunger in hand, I saw that she'd stuck a piece of newspaper under the seat. I'm not sure what she thought that would accomplish, but it was the funnies, so maybe she thought I'd find it comical.

Then one day I missed a call from my accountant. He'd left a message on my answering machine saying his name and that he needed to talk to me. Afterwards, I got a second message, this time from my son Jason who, knowing I'd know his voice, did not give his name, but just said that he loved me and missed me and, by the way, thanks for lunch. I listened to both messages, and then deleted them.

Unbeknownst to me, my mother had been listening too. She decided that both messages were from my accountant and that I was having an affair with him. Nothing could have been farther from the truth, and if you knew my accountant, you'd even see the humor in it. But Laura couldn't be budged from what she thought. She accused me of having an affair and threatened to tell X2. I couldn't even put the pieces back together because the messages had been deleted. I just told X2 about it.

I don't know why my mother thought something like that of me, or why she wanted to use it to try to destroy my marriage. At that point, I suggested that she needed to leave my house. She went back home and we didn't speak for some time. She started going through the insurance money very quickly and was living in a dangerous neighborhood. After some time had passed, I had her come back, but it was not until after I'd found her a condo and furnished it for her.

Laura read the newspaper from beginning to end every day of her life. She'd tear out scraps of advertisements and pile them on every flat surface she could find—everything from lotteries to grants—anything she thought might make her rich. Luckily, she didn't follow up on most of them, but I never knew what she was going to do next.

Once she was in the condo, I had a joint bank account with her so that I could monitor her spending, and after I paid her bills, there was only enough left in the account for groceries. One time when the bank statement came I found deductions for several hundred dollars in foreign lottery tickets. She'd given them her account number and they just helped themselves. I arranged with the bank to no longer allow this, but there was nothing they could do about the money that had already been withdrawn. I had to cover several checks she'd written that had bounced.

Her phone rang when I happened to be at her condo one day shortly after this episode. I answered it, and it was one of these lottery outfits looking to sell her more tickets. The phone was in my name, so

I had the number changed. I never told her I'd changed it, and I never told her the new number. There were very few people who called her anyway, and I gave them the new number with strict orders not to give it to her.

After a few years in the condo, my mother started becoming dangerously forgetful. She'd stick a half-gallon box of ice cream in the refrigerator or leave a $7 leg of lamb sitting in a pirated shopping cart for several days in the living room. She did have one amazing talent, though. She could stand outside the store with four bags of groceries looking like she needed a ride home and darned if someone wouldn't give her one.

She then started to be incontinent, but she refused to wear any type of protective undergarment. The sad part is that several years after she died, I discovered that most of us in my family have some sort of sinus condition, largely driven by allergies. In my mother's case, her sinuses would drain into her throat, causing her to cough uncontrollably and wet her pants. The dilemma is that it has little to do with the lungs themselves, and so coughing doesn't solve the problem. It's just a tickle in the throat. I have the same condition, but mine was not so advanced at that time, so I didn't relate to what was happening with her. A simple daily allergy pill would have done much to improve her life.

Nevertheless, she could not be on her own any longer, and I found a nursing home for her, where she lived for the next ten years. That was an experience. Laura refused to even consider going to a nursing home. She'd become severely incontinent, to the degree that she was sleeping in a soaking wet cavity she'd created in her mattress. I didn't see it until after she'd gone to the home—she never allowed me to go into her bedroom and at the end she wouldn't even let me into the condo. I was the enemy.

Eventually the stench could be smelled out in the hall and someone called the health department. Of course my mother insisted that the urine smell was coming from another apartment. She even suggested that someone across the hall must have a mimeograph machine (which I, ironically, had always called a urine machine). I'm sure she didn't realize that by that time very few people would even remember them.

The lady from the health department "condemned" the apartment, which forced my mother to go to the nursing home. The lady and I were in cahoots—I knew all about it, but my mother wouldn't listen to me or do anything I wanted her to do, so I let the lady handle it. I did, however, visit a number of nursing homes and I made all the arrangements for her placement and the financing.

Everyone told me to pay attention to urine smells in the hallway. I knew first hand that old people wet their pants, and that unless the odor was extreme, that wasn't the most important consideration. I toured several places, always with the administrator. One place was squeaky-clean, modern and beautiful. And "cold." A resident approached the administrator and the administrator told her to go sit down—she'd come back and see her later. Of course she never did.

The home I chose for my mother was the one where, as we walked around, the old folks would approach us and the administrator would interrupt whatever conversation we were having to give them each a hug. It wasn't as new or as perfectly maintained, but it was "warm." Once Laura was there, I'd stop in regularly to make spot-checks. No matter what time of the day or night, I'd no sooner be in the front door than someone, be it administrative staff, caretakers, or the folks themselves, would recognize me and tell me exactly where Laura was.

My mother continued to read the newspaper every day at the home. She didn't know what year it was, or how old she was, but that didn't seem to matter to her. She'd invariably tell me that she needed to "hunt a husband," or "hunt a job," or "buy a car." I pointed out that she had no money for a car, no money for insurance, and no driver's license. "I'll just drive without one," she said. I finally figured out that I didn't need to argue with her. I'd just say, "Okay." That realization was huge. I no longer had to be afraid of what my mother might do. She couldn't do any of it. I remember heaving a huge sigh of relief as I left that day.

When my mother's sister (my aunt) Ruth died, I debated whether or not to even tell her. Laura had always said that she just didn't know what she'd do when Ruth died. My cousin Judy, Ruth's daughter, insisted that my mother needed to know and so, the next time Judy was in town, I dragged her to the home and made her tell her. My mother cried a bit, but she got over it quickly enough. Of course afterwards, the first question she'd ask me every time I went to visit was, "Have you heard from Ruth?' When I'd hesitate, not quite knowing what to say, my mother would say, "Oh, don't tell me she died!" And then she'd cry all over again.

One family Thanksgiving, my granddaughter was at my house and so was her little cousin Krissy, both just two. They played together all day, and then had a bath together. I missed seeing that because I was busy taking my mother back to the nursing home—she'd wet her pants along with my tapestry dining room chair (the same chairs we'd had poor Shai declawed to protect!) Although she'd arrived wearing a diaper, she'd immediately snuck into a bedroom and taken it off, hiding it in a dresser drawer, where I found it several weeks later. I suppose that was fair revenge for all the food she found that I had fed to the buffet when I was a kid.

The girls wore themselves out running up and down the hall in their blanket sleepers and then they both fell asleep. Mike and his wife loaded my sleeping granddaughter into the car and left. When she woke up at home the next morning, the first thing she said was, "Where's my Krissy? I have to go back!"

A few years after that, Mike and his wife brought both my granddaughters to a luau at my mother's nursing home. It was entertaining for the girls, while giving my mother an opportunity to see her little great-granddaughters. The younger one has never been a hugger, and I couldn't get a hug out of her for anything that day— she didn't even want me to pick her up. When I was trying to get her moving towards the front door so that we could leave, I told her that I'd not pick her up if she'd walk. She said okay and she walked.

The girls both sat with me on the grass to watch the Hawaiian show—the older one on my lap, so I got a good snuggle with her, and the younger one next to me, taking bites of my fruit. When it was time to leave, the older girl, at Mike's request, somewhat hesitantly gave my mother a quick hug and kiss. The younger one, who was only two then, walked right up to my mother and gave her a big hug and a kiss. It was *dear* and it touched my heart.

She's now thirteen, and she still won't give anyone a hug. Hugs are just not her thing. That makes her giving her great-grandmother a hug even more poignant.

There are a couple more notable stories about my mother. One time when I was at her house helping her after she'd had some surgery,

I called a local HVAC company to come clean her furnace. When the fellow removed the lower panel, we saw a carcass inside on the floor. My mother knew it was there; she'd seen it when she changed filters. She'd told herself it was a "grinny," (chipmunk), but I was pretty sure, and the HVAC guy agreed, that it was a rat. He agreed to remove it and I thought he'd take it away with him, but no. He left it in a box next to the furnace and guess who got to carry it out to the trash.

This was the same house where we lived when I was little, and I remembered the time we found a dead rat in the toilet. I can't imagine how that rat managed to get up to the second story of the house, but he apparently managed to climb up from the sewer and then drowned in the toilet. Or, I suppose it's possible that the rat was loose in the house and jumped into the toilet to get a drink of water. In any case, my mother paid the kid next door to take the rat away. Shudder!

There were some bigger rats around too. One of them was a neighbor kid who'd previously done some work for my mother. Armed with a rifle, he kidnapped her at gunpoint one night and made her drive him some miles on the Interstate in her car. She didn't have much money in her purse, so when they started to get low on gas, he made her turn around and go back. He refused to allow her to stop at a rest area, so she had to squat on the side of the road. I have no idea what he was thinking, but he certainly wasn't thinking clearly. She knew who he was. Once back home, she called the police and he went to jail. The scariest part of it, though, was that at one point during this ordeal, they were in the kitchen and he was pointing the rifle right at her. She reached over and pushed it aside, telling him to get it out of her face. My mother could be pretty ballsy when she needed to be.

Shortly before my mother died, my cousin Johnny brought Uncle Jim and Aunt Becky to see her at the nursing home, knowing that it would probably be the last time. My mother knew who he was and interacted reasonably well, but Aunt Becky, who was much less with it, told one story over and over during the visit.

Apparently Aunt Becky and Uncle Jim had years earlier been on an airplane, and for some reason, after taking off, the plane could not gain altitude. They cruised briefly just above the water and returned to the airport. Becky's comment was, "Jim, you could hang a pole out that window and catch a fish." Every time she repeated the story, my

Uncle Jim laughed as if it were the first time he'd ever heard it, not to mention that he'd been there. He didn't laugh at her, but with her.

I was very proud of my Uncle Jim. The two of them were married for sixty-one years and he loved her all his life. It touched my heart, especially since, these days, it seems to be "till death do us part or until I change my mind."

NIGHT THOUGHTS ON MY MOTHER

I originally wrote this one sleepless night while my mother was living with me for that month or two after her house burned. All the years of mixed-up emotions surfaced as open hostility on both our parts with our being right there in close proximity. There were two of us living her life and no one living mine. I played the "mother" in the equation, not because she wanted me to, but because I saw it as my chance to "fix" her. I suppose I was trying to get her to be the mother I'd always needed, or if that wasn't possible, to at least get her to be less of a threat to me. She, of course, resisted. It wasn't a pretty time. What I thought she needed was not the same as what she wanted. As I struggled to help her get to a place of sane and healthy independence, she struggled to get to a place of . . . well, I'm still not exactly sure what. Writing this helped me to get a bit of a handle on it. I've updated it and added a few additional thoughts and explanations.

I have seldom "felt" guilty about much of anything except perhaps not "feeling" guilty. There is no doubt that my mother wanted me to "feel" guilty. It's hard to look deeply at this mother stuff. It's like looking in a mirror and getting in the face of my own depravity. I don't like my depravity—it's ugly and it's scary.

My mother, or perhaps it would be kinder to say her illness, has always been my enemy. I came to grips early on with my grandmother being my enemy. That was easier. Looking at my mother is horrifying. I don't know when I became consciously aware that she was my enemy too, probably not until I was an adult. As a child, I felt it on some vague and deeply subconscious level—something wasn't right—but I had no idea what right was supposed to look like. As I was got older, it became more and more apparent, and I withdrew from her gradually as time went on. Living five hundred miles away from her from the time I was a senior in high school made it easy to mostly ignore her. Then suddenly, there she was.

My mother was amazingly functional on some levels, typical of schizophrenics, and yet completely out of touch with reality on others. Among the many lasting effects she's had on me, confusion has always been the greatest. She's said some of the most brilliant things I've ever heard, and all of the most ludicrous—an extremely intelligent mind gone haywire. She could take shorthand[48] as fast as anyone could dictate, and could type it up even faster. One time we argued over the spelling of the word *seize*. She was right. She also gave me one of the best pieces of advice I've ever had—"If it won't matter to you in twenty years, why let it matter now?"

One day we were looking at an old picture of the two of us on the beach in Atlantic City, and she said, "You sure did love your mommy." I was three or four in the picture, and we were holding hands. She was right. I did love her then. But she was never "Mommy."

I was the "safe" outlet for the ugliness inside her. Apparently she banked on my always loving her anyway. Trouble is, it didn't work. Hatred as deep as I grew to feel for her can have only come from deep love—and deep fear. I suppose she verbally attacked everyone else like she did me, but she wasn't their mother. She could reach deep into my heart and rip it out with her teeth. I could do the same to her; I had a good teacher. She was more than my enemy; she was my mortal enemy. And I, in my need to survive, became hers. She was able, in all of her weakness, foolishness, and helplessness, to render me all those same things—in a little pile of ashes at her feet. I was terrified of her.

This is not to say she was completely worthless—I know that she mattered to God. If I was not worthless in His eyes, neither could she

---

[48] Secretaries used shorthand in my mother's day. Wikipedia defines it as "an abbreviated symbolic writing method that increases speed and brevity . . ." My mother used the one invented by John Robert Gregg in 1888. There are other methods, some earlier. Her red Gregg Shorthand book was always around when I was a kid, and it's one of the things she hung onto when her house burned. She even had me bring it to her in the nursing home. Examples of shorthand are on the Internet.

be. It's just that the little girl who still lived inside me wondered why *her* mother had to be crazy. And why *her* mother was never healed. And why *she* had to pay so dearly for her mother's illness, and never had a real mother—only a duty, a responsibility, a loathed thing that to her was only an illness personified, not a person.

I could not find a mother, or anything even recognizable as alive in that pile of skin and bones that seemed to need to tear out my heart and suck out my life. And I was guilty of not being able to stand, let alone love, this thing, and I was guilty of selfishness, or at least extreme self-protection from her. I wanted God to change me, to give me love for her in spite of it all, but I couldn't find any, no matter how deeply I'd reach. I couldn't even offer her His love—I wasn't sure I wanted her to have it, at least not from me, and I questioned whether I myself even had it in light of that.

My mother once said that if black people would be in heaven, she didn't want to go there. I hope God wasn't listening right then, and I sure hope He wasn't listening when I, in myself, was not sure I wanted to be there if she was going to be there. I didn't relish the idea of having to spend eternity trying to survive her!

It was more than just my having to deal with a crazy mother. It was also that she'd had to live that way for most of her life. It was no comfort that she always thought everyone else was crazy and probably didn't know the difference. But she did in a way. Even though she always made it sound like she left the jobs, the relationships, she had to have recognized on some level that she was rejected, left behind, unwanted. She always chose to isolate, but I can't believe it was entirely volitional—rather a way to survive being rejected. Her emptiness was apparent.

I didn't get my survival instincts accidentally. My mother survived in spite of it all. I have to give her credit where credit is due. She did, on some very basic and practical levels, provide for me when I was a child, and not all that badly, considering what she had to work with. To be truthful, I don't know how well I would've done on her limited resources, and it wasn't entirely fair to look down on her from my tower of blessing. I was guilty of that. On the other hand, many of the choices she made based on the faulty thinking of her illness caused both of us to be deprived of things we needed.

I moved on and away. She stayed stuck. I had a tendency to expect her to "pull herself up by her own bootstraps," a concept made popular by the late Mayor Richard J. Daley of Chicago.[49] To a degree I had done that myself, but to an infinitely greater degree, God had blessed and taken care of me.

Which of course led me to wonder why, at least as I saw it, hadn't He blessed and taken care of her? Didn't God love my mother? It would've been different if I'd felt any presence at all in her life on His part. There seemed to be none. Not even to help her necessarily, just to be in it with her. Somehow I got down to maybe that was supposed to be my job, to be Jesus to her. And that was where I failed so miserably. It was my vengefulness and selfishness *and* it was my woundedness and fear. I didn't want to be the one He used to touch her. Selfishness and self-protection aside, why was I not, at least in Him, able to rise above all this and "do' love, even if I didn't feel it? Yet I did do much of what I could do, and I did talk to her about Jesus a number of times. She didn't want to hear it—not from me, and perhaps not at all.

I struggled the most with what I couldn't do. Even as I prayed for God's grace, I could not seem to extend it to her. And this broke my heart. She desperately needed me to forgive her, or to at least be merciful, and it was so hard.

The problem was not going to go away; that I had to allow first of all. I was angry at this illness that was my mother and I was mad at God for not making it go away. And I was mad at God for not lifting me above it so that I could do what I thought I should be doing, which was to love her anyway—even as I begged God to love *me* anyway, and even as He did.

I had to address my need to forgive God, too. The adult (if not overly mature) me said that I had no business even thinking about forgiving God—who did I think I was? I wanted to stuff it, not allow it, especially if it meant feeling something about it. Guilty? I *am* guilty, and Christ died because of it, let's get clear on that once and for all. The truth is that I do sometimes get mad at God. He knows it. He can handle it. I'm sure He'd just as soon I acknowledge it rather than stuff

---

49   "Look, Sister, you and I come from the same background. We know how tough it was. But we picked ourselves up by our own bootstraps." http://byliner.com/david-halberstam/stories/daley-of-chicago

it. And it's easy for me to forgive God. I need Him too much to let myself stay mad at Him.

It was not so easy to forgive my mother. I couldn't get past the accusation in her eyes. In them, I saw my own failure as a daughter and as a Christian. And she was right. I had been neither a daughter nor a Christian to her. I definitely didn't want to be her daughter, but I didn't think I could get away with not being a Christian to her. How could I be a Christian in any respect and not be one to her? That didn't fly. I didn't even want it to fly—I just seemed to run up against the wall. My heart was full of contradictions. I was enough of a Christian to want to be right with God and enough of a selfish, depraved, hurt, scared little girl to run like hell. I was afraid I was running to hell. I didn't want to pay that price too for that damned illness that had ruined her life and was working to ruin mine! But I couldn't get clear on what was really expected of me by God versus her unrealistic expectations of me.

The fear I felt had a lot to do with my wanting to be alive. I did not want to be dead like my mother was dead. I was afraid she was contagious. I had a life, but it was mine. Maybe a good question to ask her would have been, "What are you accusing me of?" I suspect the answer was of my having a life. I had done things to help improve her life. It was she who wouldn't do anything to improve her life. I'm not saying that she could have, although I think there were some things, but that didn't make me responsible to do it for her. I could not live her life for her and there were no pieces of my life that I could give her that she could own. She could only look at me being alive and mourn her own lifelessness. But I didn't cause her illness, and I didn't make her get old, and I didn't take her life away from her! I just didn't put mine aside for hers. I had not really been her enemy, regardless of how she saw me. I was only the stick by which she measured her own loss.

Her eyes said, "How dare you have such a good life while I have nothing!" I couldn't face those eyes; maybe I believed the lie in them. The truth was, that if I'd died right then, it would not have improved her life. If I hadn't been born, it would not have improved her life. If I'd lost all I had it would not have improved her life. I could at least know that much and perhaps confront those accusing eyes with that truth, if only in my own mind. And I could answer the question for myself with this: "This is the life God has given me and I am grateful for it and for who I am and for all I have. All I can do is live my life and praise Him for it. I am not responsible for your life—you are and He is. Maybe He's wanted to come into your life too and maybe you haven't let Him."

A therapist had told me that if I didn't get resolve in regard to my mother before she died, I could be in trouble. I didn't think my mother's death would be the solution to my problem, but I needed the death of the anger and hatred in my heart. I didn't want my heart to die with her.

In the middle of all of this agonizing, God gave me the answer. He reminded me that He's got that all covered. I'm not perfect here either, but I will be perfect someday in heaven. So will she, and we will be reconciled in Him. So I handed my fear over to God and replaced it with prayer that she would ultimately wind up in heaven, trusting that He would heal us both. Call it a heavenly attitude adjustment. I had to let go of my need to have it here in this life. I had to get over His not doing it my way.

Update: This all ended quite well. Of course it did—God had it under control all along, just like He said. In the last week of her life, the Hospice chaplain led my mother to the Lord Jesus Christ. In her confused mind, she thought that the chaplain was my Uncle John, who'd been with her when I was born. God used that old memory of someone being there for her to get through the fog and into her heart. The chaplain assured me that she had understood and believed.

Jesus was with her when she died, as were Mike and Jason and I. She is whole and healed in heaven now, and enjoying life, perhaps for the first time ever. And, when I get there, I'll be whole and healed too, and we'll have the mother-daughter relationship God always meant for us.

Best of all, she was there to greet Jason when he arrived.

EAGERNESS
Crissy Shreve

I never saw such eagerness,
Such anticipation,
On the day we wed,
Nor when we traveled together,
Or loved at home or far away,
As I see now—just before you go.

Chapter Twenty-Six

Ministry Widow

Life took some significant turns in those years. My dream of X2's and my having lots of time together and traveling in the motor home never quite materialized.

Our pastor had a speaking engagement overseas, and shortly before he left, he got wind of X2's having grown up in Europe. He asked X2 to travel with him as his facilitator. During one of his speaking engagements, he talked about a businessman who'd found the Lord, and then, without any notice, invited X2 to the dais to talk. That was the beginning of X2's ministry overseas.

X2 began traveling with increasing frequency. The motor home and I spent winters in Naples and Hilton Head, where he'd return between trips. He made an effort to live with one foot in each scenario, with some success. We still attended motor home rallies and took a number of trips as well. It was a good time in many ways.

I got into genealogy and as part of that I came into contact with cousins all over the country. We were all researching our connection to our common ancestor who'd come to America in 1685. I got deeply involved with this in a number of ways. Our ancestor's daughter had gotten married in 1699 and we started planning a reunion of the descendants of both families around their 300th anniversary. I spent a lot of time working to connect cousins and also on making plans for the reunion.

This kept me very busy and fulfilled. I discovered that I had a life outside of X2. This turned out to be extremely important in the years ahead. I was becoming aware that my marriage was not all that I'd hoped it would be. My desire to be with X2 and his desire to not be with me any more than absolutely necessary began to more openly conflict. We did the dance. The more I wanted him, the less he wanted me, and vice versa.

I struggled to reconcile the good parts of my life with the not-so-good parts. I struggled to be okay with what God was doing. Here's a piece I wrote at the time that I called "Ministry Widow."

You've heard the term "golf widow." When God made it apparent that He was planning to send X2 on frequent and extended ministry trips, I became a ministry widow, practically overnight. "But what about me?" I asked God—and X2. "Who will take care of me?" I'd gotten pretty used to having X2 around, and I wasn't sure I could survive his extended absences. It's easy enough to ask your husband not to play so much golf, but can you really ask him to ignore God's calling? And even if you can, how do you argue with God?

As badly as I was tempted to argue with God, the truth is that I really didn't want to. I've always been a strong believer in the perfection of God's will, and the whole thing was so clearly His will. Apart from worrying about who would take care of me, I was in fact very much behind what God and X2 were up to. I began praying that God would not let me be a stumbling block. I began to allow God to take care of me. I invited Him to teach me what He would in the process. He did.

I will admit that I did some arguing with X2, though. I did not become a reasonably content ministry widow overnight, and I certainly didn't do it very gracefully. It was a process, and each time X2 was gone, one time for seven weeks, I learned something new and moved into a new phase. One of these phases, about mid-way through the process, was discovering that it was not his being gone that was the hard part. The hard part was knowing what to do with him when he came back. One of the ways we'd "prepare" for a long separation was by distancing, often accomplished by having a fight. Weeks later he'd come home and I'd have been independent and distanced for weeks, so it was hard to let him back in to my heart, especially knowing that he would soon leave again. It didn't help that he came home with a suitcase full of dirty clothes for me to wash.

It was difficult having to make the transition from being a fully functional wife to being a fully functional ministry widow and vice versa. Sometimes it felt like I was no good at being either one. These two parts of my life were very different from each other and just about the time I'd get used to one part and its habits, it would change again. I'd forget which hat I was wearing. One morning I was in my office and I dialed the phone to call X2 overseas. He answered from our bedroom where he'd been sleeping—just down the hall.

To further muddy my waters, someone pointed out that I was "in the situation of a pastor's wife." Whoa! Me? You've got to be kidding. I didn't ask for the job. I didn't want to be a pastor's wife. I didn't care that God was turning my husband into a pastor; I was not cut out to be a pastor's wife.

During a workshop at our church, our pastor's wife said that she'd always wanted to be a pastor's wife, even as a little girl. I thought, not me! Never in my wildest dreams did that idea ever cross my mind. She talked about having been a "good girl," and said that if there was a rule, she'd follow it. Well, again, not me! If there was a rule, I'd always tended to break it.

All I'd wanted was a Christian husband. I'd tried the other kind, and it didn't work. I became a Christian during my first marriage and the marriage fell apart. I thought that having a Christian husband would be a guarantee of a successful marriage. And, I wanted X2 to be that Christian husband. It was completely about me and what I wanted.

It was one of those times when God . . . well, perhaps "over-answered" a prayer. Of course He did. He does things His way, according to His will and His purposes. It was as if He said, "Crissy, I'll give you that Christian husband, but I'm going to use him, too." That's just God.

X2's return did not always mean that he was actually "there" either. He had much to juggle in many areas: details of his ministry, business, everyday personal needs like finding time to get a haircut, time with friends and family, quiet time with the Lord, and time for himself to just unwind. He had to live a whole year's worth in the half-year he was at home.

I struggled with this perhaps more than his physical absence. So often it felt as though I no longer fit into his life or mattered to him at all. So often I felt lonelier when he was at home than when he was away. It's easy to understand physical absence; not so easy to understand what feels like emotional absence. I had to choose to believe that he did love me, that he did need me, rather than what I was feeling.

With each trip X2 made, I became increasingly aware of being in a sort of "protective bubble." I felt God's presence so deeply during those times. Not only did He watch over me with loving tenderness, He gave me a great privilege in allowing me to watch Him in action. Without fail, each time X2 returned, there was one special story he'd share with me. I'd take a deep breath and remind myself that it was worth it.

The most precious of those stories was the time X2 was speaking in front of a group of church members, both men and women. It was a somewhat casual setting and there was a table behind him. He was leaning back on it as he spoke. One woman had been unable to find a babysitter and had brought her little girl with her. The child was mentally handicapped. She was not disruptive, but she was fascinated with X2, and she went up to him as he was speaking. The mother was clearly distraught, but X2 just stopped for a moment, and asked the little girl whether she might like to sit with him. She said, "Yes," and so he picked her up, set her on the table next to him, put his arm around her, and went right on with his talk. The little girl fell asleep and remained there next to him until he'd finished.

God's work wasn't limited to the ministry, either. He did amazing things in X2 himself and with other people in our lives. And in me. Although I was pretty sure before that God existed, I was taken one step further. I know for sure that God is passionately involved in the lives of His children and His world. I've seen the "work of His hand."

The question of who would take care of me became recognition that God did take care of me, much more and much better than I could ever have imagined. I learned so much about God and myself; it was like sitting at His feet and receiving private tutoring.

One of the best lessons I learned is that when I invite God into my life and my concerns, He comes. I got a new awareness of the tragedy of so many people living life without Him. I was given opportunities to share Him with non-believers and to encourage believers to invite Him into their life situations.

Amazingly, and entirely too frequently, I've heard believers as well as non-believers, when desperately in need of His help say, "Oh, I never thought of inviting God into it." Just as dismaying is hearing someone say, "I lost my faith," when things go wrong in their lives. They get mad at God and then turn their backs on Him right when they need Him the most.

And I learned about myself. I am part me, still very obviously a sinner, and part new creation in Him. The habits of the sinner have been with me for a long time; they are deeply ingrained from life experiences, from my basic temperament and personality, and from just being human. God hasn't finished with me. I am still learning new habits, new ways of seeing things through His eyes. Some days it is "me" who is in control, some days it is He, and some days we get in each other's way.

But I find myself coming closer and closer to wanting His ways more often than I want my own. Now, even as I instinctively do those things I've always done from habit, I find myself praying for His ways to overshadow mine. I have no illusion that I will ever be perfect this side of heaven, but I need only to look over my shoulder and see where I've been to realize just how far I've come. And it's nothing I've done; I know what I do when left to my own devices. It's what He's done.

People would often ask if I were crazy—how could I let my husband go away for such long periods of time? And I would answer, "How can I argue with God?" After a while, I became able to say, "I wouldn't have missed it for anything." I lost so little, but gained so much. I got to know my Lord more intimately and more fully than ever before. I heard His voice as He spoke to my heart. And as if that weren't enough, I saw people I love, one by one, coming to Him. It was as if God were saying, "You guys, do you really think I would use you to touch strangers with My love and then leave your precious ones behind?"

Then it all changed drastically. Life has a tendency to be a two-edged sword. It took me a while to figure it out, though. It never crossed my mind that there might be someone else. I was in my "protective bubble," experiencing God's hand on me, still believing that when God is behind a ministry, He protects it, and protects those involved. Sometimes, though, He winds up having to pull the ministry and the people involved out of the ashes of fallen man's free will.

As tempting as it is to try to analyze X2 and his behavior, and of course I've done a fair amount of that, it doesn't belong in this book. I'm trying hard to stick with what happened and what was about me in it.

I ran into something I wrote in 1992, ten years before X2's betrayal became known. In hindsight, I was not surprised to note that it was written right at the same time as X2 met a woman, his colleague's wife, in Germany. I remember his coming home and talking about her, even telling me that I'd like her! I didn't see the writing on the wall.

I willingly own my own neediness. It was certainly something of a contributor to the demise of my marriage and it has always been my own form of insanity. But I'd worked hard on it and I'd made progress by that time. If not completely removed from the equation, it was at least no longer an excuse for X2's behavior towards me. I had a life and was able to be quite fine on my own. X2's not-surprising response was to seem glad to have me out of his hair. A touch of paranoia in me even allowed for the possibility that he was plotting to get rid of me.

Now I don't really fool myself that I personally was so important to X2 that he needed to plot my downfall. Anyone married to him would have received the same treatment. His first ex had even said to me, "You'll find out what he's like." I was caught up in a charade not of my own making.

X2 held tight reign over the charade. He was very good at it—so good, in fact, that I for years believed that I had the problem, that I *was* the problem. It was terrifying in its subtle power, but I was beginning to catch on.

X2 had his own particular brand of insanity, and once I began to see it, I had to figure out how to limit its damage to me. It became clearer once my own stuff was, if not entirely out of the way, at least over to the side. It was now largely his stuff that was clogging the arteries of that ephemeral "us" that I'd chased over the years, dreamed of, hoped and prayed for.

It was becoming increasingly evident that "us" no longer existed. For whatever reason, X2 had no need of it. Although "us" was still part of his facade, it was far, far from being part of any reality. He would hold my hand as we walked into church or put his arm around me when someone was watching. Everyone thought we had the

316

perfect marriage. Several of my friends even talked about how they wished they could find someone just like him.

It started feeling as though he was trying to drive me away or drive me crazy—my choice—either way would be fine for him. As I revisit all of this, it strikes me that after all those years of my mother, you'd think I'd have caught on a lot sooner.

X2 said on several occasions that he had what he needed from our marriage. What was that—someone to keep him from falling out of my side of the bed? He also told me that I needed something he didn't have. Maybe that was true. Or perhaps he just didn't care to give it. It was probably some of both.

He liked having a wife and a home and someone to wash his clothes. He liked to know someone would be there to take care of him if he were sick or injured. I was the one he was married to, and as such, I was that someone by default, but I'm sure he felt stuck with me. Starting over with a new wife wasn't an option for someone in ministry.

I wrote, "X2 is coming back today—bodily, at least. And I don't know what to do with him without him." When he was away, I was honestly without him and I could function reasonably well. When he'd come home, I'd have to deal with his empty, unreachable, untouchable, withheld presence, and that was the hard part. And yet I'd still have to allow him "in" to the few areas where he still wanted in. He still wanted sex. I felt reduced once again to just a body, to be used and tossed away. And I screamed silently, "If you can't love me, at least leave me alone; stop tormenting me!"

That was a new scream for me, one perhaps even scarier than my old, "Please love me." The lesson was there to be learned, but hope still kept cropping up to haunt me, only to be dashed again and again against the rocks.

I started thinking, "What are you doing here, and what do you want from me?" As similar as all of this is to my "Ministry Widow" story, the twist is entirely different. I lost my ability to see it from any positive perspective, let alone what God wanted.

Now I feared his return. How was I to maintain the illusion of marriage, while protecting myself from his withdrawal, withholding, and indifference? How was I to keep it looking like our marriage was alive and functioning? I knew it wasn't. It was a joke—a horrid, nasty, dirty little joke that threatened to undermine me in every way. And yet I thought I had to maintain the illusion, for the sake of his ministry, which at that time, was flourishing.

And X2 was angry with me, had been for years. My cousin John always says that men need to forgive their wives and then to forgive them again. There's a lot of truth in that. X2 never forgave me, or perhaps he did in his own way, but not in a way that set him free from the accumulated bitterness. And being unable to voice his anger, he resorted to punishment. Silent violence is a subtle, subversive form of abuse. He'd tell me he loved me even as his actions made it clear that he hated me.

I saw a movie about abuse right at that same time. Even as he beat her, he said, "I love you." I recognized the look in her eyes as he said it, felt her feelings as she said, "I love you too." The utter confusion, the horridness of being slapped in the face by "love." Saddest and scariest of all is that X2 quite possibly did love me, or believed he did, at least for a time, just like the man in the movie.

I had only two choices: to leave or to find a way to stay in it.

For me, leaving would be final. I couldn't attempt to use it to manipulate X2 into giving me what I wanted—even if he did, I'd never be able to believe it was real. By then, I wasn't even sure that anything up to that point had been real.

I asked myself would I be a fool for staying in it solely for the financial support, or an even bigger fool to let it all go? After all, I was already alone, and wouldn't it be better to be alone rich than poor?

To a great degree, I had built my world within the marriage and was largely free to do what I wanted. The only problem was when I'd start to feel his negative presence and resentment. I knew that being alone would be survivable, and preferable to being alone in a crowded room, and I was also starting to feel crowded myself. There didn't seem to be much sense in remaining in the confines of marriage without a husband. If I'd known I'd have enough money to be okay, I would have more seriously considered leaving at that point.

I turned to Scripture. Ephesians 5:22-33, 1 Peter 3:7, and Titus 2:6 reminded me that my needs were the normal God-given needs of a woman and of what God has said to be the appropriate behavior of a husband. What I needed was entirely normal—I needed a husband. I still really wanted it to be X2.

I realized that I could not make X2 love me the way God intended. And, to use those Bible passages as moral bribery would not succeed, and even if it did, it would not be satisfactory. Only God could make the changes in X2's heart that He wanted made. He had already made many of the necessary changes in me, although I'm sure there were plenty more.

I did decide to stay in the marriage, see what God might do. On hindsight, I see that it was already too late. I didn't know what was really going on. X2 had already begun to move towards this other woman and even farther away from me.

A friend sent me an article that appeared for a while on the Internet called "The Mind of the Betrayer." It said, among many amazing insights, that "The certainty of the impending death of the marriage may be a secret known only to the betrayer, but the knowledge is ready to be used when the unsuspecting partner is most off guard. Many of the emotions arising from a divorce are worked through at the betrayer's leisure until the right time is chosen to act. Any negotiation between either spouse at this point is fruitless."[50]

Knowing none of this, though, I decided to recommit in my own heart to loving X2 no matter what, while at the same time asking God for a way out of it that He would be okay with if that was just not going to work. God hates divorce.

To love X2 full-heartedly, without reserve, yet not with my eyes closed, I'd need God's strength to be okay in the process. This meant giving my heart entirely up to God for protection, owning and feeling my feelings of sadness, betrayal, anger, and giving them to God as they happened. It meant asking Him to meet my needs, through the Holy Spirit and through myself and others, so that those needs wouldn't get in the way of my loving X2. It meant asking Him for complete healing of past issues, my own and those resulting from the marriage—not blindness, but awareness and real forgiveness and hope in Christ, not in myself or in X2.

It meant asking God to do His will and to help me trust and believe in His faithfulness, no matter what the results. It meant asking

---

[50]   http://www.geocities.com/divorceusa/thebetrayer.html was the link, but Geocities apparently no longer exists, and I can't find the article online elsewhere as of this writing. I don't know the author's name, but he or she certainly deserves credit.

Him to help X2 see his stuff and start to act in awareness of it. It meant asking Him to give X2 a heart of forgiveness for me, and for him to be able to face the things he's angry with me about, confront me if necessary, deal with it, let it go. And to give me the grace to hear him when he did and to ask forgiveness and truly allow God to work in me toward changing those things He would have me change. It meant asking Him to help me see and acknowledge change and growth when it happened.

With God's help, I did manage to hang in there for some years, even though it got harder and harder. God said, "Enough" before I did, but of course He'd known the whole picture all along. God clearly wanted the marriage and the ministry to survive. It was X2 who had other plans.

Twenty years later, and our having been divorced now for many of those years, I can still confess to a great sadness and regret that we didn't do the work together that might have restored us. I wish we'd been able to share both the pain and the joy of allowing God to heal us.

I accompanied X2 on a ministry trip in June 1997, hoping that there would also be some time for just the two of us, perhaps for some sort of reconnection. There wasn't. By this time, things between us had deteriorated even more, but I still didn't know what was behind it all—I still believed that X2 was just busy doing ministry.

I stood on the bank of a small lake near Berlin called the Wannsee. I leaned on the wooden railing and I felt the sun shining through the trees behind me, warming my back. I watched my shadow floating on the water and it suddenly occurred to me: "That's me! I'm a shadow in the sun."

I thought about what that meant for me as I gazed at that shadow rippling in the water. Flat, lifeless, dark, shallow, and ready to fade at the whim of the sun, yet with the added dimension of the shadow falling on the water. Shaky, dim, and not very well defined.

I was following X2 around like a faithful shadow, like a little puppy dog hoping for a pat, begging for a scrap. Feeling like my life was just one big changing metaphor. Wondering, who am I?

In hindsight, I now know, or think I know, exactly when X2 became sexually involved with the other woman. It wasn't right away. I can imagine that the attraction grew over time and that he even made some attempt to fight it.

320

For a number of years, God had blessed our business tremendously, allowing X2 the freedom to travel for his ministry, at his own expense, while still maintaining our income and lifestyle. And He did it despite economic conditions and X2's minimal involvement in the business.

Then one day, an employee left to start his own business, taking one of our critical employees with him. That was the beginning of the end, and the business limped along in a downward spiral until it could no longer go on. It's been said that God will hit a man where it hurts most—in his business—to get his attention. All the signs were there.

MEN

Friends recently gave me a copy of the book THE MYSTERY OF MARRIAGE.[51] I got stuck on page 38 where the author says, ". . . they shall have no business whatsoever in being together at all unless it is first and foremost the business of continuing this same gazing into one another's eyes . . ." I couldn't get past this. I read the page at least 20 times.

If Mike Mason is right, which still remains to be seen (is it just a fantasy?), it contradicts my thinking that I was wrong in loving X2 so much. He was defining what I longed for and never felt. Maybe I wasn't wrong. But X2 didn't love me that way, or didn't after the initial "gazing" phase wore off, and I felt it sorely for the rest of our years together.

What I lacked were words to define what felt was missing, although I tried. But really, no matter what I might have said to communicate what I needed, the words wouldn't have made a difference. It just wasn't there. Going through the things I wrote while I was married to X2, poems and pieces I used to try to get to what I was feeling, makes that clear to me. What the marriage book talks about is exactly what I was trying to get to, trying to understand. Turns out I understood it just fine.

---

[51]   THE MYSTERY OF MARRIAGE, Mike Mason, Multnomah Books, 2005.

My heart is breaking for that shattered dream, for all that was meant to be. And I don't know whether I'll ever be able to believe in the kind of love Mike Mason talks about, whether God's in it or not. I only know that I will continue longing for it all my days.

I have come to recognize one thing about myself, though. That very longing has been my undoing for most of my life. I've never done very well with men, but definitely not since my divorce. And it's my own fault. I realize that I've broken my own heart on behalf of the several guys with whom I've had interaction in the past couple of years. What I've missed when things didn't work out hasn't been these guys themselves, but the potential I had projected into the equation. It was potential that wasn't there; it was only what I "saw" in my longing.

The first was a guy I met in divorce recovery. He talked to me. That was huge, and something I had so sorely missed in my marriage. I never wanted it to stop. One day he flashed me the biggest, most beautiful smile I've ever seen. That smile said, "Welcome." It was so exactly the opposite of what I'd always felt from X2—unwelcome.

This guy wasn't interested in me romantically, but only as a friend, and he always made that clear. It wasn't clear in my mind, though, and when he began dating the woman he eventually married, I broke my own heart over him.

I ended our friendship on what I thought would be a permanent basis. A few years passed, and then he and his wife both insisted that we be friends again. They didn't let me go! And I can honestly say today that I'm sure glad he married her and not me. I've seen that they are right for each other whereas he and I would not have been. The best part is that he still talks to me, and every so often I even get to see that smile.

The second was a guy I knew from high school. We met again at a reunion and I really liked him. He unfortunately has a serious heart condition and he told me that it would be unfair for him to get into a relationship with anyone. Once again, I had to grieve the loss of my projected potential and of course, once again I broke my own heart over it. What's worse, I came home and ate ice cream for two months straight, gaining in the process a lot of pounds, too many of which I've still got. Hardly a desirable souvenir.

The third was a really romantic encounter. I was back in my hometown on vacation, and a friend and I were at the local park the first night of their annual weeklong 4ᵗʰ of July celebration. There was a really great doo-wop band playing in the band shell. As I was sitting in the grass listening, I said, "You know, Lord, it would be so nice to have someone to share this with."

No sooner was that prayer out of my mouth than I noticed that a little black guy who was part of the doo-wop band was motioning in my direction. I looked behind me to see if he was motioning to someone else, but there was no one there. I pointed to myself and shrugged my shoulders. Did he mean me? He pointed to me again, smiled, and nodded his head.

I walked up and he danced with me, sang to me, and he even kissed my hand at the end. If he hadn't been a head shorter than I am, I might have thought it was the answer to my prayer. As it was, I simply giggled at God's marvelous sense of humor.

But, unbeknownst to me, while I was dancing with the little guy, another guy, who was very tall and quite cute, approached my friend and said, "I want to dance with *her*!" She told him to ask me, so the minute I sat back down beside her, this guy walked up and simply held out his hand to me. Oh, boy! I have to confess that it didn't hurt my ego one bit that, out of all the women there, he picked me.

So I got up, took his hand (it was a good fit!) and we walked to the dancing area in front of the band. We both kicked off our shoes and danced barefoot in the grass. We danced until the band quit, and then we talked a while and made a date for the next day. And we kept on holding hands. Neither of us wanted to let go.

We fell, as he put it, into infatuation. I fell in love with the romance of it and of course I immediately started envisioning our doo-wop wedding—right there in the park.

The next afternoon, he called me to confirm our date and asked what I'd like to do. There was a larger park near my hotel, and I suggested that we have a picnic there. It turned out that that park was one of his favorite places and he'd been thinking exactly the same thing.

He picked me up and he brought a kite along. Unfortunately, there wasn't much wind that day, and we couldn't get it to fly. We walked around holding hands and talking for several hours, and then he asked whether I might be willing to accompany him while he ran some errands. I said, "Sure," so off we went.

When we'd finished with the errands, we stopped by his house and he gave me a hoody to wear that night in case it got chilly. Since his house was only a few blocks from the park, we walked back there to see that night's entertainment. Still holding hands.

After we'd been at the park for a few minutes, he said he wanted to jog back home to get us some chairs. He returned with not only the chairs, but also with a drink for himself. Although no alcohol was allowed in the park, he had disguised his rum and orange juice (who on earth drinks rum and orange juice?) in a water bottle, and he proceeded to sip on it for the rest of the evening.

He got fairly tipsy. At one point, I asked him whether he was an alcoholic and he said, "Probably." He wanted me to go drinking with him, but I didn't want to do that. First of all, I don't drink, and bars are noisy places, so we wouldn't be able to talk. Plus, I wasn't about to get into his truck with him driving once he'd started drinking.

He also wanted me to have sex with him, which I wasn't interested in doing. Well, that's not quite true. I would have enjoyed him immensely, and was certainly tempted, but not in the back of his truck, as he suggested. And anyway, I'm not into casual sex. I know it's not what God wants me to be doing, and with my having been so promiscuous in my earlier years, I don't want to be that person any longer.

Finally, on our third night together, and with his having once again had too much rum and orange juice, he said to my friend, "She won't have sex with me. Will you have sex with me?" That was the end of it for me. I walked away and didn't meet him the next night for the fireworks as we had planned.

I'd quit smoking for several months, but took it up again after that. And once again, I felt the loss of potential and broke my own heart. I do have to admit, though, that even after several years, I still wish he'd show up on my doorstep telling me that he's off the sauce and that he has found the Lord. I still love the idea of that doo-wop wedding.

So, I recently decided to try a foray into the world of Internet dating, just to see what was out there. I found a guy I really liked. Within the space of about a week, we went from emailing through the site to emailing privately to talking on the phone. I asked my friend who lives in the same town as this guy if he might know him. I was hoping to set up a casual evening for us to meet with no strings attached. My friend "Googled" him. Turns out he's a registered sex offender. He wasn't nearly as attractive in his mug shot as he was in his dating site photo. Of course I had to walk away from him, too.

You think I need to swear off men?

A New Mirage

Crissy Shreve

It might have been different,
Had I not found you.
And yet still it's just the same bloody same
Old thing.

Phones that never ring.
Times foregone that all your money
And all your plans
Will not regain.

I need you so badly!
My tongue is wet from the taste of you.
And though I drink my fill on those rare occasions,
The desert stretches hot before me.

I must let go!
Oases needed are oases seldom found.
But should I take to my camel
And give him lead
Perhaps he'll find me a new mirage.

CHAPTER TWENTY-SEVEN

TRIPS AND THINGS

Sometimes I would accompany X2 on one of his trips, and when I did, we'd usually take a vacation somewhere in Europe. On one of them, we took a carriage ride across the North Sea.

Huh? Are you scratching your head?

If you've ever wondered what the ocean looks like without any water in it, you can easily find out. When the tide is out, you can walk 13 km (about seven miles) from Cuxhaven, in north Germany, across the North Sea to an island called Neuwerk. We chose to go by horse-drawn carriage, a two-hour ride over what might best be described as very wet desert. As it was quite foggy at 7 AM when we set out, we could not see the island until we got fairly close to it. I kept asking, "Are we *sure* there's an island out there?"

Science fiction has nothing on the North Sea in the fog. Figures would suddenly materialize out of nowhere, walking in the other direction, and then just as suddenly disappear back into the fog. There were tall buoys at intervals along the route to give people a place of refuge should they not make it to shore. The tide waits for no one.

And it was cold. The ocean winds were not the least bit diminished by the lack of ocean beneath them. Even wrapped in several wool blankets, I was freezing. The driver and everyone else in the carriage would shush me in unison whenever I'd say, "Brrrr." What else would you say to a German horse to make him stop? So, every time the wind kicked up, I had to say, "Whoa!"

Visibility limited, our view consisted literally of the south end of two northbound horses. The dubious joy of learning the excremental habits of a horse included the fact that when a horse has to urinate, it will stop cold—as our driver put it, for a *"Pinkle Pause."* It occurred to me that many an outlaw in the old west either got caught or escaped thanks to the *"Pinkle Pause."* They don't tell you about that in the movies or the history books. The horse on the left made several such pauses during our crossing, the other not one—he waited until he was back home in his own driveway. I can't decide which of the two I think was better behaved.

Another time, X2 and I went to Paris! The thought was exciting and scary at the same time. I was a bit afraid because I knew virtually no French, and I'd heard that the French people dislike Americans and Germans. The day before we left Germany for Paris, we had brunch at a friend's house. She had lived in Paris and was fluent in French. I mentioned my concern.

"Don't worry," she said, "Just remember one thing: '*Ils sont fou, les Parisiens.*'" It means, "They're crazy, the Parisians."

I thought this was pretty funny, so I practiced saying it out loud. When the train from Frankfurt to Paris stopped at the border in Strasbourg, the German train crew got off and a new French crew boarded. Suddenly everything was French, even the menus in the restaurant car. Shaky, but undaunted, I simply resorted to, "*Ils sont fou, les Parisiens.*"

We loved Paris. I got to seriously screw up some French. At one point, I asked a cop how to get to the Seine—actually, I just asked, "Where is the Seine?" in French, but then I couldn't understand the directions he gave me, and so we headed off in the wrong direction.

I practiced my little phrase all weekend and by the end I despaired that I'd never get to use it. After a wonderful couple of days, it was time to board the train back to Frankfurt. The station had one of those big green boards with clacking numbers that show the particulars for each train. We were early, and our train hadn't yet been posted, so we sat down at a table near the board to have a final *café au lait* and wait for the info to appear.

The waiter was another of those guys who could take one look at you and know where you were from and what language you spoke. He addressed us in English. I ordered our coffees in French anyway, and he started off to fetch them for us. I hadn't fooled him, but we did get what I ordered.

A young woman sat down at the next table. She ordered a drink and then proceeded to take a sandwich and an orange out of her backpack. We drank our coffee while she ate her lunch and had her drink. When she was finished, she got up, leaving her sandwich wrappings and her orange peel on the table.

The waiter returned and stood there, arms akimbo, looking disdainfully at her mess. It was great. He looked at it from one side of the table, then moved to the other side and looked at it again. He grimaced. He muttered in four different languages—French, German, English and Spanish. He was clearly not amused.

I caught his eye, smiled sweetly, and said, *"Ils sont fou, les Parisiens."*

He broke into a huge grin and replied, *"Oui, Madame, oui, oui."*

Back at home, when I was telling my friend Sue about it—she's pretty good at French, so I knew she'd love the story—she pointed out that what made it even better is that I was an American tourist, saying that to the Parisian waiter.

By the way, there's just something about making love in Paris. I think it must be the water.

Daughter-in-law Martha comes from a huge family, and they all think they can speak German. To be fair, the grandmother actually could. In any case, they have this crazy sense of humor, which they combine with their own version of "German." The result is things like "shoes" for *"tschuß"* and "our feet are the same" for *"auf wiedersehen,"* both of which mean good-bye or seeya later.

You can't literally translate much from English to German or vice versa. The phrases we use are just not the same as theirs—they think differently than we do. We say, "How are you?" and the Germans say, "How goes it?" or *"Wie gehts?"* Martha, upon meeting step-Mike's *Grossmutter* (grandmother) for the first time said, *"Wie alt bist Du?"* The direct translation for "How are you?" would be *"Wie bist Du?"* which you'd be unlikely to say in German anyway, but *"Wie alt bist Du?"* means "How *old* are you?"

We visited wet, rainy, cold Germany one June, step-Mike and Martha in tow. Martha got seriously constipated between the time change and the long plane flight. So, shortly after we arrived, the four of us went to the local town. I was given the job of finding a *Drogerie* where we could get Martha a laxative, while X2 and step-Mike headed off to the tavern to drink some German beer. Although I was enjoying being able to speak significantly more German than Martha could, and was thus feeling pretty "smart," I was at a loss when it came to telling the salesperson what I wanted—well, without using vulgar language, at least. Fortunately, after I made several false starts, the salesperson took pity on me and asked in English what I needed.

This was my favorite of all my trips to Germany. Because we had step-Mike and Martha along, we did touristy things, and X2 had no choice but to pay attention to them and speak English. Plus, put Martha in any scenario and fun will be had.

A friend lent us a car to use. It was an antique Mercedes that had once belonged to an ambassador. There were controls for the radio in the back seat so that the ambassador could listen to whatever he wanted without bothering his chauffeur, who'd had, apparently, no say, or maybe just no taste in music.

We were stuck in traffic between Innsbruck, Austria, and the Italian border for several hours, and X2 thought he'd see if he could get a traffic report on the radio. After doing that, he tried to turn off the radio, but it kept coming back on. He'd scratch his head, mutter to himself, sigh in resignation, turn it off again, but the thing kept coming back on. Once or twice he thought he finally had it off, only to have it come on again a minute later. He was terrified he'd broken the radio.

Meanwhile, step-Mike, Martha, and I were trying our darnedest not to laugh too obviously. Martha was sitting next to the back seat radio controls.

I've often said that hearing Germans try to speak English is the best way I have of learning German. Someone from Germany is always asking me if they can become a napkin. I usually say something like, "No, but you're welcome to try. I'll watch." (The German word for *to have* or *to receive* is *bekommen*).

X2 and I were playing Rummy with Thorsten, who stayed with us for a summer. He went out suddenly and turned to X2 and said with great vehemence, "I hope you have four asses!" X2 calmly replied, "No, only one."

One German woman told me that her husband was at home in Germany "looking for the children." I replied, "Well, I hope he finds them."

The greatest mistranslation story is that of Andreas, a German fellow step-Mike met at college. Andreas was in this country for a year on a work-study program. He had completed his studies and he came home to our house with step-Mike for the Thanksgiving weekend. Step-Mike went back to school, but Andreas stayed for three months. Once he finally found a job, he bought a car and moved in with a single German guy named Charlie. During the course of Andreas's stay with him, Charlie put on a few pounds. Andreas's comment was, "Charlie's gotten so fat he can no longer fit into his dresses." (*Clothes* and *dresses* are the same word in German).

Andreas was also known to ask for bag teas, and one time, upon hearing a loud noise, said that a car had misfired, which I suppose is technically true, but of course we say backfire.

There was a couple who stayed with us, and one morning while they were there, I tried to get downstairs to grab a cup of coffee before they showed up for breakfast, but the wife beat me to it. I said to her, "I'm not talking to anyone yet, I haven't brushed my teeth." She said, "I haven't either, I'm waiting till after lunch."

A very nice lady, who spoke English very well—in fact she had studied *American* English, which is unusual—told us that she and her husband had visited a ranch in South Dakota run by a retarded couple. It was actually a retired couple.

Ulrike, when she first decided to try speaking English, said, "I'll be ready in 14 minutes."

Another fellow from Germany, who stayed with us for a month or so, was a *big* guy. I had to measure him since he didn't know his height in feet and inches, only in meters (two of them). He was six foot six. He was bald-headed, wore an earring, and looked a lot like a Hell's Angel, except that he was really very sweet. One evening he came to me with a request: did I have any "bug spray?" So I asked him if he wanted the kind you put on yourself to ward off mosquitoes, or the kind you spray in the yard, or what? He said no, that there was a spider on the wall. So, I told him that when there's a spider on the wall, you just take a tissue and squish it. He said that he couldn't do that—he was afraid of "those animals." Sigh.

A little girl named Priscilla, who was about five, came to a picnic at our house with her rather large family—if I remember correctly, nine of the ten kids joined their parents on the trip from Germany. We served them our typical picnic fare—burgers, potato salad, etc. An hour or so after dinner, Priscilla told her mother that she was hungry. The mother suggested that perhaps I'd give her some more of what we'd eaten, to which Priscilla replied, in German, of course, "*Es hat nicht geschmecht, aber ich habe es trotzdem gegessen.*" (It didn't taste good, but I ate it anyway).

One time I asked a visiting German fellow about his family and he replied, "We are seven sisters," a mistranslation of *Geschwister*, or brothers and sisters.

Another woman who stayed with us put her coffee into the microwave complete with spoon every day for a week before I noticed.

Germans typically drive stick shifts and seldom have any experience with automatic transmissions. When they'd use our Jeep, we had to be very careful to make sure they understood how it worked. The same woman who'd put the spoon in the microwave would shut off the car while it was still in gear. Another kept putting her left foot on the brake as if it were a clutch and couldn't figure out why she wasn't moving. Somehow, the microwave and the Jeep both survived.

I had the pleasure of spending an afternoon with X2's mother in Bremen (in northern Germany). We went to lunch at a place where there were many small take-out shops specializing in different types of food. We walked around several times trying to choose, until finally I suggested we eat Bavarian.

I ordered *Leberknödelsuppe* and *Weißwurst* (liver dumpling soup and white sausage). *Mutter* (Mother) told the fellow behind the counter to split my soup into two bowls because she wasn't that hungry. I was not amused. I really wanted that liver dumpling all to myself. We sat down and next thing I knew, there came *Mutter's* fork, aimed at my *Weißwurst*. When I suggested that perhaps she might order her own, she said no, she only wanted to try it. She'd never eaten it before because it was from *southern* Germany!

Another morning, at her house, I caught *Mutter* pulling the soft white doughy centers out of the *Brötchen* (rolls). It was all I could do not to smack her hand—that's the best part!

One evening at *Mutter's* house I was out in the yard taking some wash off the line. The boy who lived upstairs was outside too, and he said "*Moin*" to me. I had no clue what it meant; it didn't make sense, and I just looked at him and didn't answer. He probably thought I was nuts—or stupid. I finally figured out that it might be a form of "*Morgen*" in the local dialect. As it turns out, I was more or less correct, but *Morgen* means morning or good morning, and it was 7 o'clock in the evening. *Moin* means "hi."

It's only fair that I tell a mistranslation story on myself. One day I had to go somewhere before X1 got home from work, and I left him a note to let him know I'd fed Sheppie the dog. I wrote, "*Ich habe der Hund gefressen,*" followed in English by, "I hope that doesn't mean I ate the dog."[52] Of course that's exactly what it meant.

---

[52]   In German, people eat, and animals feed. I thought I was pretty smart to know the difference between *essen* (eat) and *fressen* (feed). So I used the past tense of feed (*gefressen*) as one would in English—I fed the dog—except that there's another word in German for the act of feeding an animal—*füttern*. I should have said, "*Ich habe den Hund gefüttert.* And yes, it should have been *den Hund,* not *der.*

LIFE BESIDE THE SILENT MAN
Crissy Shreve

Life beside the silent man,
Is loneliness in bones and skin,
An emptiness that never ends,
A dream that never did begin,
A nightmare which I cannot wake,
A sugarcoated lie, a fake.

Life beside the silent man,
Whose walls are thick,
Whose heart is thin,
Who's built a wall to keep me out,
That only serves to keep him in,
That only serves to keep me sick.

The silent man speaks not a word,
Though silence carries its own voice,
Disdain so loud can't be misheard,
An understanding of my choice,
Misunderstanding it may be,
There is no truth that's told to me.

The silent man seeks to control,
While saying softly, lead the way,
I may not follow, or I may,
But only if I like the way,
You go, oh, I will sound sincere,
But never as I may appear.

And weeding through the lies did I,
Awake one day to find he'd gone,
Long years before; I knew it then,
His words at last were ringing true,
So many things he had to say,
As silently he slipped away.

Chapter Twenty-Eight

Ending

For some reason, X2 insisted that we get a new motor home. I had major mixed emotions about it. Certainly the prospect of designing a new coach from nose to tail was right up my alley. At the same time, though, I cried at just the thought of giving up the one we had. That was so unlike me; I've always been one to get excited about something new, and getting a new coach was definitely exciting. Still, many of the best times of my life and of our life together had been in the coach we had.

To make it worse, I had a feeling that getting a new coach would be the end of X2 and me. To this day, I don't know where that feeling came from, nor can I tell you exactly what it looked like, only that it was strong. On hindsight, I know that all that happened would have happened whether or not we got a new coach. The end was already in the works. I alternated between watching for signs and trying to convince myself that it was just my imagination.

It wasn't my imagination, but the signs were subtle. I agreed to the new coach and squelched my fears as best I could.

There was a coach available for fairly quick delivery; it was already on the production line. I had to get my ducks in a row in a hurry to design the interior layout and pick colors. After a few weeks at my drafting table at home, our old coach and I moved to the campground (called the Bird's Nest) at the factory and we stayed there for seven weeks. X2 took off on one of his trips. I was in charge.

Those weeks were bittersweet. Even as I watched the new coach being built, I grieved the loss of the old one. I'm a hugger, and I'd hug it every morning on my way to the factory. Hugging a 40-foot long vehicle is a bit of a trick, and I'm sure I looked silly, but I didn't care. I was hurting and grieving and already missing it. I suspect that, on some level, I was grieving the end of my marriage too, even though it hadn't happened yet, at least not on the surface.

I've defined certain experiences in my life as "hit the ceiling—hit the floor." This was one of them. I was so up about the new coach even as I was devastated at the loss of the old one. In most cases, ceiling-floor experiences happen in that order, a major up followed by a crash. This time, I was bouncing—hit the ceiling, hit the floor, repeat often.

It only took me a few days to train the people at the factory. They quickly figured out that it was more cost-effective to ask me how I wanted something done, rather than doing it their way first and then having to redo it. Sound familiar? I seem to have to teach that lesson every time. So when I'd turn up at the factory at 8 AM, there'd be a line of various installers waiting for me, saying, "Miz Cris, how do you want . . . ?"

I wanted the laminate window casings stacked a certain way. I was told it couldn't be done. Ha! Bet me. Half an hour later, I was back, diagram in hand. It wasn't even close to rocket science. The window casings turned out exactly as I wanted them.

While our new coach was being built, I happened to mention to the customer liaison that I write poetry. She suggested I write something about my experience at the factory and living in a motorhome. I had a lot of fun with it and got to read it at the talent show the following fall. It's called "Yankee Bird." It may not all make sense to you, but it would make complete sense to anyone who's over owned a Blue Bird motor coach or even any motorhome at all.

YANKEE BIRD
Crissy Shreve

That southern charm is still alive, you hear, "Yes, Ma'am" and "Suh."
Don't bother asking questions 'cause the answer's always, "Huh?"
"How ya doin'?" seems to be the way the locals greet,
But no one really wants to know, shoot, they're already down the street.

There isn't much that you can find, beats lunch time at the Nest,
Monday, Tuesday, Wednesday, Thursday, what about the rest?
A restaurant just can't be found, no matter where you look,
Try the Piggly-Wiggly? You mean I have to cook?

You wake each morning with the "Birds," their diesel engines purring,
And pity all the "SOBs"—Some Other Brand preferring.
But even those who sleep like logs through anything at all,
Will wake right up at 7 to the factory whistle's call.

Rally in the Valley is the highlight of October,
You get a high on fun and friends even if you're sober.
Can't wait to see what's waiting in the goody bag, you say,
Clutch it tightly in your fist, throw most of it away.

The hillbilly casino at the Nest is mighty fine;
Instead of playing Twenty-one, we all play Ninety-nine.
The game itself is fun to learn, it isn't very hard,
The problem is remembering to take another card!

The laughter in the clubhouse can reduce a man to tears,
When someone tells a joke you haven't heard for twenty years.
Senior citizen humor pokes great fun at its own plight,
"My wife shut me off six months ago, but I just found out last night!"

A Wanderlodge comes well equipped, including an altimeter,
That fact that none has sprouted wings is these birds' only limiter,
We drive around undauntedly, we try to make 'em fly,
Like New York taxi drivers, people cringe when we pass by.

Birds are happy campers, and we always wear a smile,
Until it's time to stop for gas, six gallons to the mile,
We'll drive an extra hundred miles, to save a dime a gallon,
Spend half a million on a coach, but gas prices get us scowlin.'

Guys, here's a thought to comfort you, if gas mileage makes you grouse,
You're right, it's not that great for a car, but it's *real* good for a house!
So if you're driving in the car, just think about that when,
She says, "Oh, Honey, we've got to stop. I've got to go *again!*"

We'll spend the night in an outlet mall, road music helps us sleep,
If we've got twenty dollars in our pockets we can keep.
A little inconvenient? Run the generator, honey,
If it's a little noisy—what the hell, we've saving money!

A factory tour gives meaning to the words "Arrive alive."
Rolling benches, tractor pulled . . . Wait! Who let Brenda drive?
But there's no where else where you will see a sight that's quite as classy,
As some poor fool driving 'round the plant on nothing but a chassis.

Wasted space in a motor home can really get me bitchin',
You'd think these cabinets had been built for a 20 x 30 kitchen!
Grand designs, well-engineered, their very best they're givin' it.
One tiny detail overlooked, *they* don't have to live in it.

It's easier, they love to say, it's the way we always do it,
It seems to me they ought to figure out sometimes they blew it.
It doesn't make a lot of sense, no reason and no rhyme,
To do it their way first, and then my way the second time.

Of course as owners, we all know ten ways to do it better,
We rant, we rave, we bang our heads, we write another letter.
For our advice, what do we get? Just what they think it's worth:
"Thanks, but we don't care to know how things are done up north."

Homeless people, coaches in for service, all around us,
How long can it take to change a fuse? It really does astound us.
High-level conversations emanating from this bunch,
Who spend entire mornings sitting there discussing lunch!

These little imperfections are just things we'll keep ignorin',
The notion of the "perfect coach" is just an oxymoron,
So I'll shut up, it's time for this to be my final word,
When all is said and done, there still is nothing like a Bird.

After those seven weeks, our new coach was finally done. X2 returned, and it was time to leave the old coach behind and drive away in the new one. The time I'd spent grieving helped me make the transition without too much sadness. Step-Mike's "cow" (Condo On Wheels) even better described the new coach. It had a dishwasher, a disposal, and a washer/dryer! What wasn't to love?

We had a lot at a motor home resort in Hilton Head, and another in Naples. X2 and I would leave home right after Christmas and head for Naples. He'd stay a week or so, then take off on a trip, and I'd "winter" on my own. When it started getting too hot in Naples, some time in March, he'd come back, move us to Hilton Head, and repeat the process. When it started getting too hot there, we'd head back home.

I'd have my laptop along. We had phone lines in both locations. Those were the good old days of dial-up Internet. I was busy with my genealogy—it kept me out of trouble.

We took X2's mother along on a trip one time. *Mutter* was a bit of a disaster in the kitchen. She loved to cook, but she always made a huge mess and refused to clean up afterwards. There was a small stove in the motor home, but it was under a hinged piece of the countertop. I never showed it to her. She was afraid to use the microwave, so she made herself bread and honey sandwiches every day, and still managed to dribble that lovely, sticky honey all over anything within her reach. We did take her out to dinner every night, though. Fair's fair.

After we got the Chihuahuas, I discovered that there were snakes in Hilton Head. The lots were covered with pine straw around the trees, to keep the weeds at bay. My little rascals would always find a snake. Fortunately, they were baby snakes, but I quickly figured out that I needed to keep the dogs on the grassy areas and out of the pine straw. I loved Pampas Grass and was thrilled to have some of my own planted on our lot. After a few years, someone told me that copperheads lay their eggs in Pampas Grass. I had it yanked out. I like snakes, but I don't like copperheads. One of my neighbors killed a huge copperhead that was in his tree, and he showed it to me. It was a beautiful snake, but I was very glad it was dead.

I did my third Heimlich in Hilton Head. Toby was just a puppy and he still liked to chew. He got hold of a tiny stick and it got stuck in his throat. I very gently did the Heimlich using only my fingers. It worked.

One time when we were in Hilton Head, X2 was up on a ladder washing the motorhome, and the ladder started to tilt. X2 grabbed onto the awning support and his wedding ring got caught. He nearly tore off his finger. I had just left the resort to run some errands, but I'd told him I needed to stop at the office on my way out, so he got on his bicycle and, bleeding profusely, pedaled down to the office looking for me. He walked in and nearly passed out.

I'd not stopped at the office because it looked too busy; I'd decided to do it on the way back, so I wasn't there. The lady in the office took him to a local clinic for finger repair. They had to cut off the ring. After his finger healed, it remained swollen and there was scar tissue, so he refused to get a new ring and never wore one after that. That in itself could have been construed as "it is what it is," but after his finger had healed, when I suggested he get a new ring, he responded with some hostility, saying, "What? You want me to tear my finger completely off the next time?"

I was pretty sure by that time that X2 no longer wanted to be married to me. The signs were becoming less subtle. He was more withdrawn from me than ever. I called it silent violence, and I would say, "I don't know how to interpret your silence." At midnight, when 1999 turned into 2000, he perfunctorily wished me a happy new year and a happy birthday, then immediately called a ministry colleague overseas and spent a lot of time on the phone with him—except that is was really with her. He was already involved with this man's wife, but no one else knew it yet.

The new coach was sweet, and we loved it—there were so many little things that worked much better than they had in the old one. It still took me a while to get over the old coach, but the new one, having turned out exactly as I'd imagined and designed, won me over pretty quickly.

A typical scenario would be X2 driving this huge rig (43 feet and seventeen tons of coach, plus a tow vehicle) down the road, with a cigarette in one hand, a cup of coffee in the other, one eye on the GPS, one eye on the road, and two Chihuahuas asleep in his lap. He'd even manage to talk on the phone at the same time. Talk about multi-tasking.

He'd also pass everything on the road. If we were approaching an exit we needed to take, he'd insist on passing at least two other vehicles before he would even consider pulling over into the right lane. This got to be funny—I'd be certain that one of those times he was going to miss the exit. He never did. We knew another couple that had "Blue Bayou" painted on the back of their coach. Get it? Blew By You. I wish I'd thought of that before they did.

One time in upstate New York, we got pulled over for speeding. The only option was to open the front door and let the cop come in. I suspect he was just as interested in seeing the inside of our coach as he was in giving us a ticket.

"Sir, did you know you were going 85 miles per hour?"

"Gee, I didn't think this thing could go that fast."

"Sir, you've got a 500-horsepower Series 60 Detroit Diesel pusher in this baby. We both know it can go that fast."

"Oh."

That cop had done his homework, and we got the ticket.

On another of our motor home trips, X2 was cheerfully barreling down a four-lane divided highway, but it was out in the boonies somewhere, not limited-access, so there were side roads and cars entering the highway from the right. X2 was in the left lane so that he'd not have to deal with them. I was riding farther back in the coach at my desk, doing something on the computer. I happened to look up and there was a school bus on a side road, about to pull out onto the highway.

In front of us was a tiny black car with three baby kids in the back seat, while in front of that car was a van, all of us in the left lane. Now, X2 didn't grow up in this country, so watching out for school buses wasn't high on his radar. I hollered up to X2, "Watch out for that school bus! He's going to pull out."

At just that moment, the school bus entered the highway, only a little ways ahead of where we were. That wasn't so bad, except that it immediately stopped and the idiot driver put out his side stop sign.

The driver of the van, two vehicles ahead of us, slammed on his brakes and stopped. The black car with the baby kids in the back seat had no choice but to do the same. X2 *stood* on the brakes. Stopping a thirty-five-thousand-pound vehicle is no small feat. Doing it in a hurry is next to impossible. We stopped a scant inch from the rear bumper of that little black car and those three baby kids.

I know for sure that God nudged me to look up at just that moment, and that my warning gave X2 the few critical seconds he needed to react to the school bus. Had he been adrift in thought, or even slightly less focused, that little car would have been the filling in the Oreo cookie between us and the van, and those baby kids . . . well, I shudder just thinking about it.

I would occasionally write for X2, especially when he'd unexpectedly be asked to speak and had no time to prepare something. Of course I'd write in English and he'd translate it into German. It was really neat to hear a tape of him giving "my" message, and since I knew what it was about, I could understand it perfectly. Sometimes, God would even speak to me through it, even though I'd written it. The ups and downs continued, and that made it hard to get any clarity on what was true and what wasn't.

I continued to sense the growing distance between X2 and me, but I had no idea what was to come and was totally unprepared for it.

Although X2's ministry was primarily overseas, we got to know pastors from various churches in the U.S. One of these churches was near where I'd grown up. X2 was asked to speak there at a mid-week service. It was his first time speaking in the U.S., and I was excited to hear him in English. He talked about how I'd brought him to church those first times and how that got it all started.

For the day or so before he was due to speak at that church, X2 kept saying he didn't want to do it. I couldn't imagine why not, but it suddenly occurred to me that recently, when it was time for a trip overseas, he'd often said the same thing—he didn't want to go. Something had changed. Something was wrong. Still, hearing his talk, those who attended thought that we had the perfect, God-centered marriage. Even I was fooled, but it didn't last long.

After the service, we were taken to the home of a rather unique and delightful couple from that church. They served us roasted vegetables. I'd never had roasted vegetables before and I loved them. They had an amazing house and garden. They grew Joe Pye Weed. Who ever heard of Joe Pye Weed?

On the way to their house, we passed a sign, and I saw that they lived in the same town where my mother and her husband had

342

owned property decades earlier. During dinner, I asked whether they knew the couple that had been my mother's friends, the people who had always sent us the great Christmas cards when I was little. Sure enough, they knew them well.

We'd traveled in this country several times with X2's overseas ministry colleague and his wife. One time we rented them a small motor home, and we traveled out west together, with them following us. A month after the speaking engagement above, we once again took a trip with them, but they rode with us in the motor home, and we stayed at a campground that had a motel on the property. We knew people who lived in Vermont, and we'd heard much about it, so that's where we went.

Things started getting strange. The night we arrived in Vermont, the wife said she wanted to go swimming. X2 went with her, saying that he felt sorry for her since she didn't speak English. He also mentioned that she was unhappy having to sleep with her husband at the motel. The next day, the two of them, X2 and the wife, got in the car, ostensibly to go up the road to the liquor store, which was only a mile away. X2 didn't tell me they were going. I saw them leaving and asked the husband about it. He said they'd gone for beer.

I still didn't really catch on, even when they came back over an hour later. X2 went to great lengths to explain how there had been a truck parked in front of the store, so they'd missed seeing it, and wound up miles farther up the road before they realized they'd passed it. The fact that they'd been gone so long might have missed my radar, but the long involved explanation did make me a little suspicious.

I was still pretty much operating under the belief that when God calls us to do something, He protects us. And it's not untrue, but it does not preclude free will. I had some pretty thick blinders on my eyes. On the several occasions when I started to pick up on a clue, I said to myself, "Nah. God wouldn't let that happen. He's protecting us, and more importantly, He's protecting the ministry."

One of the things that had made me believe this was that He'd prospered our business so that it would continue to support us in X2's absence. I said before that I was later able to pinpoint exactly when X2's free will took him away from God's intention, because there was a specific point when the business took a nosedive. By the time we went to Vermont, the business was definitely tanking.

The next day, I was sitting next to X2 at the picnic table, and the wife was sitting across from him. I dropped something, and when I bent down to retrieve it, I saw that their legs were intertwined. That was when I knew.

Some ten years earlier, when X2 started going on his ministry trips, he'd mentioned this woman and that he really liked her, and that I would, too. As things progressed, he began staying at their house, and often the husband would go away for several days on his own business, leaving them alone together. Just a month before our trip to Vermont, the husband had left as usual, but, having forgotten something, he returned unexpectedly, and he caught them in bed together.

I didn't find out this part of it until nearly a year later, but I confronted X2 after the picnic table incident, asking if he was sleeping with her. He denied it and continued to deny it for months. But I knew. All the pieces fell into place.

All three of them knew! They'd decided not to say anything, in hopes of salvaging the ministry, but God wasn't going to let it continue. Apparently they'd agreed that X2 and the wife could remain friends, but no more sleeping together.

I was, of course, completely distraught. Despite X2's denials, I knew what I knew, and I saw my life falling apart before my eyes. I took the pups for a walk around the campground, all sorts of terrifying thoughts rolling around in my head. God interrupted those thoughts to give me three very clear instructions:

1. You will honor Me in all you do.
2. You will remember that X2 is your brother in Christ, no matter what happens.
3. You will not isolate.

All three were exactly what I needed, and despite all that went on in my head and around me, these concepts kept me focused, if not exactly sane. Sadly, I knew that God wouldn't have said these things to me if what I suspected weren't true.

When we got home, X2 immediately took off for several weeks on another trip, and also of course to be with this woman, although still denying any inappropriate attachment. He did nothing to alleviate my pain and fear; he just left me alone in it.

I was in deep trouble, feeling utterly abandoned and hopeless. I very seriously considered suicide, to the degree that I scared myself. I had it all figured out. We'd built a pole barn for the motor home. I would take the pups and climb into bed in the motor home inside the closed barn, turn on the engine, and leave it running.[53] The pups and I would just go to sleep. I didn't want to die necessarily—I simply couldn't see how I was to navigate the hell I was in. And I wasn't thinking to manipulate X2 into staying with me. He wasn't there, and I told no one of my plan.

God laid it on my heart to write a letter to my little granddaughters to tell them why I would no longer be in their lives, why they'd never get to know me. I couldn't write that letter. I simply couldn't come up with a good enough reason. God reminded me of His promise, that He had a plan for me, for hope and a future.[54] As bleak as the future looked to me in that moment, I decided to give Him a chance to show me what He could do.

I should not have been alone. I wasn't alone. God was there and He used that letter to bring me back to His way of thinking. He would walk with me through hell; He would carry me as necessary.

I sent out an email telling a few close friends what was going on. X2 had wanted me to keep quiet about the whole thing. I realized that keeping quiet was isolating, and God had specifically told me not to do that. In the email, I said that I'd come much too close to killing myself but had chosen not to. At church the next morning, my dear friend Ruth-Ann, one of the people to whom I'd sent the email, came up to me, put her arms around me, and started crying. I thought something bad had happened to *her.* Then she said, "You scared me."

Ruth-Ann became my "angel." She slogged through it all with me, even going so far as to attend several seminars at church so that I wouldn't have to go alone. I had a key to her house in case I needed her—no matter what time it was, day or night.

The woman with whom X2 was involved had given me various gifts when she'd stayed at my house or when we'd travelled together with her and her husband. Some of these things were really quite nice,

---

[53] I later was told that diesel fumes are much less toxic than gasoline fumes; it probably wouldn't have worked all that well anyway.

[54] For I know the plans I have for you, declares the LORD, plans to prosper you and not to harm you, plans to give you hope and a future. Jeremiah 29:11 NIV

but their very existence in my house felt icky. Ruth-Ann and I carried them out to my yard and burned them.

Ruth-Ann's husband Dave is an industrial-strength shrink. I'm only half joking. He really is an industrial psychologist; it's not quite the same as a clinical psychologist. When I'd been in therapy years before, I'd learned how to cry effectively. Imagine a wounded animal caught in a trap. It's a gut-level wailing and keening that isn't pretty. This kind of crying is scary—not only to the person crying, but to most people who would hear it. In order to reach this depth and purge the pain, a person crying this way can't be completely sane in the moment. The question for the one crying and the one hearing is whether there's a way back. There is, of course, but it's not something to do alone or with someone who doesn't understand it.

Dave understood. On several occasions when my pain was so overwhelming that I thought I'd explode out of my skin, I'd go get in Dave's arms and wail it out. He'd just quietly hold me through it.

Ruth-Ann and I talked a lot about my neurotic dependence on X2. I nearly got stuck in my typical desperation to find another man to replace him, and as quickly as possible. I certainly needed *something*. Ruth-Ann, in perhaps her finest moment ever, asked me, "Does it have to have a penis?"

An amazing question, and one I'd never considered. Family and friends who loved me surrounded me. Could I not count their love and friendship as valuable? And certainly God was with me. Did I *have* to have a man?

I didn't. And, of course, that would have been the worst thing I could have done. Focusing on finding a replacement for X2 instead of on healing would have been a disaster. My focus needed to be on God. He, along with those who loved me, was what I needed.

I went to see one of the elders at our church who was most closely involved in X2's ministry, and I told her what was going on. When X2 returned, she and another elder called us in to discuss it further. X2 had been the fair-haired boy, and his ministry had been highly successful and effective. He continued to deny what was going on, and they didn't want it to be true. They didn't want to believe X2 could be living a double life, and they sure didn't want to have to deal with that particular can of worms.

The second elder didn't believe me, and in that meeting she pretty well nailed me to the wall. She even went so far as to ask me whether I was "healthy enough to be married." I was in shock and speechless. It took me several hours after we left to be able to say a word to anyone about anything. I couldn't even cry. It was a trauma on top of a trauma and it nearly put me over the edge. X2 was gracious enough to say on the way home that he'd actually felt sorry for me in that meeting. Gee, thanks.

God came to my rescue yet again. He reminded me that it's never a good idea to confuse Him with people and what they do or say, even people in authority in the church. They are not God. Once I got past the shock, I was able to see that it was about her, the elder. She didn't want it to be true, so she tried to make it about me. It wasn't her most shining moment.

But this same elder did suggest that I get some praise CDs and play them in my car. I did that, and it was exactly what I needed. God worked in my soul. I discovered the comfort, and yes, even joy, of praising God in the midst of my despair. It was a way to let Him into it, to allow Him to carry enough of it that I could stumble forward. And stumble I did, until that day when he set me back on my feet, wobbly, but able to walk again.

Life went on, with X2 continuing to deny what I knew to be true, while I continued to vacillate between not wanting it to be true and knowing that it was. X2 began telling me that he no longer loved me, no longer wanted the marriage, and, after nearly twenty-five silent years, he started telling me all that was wrong with me. He'd always been one to say what he thought someone wanted to hear rather than what was true. He had a few sessions with a guy shrink and came home one day saying that he'd "learned" that doing that was actually lying. You think?

As hard as it was to hear about how flawed I was, that time was the most honest in our entire marriage. There were no holds barred. It was actually rather refreshing. The reality is that some, maybe even much, of what he was saying was true. How I wish he'd done some of that years earlier, even perhaps dragging me to a counselor.

I threw a huge catered party for X2's 60th birthday, and all his buddies from church came and honored him.

Finally, the colleague (whose wife X2 was involved with) tried to blackmail X2 into giving him a job in the ministry for which he was entirely unsuited. If X2 didn't give him the job, he'd tell our pastor what was going on. X2 had no choice but to come clean. He talked to our pastor first, who encouraged him to give up this woman and make his marriage right, and then to get back to his ministry. Then he told me. By that time, it wasn't even much of a shock. He continued to make it very clear to me that he still didn't love me or want the marriage. He wanted this woman.

Not to excuse his behavior, or my own, but I think it's safe to say that the evil one had a hand in the whole thing. He had been working behind the scenes all along. He didn't care whether he destroyed X2 or me in the process. The ministry was bringing people to Christ, and the evil one just couldn't stand it.

X2 trashed his entire life and everyone and everything in it for this woman. I asked him whether she was really worth it. He wouldn't answer me. Apparently he thought so.

It took a few years, but thanks to good teaching at Divorce Recovery, I was finally able to forgive X2. It wasn't a one-time thing, either. I had to do it over and over until I was finally free of it. Then I was able to forgive myself as well. The two go hand in hand. I certainly was not without fault in the failure of the marriage.

I often ask divorced people I meet to tell me what was their contribution to the demise of their marriages. They invariably answer, "He did this . . . ," or "She did that . . ." So I patiently try again—"Okay, I get that, but what was *your* contribution to the demise of your marriage?" The concept of their having had any fault just isn't on their radar.

PEWIE LEWIE
February, 2012

Valentine's Day again approaches, and I am sitting here in my finally finished all-season porch-*cum*-nature observatory enjoying the spring-like weather we've all appreciated this winter. The grass may be brown out there, but at least you can see it. My mantra has become,

"If this is global warming, I say bring it on." Please don't shoot me—I'm just trying to be funny.

It's about 7 AM and a good-sized skunk just cruised past my window, not an unusual occurrence. It reminds me of something I wrote a few years ago.

"There was a tragic end to romance this Valentine's Day. Pewie Lewie and his sweetheart were busy mating late last night, right on top of my "el cheapo" plastic window well cover. The cover, including Lewie and his lady love, fell in. They apparently couldn't get back out. Hence, a call to the animal removers who told me that, by law, they had to kill skunks, due to the potential risk of rabies. No more Pewie wandering by at dusk and dawn. And no new skunk babies, at least from those two. I have to admit to some sadness. R.I.P."

My son Mike and I could see the skunks through the basement window. They were no more amused with the situation than we were, and they sprayed like crazy. It was not pleasant. Mike cleverly put a board into the well, but the skunks weren't so clever—they didn't figure out that they were supposed to climb up and out. I have since replaced all my window well covers with the more rigid ones.

Despite the demise of those two, there are still plenty of skunks around. They continue to show up at dusk and dawn, and I have to confess some small fondness for them. They really are beautiful creatures.

One summer night as I was on my porch talking on the phone, Pewie or one of his cousins was busy eating seeds that had fallen from my bird feeder. He was only about ten feet from me, and we were separated by nothing more than the screens on the porch. Had Pewie decided to get "gassy," those screens weren't going to do me much good. But we peacefully coexisted for over an hour.

Another time, I watched Pewie digging in the front yard the entire evening. Apparently there were grubs in the grass, a skunk diet delicacy. It was really kind of cute—his butt and his tail sticking straight up as he buried his nose in the ground. The next morning, there were divots all over the lawn. Actually, Pewie was doing us a favor—grubs eat the roots of the grass.

A bit of skunk trivia for you: Skunks don't hibernate; they sleep more, but come out to eat when they're not snowed in. I can relate to that. Skunks come in a number of colors, including lavender, apricot, and brown, along with the standard black and white. Pewie's sweetheart was brown—the only brown one I've ever seen.

Skunks have their own web site. It's skunkhaven.net. Through Skunk Haven, you can sponsor a skunk, something I'm sure you'll want to do this very afternoon. And you can find out all about Skunk Fest, held in Ohio in September. All are welcome—you don't need to be a skunk owner to attend. And yes, it's legal to own a pet skunk in eight states.

If Only He Had Died

Crissy Shreve

If only he had died, Mikey,
You and I, we could have wept as one,
And grieved,
Wounded, yet strengthened in each other's arms.

But, instead, he stole himself from us,
From God, from all that not just should have been,
But was,
And is,
Sacred.

Even that I could have one day learned to forgive.
But not the way he stole us from each other.

CHAPTER TWENTY-NINE

FALLOUT

For a time after X2 and I ended, step-Mike struggled with his feelings about the situation, and for reasons of his own, he wasn't comfortable being with me. It wasn't about me, and I understood. Still, it hurt to lose him for even a few months. Step-Mike has always been special to me, and his loving me is one of my dearest blessings. I wrote the poem "If Only He Had Died" during that time.

My friend Barry uses the term "divorce fallout" to define the secondary losses that result when a marriage ends. At first, I didn't know whether I might lose all of X2's side of the family. As it turned out, I lost none of them, but I didn't know that in the beginning.

It was not only I who lost; in our various ways, we all lost X2. He quickly left the country, leaving everything and everyone in his dust. For several years, even as I was dealing with my own pain, I'd run into old friends at church who hadn't heard that we'd split up. They'd ask how X2 was doing, and I'd have to tell them what had happened. It hurt me to see the look of devastation on their faces.

I did consider for myself the question of whether it would have been easier on me had X2 died, rather than betraying me, and it certainly felt that way at first. That, however, was not God's plan, and as much as I wish what happened hadn't happened, I'm glad he didn't die.

It's been said, "Don't get even, get even better."[55] By God's good grace, through the healing process I did just that. My prayer throughout the entire ordeal became, "Lord, if I have to go through this, You've *got* to use it." And He did. He used me to shepherd a friend who, a year later, went through the same heartbreak. She

---

[55]   Karen Salmansohn, in THE BOUNCE BACK BOOK

commented on several occasions that she was grateful that my having "gone before" helped her to see that it is possible to get back up out of the ashes of a broken heart and a broken marriage.

Please don't misunderstand this. I am not saying that God makes one person go through hell in order to be able to help someone else go through it a year later. He doesn't have to. We give Him plenty to work with. I'm only saying He keeps His promise to work all things together for good.

One of the things I've struggled most with as a Christian is getting God to do what I want Him to do. What makes it hard is knowing that He *can* do anything. Even as I pray for His will, often what I really want is my own. I've always been quick to say that God isn't Santa Claus. He's not there to answer to my every whim. And yet, I am often guilty of looking for Christmas morning handouts—quick fixes. In looking for what I think I need from Him, I too often miss what He's really doing in me. And what He's doing, of course, is what He knows I really need. God doesn't make mistakes.

He's just not the God of the Band-Aid. When God fixes something, He goes deep, and He works on healing the underlying disease, not just the surface symptom. Usually that takes a while. A doctor may have to cleanly re-break a jagged bone so that it can heal properly. It's said that it will even become stronger than it was originally.[56] Sometimes God has to re-break me in order to help me grow stronger.[57] This is not a pleasant proposition, especially when I'm in the midst of my already brokenness.

Hindsight is a useful tool. I can't count the times I've realized that He did, in fact, fix something in me when I wasn't looking. One day I'll realize that He's been working on it for some time, and in ways I'd not expected or even noticed. I'll find myself feeling or thinking in a way that is no longer my way, but His. This shouldn't surprise me. For years I've sung words like, "Break my heart for what breaks Yours."[58] I've even meant them. And yet, no one is more surprised than I when

---

[56] ". . . the bone is actually stronger until it completely remodels back to the normal, pre-fracture state. Answerbag.com

[57] "So do not despise the discipline of the Almighty. For He inflicts pain, and gives relief; He wounds, and His hands also heal." Job 5:17-18 NASB

[58] "Hosanna," Hillsong United

I am touched deeply by something that previously wouldn't have even hit my radar.

In the days and months after X2 and I ended, I did a lot of stumbling around, mumbling, and being pretty much just numb. Then one day, I was driving around a neighborhood I'd targeted as the place I wanted to live. Suddenly, God broke through my fog saying, "You've been worshipping X2 for a long time. Now I want your worship all for Myself."

Whoa! I had to pull over to the side of the road. He was right. God knows all about this. He says, "And she will pursue her lovers, but she will not overtake them; and she will seek them, but will not find them."[59] All those years I'd chased love, particularly X2's love, instead of pursuing my God, who might have made it happen. Instead, I did just the opposite. Again, no surprise to God—". . . 'and follow her lovers, so that she forgot Me,' declares the Lord."[60]

Although I had been baptized when I first became a Christian, I now had the opportunity to be dunked in the lake at my church. I felt as though I was beginning a whole new life and a whole new relationship with my Lord. What better way to start? Just before dunking me, the elder asked me why I was there that day. I confessed that I had spent the past 25 or so years worshipping my husband, and that from that day on, I would worship only the Lord.

"Good answer," she said, and under I went.

I felt truly clean for the first time in my life; it was a huge part of my healing. God removed the thing that had stood in the way of my being fully alive and becoming who He meant me to be. I should say quickly here that the thing God removed wasn't X2; it was my perception of who X2 was supposed to be to me.

A good example of the way things worked (or didn't work) between X2 and me happened the day before he finally owned up to his infidelity. I don't remember exactly what he said, but it was something to the effect of wanting us to have a good day together. I don't know what that was about, really. He already knew what was to come the next day.

We decided to go to the mall to have lunch and just walk around, something we had always enjoyed doing together. I also needed to

[59]   Hosea 2:7
[60]   Hosea 2:13

stop at Best Buy for something. While we were driving there, I'd no sooner had the thought that we should go to Best Buy first and then go to the mall afterwards, when X2 piped up with the same idea. I was curious as to whether his thinking was the same as mine—that doing things in that order would give us more time in the mall to enjoy our time together. It probably even was his thinking. But I made the mistake of asking him, "Why?" I maybe should have said something more specific, but I didn't. He didn't reply, but instead drove straight to the mall. When I asked him why he'd not stuck to his first plan, he said, "You questioned me."

Questioning him was never my intention at all. I'd just not wanted to make it a multiple-choice question. I wanted to hear what he would say. I was really hoping he'd say something that would indicate he was considering staying in the marriage. Going out together had been his idea, after all. And we did wind up having a nice time.

I asked the shrink I was seeing about it and she said that "Why?" can be interpreted as a challenge. Our entire marriage went like that. I never caught on until that day. I'd been trying all those years to understand what X2 was thinking, what he wanted, and apparently all along he'd just felt "questioned."

We never learned to communicate with each other, never learned to know and appreciate each other. I guess what I'm really trying to say is that I wish he'd liked me. I wish he'd known how much I liked him, because I really did. In hindsight, I think I can safely say that he never did like me much and I, in trying to get him to like me, made him feel that I didn't like him, either. What a sad dance we did.

When X2 was explaining why he wanted out, he said to me, "It's not what you've done, it's who you are." I see now that that was his attitude towards me for twenty-five years. I'd always felt it, just couldn't quite identify it. Finally, at the end, with his escape route in place, he no longer held back his built-up hostility towards me. When he was finally able to be honest, it came out in cruelty.

That attack on who I am might have done me in, but instead God used that very cruelty to get through to me. I was shocked by it—X2 had never been overtly cruel. The irony was that I was not who I am. In my effort to get X2 to love me, I had shrunk into someone I wasn't. Parts of me had just disappeared and I hadn't even known they were gone. Other, newer parts had been waiting for room to grow. Once

I no longer had to shrink, I was free to rediscover myself. And, to be honest, I kind of like me.

You can't shrink so that someone else can grow!

John Ortberg wrote a book called THE ME I WANT TO BE. I was a bit surprised that what I got from it was not advice to be or pretend to be who I wanted to be or even who I thought God wanted me to be, but to simply be who I am. This is exactly why I need God and His perfect will for me. He knows who I am; He made me who I am. The things about me that need fixing are not the things he made me to be. The things that need fixing are the residue of years of shrinking. God's not confused about which are which.

I'm not blessed with self-discipline, so it's a bit silly for me to try changing myself anyway. I don't bother making New Year's resolutions because I know I'm not going to keep them. I know people who are highly disciplined—I'm just not one of them. If I am to be who He wants me to be, if I am to do what He wants me to do, it has to be by His hand.[61] Rather than trying to fix myself, I do better to invest in my relationship with Him.

When it became clear that God wanted me to write this book, I put it off for nearly a year. After a rather strong nudge from Him to get on with it, I told Him that what I lacked was discipline. Then I sat down in front of my laptop, fingers poised above the keys, and now you're reading it. It has to be God, because left to my own devices, it never would have gotten done.

Shortly after X2 and I split up, I made my annual pilgrimage with my friend Sue to a nearby town to do their historic house walk. When we arrived, the parking lot was full, but I spotted one place in the back corner grass where, with some imagination and maneuvering, we could park. As we were getting out of the car, a cute cop cruised by, but he didn't seem inclined to argue with our parking scheme. He moved on and we locked the car and went about our business.

---

[61] On the other hand, discipline yourself for the purpose of godliness; for bodily discipline is only of little profit, but godliness is profitable for all things, since it holds promise for the present life and also for the life to come. 1 Tim 4:7-8 NASB

There was a bus that would take people from house to house, but we opted to walk. And, typical of the two of us, we took the route less traveled, which, unbeknownst to us, took us down one somewhat seedy block. The day was hot and it was a bit of a hike to the next house.

About halfway along that seedy block, the same cute cop pulled up next to us. I thought at first that he would make us go back and move the car, but he was just concerned that we might be lost. We assured him that no, we were just taking the "scenic" route. As he was about to pull away, I said to him, "And here I thought you were going to offer us a ride."

I was only kidding, but to our surprise and delight he said, "Sure, hop in," and got out to open the back door for us. I'd not ridden in a police cruiser since I was a teenager. It was less than posh—the upholstered back seat had been replaced with a hard bench, and there was a strong metal grate between the front and back seats. And, there were no inside door handles—we were well and duly "prisoners."

It was great! We were delivered in style—he pulled right up in front of our next stop on the tour. Those already in line couldn't imagine why we'd arrived in a police car. We had a good laugh together with the cop and then he again went on his way. He really was cute, too. Darn! I wish I'd thought to ask him for his phone number.

Although this may not be the funniest or most remarkable of my stories, its significance is that my friend Sue said to me, "You're back." Yes, I was. Sue saw me as she hadn't seen me in years. It was good to be wacky, fun me again. No more shrinking!

THE KIDSICLES

This is my absolute favorite story about God's perfect will. It is not technically my story, but it is one I share intimately with my daughter-in-law Martha. It is not about Martha or me nearly as much as it is about our very good God and how He works things together for our good. This is an "Only God" and a "Yea, God!" story all rolled into one.

For the first few years of their marriage, step-Mike and Martha tried to conceive a baby. Martha had had an ovarian cyst as a young teenager, and as a result, the "soldiers" were unable to reach an egg. Martha went through all the procedures and ultimately produced 32 eggs, which were fertilized in a dish. Most of them were implanted over several attempts. None of them took. Between implantations, the extra fertilized eggs were kept frozen, and we called them the "kidsicles."

I was privileged to be Martha's support person through this time. I shared her heartbreak as one set of implants after the other failed. I wracked my brain for some words of comfort for her and step-Mike—and for me.

God laid it on my heart that these fertilized eggs were little people—unfinished, but fully designed, that they had souls, and that He knew each one. As Martha remembers it, I told her that they were all sitting in the lap of Jesus, waiting for us to arrive in heaven. And, as she says, she's going to have her hands full on that day.

During that same time, I had to tell Martha on two occasions that another of my daughters-in-law was pregnant. There was no way gentle enough to sooth Martha's pain—and anger. She joked that I had been praying for the wrong daughter-in-law. I'd actually been praying for God's will for her, while her thought was "I don't want you to pray for God's will; I want you to pray I get pregnant!"

I have learned over the years to pray for God's will. It's always better than mine or anyone else's. Yet I understood. I think of Christ asking just before going to the cross whether "this cup" might be taken from Him, and yet affirming to His Father, "Your will be done." When I tell God what I want or need, I have to trust Him to do His best.

I stepped out on a limb, which is always safe when God's in it, albeit scary, and I told Martha that the final chapter had not yet been written. That we would yet see the day when we would holler, "Yea, God!" together.

They then began the process of attempting to adopt an infant. One day Martha was sitting in a waiting room while her car was being repaired. On the TV, there was a program showcasing a child with exceptional talent. As she listened, she heard God's voice telling her to "Go work with kids." Martha swears it was audible. I believe her.

Then, shortly thereafter, Martha was talking to someone in the grocery store who suggested a nearby children's home. Step-Mike and Martha went there to visit. The little boys and girls came running in—the boys to step-Mike wanting to wrestle, the girls to Martha. Several asked their names, and when they said, "Mike and Martha," a little eight-year-old said, "I'm Margaret. Hey! M, M, & M." And Martha knew this was to be their child.

Still, she didn't say anything at first. She just went home and cried out her heart to God, asking Him how He dared put her around all the kids who so desperately needed to be loved, but didn't allow her to have a child when she had so much love to give. I can just hear God saying, "Hang on. Daughter, you ain't seen nothing yet."

The next day, Martha had lunch with a friend who told her all about her own experience with infertility and how God had wanted her to heal before blessing her with a child. The friend did eventually become pregnant. Martha had an "a-ha" moment and realized that God wanted *her* to heal.

Meanwhile, God was hard at work. The next night, while they were at church, their pastor mentioned a place to visit that was great for families. Step-Mike whispered to Martha, "I sure would like to take Margaret there with us." They'd both fallen in love with the same little girl!

Martha began tutoring at the children's home and would always see Margaret, yet she was afraid to ask whether Margaret was available for adoption, despite step-Mike's nagging her to do so. She feared the answer would be no. Finally Martha got up the nerve to ask, and the caseworker was astounded. The very night before, the staff had prayed for a family for Margaret. Soon Margaret was living with Step-Mike and Martha on a trial basis.

Margaret's brother Bobby was also at the home. He started coming to stay with them on weekends. He was a bit more difficult than Margaret, but when it came time to take him back to the home the Sunday night right after Halloween, he told them he couldn't take his jack-o'-lantern along because it wouldn't be allowed there. This broke Martha's heart, and by Thanksgiving, they'd decided to adopt Bobby as well. The adoptions were finalized a year later.

I will never forget Margaret and Bobby walking through my front door that first Christmas, and straight into my arms, shouting, "Oma, we're yours!"

Yes. Only God.

A few months later, Martha finally admitted to step-Mike that she'd actually been afraid of pregnancy—afraid of not being able to lose weight afterwards and of being confined and isolated at home with an infant. She realized that she'd never been all that fond of babies anyway.

Here's how I remember it: Martha, who admittedly had avoided pregnant women and women with young children because it hurt too much to see them, saying to me, "Who'd want a baby, anyway? Older kids are *so* much better!"

And that's when we hollered, "Yea, God!"

I Live Alone
Crissy Shreve

I live alone, you see,
Even after all these years,
My own best friend,
My only company,
And the only one,
Who cares to know me.

I was born alone.
Sure, my mother grew fat and pushed,
Then was led away to live in the world as only she saw it.

Somewhere along the line,
Little pieces of who I was to be got torn from me,
And like my vegetables, thrown away.
It didn't take long until I began to do the tearing myself.
It just seemed easier to be alone.

I think I'd just rather be alone these days.
I've gotten good at it over the years,
And if it's not who I was meant to be,
It's who I've become and it seems to fit well.

I've noticed that those lined up at my door,
Seek not what they can do for me,
But rather what I can do for them.
Why can't they just leave me alone?

My son tells me I will be a lonely old woman.
He seems to think that should scare me.
What else would I be?
I've always been alone.
It's what I do; it's what I've known.

Or maybe this is all just a defense,
Against the next year,
When I will be alone.

Think of all the conversations
I won't be compelled to initiate,
All the empty silences to fill with thoughts,
Yes, thoughts, no feelings allowed.
They too are dead, torn from me and
Tossed away,
Too painful to keep,
Alone.

I don't ask anyone to change it.
Only One to understand.

Chapter Thirty

Alone

To quote a line from a song called "What Can I Say" by Brandi Carlile, "Alone is the last place I wanted to be."

I moved out of the house. I couldn't stay there any longer. In my mind I kept seeing X2 and his woman there together during times she'd stayed with us. These scenes had taken on a whole new meaning and were keeping me stuck in the pain. I needed a fresh start and a place to grieve.

I moved into an apartment near my church and a few blocks from the townhouse complex where I wanted to live. I'd been looking for a screened porch with an attached townhouse, and every unit in this complex had one or could have one added. But nothing was available at that time.

The apartment was small, so I packed up only the necessities. Knowing that we would most likely sell the house, I tried to maintain its appeal and not leave it empty.

People from my small group at church, several other friends, and my sons helped me move. I think it was Jason who said it was remarkable that I had people who cared enough about me to give up their Saturday to move me. He was right. Two of the women set up my bathroom, made my bed, and put enough kitchen items in place for me to be able to function until I could unpack everything. After everything was in, they all gathered around me, laid hands on me, prayed, and blessed my apartment and me.

That apartment was on the second floor of a mostly wood building, and I was right under the roof. The night I moved in, there were tornados in the area. The warning siren was less than a block away, and apparently it was going off throughout much of the night. I was so exhausted that I fell asleep, slept like a log, and never heard the siren. The next morning, I had several calls from friends checking to make sure I hadn't been blown to Kansas. All I could say was, "What tornados?"

With the handwriting on the wall, I started attending Divorce Recovery at church. I met a guy named Barry, and we hit it off. God used us in each other's healing. Barry, too, was broken-hearted at the loss of his marriage. He'd call me up at 10 o'clock at night, saying that he had to make it short because he had to be up early the next morning. I'd say fine, then half an hour later I'd remind him that it was time to say goodnight. He'd say okay, then he'd start in on a whole new subject and we'd talk for another hour. It was exactly what I needed. After X2, it was wonderful to have a guy around who actually talked, and liked talking to *me*.

My apartment was my place of grieving. I'd be on the floor, on my face, at varying times of the day, begging God to let me die, then the phone would ring. It would be Barry, just checking in. This happened several times. It was God, through Barry, saying, "No, I don't want you to die. I want you to get up off the floor now and get on with the life and the tasks I've given you. I'm right here with you."

My son Mike reminded me of one of my favorite poems, Edna St. Vincent Millay's "The Suicide." [62] After many verses, the woman in the poem finally kills herself and goes to heaven. She watches others serving the Lord, while she can merely enjoy all the accouterments. She asks God if there isn't some small task she can do for Him. His reply:

"'But as for tasks—' he smiled, and shook his head;
'Thou hadst thy task, and laidst it by,' he said."

I got off the floor. It wasn't easy.

Around that time, a friend emailed to tell me that her daughter-in-law had committed suicide, under circumstances similar to mine. Her husband had told her (on Christmas Eve!) that he was leaving her. She'd assured everyone that she was doing fine and was planning her

---

[62] From Collected Poems by Edna St. Vincent Millay, published by Harper & Brothers Publishers. Copyright © 1956 by Norma Millay Ellis. You can find the entire poem on the Internet.

future. A week later, on New Year's, she was dead by her own hand. I hadn't known this woman, this sister, but I grieved her death. Had I been able to talk to her, I'd have begged her to allow God time to show her He could bring her through it too, as he had with me. I wept because it was too late.

I was only in the apartment a few months. God used that time to help me do enough grieving to be able to love my house when I finally found it. One of the reasons I'd picked that particular apartment was that it was so close to the complex where I wanted to live. Every day, I'd hop in the car and scout for "For Sale" signs. I also had a realtor friend watching for available units. Nothing came up except inside units. I wanted an end unit.

When I saw that there was an open house on one of the smaller inside units, I figured I might as well take a look. I didn't like it, but, on my way around the block, I saw another that was open and stopped to see it. The moment I was in the front door, I knew it was the one, inside unit or not. The price was right, and I figured that, if no end units were available, I'd be in a better position to find out when one did go up for sale.

Also, winter was fast approaching, and I didn't relish the idea of no garage and having to make several trips up and down and through the snow carrying grocery bags. I like my creature comforts. Being on my own, I didn't like the idea of dark coming earlier, either. While in the apartment, whenever I'd come home in the dark, I had several people who would "walk me home." I'd call one of them on my cell phone before I got out of the car and have them stay on the line until I was safely inside.

Another major concern for me was finances. While still in the apartment, I went to see an attorney and discovered that half of our marital assets belonged to me. That was a relief, and it made the divorce less painful in the long-term, as well as making me comfortable buying the house. Still, there were assets I could have gone after but didn't.

I hired a mover and had him pick up the rest of my stuff from the house along with what I had in the apartment. Right after that, step-Mike and Martha came to town and stayed with X2. Martha's comment was that the house felt dead to her—that when I left, I took the life out of it. X2 said the same thing. Well, yes. I took *me*.

Amazingly enough, X2 and I had never become full members of our church. Deep down, I don't think either of us perceived ourselves to be living the way God would want us to live, and we were right.

In my grieving time in my apartment, I learned first-hand the meaning of "Footprints in the Sand." God carried me in His arms until the time came when He would gently set me back on my feet—my hand grasped tightly in His.

Interestingly, God didn't spend that time showing me X2's sin. He showed me mine, and we dealt with it together—me sobbing my remorse in His arms. He showed me seven distinct areas in which I had sinned against Him, the worst, to His way of thinking, being that I had worshipped my husband instead of my Lord. I had trashed God, myself, my kids, and everyone else in my life for X2, in a futile effort to win his love. Twenty-some years later, I still didn't have it. I wasted the best years of my life following a dream that was in fact a nightmare, and doing very little to serve the Lord or his beloved. And yet God still loved me.

I recognized in the membership class that after my time of private tutoring by God, I had finally reached the place where I knew for sure that all I wanted in my life from then on was what God wanted. He gave me back everything I had trashed. I have everything I need and most of what I want. I am exactly where I am supposed to be. Best of all, I have His peace, which is peace when peace makes no sense whatsoever.

My prayer continued to be, "Lord, if I've got to go through this, You've got to use it." God got right to work. He brought a friend I'd not seen in 38 years back into my life just as this was all happening. Even as she gave me worldly, vengeful advice, I was able to say no to it, and to tell her what I believed God was leading me to do. When I visited her in Florida, she said, "I want what you have."

If I had killed myself, I would have gone to heaven, but she might never have shown up. When my friend Marie came to visit, and I was telling her how close I'd come, she said, "I'm so glad you're still here. Think of all the things that couldn't happen if you weren't here." We cried and cried.

2003 was the worst year of my life—and also the best. There are no words to adequately describe God's incredible goodness to me when my soul was shattered and my heart was broken. He is awesome.

All that matters to me now is who, by His grace, I can take with me to heaven.

X2 was a bit surprised that I pursued church membership. Apparently he expected me to leave the church in shame or embarrassment. He'd even told me he felt bad about how what was happening would affect me at church. Truly, that never crossed my mind. It wasn't about me.

On the day we signed final divorce papers, our beloved Chihuahua Tory died. I thought that this was a clue for us both that maybe God wasn't pleased, and it probably was. Tory was the last thing that we shared, the last thing that connected us. Perhaps God was just cutting the strings altogether. For me, though, losing Tory was the worst of the divorce fallout.

My mother died a year or so after the divorce. I'd never told her about it. She would have somehow made it my fault. There's a word in German, *Schadenfreude*, which means pleasure in others' misfortune. My mother, who was always telling me that I would "lose him," would have been so pleased that I finally did. I'm glad it happened after Grandma Ruth died too. She'd adored X2 and our divorcing would have broken her heart.

After I was gone, X2 had a termite infestation at the house, and the little buggers ate a good portion of one side of it. God had apparently run out of locusts.[63]

---

[63] Locusts were one of the plagues God sent upon Egypt prior to the exodus.

COME INTO MY PAIN
Crissy Shreve

Come to me, Lord,
Come into my pain.
Hold my heart, my Lord,
Until I'm whole again.

All that I have suffered,
All that I have lost,
Finding you between my tears,
Was worth all that it cost.

For when my soul was shattered,
And my heart broke in two,
That's when I fell into Your arms,
And knew the best of You.

And so I gladly bear my cross,
And all the hell I've known,
For through it all, You've been with me,
I've never walked alone.

Chapter Thirty-One

Jason

The summer before the real estate market took its nosedive, an end unit became available in my townhouse complex. I put my little inside unit on the market and started negotiating with the owner of the end unit. He was waiting for his new place to be finished and said that it would take nearly a year. By the time he was ready to move, the real estate values had come down significantly, and so had the price of the end unit. I got a great deal, but I wasn't able to sell my little unit. I rented it out instead, and that worked well enough.

I moved eight doors down the street. It was delightful to finally have enough room for all my "stuff." I wound up with two and a half times the space I'd had, including a full basement. Mike had been waiting for me to move because he needed to leave his marriage, and he, too, had "stuff." There was no way he'd have fit in the smaller unit. Neither of us is either a pack rat or a hoarder, but we are both collectors, and we do both like our stuff.

Jason did odd jobs for me, both in the new unit and getting the small unit ready to sell. The townhouse complex was about twenty years old and my new place had not been updated, which I liked, because I could do what I wanted without having to settle for or tear out whatever someone else had done. My head was full of plans.

Barely five months later, the middle-of-the-night phone call that every parent dreads came. Jason had been in a car accident; I needed to get to the hospital. The hospital chaplain who called told me to breathe and to drive slowly. Good words, and right ones. I'd have thought of neither.

I threw on some clothes and got in the car. About halfway to the hospital, I woke up enough to wonder whom I might have called to take me. Although a number of people crossed my mind, I realized that I was not alone, that Jesus was in the passenger seat, and that He was all I needed.

When I arrived at the hospital, the news was not good. Jason had suffered a severe head injury and was in surgery to determine his condition. The doctor had already told Jason's dad that it wasn't likely Jason could survive. As it turned out, he couldn't. He wasn't just brain-damaged; the top of his head had been torn off in the accident. Step-Mike, who's a doctor, flew in to be with us. Having him here was a tremendous blessing. He helped us understand that there was no chance of a recovery, and that we could, in fact had to, discontinue life support.

When the hour came to do so, I saw Brent, the young man who'd been in the accident with Jason, walking behind us into the hospital. Only family was allowed in the ICU and I really didn't think I could handle Brent's deep grief along with my own. "No, God," I said, "I can't help Brent today." But God had a different idea. He said, "Take Brent into the room to say goodbye to Jason. He needs it and you're the only one who can do it. I'll take care of you." So I did, and He did.

We'd hoped that some of Jason's organs could be used, but he stayed alive too long. As we all sat in his room waiting, I imagined him lying on top of the hanging cabinet, propped up on his elbow, watching us. After a few hours, we'd all had enough crying and grieving and needed some comic relief. I asked X1 to explain to us how he'd gone to the store, gathered two full carts of groceries, and wound up getting back forty cents instead of having to pay for them.

It went something like this. Between buy-one-get-one-free deals, coupons for amounts larger than the price of discounted or clearance items, free trials, and mismarked items, he managed to save more than the cost of the groceries. This takes real talent—talent I certainly don't have. My motto has always been "Every man needs a good woman to spend his money," to which I add, "and I've never met a man who could make it faster than I could spend it." X1, however, is the ultimate cheapskate, and I mean that kindly; he's proud of it. He can regularly be seen stopping his car in the middle of the street to pick up a penny. If they ever take pennies out of circulation, I don't know what he'll do for entertainment.

X1 laughed as he told us about his shopping spree—laughed so hard that he had tears running down his face. That got us all laughing. I imagined Jason laughing with us. It was just what we needed, particularly what X1 needed, to relieve the tension we were all feeling. I watched his face go from chalky white to living red. I think in that moment, we all began to believe that we could go on.

Finally, hours later, Jason left us. I'd gone home, as had most of the others, leaving only X1 and Mike. Mike said later that he figured Jason hadn't wanted me to see him die. I think he was right.

I've talked about how, during the ending of my marriage, I'd learned to hang on to and praise God through rough times. From the moment the phone rang and for some time afterwards, God carried me. There is no other way to describe it. There was nothing I did volitionally; I just melted helplessly into His arms.

I discovered many things in the days that followed. One was that people are who they are, regardless of what's happening to you or me. There were certain people I wanted around me, and others I did not. I found myself being able to not only distinguish between them, but to intentionally choose the ones I needed to walk with me, and gently send the rest away. As an example, one friend called me repeatedly in the weeks after Jason died. She'd start out by asking me how I was doing, and after the first time, I realized that I had maybe thirty seconds to tell her how I was doing, and then I'd get to listen to her woes for the next hour. Caller I.D. was helpful.

It was humbling for me to suddenly be the one in need. I have always been the "go-to" person when my friends have needed someone. Some who were used to me in that role couldn't put it aside and I too easily fell back into it myself. That wasn't what I needed.

I recognized a huge need for normalcy. The whole experience was surreal, for lack of a better word, and after the first few hours at the hospital, I needed to get outside just to breathe, to escape the intensity. I needed to go home and take care of my dogs and take a shower and read email. Normal things.

I came to see that words were useless. There were none worth saying. I just needed arms around me. I gathered hugs unashamedly.

Still, I often found myself in the position of comforter. Many people wept in my arms. That seems counterintuitive, doesn't it? I came to see that they were crying my tears, feeling the pain that I, in my numbness and denial, wasn't yet able to enter into. I think the greatest gift in this was that others were crying for my Jason when I couldn't yet do it.

I didn't cry much in the first days. I stayed busy and perceived myself as being strong. I remember thinking that I would miss Jason every day for the rest of my life. It seemed wiser to me to let it out in little bits rather than to have one or more serious meltdowns. I think the truth is probably that I was afraid to get too close to a grief that felt insurmountable. I'm not sure how well that worked, but it's what I did. And I was right; I do grieve Jason every day.

Everyone grieves in his or her own way. There are no rules. Even as I learned to allow my own grief process, I've learned that I need to allow others theirs.

Several people sent flower arrangements to the house. I allowed one to just dry out in its vase and it remains, still beautiful in its way, on my dresser. Throughout the ordeal, I kept envisioning one picture I have of Jason at about age three. His face in that picture is pure sweetness. It now hangs above my bed, where I can imagine him helping God watch over me as I sleep.

I had Jason cremated. That had been his wish, and it still astounds me that I knew about it. Only a few months before Jason died, we'd gone together to a baseball game. The game was in the city, near the lake, and Jason had wanted to scatter my mother's ashes in the lake. He'd promised to take my mother there and he never got the chance. Jason conducted a beautiful little lakeside service for my mother, praying for her and remembering her.

During our time in the car that day, I told Jason what I wanted when I died, and he told me that he wanted to be cremated, and to be scattered near a small stream in Germany—that Mike would know where it was. X1 did it at a later date.

I kept a small handful of Jason's ashes, as did Mike and their dad. Mine are in a small urn on my mantel, next to a sleeping resin angel. Jason died in early November, and just the day before, I'd received a package containing the angel. I'd ordered it as a Christmas present for a friend, but it was broken, so I ordered a replacement. For some reason, I didn't feel right about throwing away the broken angel, so I stuck it on my mantel. The top of the angel's head had broken off, but it was intact otherwise, just as Jason had been.

We held a memorial for Jason at my church. The first part of the service was "God's Song," held in the chapel. I gave a eulogy, as did Mike and X1. At first I didn't think to ask X1 whether he wanted to speak at the memorial. I didn't perceive him as someone who would. As it turned out, his eulogy was magnificent. His first words were, "Jason, Jason, Jason," something he'd said frequently over the years. He got us all bawling with that, and then he talked about how Jason had always called X1's summer home the "Happy Place." That now Jason was really in the happy place.

Afterwards, we went downstairs to the room below the chapel. My neighbors had rallied around me with hugs and love, and were responsible for much of the food at the memorial. X1 and others brought food as well. I never even saw the food or ate any of it. There were at least two hundred people there, and I was too busy greeting and hugging them all. Downstairs was "Jason's Song." We played his music and had a microphone set up so that people could tell their stories.

The whole thing was a bonding experience for X1, his wife Amy, Mike, and me. We became and continue to be family.

Many people said to me, "Your faith carried you through this." True, of course, but I always answered, "No, it was my God in whom I have that faith." They got to see firsthand God's amazing grace and presence when I needed Him most. God using what He allows. It is my prayer that those people, in their own moment of grief, whatever it looks like, and whenever it comes, will remember and grab onto Him for themselves.

Here are some pieces of my eulogy to Jason:

Well, here we are. I think we'd all agree that we'd rather be just about anywhere else, doing just about anything else, rather than what we're doing here today. How on earth did we get here?

The word that keeps coming to my mind is choices. Each of us in this room is here because of at least one choice, or, more likely, a series of choices. It's something to ponder, really, the choices that brought each of us here today. Choices that led us to know Jason, led us to know each other. Choices we made ourselves; choices made by others that trickled down to us.

Choices. We make them all day, every day, and most of the time, we're not thinking a lot about possible consequences. No one has a crystal ball. We're all just, as Jason always said, ". . . making it up as we go."

And here we are.

If you've ever tried installing a computer program, you've come to at least one screen that requires you to choose one of several options. And, of course, nowhere, not in the manual or in "Help," does it tell you what happens when you choose one option over another. So, you pick the one that seems most logical and you go from there. The thing is, though, if once you begin working with the program you discover that something's just not right, you can always go back and try a different option. But life doesn't work that way. The consequences of choices we make can jump up and bite us in the butt years after we've forgotten we even made the choice in the first place.

Even outside of choices, life beats up on us. It beat up on Jason. Even so, his heart stayed strong, his spirit tender, his love apparent. If Jason loved you, you knew it! If you needed a hug, he was the man to see.

Jason's choice to drive that night was a choice that ended his life. It was a big choice, a defining moment. But other choices, perhaps one as small as leaving the concert five minutes earlier or five minutes later, might have made all the difference. I don't know how to get around all of that, but here's what I do know:

Somewhere along the line, Jason made another choice. He chose to trust the Lord Jesus Christ for his salvation. When all is said and done, it was the only choice that really mattered. And because of it, we can know where he is—he's with the Lord. Jason understood that he didn't have to be "good enough" to spend eternity in heaven with God—he only had to trust Christ's death on the cross to be enough.

A few months ago, I had a ceiling fan installed. Part of that involved replacing some drywall where it had been cut out to get to the electrical piping inside the wall. Jason patched the drywall. He did a perfect job. You can't even tell it was ever gone. A day or so after Jason died, I was cruising past that wall and I stopped in my tracks. See, Jesus says, "In my Father's house there are many mansions . . . I go to prepare a place for you."[64] And in that moment, I knew exactly what Jason's doing. He's up there helping Jesus build my mansion.

---

[64]   In my Father's house are many mansions: if it were not so, I would have told you. I go to prepare a place for you. John 14:2 KJV

And I know it's going to be perfect, just as I know Jason is now perfect.

I'll miss my little boy every minute of the rest of my life. I'll miss that strong, tender heart and that gentle spirit.

The chorus to one of my favorite country songs[65] goes,

"If you get there before I do, don't give up on me.
I'll meet you when my chores are through,
I don't know how long I'll be,
But I'm not gonna let you down,
Darling, wait and see,
And between now and then, till I see you again,
I'll be loving you . . .
Love,
Me"

I'm not here today to say good-bye to Jason. I'm here to say, "Seeya later, Kiddo."

Knowing that I'll see Jason again is the only thing that keeps me going. I can't imagine living with the loss of a child without that reassurance.

Brent, who was in the accident with Jason, has kept in touch with me. We attended Grief Support at my church together. Recently, I was telling Brent about this book and that he'd be mentioned in it. He said that, if it were ever made into a movie, he'd like to be played by Brad Pitt.

I had the opportunity to teach one night at Grief Support after I'd attended for a year or so. My topic was "And." Here are some of the highlights:

I think that, for me, the most confusing part of dealing with my son's death was just that—confusion.

In the third century BC, Aristotle speculated that thunder was the result of two clouds colliding. Although there are later, more scientific explanations for what causes thunder, the idea of two clouds bumping heads is as good a way as any to think about confusion. Confusion is

---

[65] Collin Raye "If You Get There Before I Do."

two or more feelings colliding. Bumping heads, as it were. Usually our heads. So many feelings bombarding us at once. And they're not all complementary; in fact, they can be pretty contradictory. Confusion.

My son Jason lived, by his choice, "on the edge." And because of his lifestyle, there was a certain inevitability in his death. We'd all dreaded the thought of that phone call in the middle of the night. And one night it came.

Perhaps you know someone who's terrified of flying, or perhaps you yourself are. I have a friend who describes it as wanting to jump out the window at 30,000 feet, just to get it over with—to get relief from the fear. As awful as it sounds, we all felt a sense of relief that we'd no longer be living in fear of that phone call. Did that mean we didn't feel deep heart-wrenching sadness? Of course not.

It wasn't an "or" proposition. We felt both sadness *"and"* relief, along with a million other things. Years ago, I heard a theology professor say that when two things in the Bible seem to contradict each other, believe both. That's where the idea of "and" comes in. When it comes to contradictory feelings, we need to own them all and feel them all.

If we get stuck in "or," if we think that we can't possibly feel sadness if we feel relief, or that we can't possibly feel love if we feel anger, then all we can do is get lost in confusion. How can I feel relief when I feel such sadness? Is it okay to feel relief when I "should" be feeling sadness? It *has* to be okay, because I'm feeling what I'm feeling. By replacing the "or" with "and," I can allow all my feelings.

Life is peppered with "ands," especially in relationships. We love people, *and* often we hate the things they say or do. It's when we think we have to choose one feeling over another that we get in trouble. If we live in "or" thinking, we're not free to fully love someone whose behavior hurts us, or to truly enjoy the things we do. It's too easy to focus on the negative feelings and lose sight of the good feelings when we get stuck in "or."

"And" thinking can help us work through the tough questions:

Can I be angry at God *and* still love Him? Yes!

Can I be angry at the one I've lost *and* still feel my love for him or her? Yes!

Can I be so shattered *and* still believe that life is good? Yes!

Can God have allowed this to happen *and* still be worthy of my trust? Yes!

Can I be in such excruciating pain *and* still feel joy? Yes!

The answer is always yes, because with "and," no feeling precludes another! They're simply both, or all, real.

I have many stories of how people surrounded me with love and support and comfort when my son died, but here's the most poignant: A few years ago, my friend Marie (who was living in another state) gave a couple of gorgeous, black and yellow suede, Steelers bomber jackets to friends of hers named Laura and Jeff. I went to visit Marie and I met them. When they showed me those jackets, I drooled; I mean my tongue was on the floor. I *wanted* one. Well, by then some time had passed, and the only size still available was a 2XL, but I ordered one anyway, hoping that perhaps they ran really, really small. They didn't. In fact, the jacket I got would have fit Refrigerator Perry with room to spare. Sadly, I returned it.

Right after my son's death, I met up with Marie again, and I just happened to mention that I *still* craved that jacket. Marie told Laura. A few weeks later, I found a package on my doorstep. I didn't even have to open it. I knew what it was. And I sat down on my front stoop and bawled.

Such a simple thing, and yet, as I wore that jacket, even when it was just hanging on the hook by the door, every time I looked at it, my depression lifted and I was reminded that *life is still good*. Laura loved that jacket every bit as much as I did *and* she made a loving sacrifice that played a huge part in my healing. The jacket hung on the hook all winter long until spring came, when I finally hung it in the closet.

(There is a sad epilog to this story. About six months before I finished this book, Jeff died of cancer. Laura just couldn't get past it, and she committed suicide. Now the jacket once again hangs on the hook by the door, in loving memory of two of the most beautiful and generous spirits I've ever known.)

Grief can make us a little goofy. The whole first week after my son died, I kept trying to put toothpaste under my arms instead of deodorant—every morning. I'd look down and giggle and tell myself, "This doesn't work!" I'm not making this up; I really did that.

Yes, we can be in the deepest shock and grief *and* still laugh at ourselves. You've probably heard the old saying: "Blessed are they who can laugh at themselves, for they shall never cease to be amused." (That's not in the Bible, by the way).

Of course, the concept of "and" doesn't always work. Some things are simply "ors" and there's not much we can do about it. For instance, you're either a man *or* you're a woman. You're either here *or* you're there; as helpful as it might be, I haven't yet figured out how to be two places at once, and I don't suppose you have, either.

I know one thing: life seldom makes sense *and* God *always* makes sense.

A few years ago, I attended a talk given by Valerie Bell on the subject of "Fear." She quoted 2nd Timothy: "For God did not give us a spirit of timidity, but a spirit of power, of love and of a sound mind." And she made an amazing statement that changed my life. She said that the best, the *only* real source of power, is surrender. Surrender to God. Power in surrender? That sounds counterintuitive, doesn't it? Definitely an "or," right? Until you apply the concept of "and."

God says this, "My grace is sufficient for you, for my power is made perfect in weakness."[66]

One big "and" that many people have trouble wrapping their brains around is that Jesus was fully God *and* fully man. In His humanness, Jesus felt terror in the Garden of Gethsemane as He faced His crucifixion. He prayed that the cup might be taken from Him. But as God, He prayed for His Father's will. And, because He was Himself fully God—it was His will, too. See, Jesus didn't just "give in" and go to the cross. He *insisted* on it. For you and for me. Jesus wasn't confused. He felt His feelings *and* He applied truth and intellect.

When we lose a loved one, it can feel like we, too, have died—and a part of us *has* died. *And*, it's our job to go on living. Ultimately, it's even our job to go on living abundantly. Jesus says, "The thief comes only to steal and kill and destroy; I came that they may have life, and have it abundantly." [67]

Crap happens. We're not in control. All we can do is reach up and grab onto God's hand. With God, even the impossible is possible. I

---

[66] 2 Corinthians 12:9
[67] John 10:10

know this—He brought me through my divorce and then through the death of my son.

Life is just too complex to settle for "ors." And it's definitely too complex to do on our own.

As part of this teaching, I handed out a sheet with some of my favorite quotes . . .

"I'm never down: I'm either up or I'm getting up."—much quoted, original source unknown. One source says it came from a boxer. Makes sense.

"Don't cry because it's over, rejoice because it happened."—Dr. Suess

"Jesus knows me, this I love."—Morgan Easter (song)

"When life makes no sense, God *is*."—Me, I think.

"It is well with my soul."—Horatio Spafford

. . . and my favorite prayers . . .

My old standard, "Lord, if I have to go through this, You've got to *use it*!"

"Thank You, Lord, for everything, just the way it is."

The second prayer is a hard one, but one that is amazing in that, even as it tells God that we're trusting Him, no matter what's going on, it speaks even more strongly into our own hearts and attitudes. This is where we start to find the strength and the power we need in the hardest of times. This is surrender.

I was at a seminar at church about three years after Jason died. The speaker just wasn't capturing my attention, so I decided to go home. Then I had a rather surprising nudge to go *right now*. I quickly gathered my stuff together and headed out. As I walked through the lobby, I looked up at the banners hanging from the ceiling, representing the current series we were in. Another woman was admiring the banners too, and we started talking. At some point she said, "I have a son in heaven." I just put my arms around her and said, "I have a son in heaven too." We held each other and shared a little cry.

I never cease to be amazed and delighted by the divine appointments God arranges for me. This one was a gift straight from

His hand—not only a moment to share my grief with a sister who understands, but the words she gave me. I have a son in heaven. I have a son in heaven!

FROM THE ANALS
JASON STORIES

I picked up my mother at the airport on a very cold night. It was the Christmas when Jason had just turned three. He went along and he held her hand on the way to the car. She remarked at how warm his hand was, that it warmed her hand right through his mitten. I think that hand must have been attached directly to his heart. Jason had the dearest, warmest heart I've ever known.

Jason was always a trooper. When he was about five, we went to my friend Kathy's for dinner. She served asparagus, which I was smart enough not to eat. Dear Jason just ate what was on his plate. He'd certainly never been served asparagus at my house—he just thought it was "yucky beans." He threw up immediately when we got home. I don't blame him.

"That's bidiculous!" said Jason, at around age four.

"Look, there's a station wagon limousine!" he said, upon seeing a hearse for the first time.

One time Jason and Mike were shopping at Sear's, and Jason put his five-dollar bill down on a counter while he looked at something, and then forgot to pick it back up. They innocently thought someone would turn it in, so they left our name and phone number at the service desk.

"You're da best grandfodder I never had." Jason told X2.

"I mean, things have changed that dramastically." Jason was about twenty at the time he said this. He also liked to say, 'No ands, if, or buts . . .'

Mike, being almost five years older, although generally smaller in stature, was much bigger than Jason until he (Mike) went off to college. He arrived home at break time, tackled Jason in the yard, then looked up and said, "Oops!" Jason had sprouted up to over six feet tall.

Jason, when he was around four, said, "I've got the problem to your solution."

"I won't be there before 9 o'clock irregardless anyway," said Jason, master of the multiple redundancy. He often created his own words. One of his best was "profuciously," in the place of profusely.

Jason once described a mirror as ovular. He meant oval, of course, but I wondered at the time whether he mightn't have thought the mirror would reproduce little ones just like itself.

His very best, though, was when he combined Worchester Sauce with horseradish and called it "horse-shitster-sauce."

A ROSE
Crissy Shreve

A rose is a rose for a moment;
It cannot last.
Smell its sweetness,
Feast on its beauty,
Now,
Today.
Grieve its fading if you will,
But know:
There will always come another.

CHAPTER THIRTY-TWO

RESTORATION

My son Larry, whom I had placed for adoption in 1965, found me July 3rd, 2010. It had been forty-five years since I'd last seen him.

Here are some snippets from his first email to me, and my response.

Larry: I guess I found you by accident . . . not knowing what your married name was . . .

Crissy: Larry, oh, Larry!

You must be my kid; I too am into the dot dot dot thing.

First, most important, I am thrilled beyond words that you found me. I'd like to move a bit slowly to begin with, though, if it's okay with you. I'm not sure what you envision, but I am open to the whole nine yards, just not too quickly. Part of me wants to head to the airport and part of me says "slow down."

I got married in another state.

Larry: . . . not to mention not one record from the DMV . . . .

Crissy: I had a learner's permit there, but didn't get my license until I came here.

Larry: . . . but I happened to talk to somebody in the tax office . . . and asked them about who lived at your address in 1965 . . . and she gave me Laura's name to go with the Christina name that I've had for years . . . .

Crissy: My name is Cristina (no h). I suspect that your birth certificate probably has an h in my name. People just don't seem to be able to believe me that there is none. In fact, a lot of people call me "Cris no h." It's the Spanish spelling—I found that out when I was in Spain some years back and bought a package of Santa Cristina coffee. Imagine that, I'm a saint. LOL. Laura never knew that it was the Spanish spelling, though; she was just trying to be creative.

Larry: . . . like I said, I met Laura once at her house . . . but at that time I had no clue she was related to me . . .

[Larry was picking up a sink my mother no longer wanted. Someone who was working at the house knew she had it and told Larry's ex-wife. My mother didn't recognize him, but since he looks so much like me, you'd think she might have wondered. Larry finally tracked her to that house, but it was years later, and by then she'd moved away].

Larry: I happened to find your married name on the high school roster . . .

Crissy: I didn't actually graduate from that high school—I left right after you were born . . . That high school website has been the source of my reconnecting with my best friends from back then.

Larry: I don't know whose idea it was for you to be so hard to find . . .

Crissy: Not my idea. I sure wasn't hiding from you. I never felt it was appropriate for me to try to find you. I didn't know whether you knew you were adopted. Things were done differently in those days. I didn't want to interfere in your life or that of your family. But I always knew you'd find me eventually—if you wanted to.

Larry: . . . but it's been 45 years now . . . there's nothing that I want . . . other than to know about my real family, like brothers and sisters, anything like cancer or heart problems that run in the family . . .

Crissy: You have one brother living and one who died not long ago in a car accident. I am so sad that you and he will never meet. Two stepbrothers from my second marriage. I was an only child, so you have no aunts or uncles, but several cousins and their kids and grands. You are part of a delightful family and they are all thrilled at the news. Oh, and two Chihuahuas. Nothing to get concerned about health-wise.

Larry: I sort of knew (where you were) when I found Laura's death notice . . . but anyway please respond . . . I was born June 13, 1965 . . . and have heard I was put up for adoption as soon as I was born . . . which I do not hold against you in any way . . .

Crissy: Now I'll get mushy . . . you were adopted out of the Florence Crittenden Home, which was right across the street from the hospital. I brought you back to the home from the hospital and we were together for two or three days. Apparently that was the policy, for whatever reason. I changed your pants, powdered your butt, and held you in my arms and absorbed all the love I could squeeze out of you. I loved you with all my being and a very big piece of my heart was torn out and stayed with you. I have missed you for 45 years.

Thank you putting my heart back together. I don't know whether you'll understand this, but I had to harden my heart in order to be able to let you go. Now I feel like I can finally allow it to soften up a bit. Now I feel like I can finally weep.

I wanted so much better for you than I could have given you, so I'm on-my-knees grateful that you don't hold it against me. I've always been so glad that abortion wasn't an option. I have been able to live with the knowledge that you were out there somewhere.

Larry: I have had a great life so far . . .

Crissy: I am so glad. Bless your parents. It's been hard to not know whether you were okay and to be completely powerless to help you if you weren't. I think right this second I could die happy just knowing you're okay. But I probably won't.

In about 1972, I trusted the Lord Jesus Christ to be my Savior, and you've been in His hands ever since—whether you knew it or not. When I wrote to my cousin Judy that I'd heard from you, she was so pleased, and reminded me that she and a friend had been praying for years for you to turn up. I, too, have prayed for you all these years. The only way I could survive the not knowing was to surrender you to Him and to trust Him.

Larry: . . . but I feel that I am missing something by not knowing you . . .

Crissy: Wow—that's so something I would say. Yep, you really must be my kid.

Larry: If you want . . . you can call me . . . your son . . . Larry . . . I hope to hear from you.

Crissy: As a starting place, if you are agreeable, two things: First, I'd really like to see a copy of your birth certificate, and if they issued you a revised birth certificate, a copy of that. Second, I'd like to have you meet our cousin John who lives near you. I'd feel more comfortable with it all if you would do that. This is all still such a shock, a wonderful shock, but a shock nonetheless. Just let me know and I'll have him call you.

I have all kinds of information on your ancestry. We'll get to that at some point, too. It's really fascinating stuff. A quick teaser: you've heard of Old King Cole? Well, he's not just a nursery rhyme any longer. He's your 64th great-grandfather.

Of course I want to know everything about you . . . hair color, eyes, height, married, kids, siblings, education, job, etc., etc., etc. When you're ready. Oh, and a picture. You looked so much like your father when you were born.

I think I should just be Cris to you—? Your parents are your mom and dad. But whatever works for you is fine.

We had a few further emails and then we discovered instant messaging. We burned up cyberspace for several hours every night for three weeks.

Larry insisted that he call me "Mom." That's when we thought of AMom for his adopted mother and BMom for me as his birth mother. He did send me copies of his original and adopted birth certificates, plus a letter from the attorney to his adoptive parents that had my name in it.

While on his way to the restaurant for their first meeting, my cousin John was waiting to turn into the parking lot, where Larry was standing next to his truck. John thought for a second that it was I he was seeing. Then he remembered that he and I just talked on the phone half an hour before and that I was five hundred miles away. The resemblance really is amazing, and it pleases me because neither of my other sons looked like me.

John asked Larry, "How long have to been looking for Crissy?" Without missing a beat, Larry said, "Forty-five years." Imagine his getting a whiff of me, his mother, for a few days, and then suddenly I was no longer there. I believe that that, more than anything else, engendered his lifelong desire to find me.

The first question most people ask me is how Larry found me. He worked with a lot of bad information for a long time. He finally got hold of his original birth certificate, but it had an "h" in Cristina, which made the search more difficult. He called everyone in the phone book who had the same last name as mine, but none of them had ever heard of me or my mother.

My mother had lived in several places and had always moved on before he got there. It wasn't until he found her death notice online that he figured out where I was and the correct spelling of my name. Then he found me on the roster of the local high school. He searched my email address and found my name again on my family website and knew he'd hit pay dirt.

He wrote, "For years I really thought that you didn't want to be found . . . or that your family didn't want you to be found . . . shows how wrong I was by thinking that . . . I just was looking in the wrong places all those years." Larry didn't totally believe I hadn't been hiding from him until my son (his brother!) Mike told him that he'd known about him all his life.

Larry had also looked at several adoption reunion web sites, but unfortunately not at the one where I'd listed us, and he was searching for my name. Had he searched his birth name, he might have found me at least five years sooner.

My cousin Judy's comment, after praying for years that Larry would turn up was, "Well, it's about time!"

ABORTION

Abortion wasn't available when I was a pregnant teenager. I wish I could tell you that I wouldn't have had one, but had it been an option, I very well might have. In hindsight, I'm so grateful that it wasn't. When abortion was legalized not very long afterward, it was a comfort to me knowing that Larry was out there somewhere, presumably alive and okay. However hard it was, I could live with that.

If you disagree with me and you're tempted to put this book down, or throw it away, please don't—not yet, at least. I think you'll be glad you didn't. If you've had an abortion, know that I am not judging you. Please keep reading.

I have several friends who've had abortions, and it's affected them—subtly perhaps, but it has. What surprises me, although maybe it shouldn't, is knowing several men who have also been affected by their girlfriends' having had abortions, particularly when they'd encouraged them to do so.

Deep inside a woman's soul, and also inside a man's, is a God-given instinct to protect and nurture his or her children. We may apply intellect and say that a fetus is only the "product of conception," but every cell, every nerve in a pregnant woman's body screams, "protect this child." It's a part of her. When she destroys it, she destroys a part of herself. Although she may appear to walk away relatively unscathed, her soul will be shattered. Killing an unborn child is utterly counterintuitive, utterly unnatural, and potentially devastating to the psyche of a mother. It is not without its cost.

There was a time when the idea of abortion was abhorrent. Then, abortion became acceptable within the first trimester of pregnancy. "As it stands today, American women have the legal right to obtain an abortion in all 50 states, through all nine months of pregnancy, for virtually any reason at all. This has been true since January of 1973 . . ."[68] The idea of the sanctity of life started out the window with the acceptance and legalization of abortion.

In the past decade or so, there have been several incidents of mothers killing their living children. Now, I absolutely do not think this is a good idea, and I certainly don't condone it. I do wonder, though, why anyone is surprised that it happens. If it's acceptable to kill a baby one day before it's born, why is it any less acceptable to kill it one day after it's born? Again, I'm not saying I think it's okay. I'm only asking, what's the difference?

Once something becomes acceptable, it opens the door to the next step. We've lost our sense of morality, of sin, and of outrage. These days, practically anything goes. When an attempt is made to right a wrong, often the pendulum swings way too far in the other direction as a result. Sometimes, over time, balance is achieved, but I fear that, even so, our sense of right and wrong often gets lost in the process and never returns.

The treasure of knowing Jesus is eternity with God and with those we love who've trusted Him for salvation. Women who have had an

---

[68] http://www.abort73.com/abortion_facts/us_abortion_law, May 26, 2011.

abortion can be comforted that, one day, they can be reunited with that little person who never had a chance at life. Abortion is not the unforgivable sin, and God is big enough and gracious enough to cover it, if they allow Him into it. If Christ's blood isn't sufficient for the sin of abortion, it's not sufficient for my sin.

It is sufficient.

Still, why not give *God* a choice? Abortion irrevocably shuts the door on a life. Adoption leaves that door open. I firmly believe that when we make right choices, God honors those choices. He certainly did for me and for Larry.

If nothing else, doesn't it strike you as ludicrous that we destroy our own babies in the womb and then adopt others from overseas?

UNDER THE BEND IN THE RIVER

Crissy Shreve

Under the bend in the river,
I found myself again,
In water pure, my soul was cleansed,
My heart began to mend.

For by His hand, He set me free,
To splash and play and heal,
I am His child, safe in His love,
His promises are real.

And when I climbed up on the shore,
And sat in sun and dew,
My shattered soul was whole again,
And I was all brand-new.

CHAPTER THIRTY-THREE

REUNION

Our first meeting! When it finally happened, it was sweet and tender and poignant. Perfect. We simply walked into each other's arms. No words were needed.

Once I'd scheduled my trip to meet Larry, I started fantasizing about how it would be. Would I be so nervous that I'd laugh hysterically? Would I weep uncontrollably? Would I stand there doing the "Chicken Dance?" Would I be utterly speechless? Would whatever I did be the right thing?

The Christian group MercyMe does a song called "I Can Only Imagine."[69] It's about going to heaven and experiencing that first meeting with Jesus. The chorus played over and over in my mind.

"Surrounded by Your glory, what will my heart feel

Will I dance for You Jesus or in awe of You be still?

Will I stand in Your presence, or to my knees will I fall?

Will I sing hallelujah, will I be able to speak at all?

I can only imagine. I can only imagine."

Although of course I wasn't going to heaven or meeting Jesus, this would be, for me, the most sublime of moments here on earth—the culmination of forty-five years of missing my baby, and three weeks of pinching myself—when I wasn't flapping my arms and saying, "Oh, my goodness, oh, my goodness," which I called doing the "Chicken Dance."

I had no clue what my heart would do, what my mind would do, or what my body would do—and I didn't want to even think about those possibilities. I could only imagine, and my imagination knew no

---

[69]   "I Can Only Imagine," MercyMe, © 2005 Sony

bounds—the scenarios flashed through my mind, many and varied and sometimes pretty crazy.

My son Mike came to my rescue. I was telling him about how I was afraid that I'd not show the right amount of emotion, or that I'd show too much. Mike pointed out that it would be what it would be, and he suggested I plan to just be in the moment. Good advice, which I tried to follow as best I could.

FRIDAY

Thankfully, the flight only lasted just a little over an hour. I wasn't sure exactly how I was to contain my excitement within the confines of a seatbelt. My son, my precious baby, was at the other end of that flight! Just before we took off, I texted Larry that, if he heard on the news that some crazy lady was arrested for doing the "Chicken Dance" on an airplane, I was counting on him to bail me out.

God's good. He's got even our smallest details in His hands. I sat next to a delightful woman on the plane and we talked the entire flight. I can't tell you what we talked about, only that before I knew it, I was there!

Somehow I managed to collect my suitcase, pick up my rental car, and drive to the hotel. I called Larry from my room and he said he'd be right there. My room overlooked the front entrance, so I watched from the window. I knew he had a white pickup truck, and I knew, from pictures, more or less what he looked like. He fooled me, though. I saw his truck drive in, but he parked over on the side of the lot that I couldn't see because of the canopy over the hotel entrance, so I didn't see him walk up. He called me and said he was downstairs.

I went down, thinking he'd be in the lobby, but he was outside, under the canopy. He looked happy and nervous and scared—much, I suspect, like I looked, and certainly like I felt.

I'd warned Larry that I was a hugger; in my (his!) family, we are huggers. So, he was forewarned that he was going to get hugged, but I don't think either of us was prepared for the power of that first one. We were both pretty overwhelmed. Larry was making some sort of "huh-huh" noises, while I was simply speechless, which is basically not like me at all. Neither of us knew what to do next and so we just hung on for a bit.

When we finally let go, we were both beaming from ear to ear. I suggested we go sit in the breakfast room inside the hotel, which we did. After some small talk, Larry went to get the photo albums and baby books he'd brought along for me to see. He'd left them in his truck, which was a good thing. It had left both his arms available for that first hug.

We spent some time going through the albums, and he told me bits and pieces of his life. I pulled out a number of pictures to copy and take home with me. By that time I seriously needed a nicotine fix, and Larry went outside with me. There was no break in our conversation or our smiles.

As we stood outside under the canopy, a bug dropped from an overhead light into my shirt. I sort of brushed at it and thought it had moved on, but when we got back inside the hotel, it was still in my shirt. In the process of trying to squish it and shake it out, Larry finally got to see me doing an unplanned rendition of the "Chicken Dance." He laughed so hard.

We both laughed the entire weekend. Of course, many of our stories were, in fact, funny, but that laughter was also a release of forty-five years' worth of joy—joy that neither of us had ever known we'd get to feel. And we talked. And talked. And talked. I may have done most of it, I usually do, but he managed to get in a few words edgewise, too.

We hopped in his truck and went to a local restaurant for "late breakfast." Larry just had some fries, while I had eggs and toast. We both love sweet tea, and between us, we must have drunk a gallon of it. We stayed there until the wee hours, talking and just looking at each other. Larry looks a bit like a chubbier, scrubbier Billy Ray Cyrus. And me! To see this near mirror image of myself across the table was amazing. We are much alike in many ways. We are also very different in other ways. I think, though, that our similarities are largely in the core of who we are, while our differences derive more from our life experiences.

We did a lot more hugging that weekend. He was slightly bigger (by close to six feet) than he had been when I last held him, but I didn't care. I had forty-five years to make up for, and so did he. I gave him one of the buttons we'd passed out at a recent family reunion. It was a way of grafting him into something even bigger than just the two of us—his (!) family.

Larry's adoptive parents had been older, and most of that family is gone. Growing up, he'd not had young cousins. AMom was forty when they adopted him, whereas I was only sixteen, so I was really pleased to be able to give him a younger family who would be in his life for years to come.

One of the things that Larry had said in his first email to me was that he thought he was missing something by not knowing me. I wanted him to know me. I wanted to know him. We told each other some of our stories. I told him my "Paris Coup" and "Catheter" stories, to give him an idea of my sense of humor and my spontaneity. He told me of his days as a cop.

Since I'm only sixteen years older than he, we could almost be brother and sister. We certainly look like we are, and maybe even twins. We finally decided, at about 3 AM, that maybe it was time to adjourn for the night. As we were leaving the restaurant, the hostess told us to "have fun." I think she thought we were on a date. I'd often been mistaken as Jason's girlfriend, so it wasn't a huge surprise to me. I was twenty-five years older than Jason, so with only sixteen years between Larry and me, I suppose it was a reasonable assumption. Larry's plenty cute, and if he were anyone other than my son, you can be darn sure we would have been on a date!

We drove back to the hotel and finally parted around 3:30 AM. Neither of us slept much. Must've been all that sweet tea.

SATURDAY

We met again at the hotel, early afternoon. Larry brought us both bottles of sweet tea he'd picked up at a local convenience store. We started out in the lobby again. Larry gave me his lieutenant's bar and another police pin. I gave him a Yoda birthday card—his birthday had been in June, just a few weeks before he found me—and a copy of Jason's memorial picture montage.

Then we took my rented Charger and did the tour. We drove to the apartment building where I'd lived when he was born. I showed him the house where his father had lived, and also the house where he'd probably been conceived while I was babysitting. We went to my grandparents' house where I had lived as a young child and where my mother had also grown up—the same house she'd later owned and lived in until the fire.

We drove around his teenage stomping ground. We passed his high school, but the gate was closed, so we couldn't get on the campus. We drove past his grandfather's house and other houses he'd lived in.

Finally it was time to pick up Larry's girlfriend Jas from work, and I met her for the first time. We went to his house where I met and had a delightful visit with AMom. I saw where Larry had sat while we instant messaged all through July. I saw his gun collection and the bathroom where he showers. Every night he'd signed off saying it was time for his shower, so seeing these things were part of seeing him. I saw pictures from his first wedding and borrowed one to copy. Every mother needs a picture of her son in a tuxedo. AMom took a picture of Larry and me, then we all went out to dinner at Red Lobster.

As we drove back to the hotel, I told him I'd noticed that he's rather hard on himself, but that I could see right through his badass persona to the sweetness inside, a trait he shared with Jason.

I wrote in my journal: "Lord, I love this boy, this man, my son. Thank You!"

SUNDAY

Larry and Jas came to the hotel to pick me up for church. They were early and I wasn't ready, so I hurried to finish my ablutions and headed downstairs. We sat in the lobby for a while; it was too early to leave and too hot to be outside. Larry, who typically wears a sleeveless t-shirt, was wearing a long sleeve, white dress shirt with his jeans.

I gave him a copy of THE MESSAGE Bible that I'd inscribed to him from me. I also gave him a silver-plated pin box that had been his great-grandmother Laurena's. It was tarnished, but I hadn't polished it; I thought it should look just as it had looked all the years it had been in the family. Whoever had given it to Nana had had her name engraved on the top, but had misspelled it Loranna instead of Laurena. Plus, Larry thinks we look like her. I also felt that the pin box was somehow reflective of Larry's restoration to our family. Nana had kept it, despite the misspelling of her name—perhaps out of loyalty to the friend who'd given it to her. When she died, it stayed in the family—no one ever thought to throw it away.

He gave me the picture AMom had taken of us the night before. We went to a church that I always try to attend when I am in town. We were early, so we walked around the facility and met the new pastor.

Afterwards, we had a delightful lunch at an outdoor restaurant where Jas and I could smoke. We had an appetizer of hummus with pita bread. Jas and I both liked it. Larry tried it and wasn't impressed. We sat there for two hours talking and laughing, and then we drove around in the area. I showed him both houses where Uncle Austin had lived.

We went back to his house and picked up AMom. I called her "Mom" three times, to which she didn't seem to object. Larry said she liked me. I was pleased about that. We took AMom out for dinner; she had a roast beef hoagie. Larry and I split calamari, crab balls, and wings. We were both still pretty full from lunch, but we wanted to take AMom out. Jas didn't go along; she was tired from the busy day.

We dropped AMom back off at the house. Then Larry took me back to the hotel. He had to work the next day. I prayed for him to be able to sleep.

I wrote in my journal, "I love him even more today!"

MONDAY

Since Larry had to work, I was on my own all day Monday.

He signed a text to me with his adopted name. I asked him about it, and he said he'd decided he wants to be known to the family and me by his adopted name.[70] It makes sense, although I was a little sad. But, now that I've met him and gotten to really know him, it's not a big deal. I call him "BB" for Baby Boy, anyway. Larry says he's a little too big to be "BB." I told him it's a mother's prerogative. He seemed to like that concept. My son Mike's girlfriend always says that it's a mother's duty to embarrass her kids. I take that duty very seriously.

That evening I picked Larry up at the house, and we met cousin John and his wife Sherri for a baseball game. It was a nice time. On the way back to the car, I stumbled over a curb and only barely

---

[70] I only use his birth name Larry in this book.

managed to keep myself from falling on my face by sort of "flying," nearly horizontal to the sidewalk, my arms stretched out in front of me. I came to a stop an inch from the stone front of a building, luckily avoiding a crash landing. It must have been pretty funny because everyone laughed.

Larry and I went to Denny's to eat. He told me he'd looked over at me at the game and he'd never seen anyone so happy. We laughed together constantly. It was so, so, *so* good! I loved him even more again that day. I told him it was hard for me—I wanted every precious minute I could get with him, yet I knew he had things to do, too. He said, "I know." Tuesday was to be our last day together. But just till next time.

TUESDAY

The last day.

Larry took the day off work. We started out at 9AM. I picked him up at the house. We stopped for tea, of course, and then went to Flo's, the home where I'd lived before he was born. The building is still there—it appears to be some sort of residential facility now, but there was no sign. We walked around outside—Larry wanted to know all about it—where I'd slept and where we'd eaten, etc. It wasn't easy, but we found the old part of the hospital where he'd been born. It was buried behind a lot of newer buildings and a parking garage.

Then we went up to W Street, where I'd walked almost daily, and we walked it together, from one end to the other. I suggested that, since the last time he and I had been there, and I had carried him (in my belly), perhaps it was his turn to carry me. Larry declined, but it was a good laugh. These were the places Larry and I had shared, even though he wasn't yet born. Seeing them, sharing them again together, seemed to be important to him, too. It was special—full circle and poignant.

I had looked at a pair of cowboy boots in a shop—great boots, great price, but they didn't have my size. So Larry and I drove about thirty miles to a country/western store where he buys his boots, and I found a pair there. Afterwards, Larry bought us lunch at a nearby Waffle House. We continued to talk and laugh the whole time.

At some point, Larry and I were talking about fitting everyone (the two of us plus Jas and AMom) in the car. I had a few things in the back seat that he thought would be in the way. I said, "Well, there's always the trunk," to which Larry replied, without missing a beat, "You want to put AMom in the trunk?" I nearly wet my pants.

Back in town again, Larry took me to a really wonderful antiques shop. It was especially neat because it was his idea—he'd never been there before, and wanted to see it. It's a huge warehouse that belongs to a super-rich guy who's traveled extensively, and who has collected antiquities from all over the world. We were told that he had other warehouses full of things, as well, plus several houses where he displayed his collections. Everything was for sale, but the prices were beyond impossible.

The best part was seeing what caught Larry's attention. He was particularly interested in a pair of Kentucky long rifles. I gave some serious thought to buying one of them for him, but I wasn't sure he'd be comfortable with such an expensive gift, so I decided not to.

Then we drove around downtown, and Larry showed me the building where he'd worked when he was a cop. He'd been shot and had given it up after that. He showed me where the bullet had hit him in the shoulder and allowed me to touch the scar. It was hard for me to see that my child had been so badly hurt, but I knew then that God really had watched over him.

It was getting late, but we decided to quickly run out to the cemetery to see Nana, Dadum, and Laura's graves. Larry commented that they'd recognize him—no introduction was necessary. Interesting comment. I can buy into the idea, though. I'm sure my mother was thrilled. It struck me then that it had probably broken her heart to give him up, especially in light of her having lost the baby boy before I was born. Asking me to name him Larry had been her way of keeping him in her own heart.

We stopped to get *pierogi* for dinner. I made the mistake of asking them to heat them, which took a lot longer than they said it would, and it turned out that we were 20 minutes late picking up Jas. She was not amused.

Back at the house, we ate quickly. Everyone seemed tired except AMom, who wanted to go out for ice cream. I will take her another time. By that point, I could barely contain my sadness at its being our last night, and I needed to leave right after we'd finished eating. I knew I was about to lose it.

During the four weeks between when Larry found me and when I finally met him, I was so happy, so full of excitement and anticipation that it never occurred to me until Sunday night that it was going to be hell to leave him again.

I said good-bye to AMom. She said, "We did good, didn't we?" about Larry. I apologized to Jas for our having been late picking her up. I didn't want her to be mad at Larry.

He came outside with me and we said good-bye in the driveway. It was hard to hug him, hard to hold him, and excruciating to let him go. I cried a bit. Larry reminded me that he would only be a phone call away. Once I got around the corner and out of sight, I sobbed all the way back to the hotel, and for the first two hours after I was back in my room. Then Larry sent me a text: "Good night, Mom." It was perfect and it helped a little. I prayed, "Lord, please help me to remember how wonderful it all was and *is* and to dwell on that, not on the leaving."

I love you so much, my baby boy.

WEDNESDAY

My flight was scheduled for early evening, so I had this day to myself. Jean Ann, an old friend from all the way back in first grade, had written me a beautiful note when Jason died, and I'd promised to look her up when I was next in town. I checked out of the hotel, grabbed a sweet tea at McDonald's, then drove to her house and spent a delightful afternoon with her on her covered deck. Being with her, and knowing that early the next morning I would attend a two-day seminar at my church at home, brightened my world.

I called Larry as I was waiting to board the plane and we talked for a while. I was somewhat recovered, but still pretty sad. He pointed out once again that he was only a phone call away. Larry had written me a beautiful email, but I didn't see it until I got all the way home. I'd been using Jas's laptop while I was there, but I'd given it back, and I didn't think to check email on the computer in the hotel lobby.

AFTERTHOUGHTS

I wrote these things in my journal when I was back at the hotel on Tuesday night. It helped me to be fully present in my sadness and to work my way through it.

Larry will be in my life, but he can't and he won't *be* my life.

I must never put Larry in the middle between Jas and me.

We had a right to this time together.

Thank You, thank You, thank You, Lord.

Leaving this time is *not* like the first time, no matter how it feels. I am walking away again, but it's not forever.

I can't stretch Larry too thin. I need to be mindful of this in subsequent visits. This first visit was unique and special, but probably not sustainable, nor probably should it be.

God did *not* mean this to break my heart again!

My tears are not all sad.

Larry knew how hard it was for me to leave. I suspect it was hard for him, too. I'm so glad he sent me the email.

I was feeling so alone in it; then I got his text and saw that I wasn't so alone in it, after all.

It was a truly anointed time!

It's all good.

We interacted and enjoyed each other in a way few people will ever experience.

No one's letting go. We belong to each other—we always have. We were tied together for 45 years by a golden cord, held in the hand of God.

Mike was right; I need to just be in the moment.

This time together *was* and *is* enough—until the next time. And yet, it will never be enough.

It was hard to leave him again, but I did it, and I didn't die of it.

It's not over, it's just distance.

Thank you, my "BB," for being you.

How do you do relationship with a mother you've not seen or known in . . . well, forever? How do you do relationship with a son you've not seen in 45 years?

God promises in Joel 2:25-26 "I will repay you for the years the locusts have eaten . . . You will have plenty to eat, until you are full, and you will praise the name of the Lord your God, who has worked wonders for you; never again will my people be shamed." That's exactly what happened when Larry came back into my life.

SPECIAL THINGS

In our few days together, we discovered our own crazy catchphrases from inside the time and the stories we shared.

"Yih" and "Uh, yih." Both are things that Larry says. My phone's automatic correction function doesn't like "yih" and changes it to "yin," so I have to get creative when I try to use it in a text message.

"Ee-ven." We share a fondness for old Snagglepuss.

"Yinz." Local dialect for you all; it's fun to hear Larry use it regularly.

"Never trust a fart," a line from the movie *The Bucket List*.

"I was not amused." For some reason, Larry thinks it's hysterical when I say this. So, of course I say it every chance I get.

"French fried brains." Larry got such a kick out of the story of my mother announcing out of the blue that she'd had French-fried brains.

Larry's job occasionally takes him to the town of Homestead, home of my mother's "Homestead hunkies." He always texts me to say that he'll be saying hi to them for her.

And of course I regularly remind him not to put poor AMom in the trunk.

HEAVEN
Crissy Shreve

I don't know a lot about what will be in heaven;
I just know I'll be there.
And Jesus will be there.
But I know a lot of things that WON'T be there:
These damn cigarettes won't be there.
I may puff and hack until the day I die, but on that day,
if not before, I will leave them behind.

Along with my fears
And all the pain
And wasted years
And every bed where I have lain.

All the sin I've suffered
All the sin I've committed
My wounded soul
My anger
My broken heart
The hearts I've broken
My relational graveyard finally, eternally, laid to rest.

My weaknesses:
Of mind
Of body
Of spirit

He is preparing a place for me
A place just right for me
In that house of many mansions.
And I will be seen
And I will be known
And I will fit in
Because He lives.

CHAPTER THIRTY-FOUR

EVIL

I've learned something about myself. I'm not evil. I am a sinner—I do wrong things, sometimes even really bad things, and I definitely make mistakes. I am wounded. But I am not evil. I never even really thought much about it, until I met evil face-to-face. It was wearing a smile.

Something happened to me. I got elderly. Not old yet, just elderly. It snuck up on me when I wasn't looking. Social Security noticed, though, and now they send me money every month. Some other people apparently noticed too, and they figured that I'd make a good mark—someone they could con in some way. I keep looking in the mirror—I don't see "Stupid" tattooed on my forehead, but it must be there.

I always thought I was pretty smart. Now I find that I am capable of being abominably stupid. I joke that my sex life's been great in my elderly age. Even though I'm not sexually active, every time I turn around, I get screwed. It's a bit ironic for someone who spent so many years trading sex for love. I'm not getting any love this way, either, and I'm definitely not laughing.

Of course I've run into evil before—you can't very well live in this world without running into evil, especially in today's economy. People are desperate. In the past, though, the evil I've experienced has been of the sick variety—wounded people doing whatever it took to survive their pain, and I've certainly done my fair share of hurting others out of my own woundedness. Although this type of evil always filters down to those around the wounded one, it's still at least reasonably understandable, if not necessarily excusable. Again, as Will Bowen said, "Hurt people hurt people."[71]

But what I want to talk about in this moment is true evil—intentional evil. Evil with a smile should not surprise me. After all, didn't Judas betray Jesus with a kiss?[72]

A few weeks after my son Jason died, I got a phone call from a tenant asking to meet. I was in a bad place emotionally having just lost my son. The tenant knew my son had died, and he was duly "sympathetic," even hugging me. He then said that they needed some "relief," asking that I take a reduction in the rent to "help them stay in business."

I wish I'd said I'd think about it for a few days. I wish I'd thought to contact an attorney. I wish I'd talked to someone else, anyone else, before I agreed. I made a very stupid on-the-spot decision, and it came back to bite me over the next three years. I agreed to a 25% reduction in the rent, thinking that 75% of something is better than 100% of nothing. There's a reason why they tell you not to make any major decisions shortly after a significant loss. I didn't think it through.

The agreement was only for one year, or so I thought. Through clever wording, it could be construed as ongoing, making it contingent on the economy and the tenant's financial position. These people knew exactly what they were doing. They played me—and I let them.

After that first year was up, I received the next rent check in the reduced amount. I spoke to the tenant again. I told him that I needed more the following year, perhaps not the full amount, but an additional ten per cent. He agreed, then called back the next day saying he'd changed his mind. I told him that I might consider allowing the reduction for another month or two, but that before I did anything, he'd have to agree in writing to the forfeiture of his security deposit.

He sent me a letter, purporting to summarize our conversation, but it did not reflect anything I'd agreed to, so I didn't sign it. I

---

[71] Will Bowen, COMPLAINT FREE RELATIONSHIPS: Transforming Your Life One Relationship at a Time.

[72] While He was still speaking, behold, a multitude came, and the one called Judas, one of the twelve, was preceding them; and he approached Jesus to kiss Him. But Jesus said to him, "Judas, are you betraying the Son of Man with a kiss?" Luke 22:47-48 NASB

thought I was just leaving him in default on the lease. I was wrong. By continuing to accept the lesser rent amount, and by depositing his checks, I was, in effect, agreeing.

At the beginning of the third year, I sent him a letter stating that I needed full rent and would seek legal counsel. He replied by email, attaching copies of his financial statements and listings for other properties in the area. He stated that the company's financial position had not improved. So, for the third year, he continued to pay the reduced rent, and I, by virtue of accepting the money, agreed by default.

I thought that I could sue him after the lease ended. When I finally contacted an attorney after the tenant had moved out, I discovered that not only was the tenant off the hook for past due rent, but that I'd also have to return his security deposit.

I try not to think of it in terms of "what was done to me." I don't want to wallow in victim mentality. I was a victim, but it was my own fault that I allowed it. The question then becomes, why did I allow it? What was going on with me?

First, I suppose, was the hug. What an amazing weapon, the hug. I really didn't see that I was being played. More, though, was my emotional condition, which as it turned out, got worse as this went on. I fell into deep depression. It all caught up with me, and I was largely unable to cope with life for several years. Oh, sure, I put on a good face, but I wasn't okay and I'm not totally sure I'm okay now, either. I think I can be forgiven for this—more importantly, I've had to forgive myself for being so stupid.

I had to let it go, and I had to learn from it. That's a given. I didn't want to spend another minute perseverating over it. That just gives the evil more power than it deserves. I actually felt a great sense of relief when I dropped the check in the mail to return the security deposit. It was over then—and having given the situation over to God, I could put it behind me. Someone said, "No one but a fool trips on what is behind him."[73]

But what about the evil? What to do with that? I'm not quite ready to agree with Will Bowen about this particular man, the tenant,

---

[73]   I didn't write this—wish I had. It was on a list of quotes a friend sent me one time, uncredited. As of this writing, I don't see a source anywhere on the Internet.

being simply a poor wounded soul. I believe that he acted with intent, knowing exactly what he was doing, despite what it could cost me. He didn't care. But, I don't have to live in his skin. I will sleep at night.

As I was driving home after seeing the attorney, after having discovered that I had been well and duly screwed, I had a one-way dialog with God. I was asking Him for vengeance—His vengeance, not my own. There's really not much I could do, even if I wanted to. "Vengeance is mine, sayeth the Lord."[74] I'm His kid. You mess with God's kids at your own risk.

After venting some serious spleen in God's ear, I cooled down a bit, and much as it pained me, I had to confess that my attitude was not pleasing to Him. I was being spiteful and mean-spirited. I was legitimately and righteously angry at this man, *and* I am still responsible for my own heart in it, regardless of the circumstances.

Of course I wanted dire consequences for this man. But, and it's a big but, he has young children. I had to quickly amend my request—that whatever the consequences, they would not hurt those kids. I settled for asking God to maybe fill the man with a realization of what he'd done and to give him a few, or maybe even a lot, of sleepless nights. I think I'm sticking with that request. I'll probably never know whether that prayer gets answered.

I had to recognize that it wasn't personal. The tenant didn't set out to screw Crissy. He'd have done the same to any landlord, although chances are he'd not have been successful had it been anyone but I, or had I not had my head tucked away where I keep it when I'm not using it.

There are those who would say that it was only business; that the tenant was just being a shrewd businessman doing what shrewd businessmen do. I'm sure he, the tenant, sees it that way. I imagine he's even proud of himself. I wonder how proud his wife and children would be to know that the only way he could think of to stay in business was by bilking an elderly woman out of her retirement income.

The most important thing, and the only thing that was going to serve me well, was to forgive this man. It couldn't matter whether or

---

[74] Vengeance is Mine, and retribution. In due time their foot will slip; For the day of their calamity is near, And the impending things are hastening upon them. Deuteronomy 32:35

not he deserved it. In setting him free, I set myself free. I didn't want to drink the poison of unforgiveness, hoping he'd die. There was no other option but to forgive him and leave it in God's hands. It was too heavy for me to carry, anyway.

But I still hope he has some sleepless nights!

And then . . . as I was writing this, the phone rang.

My residential tenant up the street had been running about six months behind in his rent due to a work situation that was beyond his control. Because of my own financial situation, I now had to start eviction proceedings. He's a believer, I adore his little girl, and I did *not* want to put him out. However, I could no longer afford to carry him. He prayed, I prayed—not only for myself but also for the situation he was in, that somehow God would make it possible for him to pay me what he owed me. The real estate tax bill had just come, and I didn't have the money to pay it.

When he called, wanting to come by and talk to me, I told God that, please, *please*, I couldn't handle any more bad news, at least not that day.

Instead, this tenant handed me an envelope with every penny he owed me. Not only is God's provision perfect, He knows exactly what I need and *when* I need it. Had my residential tenant been paying his rent on time, I'd probably have already spent the money.

So a few weeks passed, and Dave Ramsey came to speak at our church. Part of his message was that it all belongs to God, and it is our job to steward whatever resources He entrusts to us. I had to confess that I had not been a good steward—not only had I not taken care of business, but I'd not set aside enough to cover what I'd need.

Even though I absolutely trust that God will provide for me, I can't expect him to just blithely replace the money I lost, at least not immediately. I need to learn to live with less for a time. I discover that trusting God comes fairly easily to me; *waiting* for Him to act—not so easily.

All these things rolled around in my head (which I'd finally taken out of hiding, dusted off, and started using again).

What I ultimately came to was this: in the Bible, the story is told of Joseph[75], who was sold into slavery by his brothers. But Joseph

---

[75] Genesis 50:18-21 NIV

gained favor with Pharaoh in Egypt and became a powerful man. Later, when famine struck, his brothers came to him for help. "We are your slaves," they said. But Joseph replied, "Don't be afraid. Am I in the place of God? *You intended to harm me, but God intended it for good* to accomplish what is now being done, the saving of many lives. So then, don't be afraid. I will provide for you and your children." He reassured them and spoke kindly to them.

What's particularly noteworthy is Joseph's asking, "Am I in the place of God?" If I continue to harbor anger, if I refuse to forgive, if I stand in judgment, I put myself in God's place, a place I definitely don't belong. This whole idea is further affirmed in "And we know that *God causes all things to work together for good* to those who love God, to those who are called according to His purpose."[76]

My final prayer became simply that God would use for good what was intended for evil. I don't yet know how He'll do that, and I don't need to know. I do know that He will.

It may seem that this was all rationalizing and spiritualizing. And, in fact, it probably was. But I got through it with my heart intact, and that's what I needed most. God tells us to guard our hearts.[77] I could only do that by clinging to His promises and opening myself to His ways. That's when I found peace.[78] I'm almost at the place where I can praise God that all I lost was some money—and I'm going to get there, too.

I can still say that I am the most blessed person I know. I have everything I need and most of what I want. Way beyond that, though, I have everything that matters.

---

[76] Romans 8:28 NASB

[77] Watch over your heart with all diligence, for from it flows the springs of life. Proverbs 4:23 NASB

[78] And the peace of God, which surpasses all comprehension, shall guard your hearts and your minds in Christ Jesus. Philippians 4:7 NASB

RED BIRD
Crissy Shreve

My Lord comes to me in a bright red bird,
Perched cockily on my window sill,
Glancing here, glancing there,
With bold black eyes, then
Snatching at an insect.

I wish him happy breakfast,
And just as quickly he is gone.

Yet still I know He's here.

CHAPTER THIRTY-FIVE

BE

July 16, 2012[79]

A long time ago, like forty years ago, when I was part of that women's singing group, we all made squares that were to be assembled into a quilt for someone who was leaving the group. Who she was or why she was leaving escapes me. What I do remember is that one of the squares someone made simply had the word *Be*. It was a directive, and it was reflective of the just post-hippie era thinking of the time. I didn't then, and I still don't quite know what it meant. More specifically, I didn't know what I or we or the recipient were supposed to do. How does one just "be?"

Today I sit before my keyboard, sadly and painfully aware that that is exactly what I'm doing today. *All* I can do today is be. Now I understand—it's a default. It's not an act but a fallback. For me, today at least, it can be no more. Maybe that's all it ever was or could be.

I just got home last night from my great-granddaughter's funeral. As if that weren't tragic enough, she was brutally beaten to death by her mother's boyfriend. She was seventeen months old. Shortly after this little girl was born, I got to meet her and hold her. I absorbed the sweet, sweet love that only comes from someone so fresh from God. Now that precious baby has been stolen from us.

Now I also have a great-granddaughter in heaven.

I don't know who or what I'm "being" today. I only know what I'm not. I'm not being wise or clever or even fully alive. But, as is my wont, I am writing my way through the pain of it.

---

[79] This happened just when I thought I'd finished this book. Apparently I hadn't, and apparently I've not seen the last of evil in the world. Oh, oh, oh.

I am remembering things I learned when Jason died. One was that I have a job to do. I have to go on living. Even as I have to go on living without Jason, without seeing him marry and have children, I have to go on without seeing that precious baby girl grow up. I will never see her walk down the aisle to her love—she will never walk anywhere again.

I've been going around for the last few days saying, "Oh, oh, oh." There are no words for something like this—no words, no way to wrap my brain around it, no way to even know how to feel about it. Yet, worthless as they may be, words are all I have. Even f-bombs, as furiously as they are dropping on my floor, don't begin to cover my pain and outrage at what's happened. Maybe they will tomorrow or next week. Today I can only "be."

My grandson, the baby's father, had called and asked me to come be with him—although of course I would have gone anyway. But the funeral was hard—I think perhaps the hardest thing I've ever had to do. My grandson was a mess. I was a mess. We were like two drunks, staggering together, holding each other up, as we approached the open casket. I touched that tiny cold hand and kissed that precious little forehead. Oh, oh, oh.

The funeral was very Christian, and I would almost say beautiful if that weren't such an oxymoron. Over the casket they showed a video pictorial of the baby. It was good to be able to look up and see her in life. Even as we cried over the casket, we were able to laugh at some of her antics in the pictures. That was well done. I remember us all laughing in Jason's room when X1 talked about his grocery-shopping trip. That was the start of our healing, and I saw that happening for people at the baby's funeral too.

God wept all through the visitation and the service, yet stopped for a time as we left the funeral home. I had the feeling in that sunshine that He was telling me the rain was not meant to punish in any way, only to share our grief. He wept again, and copiously, most of the way to the cemetery, an hour and a half drive. Then the sun came out again, to shine on the burial itself. I don't know how the mother survived seeing them put her baby in the ground. Hell, I nearly didn't survive it. Oh, oh, oh.

They released doves at the cemetery (okay, probably white pigeons, since they told us that the birds would find their way home). First four, representing loved ones who'd gone before, then the one for the baby. The birds circled several times over our heads and then flew off into the sky. It was powerful. Jason was one of the four. He's with her, helping God watch over her. They're playing with Tory, my Chihuahua. I can just hear Jason, who died before she was born, saying, "Who's this baby? Oh, she's cute. Okay." *They* are okay.

All the platitudes, all the truths. God is still good, still in control, all of it is still true. And yet this is not okay. There is nothing about it that is okay. Not to me—not today and not ever. Her organs saved the lives of two little baby kids and one elderly woman. That's a little okay. Still, I watched them shovel dirt over her coffin. And it is not okay.

My long string of f-bombs is all I have today. My mind keeps going back to Jason's friend who called me while I was in the hospital waiting room after Jason's accident. The prognosis was not good. This kid called me on my cell phone and said only one thing: "Oh, f—!" It struck me then, and it strikes me now, that it was the only thing anyone said that even remotely reflects any reasonable response to Jason's death or that of my great-granddaughter.

And yet God has a remarkable way of knowing what I need, when I need it, and showing up at just the right time. Even as my bombs were bursting on the floor around me, my cousins stopped by. Just as they were getting out of the car, Jan noticed a female Mallard on my courtyard wall. She grabbed me to come see. Mama Mallard (she was quite beautiful in her own right—I never noticed that before) started "talking" to us, and with some urgency. Then she hopped down into the courtyard. That was when I knew. There were babies in there and she didn't know how to get them out.

God truly does work all things together. Several neighbors had had ducklings in their courtyards too, and I'd heard them talking about it. So, I knew exactly what to do. I had my cousin's husband disconnect the downspout that was inside the courtyard, and that opened up the 4-inch round drainage hole in the wall.

Smart Mama figured it out quickly and quacked at the babies from outside the wall to entice them to hop through. They weren't quite big enough to make it up to the hole, though. Jump as they might, they just tumbled all over each other. I stuck a ruler between the ground and the hole to make them a ramp. A few of them figured it out and went through. But that was apparently too complicated—there were still five inside, and four of them kept following the stupidest one around in circles, all peeping frantically. I then piled some rocks under the hole for them to jump up on. Finally, the rest of them went through.

Now I'm busy praying that they won't become Coyote Chow.

The miracle is that Mike's off in Boston all week, and access to the courtyard is through his room—I never go in there, and he never opens the door or the shades. I go in and out of the house through the garage, usually in the car. No one would have known those ducklings were in there, and they would have died without water. But God knew, and He sent just the right people at just the right time.

His eye is on the ducklings—and I know He watches over me. My great-granddaughter is safe in His arms where no one can hurt her ever again.

Tomorrow I will feel the comfort of these things.

Later in the evening, just as I was about to make an early escape to my bed and my TV, armed with comfort food, the phone rang. It was my friend Christa, and we talked for an hour about her upcoming trip out here with her son in a few weeks.

I finished with Christa, thinking I'd definitely hit the wall by that point, and got all the way to my bed, food beginning to digest, when the phone rang again. It was my cousin Jan. We hadn't really had time to talk and we both needed it. Our conversation reconnected me to my life, and the next morning I was ready to go again.

God's in it all with me, and He reminds me of that. After my great-granddaughter's death, He orchestrated the ducklings' rescue. After Jason's, He sent my Larry back to me. I have some trouble crying over the most painful things in my life. Then God shows up. That's when I'm able to cry—in that moment when I find His goodness again in the middle of it all.

The day after the funeral was Sunday, and I went to church with step-Mike and Martha. Here's where God shines His brightest. I didn't connect the dots until a few days later, but at that service, a young woman sang the song "To Make You Feel My Love." As I listened, I knew it was God's love song to me. But do you know who wrote that song? It was Bob Dylan. The night Jason died, he was on his way home from a Bob Dylan concert!

A week later, I was still struggling with it all. I know that God allows stuff. We have free will. I kept saying that the baby's death was not okay with me. That it would never be okay with me. It wasn't until I realized that her death was most certainly not okay with God that I started to feel better. He reminded me that He'd cried harder than any of us.

There's more to the ducks story, which I didn't find out until afterwards, when Mike returned from Boston and I was telling him about the ducklings. A month or so earlier, Mike and his younger daughter had just gotten home from church, and as he put it:

"We came home and there were three ducks on the driveway. Clearly, two were male, and one was female. The two male ducks were fighting. Of course. My daughter intuited that they were fighting over the girl. Of course. The girl duck stayed close to the two boys fighting, and my daughter wondered why she didn't just fly away. (Good girl!).

"This went on for fifteen minutes and they covered the entire property. Well, of course one won and had his way with the girl duck. It was at this moment that my daughter remembered that she had a camcorder on her iPod. (Please, Lord, no!) Thankfully her iPod battery was dead. The boy duck finished up and both boys flew away, leaving the girl duck. I think my daughter learned a lot about life and love in those moments. She had some choice words for the boy ducks. (Good girl!) After about ten more minutes the girl duck gathered her wits and flew off toward the pond. My daughter said she was going after the boy duck. Under my breath I said 'Yup, for child support . . . '"

So, a year goes by and another Mama Mallard, or maybe the same one, again lays her eggs in my courtyard. One morning, from upstairs in my bedroom, I hear, "Peep, peep, peep, peep, peep." I look out my window, and sure enough, there are several little ones. I find the screwdriver and again open up the downspout hole and pile up the rocks underneath it.

My friend Robin was here and we kept checking on them. Finally only one baby was left and he couldn't seem to get out. I put on some gloves, scooped baby into an old coffee can and we took him across the street and put him down in the grass, right next to the pond. He immediately hopped into the water and the next thing we knew, Mama came flying across the pond to greet him. They swam off together, to join several others and Papa.

Robin and I were both in awe and there were some tears shed.

DESPERATION

I've talked about the desperation I've felt in my life. As I began to move into my teenage years, that desperation was something vague, simply a sense of needing something I couldn't define. Before long it manifested itself into a need to have a boyfriend at all times, and I would walk the streets at night hoping to get picked up. Desperation made a slut of me.

Throughout the years, that desperation stayed with me, taking various forms that kept me unsatisfied with my life and with the people in it, although I didn't recognize it as the same old thing. It hadn't really changed—it just was subtler.

When X2 and I were splitting up, my sense of desperation returned with a vengeance, once again insisting that I needed to find a new man, preferably right now! By God's good grace and the counsel of my dear friend Ruth-Ann, I was able to get past it and turn instead to God and to getting back to myself.

I can say in one sentence that I understand and yet don't understand desperation. Because I've known it all my life, I can understand its power and be empathetic to other women who experience it. At the same time, I was mostly unaware of its power until recently, and I don't know all its root causes in myself or in anyone else.

I do know that desperation is sneaky and that it feeds particularly on women—not all women, but certainly too many, and in various ways. I can't say exactly what it looks like—perhaps an unconscious longing to fill an undefined emptiness. It may simply be part of the human condition. It may just be that God-shaped hole in each of us that only God can fill. It may even be part of what motivates some of us to succeed. I think, though, that in most cases, desperation is seldom truly satisfied.

Consider various addictions, be they to substances or behaviors. It's said that, as time goes on, it takes more and more of whatever it is to satisfy. Desperation is like that, and it may well be an underlying cause of addiction.

In my case, if I had to find a bottom line, I'd have to say that I was desperate to feel loved and wanted. My whole story revolves around the things I would do to try and feel that way. Few of them worked, and those that did weren't sustainable. In that very desperation, I sabotaged any chance that I might actually get what I needed. I don't know exactly why that was, but I do know that it wasn't until only recently that I have been able to believe that I am loved and wanted—certainly by God, and even by some people.

I hadn't planned on writing this piece, actually. I didn't think I had much to say about desperation, beyond the occasional mention. And then my great-granddaughter was murdered. Now I have something to say, although I'd give just about anything not to have that reason.

My grandson was with a girl for a while and they had a baby. They didn't marry, and before long they went their separate ways. The girl was living with some other guy. He beat the girl and he beat the baby. She had him arrested and then she bailed him out. A day or so later, she left the baby with this man while she went to work. And now the baby is dead.

I can't help, and I'm sure you can't help, wondering just what on earth could possibly have led her to leave her baby with him. It defies . . . well, everything. I'm not looking to excuse her, but I need to try to understand it for myself. The only logical thing I can come up with is desperation. In her case, there was logistical desperation—she'd been kicked out of her parents' home—and there was emotional desperation. Denial and delusion seem to walk hand-in-hand with desperation.

She needed someone to help her financially and in raising the child, and she needed emotional connection. Desperation said any man would do, denial said that he wasn't really so bad, and delusion said that they had a future together. Had she chosen a different man, it might even have all turned out as she hoped. Unfortunately, desperation too often makes us myopic, unable to see clearly.

I've never been physically abused by anyone. I may have just gotten lucky, but no one's ever tried it with me. Maybe I've got "Go ahead, make my day" tattooed on my forehead. Maybe God just knew that I'd be an easy mark and protected me. Kids can't do much to protect themselves, but I honestly don't understand why any adult woman would allow herself to be abused by a man. My take has always been simply that he has to go to sleep eventually. Anyone who abused me would wake up missing an appendage—or two.

When I discovered X2's infidelity, I told him that perhaps I ought to just cut it off for him, Lorena Bobbit-style, to keep him out of trouble. He knew me well. He looked at me with terror in his eyes and asked me whether he dared go to sleep. I said, "Lock your door." Of course, in that case, I would not have followed through with the threat—it wasn't worth spending the rest of my life in jail.

Beat me up and it might be a different story.

But I'm me.

I'm too lazy to undertake a major research project, so I'm not going to try to address why some men need to abuse. And, as I said, I don't really understand why women let them, or why they think they deserve it.

One phrase that I remember hearing when X2 and I were splitting up was that there was nothing I'd done, nothing I could have done, to deserve his betrayal, even though my own behavior in the marriage may not have been stellar. The same is true for abuse.

Women, there is nothing you have done or could do to deserve to be abused. If he's an abuser, it's about him; it's not about you. You are *not* that desperate. You are a beloved child of the Creator of the universe.

Your life or that of your child is at risk. Take off those rose-colored glasses and get out!

GIFTS

Crissy Shreve
To my Children and Grandchildren
With ALL my love, all my heart.
Mom/Oma, Christmas 1999

Our "Anals" may be funny,
Or may sometimes bring a tear,
It's been my joy to write them down,
To share with you this year.

You know you've been a part of them,
And they're a part of you,
But we're all part of something else,
That's real important too.

We may not all be on one page,
Some on no page as yet,
It's true we're in this family,
But please, please don't forget.

That there's a bigger family,
One where we'll never die,
I'd like to think we'll all be there,
Together, by and by.

If I could have one wish, one prayer,
One gift from you, 'twould be,
That you'd seek to love my Savior,
Just as you've loved me.

Chapter Thirty-Six

From The Anals

Mike and Jason and I were at the drive-through at Wendy's. The guy on the other end of the intercom asked me, "Do you want cheese on that cheeseburger?" I'm not making this up.

"I know! Let's eat at Kentucky Fried Turkey," I said to X2 while driving home from Hilton Head one Thanksgiving Day.

I hate bad English, especially when I hear intelligent, college-educated, people using it. I think to some degree it's trendy; when people hear these words or phrases so often, they start to think they're correct. The word "orientated" was popular for several years (the correct word is oriented). One man, who delivered water softener salt regularly to our house, continued to use it long after the trend had passed. He took it to extremes though. In the same conversation in which he had used "orientated," he proceeded to tell me that when his son had dropped out of high school, he had been "devasticated.' I had to quickly send him on his way so that I could laugh.

When X2 and I took his boys to Germany, step-Mike and I were a team. Having studied German in school, he could understand it fairly well, and I could speak it—well, sort of. We'd rented a small motor home, and as we travelled around, step-Mike and I were in charge of buying groceries. It worked well. We'd go into a store, step-Mike would tell me what people asked us, and then I'd answer them. X1 grew up in the German state of Hessen and he'd always talked about *Schleswig Holsteiner Mettwurst*, a type of sausage, so I just naturally assumed you got that in Hessen. Step-Mike and I hit the local butcher shop in a small town in Hessen, and I asked the butcher if he had *Schleswig-Holsteiner Mettwurst*. He said, "*Was für Mettwurst?*" (*What* for

Mettwurst?) *Now* I know that you get *Schleswig Holsteiner Mettwurst* in Schleswig Holstein, a different state. Of course you do.

One night we parked in a small campground that was at the end of a long dead-end road into the Alps. The road started out in Germany and ended up in Austria. Arriving early in the evening, we spotted a small Alp right across the road and decided to climb it. It was pretty much a vertical meadow with very long grass and the occasional cow, but not especially difficult to climb. Once at the top, we realized that going back down would be a bit of a challenge in that it was nearly a straight drop. Standing at the top, it felt like we were at the edge of a cliff. I knew that I couldn't walk down it without falling on my face, so I sat down on one foot with my other foot extended out in front of me for balance, arms out to the side, and sort of skied down the slippery grass. The others followed suit and it was quite a fun ride. Once back at the campground we noticed the huge sign that said, "Please do not climb the mountain." It was, of course, in German, so we couldn't have been expected to read it.

On that same trip with X2's sons, we stayed in another small campground. The Dutch are much into tiny travel trailers and the place was full of them, with not much space between the sites. The window in our rented motor home faced the window of the little trailer next to us. As I said earlier, sex and nudity aren't the big deal in Europe that they are here. Our boys, then seventeen and eighteen, were delighted to watch the young woman in the trailer changing clothes without bothering to pull the shade. She was our dinnertime entertainment. As we all watched in fascination, she glanced up and saw us. The man with her came right up to the window, dropped his drawers, and mooned us. I suppose we deserved it.

Along those same lines, one time X2 took a fellow from our church into Hamburg for some sightseeing. He took him to the *Reeperbahn*, the well-known red-light district, also referred to as *die sündige Meile* (the sinful mile). That poor guy didn't know what to do. As he put it, "To look once is curiosity, to look twice is sin." So he just took one *very* long look and walked right into a phone pole.

One night when X2 was away on one of his trips, I decided to broil myself a burger. I opened the oven door and there were *cobwebs* inside. I don't cook. It occurs to me that if I wanted to hide something from myself, the oven would surely be the place to put it.

The freezer works well, too, especially for chocolate. I am entirely too fond of Cadbury cream eggs, which are usually only available right around Easter. I'll pick up a pack of them, and as soon as I get home, I'll stick them in the freezer in self-defense. Then I'll forget they're there. They make great treats when I finally find them again on a steamy July day.

"Oma's Sarah's boy," said my grandson Zachary, at age 2. I was snuggling with Sarah. What he meant was Sarah's Oma's girl. (Oma is German for grandmother).

"Oooohhhhh! *That's* what that's for!" Zachary, age 2 1/2, was watching his dad urinate. According to his mom, it was like a light bulb lit up in his head.

When Zachary was three, he noticed that I was taping his older sister Sarah's pictures up on the wall. He drew me something too, folded it in half, and then took a piece of tape, which he stuck smack in the middle of the paper. Then he tried to stick it on the wall, right at his eye level. Of course it didn't stick, but good Oma that I am, I taped it up properly. It stayed there for some months and was always good for a giggle every time I passed by and saw it.

"I don't like it when you talk in Spanish," said Zachary to one of our guests, whose native tongue is German. That wouldn't have been particularly remarkable had she not been speaking *English* at the time.

My daughter-in-law sent me this: "Just wanted to tell you a funny story of what happened the other morning. I always sort my laundry all over the bathroom floor, adding to and taking piles down to wash periodically. The other morning, after having just sorted the laundry, Zachary woke up and needed to use the bathroom. He maneuvered quite well on the way to the toilet, but on the way back had some difficulty and got tangled in some bra straps, tripping and falling to the floor. He turned to me and said, "Boy, watch out for that bra!" I told him it was my *"booby-trap."* The best part was that he got the humor and couldn't wait to tell Sarah when she woke up!"

When granddaughter Ellie was still a baby, and X2 was out of town, Rick and family took me out to dinner. As we were about to enter the restaurant, it started to get very dark and windy here in tornado alley, and we debated whether we'd be safer inside the restaurant or in the car. Hunger won out. We were seated in an inner room at a booth with a strong wood table that was even bolted down.

Perfect. We made a plan: If the roof blows off, everyone under the table. Last man down, grab the food—*and Ellie*!

Rick and Cindy took the kids to Minnesota to the Mall of America, and Zachary, almost seven, had $3.00 of his own. He found something to buy and he wanted to handle the transaction himself. He took the item to the cashier who told him it would be three dollars and eighteen cents, to which Zachary replied, "I don't have any cents." He then proceeded to prove it—once his parents had covered the sales tax, he left his bag on the counter.

"Alrighty . . . mmmmm . . . real good!" said Rick in his sleep one night, according to step-Mike. Step-Mike is famous for playing "air" guitar in his sleep. Mike says he's good too!

One summer evening, step-Mike and a couple of his buddies set up a tailgate band on the back of a pickup truck on our driveway and entertained the neighborhood. Couples out for their after-dinner stroll stopped to listen. It was great—until the police showed up. It was still light out, and they weren't playing too loudly. The policeman told us that the boys were doing nothing wrong, but because someone had complained, they had to stop. We never found out who had called, but I wondered what their kids were up to while they were hiding behind their curtains and complaining about ours.

Having two Mikes around in the summers was always interesting, but especially when the girls would call and ask for Mike. I'd of course have to ask which Mike. I'd get various answers, but never one that was any help at all. I finally got to the point where I'd just holler, "Hey, Mike—telephone," and whichever Mike showed up got the girl. I figured if the girls didn't know the difference, it wouldn't matter.

Of course it was great for me to be able to say, "This is my son Mike, and this is my other son Mike."

X2 gave me Norman Rockwell figurines several Christmases in a row, always with children. One was a boy playing hooky and sitting under a tree with a stalk of grass in his mouth. When Rick saw it, he said, "Oh, he's got a joint!" When we pointed out that it was grass, he said, "That's what I said."

The first time we met Bea, who ran a rib joint in Arkansas where we were on vacation, we asked her what time she closed the restaurant. She answered, "Dark-thirty." Bea was a voracious reader and later I discovered that there was a book by the name of DARK-THIRTY, which she'd obviously read.

They talk funny in the south. X2 often couldn't figure out what they were saying. One time Bea asked X2, "Do you play goff?" X2 answered, "I've never even heard of it." She also said *hep* for help, *light bubs* for bulbs, and *chirrun* for children. Bea kept us in stitches.

A fishing guide in Arkansas was telling us some story and ended it with, "That just skeert the far out of me." When the guide turned his back to bait a hook, X2, who hadn't a clue, whispered to me, "What did he say?" That same night out fishing we heard Whip-por-wills—and that *is* exactly what they say.

Fishing was great in Arkansas. Happy to drift around in the boat with a book in his hand, X2 was quite sure he didn't want to bother with it, until I caught my first fish. Then it was off to the store to get him a rod and tackle and a fishing license. We hired a guide and sped across the lake to the edges where the bass had cornered the shad. You had to get there quickly.

We went trout fishing on the White River. It was very interesting and very different. The current was just right. We sat in a long rowboat that would drift downriver, but it would want to straighten itself out due to its shape. To counteract that, the guide had a trolling motor on the front, and that kept us sideways as we floated downstream. We'd only go so far, then zoom back up to our starting spot and start down again. We used small poles, very skinny line, tiny hooks, and canned corn for bait. We sat backwards, trolling slowly with our poles hanging over the upriver side of the boat. The rainbow trout loved the corn and we hauled out our limit.

Of course it was the guide's job to clean our fish. He used an electric knife, deftly slicing the filets off the spine up one side and down the other. It was quite efficient, but he didn't kill the fish first. It was weird watching a fish get cut up while it was still breathing. The guide claimed that the fish couldn't feel anything, but I didn't buy it, and I didn't like it.

"I used to did not like it when my dad came home and . . ." said a pastor in a sermon at a little church in Hilton Head.

"We done had us one big damn downpour," we heard someone say in Arkansas after a storm.

One time I went along with X2 on a business trip to a small town about as far south in Georgia as you can get. It was so hot there that the glue that held the rear view mirror on the car windshield melted and the mirror fell down. While X2 did his business, I got the task of finding someone to fix the mirror. I found a small garage and when the job was done, I asked the guy how much. He said, "Fi dolla."

In a truck stop in the heart of Georgia, a woman had posted a notice that she was available for baby-sitting and that she was "regested" with the state. I'm sure that's exactly the way she said it, so I suppose it makes sense that she'd spell it that way.

Our small group from church met weekly for several years. One of the couples lived in a condo, and we were at their place frequently. They were very close to some young people who lived below them, and they'd usually mention to them that they were expecting our small group. The young husband couldn't quite grasp the small group concept and called us the "Little People."

We went camping one October weekend with the "Little People." The weather was crisp and clear, stars filled the sky, and the campfire was warm and friendly. I'd brought my guitar and we were gathered around the fire singing praise songs. We sang "I Exalt Thee" several times and then just hummed the tune in personal worship. Right as we finished, and just for a minute, a few light, refreshing drops of rain fell on us. I like to think that we touched God's heart and He sent us His love in His teardrops.

When X2 and I were first married, one of us passed gas in the middle of the night. X2, who is a light sleeper, woke up from the noise. I don't wake up when tornadoes go through the yard, just ask my cousin Judy, but even I woke up from the smell of that one. We never knew who the culprit was, but we decided it must've been someone in the house next door.

I've been known to run the water in the washing machine, put in the soap, and then get distracted. The washer won't go past a certain point with the lid open, and one time I noticed that it had stopped, so I dutifully closed the lid, saying to myself, "The washing machine works a whole lot better when the lid is closed." I then proceeded to set the timer so I'd know when to put the load in the dryer. The timer went off and I had a nice, clean, *empty* washer.

One time my daughter-in-law Martha put a plastic plate in the *toaster oven*. Toasted it nicely. When it was time for her wedding shower, I wrapped up the plate and gave it to her as a gift. Later on she snuck it back into my cabinet. Not long afterwards, I found another one just like it in there. Martha swears she only did it once. Hmmmmm.

My sister-in-law, whose first language is German, is the master (or is it mistress?) of the messed-up metaphor. Here are a few of my favorites:

"Jeffrey, I know you so well I can read your mind blindfolded."

"You can kill one bird with two stones."

"That's a prayer to our answers."

She once used the word Virginia in place of vagina in some crazy conversation.

One time when she wanted to assure me she was telling the truth, she said, "Cris, I would cross my fingers on a stack of Bibles."

One day she was talking about something and used the phrase, "Hersh Kissies." Later that same day, she said something about serious killers, meaning, of course, serial killers.

When I worked at the smaller HVAC firm, one of the guys' wives sent in a homemade apple pie. I called to thank her for it and of course she wanted to know how I liked it. I had to admit I hadn't had any because I didn't have a fork. No sooner had we hung up than the mail came, and in it was an advertisement for stainless steel flatware, including a sample fork. God's good and so was the pie!

One day a lady called asking to have her furnace checked. The boss liked to take these calls himself when he thought there might be a damsel in distress and he could score some brownie points. He went out there and the lady admitted to him that she'd never been down in her basement in all the years she'd lived in the house because she was afraid of spiders. When he finished his work and came back upstairs, she asked him if he'd seen any spiders. He said, "No, just a dead mouse." The lady fainted.

That same boss told me a story about how when he was in the service, he and his fellow soldiers slept out one night in the desert in New Mexico. They woke up covered with tarantulas. The tarantulas evidently got cold and liked the warm soldiers. None of them got bitten.

When I worked at the first HVAC place, there was a story told about a former employee who had had a habit of falling asleep at his desk. He'd prop his head up with one hand, hold his pencil poised over a piece of paper with the other, and take a nap. This was apparently a regular occurrence, until one day the boss happened by with a question. Upon finding the fellow sound asleep, the boss gently removed the pencil from between the man's fingers and wrote him a note on the piece of paper. He then put the pencil back in the man's hand. The note said, "Come see me when you wake up."

I heard a good story about a church that had to do two back-to-back funerals. The first was for a lady named Mary, the second for a lady named Edna. It being the age of the computer, they simply "replaced" the word *Mary* with the word *Edna* in all the printed matter, including the programs. It all worked quite well until the congregation was reading the Apostles' Creed out loud and came to the part about ". . . born of the virgin Edna."

I told this story to several people via e-mail, one of whom was our attorney, and also our good friend. He reminded me of the time he did something similar in a document he'd written for X2. He'd set the computer to replace every *his* with *its*. A computer, being only as clever as the fool who uses it, replaced *his* in the word *this* as well, which changed every *this* to *tits*.

In the days before Caller I.D., when someone would call to sell me something and I wasn't interested, I'd just lay the phone down on the counter and let them talk, going back 10 minutes later to hang it up. Arguing with them just never worked.

TO AN OLD WOMAN
Crissy Shreve

Tell me.
What were you like then,
When you were young?

Were you always so settled,
So calm,
As now when you speak of your daughter,
Who must be near my age?

Did it take you years to grow,
As I am growing now?

Years of trouble,
Years of pain,
Guilt forever,
To make you happy?

How do I get to be like you?
I am not a giver,
I am not a lover,
I am only me,
And my world closes in,
(I draw it to me).
But, what of you?
Tell me—what were you then?

CHAPTER THIRTY-SEVEN

MORE FROM THE ANALS

My granddaughter was visiting one time when she was not quite two, and she went around my house, checking things out. She discovered a bottle of Elmo bubble bath in the bathroom. For some time after that, she thought that my house (Oma's house) was *Elmo's* house.

When she was about three, she hurt her finger, and Mike asked her if he should buy her a new one. She said, "No, you can't. This one is 'in-tached'" (Personally, I think her *in*-tached makes a lot more sense than at-tached. *On*-tached would be even better.)

On her second birthday, she got a wagon. I pulled her around the block in it, and we stopped to look at all the grasshoppers in a field along the way. She was quite familiar with them; she called them "hoppers." At about the halfway point, she got sleepy and reached her arms up to me to carry her, which of course I did, pulling the empty wagon along behind us. She was still sound asleep (and dead weight, as only a sleeping child can be) when I finally limped into their driveway. It's a really long block. I carried her to the couch and just sat and held her while she slept for about an hour. I was tempted to doze off myself, but I just couldn't bear to miss one minute of that sweet snuggle time.

She, like Mike, was always on the move, and the only way to get a snuggle out of her was to grab her on the fly, and then it was usually only a quick one. I called them love attacks; she called them heart attacks.

Right at the time she was learning punctuation in kindergarten, her mom said, "I've got PMS," to which she replied, "Remember, Mom, you have to have a period at the end of that."

On the occasion of her first communion, upon receiving the wafer, she said, "Jesus tastes like stale Cheerios."

The girls were outside carefully arranging carrots for Santa's reindeer one Christmas Eve. Mike asked one of them what she'd do if Bugs Bunny came by and ate all the carrots before Santa got there. She said, "Oh, Daddy, everyone knows Bugs Bunny's not real!"

I've had great luck with granddogs . . .

Rick and family had a Sheltie named Sheldon. He was a major wuss. I called him Dudley. They couldn't take him with them on trips because he'd get carsick, so I got to dog-sit him from time to time. He wouldn't eat at my house, nor would he potty when I took him outside. One day I spent forty-five minutes outside with him without results. The minute we got back into the house, he immediately presented me with a nice little present, right on my office floor.

When their dog Casey was just a puppy, step-Mike and Martha came to visit. Casey accompanied me into my bathroom, and I looked at him and said, "I hope you aren't looking for a place to poop." This, while my own pants were at half-mast. He looked right back at me and immediately began doing just that. I just about fell on my face trying to grab him. Casey later sent me a package of Blue Cheese as an "I'm sorry" gift, and he was the perfect guest on subsequent visits.

And then there was Henry. When Mike was in college, he lived with us and worked at a local K-Mart that was connected to an enclosed shopping mall. He'd usually spend his break time cruising the mall, so he was familiar with the stores, the merchandise, and of course, the sales girls. There was a pet shop in the mall, and Mike went in there often.

One night, X2 and I happened to be at that mall, and we wandered into that pet shop. They had a number of exotic birds—several large parrots, a beautiful (and quiet) toucan, and a Mynah bird. While I was admiring the (nice, quiet) toucan, X2 walked over to the Mynah bird, which looked right at him, and said, "Hello." X2 fell instantly in love, so hard that apparently his ears clogged up and he didn't hear the following word: "Sucker." He bought the bird.

Mike's comment to everyone he knew at the mall was, "Remember that mouthy Mynah bird in the pet shop? It now lives at my house."

We named the bird Henry. Mynahs are cage birds, not hands-on birds. Once X2 figured out that Henry was never going to be his shoulder buddy, he lost interest, and Henry became my . . . problem. In fact, one of the things Henry came already programmed to say was, "You got a problem . . . problem . . . problem?" Well, yes.

Henry's wolf whistle could be heard across town, and he used it regularly. I needed a place to put him where I could close him in, and yet have him with me during the day. Since I spent most of my day at the computer, we put his cage in my office. When the phone would ring, Henry would always be the first to say hello. If someone came to the door, Henry would holler hello from my office, and then run through his repertoire of words and whistles to get their attention.

I kept a spray bottle filled with water on my desk so that I could spray him when I needed to talk on the phone. I only had to pick up the bottle and Henry would shut up—well, he'd stop screaming and whistling, but he'd still mutter to himself.

My cousin John had a key to my house. One time he came to visit and I was out when he first arrived. No problem, he just came in with his key. Henry was closed up in my office hollering, "Hello, hello." Poor John walked all around the house looking for me, and finally found Henry, who happily greeted him. When I got home, John said, "That bird talks in your voice." Of course he did.

Henry had two large dog food bowls in his cage. Every morning I'd give him fresh water and moistened dog food pellets to eat. And every morning, Henry would take a bath in his water dish, happily shaking and flapping his wings. I hung big pieces of plastic on the wall behind his cage to catch the spatters. His range was amazing. I did make X2 clean his cage, though.

We taught Henry to whistle the first line of "Jesus Loves Me." He got to be quite good at it, and it was easily recognizable. In the process of teaching it to him though, X2, Mike, and I were all whistling the tune, but in three different keys. Poor Henry got confused—he'd start out in one key and end in another. I finally told the guys to just let me teach him, and that worked well. It was a lot like when X2 would play the piano and hit a wrong chord, which he did with some regularity, in effect playing a song in two different keys at the same time. They had that in common, at least.

My friend Marie has a deathly bird phobia. One time she stopped by and came into my office. I'd just finished vacuuming, and the vacuum cleaner was still there in the middle of the floor. For some reason, Henry didn't say anything when Marie first entered, and his cage was off to the side, so she walked right past him without noticing that he was there.

We talked for a minute or two, and then Henry decided to whistle at her. Poor Marie jumped like a jackrabbit and ran out of my office, screaming louder than even Henry could scream. She was wearing four-inch heels, and she had to navigate over the spread out vacuum cleaner hose. It was actually pretty funny, but she nearly had a heart attack.

I mostly didn't mind Henry—he was kind of fun. His wings were clipped, so he couldn't fly, but he could jump out of his cage if I wasn't careful. One day when I was changing his water, he did just that—he jumped out, landed on my shirt, and tried to peck out my eye. Fortunately he missed, but he got my cheek. That was the end of Henry for me. I found him a new home.

There's a bit more to the story, though. We used ground corncob in Henry's cage, sort of like cat litter. It came in large corrugated paper bags. One day I noticed a bug on the kitchen counter. I didn't recognize it. A few days later, I saw more of the same in the bathroom. Oh, oh, is right. Cockroaches.

I had an exterminator come in, but the roaches were winning because we hadn't found the source. The guy left me a can of heavy-duty spray to use. One day when I was changing Henry's water, I noticed a cockroach in the cage. It scampered into a hole in the stand. And then I knew. X2 and I took the stand into the kitchen and sprayed the bug killer into a hole in one end—out the other end came about fifty roaches, the females dropping their egg sacks. We killed them, but I kept a few of the egg sacks and put them into a baby food jar. I did *not* put holes in the lid.

Thus began my revenge on the cockroaches. They say that in a nuclear attack, the only creatures that will survive are the cockroaches. Those egg sacks are nearly indestructible. There were maybe six egg sacks in the baby food jar. Within a day or two, they hatched, and I had a bunch of baby cockroaches. They were tiny and transparent. With no food or water or air in the jar, it became a case of survival of the fittest. I watched as they disappeared, until only one was left. He'd eaten all the others. Then, having no more food or water, he too died.

It was an interesting experiment, albeit admittedly wacky. I charted the entire process, and I'm sure that little notebook is here somewhere in one clutter pile or another. I keep it just in case, but to date no one has offered to pay big bucks for my impressive research.

X2 and I decided to bring the old antique piano that he had grown up with across the ocean and into our living room. It was a great piano—an old upright with beautiful woodwork and brass candleholders. It had a real honky-tonk sound to it. Grandma Ruth played the right kind of music and we loved hearing her play it. Before it could be played, though, it needed some serious refurbishing.

It wasn't like a typical American piano—I don't know whether it was just because it was so old or whether it was because it was European, but the innards were different. We finally found someone who knew how to repair that type of piano, and he picked it up and took it to his shop. It lived there for some months, since we were in the process of renovating the house and needed it out of the way.

One day we went to visit the piano. The shop was in a storefront in an old section of town. It had been, perhaps, a dress shop or furniture store, and had huge display windows in front. And there, sitting in the window was a square grand piano. I'd never seen a square grand in person. I loved the TV show *Family*. In the opening credits at the beginning of each episode, they showed a square grand piano with a lot of framed pictures on top.[80]

I loved seeing that piano on the show every week, and when I saw the one in the window I nearly wet my pants. I wanted it. The fellow wanted a lot of money for it, though, and it too needed extensive repair. I sadly had to give up the idea of buying it.

He finished our upright and we moved it into the house. Some months later, this fellow called me, saying he'd lost his lease, and he'd part with the square grand for significantly less money. I thought about it, but I didn't really know where to put it in the house, so I said, "No." I didn't want to spend the money to repair it either. Another month or two went by, and he called again, saying that he didn't care

---

[80] YouTube has a video of the opening credits of *Family*, but it's dark and you can't see the square grand very well. A pity.

how soon I paid him, if I'd just take it. I again said, "No." I still didn't know where to put it.

Finally, he called and said that he'd give it to me for free, but that if I didn't take it, he'd have to ax it. I couldn't allow that, so he dropped it off. Originally the piano had been a beautiful rosewood, but apparently it had lived in a window, exposed to too much sun, and had faded to a muted gray on one full side. It wasn't pretty, it couldn't be played, but it was a square grand, and it was mine.

I had him put it in the area of our lower level family room that I hoped one day to turn into a small kitchen for entertaining. I still didn't know where to put it permanently. When I'd designed the house, I'd had to include a plumbing wall to get water to the upper level and back down. This created a small bar-like area that was eventually to have a laminate counter top and would serve as a bar or eating area. One day inspiration struck and I measured that area to see if the square grand would fit. It did, and perfectly!

The young woman who was then my "gopher" and I painted the whole piano a glossy white. I had the top laminated to match and to make it impervious to spilled drinks. It became the perfect piano bar—very slick. I hoped one day to make it playable and also to convert it into a player piano to entertain us at parties. That never happened, but I hope the square grand still lives in its cubicle in that house.

Suddenly we had four (count 'em) pianos. We'd bought an electronic piano called a Clavinova, we had X2's old European piano, my Schiller baby grand, and the square grand. Collecting pianos was nearly as much fun as using one to measure a stairway.

THE SNAIL
Crissy Shreve

To a pretty shell on a windy beach,
A tiny snail did come,
Said the little snail to the pretty shell,
"May I make you my home?"

"No," said the shell, "Hope you understand,
You're just too ugly for me,
Go dig yourself a hole in the sand,
You'll be sheltered from the sea."

The little snail did dig a hole,
And nestled in quite a way.
That night the waves blew in from the sea.
The shell was gone the next day.

Chapter Thirty-Eight

The World According To Crissy

I wish I'd said it first—life doesn't come with an instruction book. So we all write our own. Garp[81] wrote his; this is mine, or some of it.

Some things just get my goat, others interest me; many are somewhere in between. These are just my thoughts on whatever comes to mind. It is not exhaustive by any means. I can wax prolific on many subjects without necessarily knowing what I'm talking about. As Monk says, "I may be wrong . . . but I don't think so."

As I approached the returns counter in Menard's one day, I noticed a woman who was standing there talking loudly and gesticulating wildly. This would have been much less remarkable had there been anyone else around, but there wasn't. There was no clerk behind the counter and the woman had no companion that I could see. I knew she wasn't talking to me because she was speaking a language I'd never heard before. Deciding she was crazy, I was just about to walk away, when I noticed something sticking out of her ear. Oh! She was talking on the phone! I'd somehow missed the advent of those little gizmos you stick in your ear to make your phone hands-free.

I suspect you've noticed that there are a whole lot of people who insist on talking on their cell phones in public places and that they always talk too loudly, often in a foreign language, and invariably it's in a hallway or lobby where the acoustics amplify their voices. And of course the person driving erratically or too slowly in front of me is invariably talking on a cell phone.

---

[81] THE WORLD ACCORDING TO GARP (John Irving, 1978)

I don't care what anyone says. When someone is driving and talking on the phone, their attention is not focused on the road. I seldom answer my cell when I'm driving. One time it rang as I was stopped at a red light, so I answered it. It was my friend Jackie. The light changed and I drove about two miles to church while talking to her. I realized after we hung up that I had no conscious memory of the drive. I don't trust my radar and I don't trust anyone else's either.

At least they've outlawed texting and driving. I've often seen people reading a book or a newspaper as they're driving along, though. That's just plain scary.

I was sitting one time in a hotel lobby. The ceiling was a rotunda. There was a couple sitting on the other side of the lobby talking to each other. It was not a small distance between us, and they weren't talking loudly at all, but I could hear every word as though I were sitting next to them. I had a similar experience in a restaurant, and I asked the owner whether anyone else had ever mentioned being able to hear conversations taking place across the room. He said, "Yes, all the time."

I take some small comfort in that now, in my elderly years, when I can't hear what the person next to me is saying, I can sometimes hear what someone is saying on the other side of the room.

One thing I can tell you from my vast store of "expertise" is that kids are *kids,* and it's ridiculous to expect them to be anything else. Once I figured out that 3-year-olds are going to behave exactly like 3-year-olds and that it's okay, I stopped expecting them to be perfect little adults. This made it much easier on *me.* I only wish I'd figured that out when my kids were little.

I was very impressed one time with my daughter-in-law Cindy. It was half an hour before her guests were due to arrive for a birthday party. Me, I'd have been rushing around making sure the house and the kids were clean and perfect. Cindy had the kids sitting on the kitchen floor making ice cream—and a mess. It was a great lesson for me.

Ever since, I've let my grandkids do whatever they want to do as long as it's not dangerous to them or to things I really care about. There are enough things in my house that they are free to touch and use and play with that they can respect those things that are off limits—as long as I tell them which is which. But I also tell them that there is nothing I have that I love more than I love them, *and* that I do like my stuff, so I appreciate their being careful with it. They are busy doing the tasks of growing up. It's much more fun to watch them and know them than to get hung up on either perfect behavior or the mess they make in the process.

There are people like me in the world who need to connect with a kid before he shows up, so any expectant mother within my reach can expect some belly patting, unless she's really uncomfortable with it. While Stefan and Katrin lived with us, she became pregnant, and I really enjoyed getting to know the baby before he was born. I patted and talked to him throughout the day. And when he was born, he knew me; he responded to my voice.

And, by the way, I cringe when I hear someone say, "We are pregnant." No, *we* are *not* pregnant. It's nuts. I've never yet met a guy who was pregnant. What's wrong with saying, "We're expecting?"

Have you noticed lately that often when you thank the young person who packs your groceries or otherwise helps you in a store, they reply, "Not a problem?" I like to mess with them. I say something like, "Oh, it never occurred to me that it might be a problem. Was it a problem?" Then I suggest that a better response might be, "You're welcome."

Sometimes I'm just trying to be funny rather than making a point, though. I was in the drive-up line at Starbucks and I ordered my usual venti, half-caff, skinny mocha, no whip, managing to remember all that. The sweet little girl who took my order asked, "Will that be all for you?" I couldn't resist. I had to say, "Absolutely! I'm not sharing it with anyone." Of course it went right over her head, so I sure hope you will laugh when you read this.

Okay, I confess. I'm a slot machine junkie. I have been ever since my first foray to Las Vegas with X2 in the early eighties. Of course they have slot machines at the airport there and of course I dutifully stuck my quarter in the first one I saw. Wonder of wonders, it gave me back two quarters, and just that easily, I was hooked.

I'm not officially a gambler, though. It's truly not about winning gobs of money, which is a good thing, because I never do. It's the game itself. I just love playing slots. And I have one hard and fast rule: I never go to a casino that's less than one hundred miles from my house.

Going to Las Vegas with X2 worked well. Whatever I'd lose on the slots, he'd win playing Black Jack, and usually more. The only time this didn't work was when we went for my 50th birthday. It was New Year's Eve and neither we, nor anyone else, was winning anything anywhere. I get that they can rig the slots now that they're computer-controlled, but how on earth did they manage to rig the Black Jack tables?

One time we went with my friend Marie and her husband. She was pregnant with their first child. She'd never been to Las Vegas before, and when we entered the casino, there stood Big Bertha. Now, I've always given Big Bertha a wide berth because I know I'm not going to win anything on her, so I went off to find some quarter slots to play.

I'd only blown a few bucks when I heard over the loudspeaker, "Congratulations to expectant mother Marie who just won ten million dollars on Big Bertha." I nearly wet my pants, but it's just as well I didn't, because it was a different Marie. That was thirty years ago, and I can still feel the adrenaline rush.

X2 noticed a casino software program one day when we were at Best Buy and we bought it. From that time on, I've been completely content to play slots on my computer. Unlimited playing money. Now that Facebook offers tons of online casinos, it's even better. They're all free! There are those who buy chips, but I can't imagine why.

I have a huge problem with "politically correct." I find it nonsensical—most particularly the term African-American—and not the least bit respectful. It's verbal segregation; most black people are simply Americans, and they are all simply people, just like I am.

When a distinction is absolutely required, the word *Black* is just fine. What happened to "Black is beautiful?" I think it still is. Not everyone who is black is African. Not everyone who is African is black. And not every black person is an American citizen. A white guy I know comes from South Africa. If he becomes a citizen of the US, will he then be African-American?

There are words that are kinder than others, and I too prefer them, but it disturbs me that we have become such a culture of denial. Terminology doesn't change or even mask reality. Pussyfooting around reality is patronizing and insulting (in my not always humble opinion).

I walk a thin line between being involved enough that my sons and their wives know I care, and staying out of things enough to avoid trouble. My rule of thumb: "Care and pray, stay out of the way."

Being a female and having had my share of mothers-in-law, I think I understand the basic competition for the "control" of the son/husband that simply happens (and which I really do want to stay out of). I figure, she married him, she can have him. The bottom line is that any daughter-in-law of mine has to love my kid—she doesn't have to love me, although I'd sure prefer it if she did.

I am aware too of the potential for emotional blackmail, both ways, particularly when grandchildren enter the scenario. I try to be intentional about not doing that to them, and I won't let them do it to me.

I can't *stand* flavored coffee. One morning a houseguest thought to "surprise" me by making vanilla coffee in *my* coffee maker before I got downstairs to protect myself. Then, as all good surprises go, of course she didn't *tell* me, so I fixed myself a great big mug, doctored it, as is my wont, and took a big swig. Nice surprise; I nearly threw up.

I am inhuman before I get my coffee, a cigarette, and at least half an hour of no sounds of any sort. There I was, right out of bed . . . you can imagine my distress. You can't kill the people God sends you to love, so what do you do? The worst part was that I then had to make my coffee in the other pot, the *slow* pot, and wait it out.

Flying first class is wonderful. I've only done it once, so the novelty hasn't worn off. I loved the linen tablecloth on my little tray table—and the napkin with a buttonhole! My only regret was that I was wearing a shirt with no buttons. Sloppy eater that I am, I'd start wearing more button shirts if restaurants would offer napkins with buttonholes.

More than once, I've gotten in trouble talking to babies. The first time was at church. I was an usher and I was just babbling inanely to a baby, telling it that I knew it was a quiet baby and we'd never have to kick it out of the service. We sometimes had to escort a mother whose baby was crying out of the room. The baby had no understanding of what I was saying. It never even occurred to me that the parents were listening to what I said, let alone that they would make a big deal out of it. I wasn't talking to *them*. They made a big deal out of it.

Well, like I said, I can be stupid. You'd think I'd learn. Just long enough after that incident for me to have forgotten all about it, I was talking to my cousin's baby. Again, it never occurred to me that anyone was *listening*. She had been a very placid baby for the first several weeks and then she got cranky. My cousin had been doing some major complaining to her mom, which her mom had mentioned to me. So I was telling the baby that she was so sweet that I could just take her right home with me.

My cousin lit right into me saying, "You can't take either one of my kids home!" What? Who wanted to take her kids home? Did she really think I wanted to take her kids home? Why was she listening to what I was saying to the baby and *then taking it seriously?* Thank heavens I didn't say the baby was so sweet I could just eat her all up!

Even more stupid was that I thought, well, at least I'll be able to say stupid things to my own grandbaby when I have one, and no one will land on me. Oops.

The first time I held my newborn granddaughter, it was in the hospital, only a few hours after the birth. I was talking to the baby, assuring her that her mommy would feel better soon. It was never intended to be any kind of criticism or reflection on her mom's *ability* to take care of her. And regardless, I was just babbling to the baby. It still never occurred to me that anyone else was bothering to listen. Then I told my granddaughter that I didn't know how anyone could love her more than I did.

I got confronted on both points a few days later in a vicious email from my son.

I was very upset, and I thought about it more or less nonstop all the following week. And I came to some conclusions. One is that while I am addressing a baby as an individual human being, which is what it is to *me*, it's not who the baby is to its parents. To them, the baby is an extension of themselves. That's logical, and it's time I caught on.

I'd made the mistake of believing my granddaughter to be "mine" too. Not in the sense of ownership—she's on loan to all of us—she belongs to God. But "mine" in the sense of blood and kinship and being my grandchild and her dad also being "mine." I had no intention of competing with her parents. The same Hand that designed her parents to be able to love their child more than anyone else ever could had designed her to love as many others as there are for her to love. She'd just come from God, she was *full* of love, and had plenty for all of us. On top of that, she was designed to absorb love.

Another mistake I made was in thinking that the relationship between us all had come to a different plane than it had been in the past. Anticipating the baby together had been, at least for me, a very special time. Suddenly I felt left out, no longer part of it.

Then there's the "Mama Bitch" aspect. At first I thought it was only "Mama Bitch," but then I realized that it was "Papa Protector" as well. "Mama Bitch," in case you've never met her, is psychological jargon for the mother's protective instinct. "Mama Bitch" isn't bad—she's normal. She will instinctively protect her young from any threat or danger she might perceive, regardless of the direction from which it comes, and regardless of whether there is truly any danger or not. She will strike out first and probably won't even bother to ask questions later.

Of course, "Papa Protector" has to protect "Mama Bitch" and the litter. All of this is as it should be. It was well-designed to protect the young and the species, and it's not just seen in animals. "Mama Bitch" and "Papa Protector" don't just notice a threat, they *watch* for it, from all quarters. If they error, they do so on the side of being overly protective and overly sensitive.

Again, this is not bad. It's great, but it *is* hard on stupid people like me. In none of these cases was there ever any intention on my part to insult or hurt or undermine or even say anything at all to any of the parents.

After receiving the email from my son, I was devastated, and spent most of the week dodging attacks of self-hatred. I learned that when one person seems to think you're crap, it makes sense to take a poll before jumping out the basement window or sticking your head in the electric oven. All that week, my great big faithful God kept sending little angels to tend me.

First, I received an email from someone whose opinion of me I value deeply. It said, simply, "You're awesome."

Then I received a phone call from a dear friend whose love is unquestionable, with an invitation to dinner.

Next I received a fax from a former "gopher" with a drawing of flowers and a reminder of how she used to put flowers on my desk when she lived with me.

So I started telling everyone I talked to about these little angels God was sending me. And then I received a snail-mail letter from a friend, and when I opened the envelope—hang on to your seat—out fell *five tiny brass angels*.

Christmas, for me, has been a chore for many years—not the real Christmas, just the tinsel and shopping malls. I hate having to buy people things just because it's Christmas, and wasting time and money buying those things when I haven't a clue what they really want or need. I'd so much rather wait and get someone something that's just right for them when I know exactly what that is.

The perfect Christmas for me is putting a wreath on the front of my car, going to church on Christmas Eve, and having a birthday cake for Jesus on Christmas Day. I realized that the cards I used to make (and that many people loved) were more about showing off what I could do than they were about the Christmas message, even though the Christmas message was usually a good one.

To me, the tinsel and cookie thing would be really great about once every five years. Of course, the stores would not agree with me, and I doubt that that will ever change. This is, after all, America. And I don't need to change America, just my own little corner of it.

Another thing about Christmas—most businesses are closed, which is as it should be, but still, it always feels a little spooky to me. I feel like the world has ended and I've been left behind. Weird, I know, but I feel that way, especially around midnight on Christmas Eve when I'm driving home from somewhere and everything is dark and deserted. Christmas Day's hard, too. I discovered that my local Walgreen's is always open—and very busy. I take comfort in knowing that, if I get too lonely, I can always run over there and rub elbows with other lonely souls out buying things none of us really need.

When I was first divorced, I dreaded all the holidays. Now, though, many stores are open on holidays other than Christmas and Easter. I don't *need* to go shopping, and I usually don't, but it sure helps to know there's somewhere to go. Plus, as I found out from my Jewish friend Jackie, the thing to do is eat Chinese and go to a movie.

When my (appropriately-named) friend Robin was here one day in early spring, she hollered down the stairs that I had a nest in my loft. Just as I was about to panic, she clarified that the nest was in fact outside the window, on the ledge. And sure enough, there it was, and in it was a bright blue robin's egg. The next day, there was another egg, followed daily by another until there were four. And then mama robin sat.

Although I found the entire process amazing and exciting to watch, the one thing that really struck me was the mud edge on the nest. How a couple of birds, with only their beaks for tools, could carry and form mud into something resembling a tiny brown snow fort astounded me.

Earlier the same week, I'd stood outside a neighbor's front door talking with her for five or ten minutes, and never noticed, until she pointed it out, a mama mourning dove silently and patiently sitting on her nest, practically right next to my head, on a leftover hanging plant basket. Apparently this dove had claimed that basket for several years in a row. I have to confess, I was a wee bit jealous; I wanted one, too. Two days later, *voila*, there was mama robin!

After about ten days, I saw the first baby robin, with the second halfway out of its egg. The other two soon followed. Now there were four of what looked like tiny plucked chickens no more than an inch long.

While mama had been patient with me peering through the window as she sat on the eggs, she was not at all patient once the babies had hatched. She actually cried in fear.

Each day the babies got bigger—and bigger and bigger. They quickly went from tiny plucked chickens to fuzzy balls with oversized beaks to little black and brown striped bodies with long necks. By this time, both mama and daddy robin were bringing them worms, and although I'd approach when they weren't there, within seconds, one or the other would come zooming back, worms in their beaks. In the nest, four sleeping fuzz balls would suddenly become four long necks reaching those open beaks up for their share. The parent would drop the worms into their mouths—often one baby would chomp off a piece and then the rest would go to the next baby in line.

Usually the sudden arrival of a parent bird would startle me, and my presence, in turn, would startle the parent. Daddy robin would give me the serious evil eye. I realized that my being there hampered the babies' feeding, so I started standing off to the side where I could still see but not be so easily seen. Soon the babies' spindly legs and feet started to show. They couldn't stand yet, so those legs were all over the place, intertwined like spaghetti, and in the way.

Most of this transpired before the spring sunshine finally decided to show up around here. But then it did, and because my loft window faces west and the hot afternoon heat reflects off the bricks, I was worried that those babies were going to broil. Mama, however, had cleverly built the nest in the one corner of the ledge that is fairly well sheltered by a tree. And I'm guessing that worms must contain plenty of water for baby birds—ah, clever creation.

I did note that the babies would sleep with their mouths open so as not to be "caught napping" when mama or daddy brought a worm. In the last few days, they began to lie neatly tucked together in rows facing outward—or should I say wormward?

As I wrote this, the babies were still in the nest, but would soon be learning to fly. It put me in mind of a song that my Aunt Ruth made up some time in the early 1930's, one that all of us in my family sang to our babies. It goes like this:

"I am a little robin and I live up in this tree,
I have a mother robin and I have some brothers three.
My mother's teaching us to fly, and she says, 'Never fear,'
But I am staying on this branch 'cause pussycat is near."[82]

Where I live, spring is often but a promise, something to be taken on faith, something to watch for so that we don't miss it as nasty

---

[82] My family assures me that Grandma Ruth (my aunt) wrote this song.

winter seemingly overnight becomes hot summer. It's in moments like these, seeing life begin anew, that I believe.

Not having any siblings, my four first cousins were like brothers and sisters to me, both as I was growing up and ever since. Having once been the youngest, it is somewhat dismaying that we are now the oldest generation in our family. It's weird watching people I played with sprouting gray hair and wrinkles.

For me, one of the hardest things about aging is knowing that from here on out things will mostly only get worse. Death and illness will be ever more a part of our lives. After sixty-some years on this planet, I've collected a lot of friends and acquaintances. They too will suffer their travails.

Recently I've begun to realize one of the reasons we have to die. The time is fast approaching when I will no longer be able to keep up with things, or no longer like the way things are going in the world. Not only will I soon no longer fit in, I'll no longer have what it takes to make a science out of not fitting in. This is how I know I'm getting old.

I am grateful that I started using a computer in my forties because if I had to start all that today I'd not be able to do it. Not only because my brain has largely caught the last train to Clarksville, but because technology evolves, builds. So, too, does learning how to work a computer or a smart phone. The knowledge bank we've accumulated over the years makes each new technological wonder possible for us to at least survive, if not completely master. These days, kids are born with a mouse in their hands. Somehow, each generation comes complete with the skills it needs. The rest of us are left to try and keep up. It's daunting.

I think about Grandma Ruth trying to use a computer and I have to giggle. To her, it just "wouldn't compute." She never even learned to drive.

My cousins tell the story of Uncle John trying to teach her to drive. For some reason, he positioned her facing upward, right at the top of the steepest street in town, and he wanted her to let out the clutch and get the car moving up the hill. They rolled all the way down the hill backwards. Apparently he had shown her the brake pedal or they'd have wound up somewhere in the next county. It was at this point that she gave up driving entirely. Personally, I'd have given *him* up, but he turned out to be a good guy in other ways.

While tracing my ancestry, I ran into an amazing thing. I am my own eighth cousin. This happens when, in an earlier generation, someone married his or her cousin. Being my own eighth cousin works quite well for me. There are days when I'm "just not myself." It is a great relief to discover that on those days, I'm just busy being my eighth cousin. When I do something stupid or ill advised, I can blame her! She's gotten me into a fair amount of trouble over the years.

Stranger things have happened. In 1947, Dwight Latham and Moe Jaffee wrote a song called "I'm My Own Grandpa." It was based on a Mark Twain anecdote, and it's been performed by a number of artists on several TV shows. If one eliminates the "step-" in the relationships, it can be done, although not consanguineously.[83]

As I've always said, genealogy can be quite genial, but it's not always logical. Here's a silly little limerick I wrote about it:

GENEAL-LOGICAL
Crissy Shreve

When we pursue things genealogical,
We sift thru a lot that's hodge-podgical,
Tho' cousins are GENIAL,
The work can be menial,
And I've not yet found much that is LOGICAL.

A friend once asked me whether I ever had visionary dreams, and it was right after I'd had one of my "nudges" from God. I have no sixth sense, particularly not dream-wise. My thing happens when I'm wide-awake.

I had contracted with a man from church to build me some cabinets. He and I had a falling out over his failure to begin the job according to our agreement, and he refused to return my deposit. We hadn't spoken for some months. I knew that he was ill but didn't know the extent of his illness. One day I felt a nudge to send him a note saying that I'd forgiven him and that I hoped things could be

---

[83] Wikipedia

right between us. He called and we had a great time of reconciliation on the phone. Not long afterward, I was in the shower (really) in our motor home, in Hilton Head. Suddenly, I looked up and said to God, "Oh, Glen died?" I sent an email to a friend and found out that yes, he had died just the day before.

There are times when I'm very aware that God is nudging me in different ways. No problem with this, but there are also times when my own brain tends to create scenarios that I would *not* want to have happen. It's my tendency to depraved morbidity—or is it morbid depravity? Either way, it's the right description. That makes it very important to me to be able to distinguish which is which, to separate the positive and the negative.

I know little of clairvoyance, but if it in fact exists, I would be inclined to wonder where it comes from. As in *who* is using that brain? To be specific, is it God? Is it the evil one? Or is it just someone's own thoughts or subconscious wishes? I don't have the answer.

I Love A Man . . .
Crissy Shreve

. . . who knows he's a man.

He doesn't need to cheat to prove it.
He can carry his love's purse through the mall.
He can cry without shame when it's crying time,
Then get up and get on with living.

He can speak his heart and he can speak his mind,
Without being diminished when someone disagrees.
He's tough on the outside and squishy on the inside.
And he's not afraid to let the little boy inside come out to play.

He understands that he needs to forgive his love,
And that he'll need to forgive her again tomorrow.
He knows that his only source of power is surrender,
To a God Who is stronger than he.

He is honest in his dealings,
He is tender in his passion,
His smile shines a welcome,
And his words touch a heart.

He knows his warts,
And he's put his past behind him.
He's willing to look at himself,
And willing to learn.

And when he does, he discovers,
What he's known all along—
That he's a man.
And he's a good one.

All he needs is my arms around him.

CHAPTER THIRTY-NINE

I'M NOT DONE YET

Once at a restaurant drive-through I had to wait a minute for Mike and Jason to decide what I should order for them, and the order guy thought I was finished. He gave me my total and told me to pull up to the window. I said, "I'm not done yet." This became a favorite catch phrase for us, and it saddens me that, with Jason gone, now only Mike and I have the memory. Yet even as I write that, I remember that Jason's in heaven. He's not done yet.

Words don't always work well. It's not my fault—I didn't invent them, although I can take credit for a few. *Ilk* is one. When someone is *of* an ilk with me, I call him or her *an* ilk. An ilk doesn't have to be just like me—he or she only has to "get" me. Not everyone is an ilk to everyone else, which is why it is so rare and wonderful to find one now and again.

I have often used the letter *e* as a word for email, as in "I'll be eeing you," or "Eya later."

I do enjoy great words. On of my favorites is the Yiddish *shmying*. To go *shmying* is to gad about. It works very well for shopping trips. And *schmoozing*—another Yiddish word. I'm good at *schmoozing*.

The Germans have some good words, too.

A rooster says (and is called by children), *Kikeriki* (pronounced key-ker-ah-*key*).

A cuckoo is called a *Kuckuck* (pronounced kook-kook).

Some years ago, I arrived in north Germany on June 21st, memorable only in that it was the longest day of the year. Around here, we celebrate the days getting longer in the spring and mourn their shortening in the fall. And then we go about our business. It's not that big a deal for most of us.

In north Germany, though, it is a big deal. The days are significantly longer in late June than they are here. Night lasts about three hours, and it never really gets very dark. You see people out taking a stroll at 11 PM. There's no sense trying to sleep—it's too light out, and anyway, what's not to like about getting some extra time for free?

But when I arrived that day, I was looking forward to giving my poor jet-lagged body some much-needed rest. I'd arrived early in the morning, after a night in the sky, and had stayed awake the whole day in a misguided attempt to adjust my body clock to the six-hour time difference. But sleep was not to be had. It just wouldn't get dark.

At 11 PM, X2 and I gave it up and headed out for a stroll in the woods. The thing about the woods in Germany is that there really are cuckoos. Oh! I get it. *That's* why they like cuckoo clocks so much. And amazingly enough, those cuckoos in the woods sound just like that cuckoo clock that's gathering dust in your attic.

The cuckoos hide in the tops of the trees and call out to each other at dusk. People play a game, betting on the number of calls they'll hear between a pair of cuckoos. Since you never actually see them, most people have no clue what a cuckoo looks like. I submit that that cuckoo on your aforementioned clock may just be a figment of some whittler's imagination.

Well, anyway, all of this (and probably my lack of sleep) inspired me to immortalize this experience in a little verse. I even wrote it in German first, and then translated it into English. I'm unashamedly proud that I managed to make it rhyme in both languages. Although I can't vouch for the correctness of the German grammar, I can claim poetic license.

THE CUCKOO
Crissy Shreve
Germany, June, 1996

Am Abend Zeit im Stenumer Wald,
Mann muß spatzieren nur,
Dort hört Mann der Kuckucks Song,

Wer braucht ein Kuckuck Uhr?

At evening time in Stenum Woods,
It's fun to take a walk,
For there you'll hear the cuckoo sing,
Who needs a cuckoo clock?

X1 always said that I speak "backwards Polish" when I speak German. He may be right. I always say I speak "survival" German—just enough to get by. I can't claim credit for the concept, though. In the mid-eighties, Florida's Miami-Dade Community College developed a course called "Survival Spanish."

I have more favorite words in German. One is *Baumschule*, which translates literally to tree school. I always think of it as the place where the little trees go to school.

Another is *Handschuh*, which translates literally to hand shoe.

And of course *Fingerhut*, which translates literally to finger hat.[84]

German is very phonetic, which makes for some interesting pronunciations. One is psychology (*Physiologie*). It's pronounced fi-si-zhi-low-gee (with a hard g as in geese).

German also has words like *Schadenfreude* that have no equivalent in English and so can only be defined. It means joy at someone else's misfortune. It's a great word and it seems to be gaining popularity with English speakers.

I quickly learned to take advantage of X2's liking to impress visiting Germans. When he and I got married, he had, at my request, given me a simple thin gold wedding band that would go well with, but not overshadow, my engagement ring. Later on I discovered anniversary rings, and I figured that having a wedding band with a few diamonds on it couldn't hurt. On a trip to the shopping mall, I dragged X2 and some visiting Germans into a jewelry store. This gave X2 a great opportunity to impress, and he bought me one.

As we were wandering around the shopping mall, I mentioned, in German, that I needed to look for a bathroom, which I mistranslated

---

[84] A *Baumschule* is a nursery—the plant kind, not the baby kind. A *Handschuh* is a glove—of course it is. And a *Fingerhut* is a thimble.

to bathroom in German. No problem, except that you wouldn't say it that way in German. The visitors thought I was looking to buy new bathroom fixtures. When I explained, they replied, again in German, "Oh, you are looking for a toilet!" That too.

While we were having lunch at a restaurant in the mall later that same day, it started raining buckets. X2 looked out the window, and remembering that we had parked quite a ways from the entrance, despaired of getting the car without getting soaked. He looked at me—I think he was mostly kidding—and asked whether I'd like to go get the car.

No fool, this kid. "Sure," I said, "for a hundred bucks." I too was mostly kidding, but he called my bluff. He whipped out his wallet and handed me a hundred-dollar bill. What's a woman to do? I went and got the car. My good leather bomber jacket, which I'm sure had cost more than a hundred bucks, was never the same again. But the Germans were impressed.

I've got another hundred-dollar story. I had a great retro silver and garnet bracelet that I loved and wore all the time. Apparently silver is a comparatively soft metal, and the connecting pieces tended to open up, allowing the bracelet to fall off. I lost it several times, found it again, and then finally lost it for good.

One night before that, though, I'd just picked up this bracelet from the jeweler's after another repair. I put it on, and then drove to a local department store to look for a new pair of jeans. As I got out of the car, I noticed a scratch-off instant lottery ticket on the pavement. I nearly passed it by, thinking it had just been thrown away, but decided to take a look, just in case. It was a hundred-dollar winner! I didn't see anyone else in the parking lot, so I stuck the ticket in my purse and went on into the store.

I tried on several pairs of jeans, bought one, and then headed back outside to my car, maybe forty-five minutes later. I noticed a guy wandering around the parking lot looking down. It's a good bet he was looking for that lottery ticket. I had a decision to make. I could ask him if he'd lost something, and if he could tell me what it was, give it back to him. Or I could claim "finders keepers" and keep it. I chose the latter. A hundred bucks, after all.

But it bugged me for several days. It wasn't a moral issue. I hadn't stolen the ticket—I'd found it, and it was fair game. Still. And I knew why it was bugging me. Years earlier, when I was still in my twenties, I was at the grocery store one day, and my neighbor got in line behind me at the checkout counter. We started talking, and we talked the entire time my groceries and hers were being rung up and bagged. I was only vaguely aware of writing a check, handing it to the cashier, and getting my receipt.

My neighbor and I left the store, still talking, and headed towards our cars. When we finally parted, I looked down and there was my seventy-something-dollar check in my hand, along with my receipt. The cashier had inadvertently handed it back to me. I packed my groceries in the trunk, went back into the store, and returned the check to the cashier.

She was ecstatic. She thanked me profusely, saying that she would have been fired had that amount been missing from her till. Above all, she was amazed and deeply touched that I'd returned it. Seventy-something dollars is, after all, seventy-something dollars, and in those days, I could have used it myself. Again, I hadn't stolen it. It had been handed to me—not my fault. But I remember thinking that it wasn't mine, and as such, I didn't want it. And I remember feeling pretty good about the whole thing.

Back to the lottery ticket. I didn't do wrong by keeping it, but I missed something by not returning it, or at least not trying to. I missed the good feeling, that's for sure. But more, I missed an opportunity to tell the man why I was returning it. I missed the opportunity to bless someone and maybe even to tell him that Jesus loves him. I don't know what I might have said because I didn't say it!

The next morning, hundred-dollar ticket in hand, I stopped at a convenience store to cash it in, and noticed that my bracelet was no longer on my wrist. I'd lost it again. Now, I'm not a believer in karma.[85] I do, however, find that sometimes what goes around does

---

[85] Today's simplistic definition of karma seems to be "What goes around comes around." I find it interesting that karma is a fundamental doctrine in both Buddhism and Hinduism, in that Buddhism is atheistic (having no God) and Hinduism is polytheistic (having many gods). The doctrine of karma, in both religions, is significantly more involved and complicated than that simple definition.

come around. And that's even a good thing sometimes, but maybe not this time. There I stood, thinking that that was what had happened, and given the choice, I'd actually rather have my bracelet than the hundred bucks. It crossed my mind that perhaps whoever had lost the ticket might ironically have found my bracelet right there in the parking lot. But at this point, there wasn't much else to do but cash in the ticket, so I did.

This starts to get funny. That night, in my sleep, for some reason I got the impression that my earring had fallen out of my ear, but I didn't wake up enough to check it out. Of course, I forgot all about it until the next morning when I was doing my hair, and discovered that it wasn't in my ear. Oh, great! So now I'm thinking that that stupid lottery ticket had apparently cost me a favorite earring too. Was there a lesson in this?

Then I sort of remembered (you know how sometimes you sort of remember things?) that idea in my sleep, and I went to look in my bed for my earring. I didn't find it, but right there on the floor next to the bed was my bracelet! Broken again, but I still had it. Okay!

I put on a different pair of earrings and went on with my day, tucking the bracelet into my purse to go back to the jeweler *again* for repair. The next day, as I was sort of straightening my bed—I never make my bed, I'm just going to mess it up again in a few hours and anyway, my dogs like to re-make it to suit themselves—I spotted my earring.

To further complicate the whole thing, this all happened right as I was struggling with having to evict the man renting my little house down the street. I'm not going to go into a lot of details because they are his details, not mine, but getting him to pay his rent—at all, let alone on time—was getting to be too much for me. I struggled mostly because I adore his little girl, and it wasn't quite so easy to deal with evicting her.

I got all hung up on the story Jesus told in the Bible about a man who successfully pleads to be forgiven a huge debt and then turns around and refuses to forgive someone who can't pay him a much lesser debt. That didn't go over very well. I was thinking about how greatly I am blessed and I wasn't sure I was supposed to kick this guy (well, his daughter anyway) out. I started worrying that if I didn't care for this man, God would withdraw His provision from me.[86] And I need His provision.

I'm not generally one to make decisions based on feelings, but I regularly sing, "Break my heart for what breaks Yours," to God during worship times. I'm pretty sure this man's situation breaks God's heart. It certainly breaks mine. However, after consulting with a number of godly friends, I was able to see that it was, as Dr. Henry Cloud calls it, a "Necessary Ending." I was simply not in a position to make this man my personal charity, and I would do him no favor by allowing him to continue to renege on his lease contract with me.

I'm still not completely sure what the lesson was, but I came away from it seeing that I can trust in God's provision, regardless of what choices I make or have to make. He's not out to get me. I can't manipulate His love for me. Good thing. I gave the tenant one extra month to move out, and then put him and his situation in much better hands than mine. I pray and trust that God will provide for him too.

One time my son Mike, who was maybe twelve at the time, was at the 7-11. He was very much into comic books, and he picked one up, plus a candy bar and a pair of sunglasses. He took it all to the counter and laid it all down, fully intending to pay for it. All the while, he was engrossed in the comic book and wasn't paying attention. He put down a ten-dollar bill, collected his change, picked up his purchases, and started out of the store, nose still in the comic book.

The storeowner stopped him and called me, saying that my son had "left the store without paying for something." I went there and insisted on hearing Mike's side of it before I would listen to hers. She was not being very nice. She was not pleased when I pointed out that it was in fact her cashier's mistake, that he simply hadn't charged Mike for the sunglasses. Mike didn't realize it, he just picked up what he thought he'd paid for and left. The storeowner was in no hurry to give in, so I finally suggested that she call the police and let them decide what had happened. She relented, Mike paid for the sunglasses, and we went home.

---

[86] The whole story can be found in Matthew 18:21-35, but here's the ending: And his lord, moved with anger, handed him over to the torturers until he should repay all that was owed him. So shall My heavenly Father also do to you, if each of you does not forgive his brother from your heart. NASB

Ironically, only a month or so earlier, I had been in this same store, and I'd purchased several things, putting a twenty-dollar bill down for payment. They'd just installed one of those new cash registers[87] where the amount tended gets entered and the machine calculates the change. It was this woman's husband who handled the transaction, and he forgot to enter the amount tendered. He wound up giving me back the amount of my purchase as change. Rather than giving me a dollar-something, he gave me back eighteen-something. I was in a hurry and didn't notice until I got home and discovered that I had a much greater handful of cash than I should.

Not having time to return to the store that day, I stuck the money and the receipt in an envelope and put it in my purse. The next time I was at that store, I returned it, explaining how it had happened. Unfortunately, neither owner was there that day, but the employee behind the counter was amazed that I'd bothered to return the money. Again, it wasn't mine, and I didn't want it. I tried to tell the woman storeowner about this during Mike's sunglasses incident. She wouldn't listen.

Mike, meanwhile, was somewhat astounded that I'd gone to bat for him, and with good reason. Not all that long before, he and Jason had tried to shoplift some Star Wars figures. They took the figures and some jeans into a dressing room, took the figures out of the packages and stuffed them into their shoes, while ostensibly trying on the jeans. They then put their own jeans back on.

My baser side thought it was rather clever and that it was almost a shame they got caught. But caught they got. The store detective told them it was the oldest trick in the book.[88] He approached them outside the store with a little gun lighter and told them he would shoot their

---

[87] The cash registers were new at that time. Apparently they were invented because no one under the age of fifty seems capable of counting change these days. Of course, as I always say, any solution to a problem usually creates a new problem. If a clerk (or a store owner!) is too stupid to count change, what's to guarantee he or she isn't too stupid to remember to enter the amount tended? It makes me wonder how much money stores lost once they started using these cash registers.

[88] And I guess it was. Years earlier, in my own shoplifting days, I'd go into a dressing room and filch whatever had been left there by the previous occupant. The irony was that those things were never my size. I never got caught, but I came close.

455

legs off if they tried to run. The little geniuses had the figures stuffed into the bottoms of their shoes and couldn't have run if they wanted to. And of course he couldn't have shot them if he wanted to.

But lest they pursue a life of crime, I thought it a good time to teach them that crime doesn't pay—it costs. I made them work for the money to cover the price of the Star Wars figures and then to work some more for the same amount to give to a charity of their choice. They did this, but Mike was disappointed that he didn't get to keep the figures.

There's one more "what goes around comes around" story. It's not my story, but it's worth the telling. A friend of mine, shortly after her divorce, got involved with a man. He was not a good man, but she was besotted with him. The long and the short of it is that, at his behest, she sold her house, they moved to another state—away from her friends and family—and he got her hooked on heroin. At the end, he was shooting her up with it. When all the money from the sale of her house was gone, he gave her an overdose and she died. It apparently couldn't be proven that he'd done all this intentionally, so he went free and immediately found himself another woman and did the same thing! Women—beware!

Now here's the come around. I don't know about God's involvement in this ending, but I do know that no one was sorry about it. Some time later, this guy got hit by a train while crossing some tracks when the gates were down. He was beheaded.

A SHOCKING STORY

Some years ago, my friend's son Shawn, then twenty, was playing in the trees at a local forest with a bunch of his buddies. Unbeknownst to them, the local power company had left an old, unused, but live, corroded green high-voltage wire running through the tops of the trees. Shawn, high up in a tree, didn't see it and unintentionally grabbed onto the wire. He was electrocuted—7500 volts passed through his body. To give you an idea of how much this was, between 500 and 2000 volts are typically applied during executions in the electric chair.[89]

Fortunately, Shawn fell out of the tree. On the way down, some forty-five feet, he was only worried that he'd break his leg. Apparently, the electrocution itself hadn't hurt, and he was at first unaware of the damage that it had done. But, his body was so hot that it burned the shirt of the girl who caught him when he fell. The fall did not cause any injury! God had His eye on the sparrows in His tree that day, the tiny one and the not-so-tiny one.

The potential for serious injury or death by electrocution is huge and terrifying. Shawn sustained injury to his hand, where he had grabbed the wire, and also to his leg. Although these injuries were quite serious, they were miraculously minimal compared to what could have happened.

Although I knew all about the accident at the time, I only recently met Shawn, who is now forty. What an inspiring young man he is! Ultimately, he lost his right hand and walks with a bit of a limp, neither of which slows him down. He's learned to write with his left hand and has figured out how to do most of what anyone else can do.

Shawn handles his disability with class and humor. He quickly dispels any discomfort one might feel upon meeting him. When I introduced him to my son Mike, Shawn had his stump covered by his jacket sleeve. Mike, of course, stuck out his right hand to shake, and Shawn offered his left hand. "Oh, a lefty," said Mike. "Nah," answered Shawn, "I just have no right to shake," and showed his stump.

When Shawn's daughter was a tot, he taught her to do "Patty-cake." She did it with one hand and one fist.

Just like Daddy.

---

[89] Baumgart, R. A. & McCuen, Gary E. Reviving the Death Penalty. Madison, WI: Gary McCuen, 1985

I Cannot

Crissy Shreve

I cannot bring myself to hate the one,
Who stole your love from me.
Nor can I seek revenge upon the one,
Who made it die.
I cannot even feel remorse at sorrow,
As yet I've more to see.
For in the midst of all the pain,
I cannot hate myself . . .
Can I?

CHAPTER FORTY

I'M STILL NOT DONE YET

Before the Berlin Wall came down, X2 and I traveled to the Harz Mountains area, on the border of West Germany and the former East Zone. We went to the border itself and saw a high chain link fence, beyond which was a wide minefield. There were guards and guard towers and dogs on patrol. Someone said that those on the other side were told that that fence and minefield were there to keep *us out*. I cried as I watched a bird flying over the fence, from one side to the other, and understood just how precious my freedom is.

A German fellow we knew (and his mother) invited and paid for a couple they knew from East Germany to come to the U.S. for a visit. This, too, was before the wall came down. The man and his wife were professional people, quite intelligent and learned. I don't know why they were invited, and I don't know how it was pulled off, but there they were, and one day they got dropped off at our house for coffee and a visit.

I served them coffee and some cake. They gobbled the cake like they'd not eaten in a week. Although they were embarrassed, they finally admitted that they *hadn't* eaten in a week—the fellow and his mother weren't feeding them and they had no money of their own. We ordered them a pizza and gave them some food money.

We asked them what kept them from just staying here and not going back. They said that they had family there who would be in danger if they didn't return. Again, I came face-to-face with the beauty of my freedom.

After the wall had come down, X2 and I visited a town called Eisenach, in the former East Zone. Up on the mountain, high above the town, is the medieval Wartburg castle and the old church where Martin Luther was hidden to avoid persecution, and where he translated the New Testament into the tongue of the common people of Germany. There is now a hotel up there, and we stayed for one night. It was magnificent and obscenely expensive, but worth it. And it was cold up on that mountain. The bathroom floor in our room was granite or marble, but it was heated, and that helped a little.

While we were in the Eisenach area, we took a side trip to the Buchenwald concentration camp. I stood inside the perimeter of a former barracks where Jewish prisoners had lived. I saw a crematorium and a gas chamber. The entire time I was in that camp, I didn't speak. The term speechless doesn't begin to define what I was feeling. There are no words to define what I was feeling. No feelings even exist for what I was feeling; we weren't designed for it. It was beyond words and even beyond tears. If I felt this way just standing in their footprints over fifty years later, how must the people who'd suffered and died there have felt? I couldn't imagine. The only thing I had to offer them was my silence.

This was perhaps the most profound experience of my life. I left Buchenwald a different person. I left whatever little innocence I might still have had behind me there. Whatever belief I had had in the goodness of mankind died in that place. A little piece of my heart remains in the dust within what's left of those barracks.

I've read the books. It's not the same. Whatever I thought I knew about the horror of the camps was nothing compared to standing where these people had stood. The only reasonable thought I was able to muster in the hours and days after that visit was that if I were in charge, every American high school senior would have to visit Buchenwald as a requirement for graduating.

I think this idea has some merit. I think it could change the world. It wouldn't necessarily have to be Buchenwald. It could be a trip to an inner city ghetto area or to a war-torn or poverty-stricken or hurricane-devastated area anywhere. Seeing the world through new and softer eyes, kids might gain a valuable perspective, one they would take with them as they become the new shakers and movers of mankind.

I fell in love with the town of Eisenach, and of course I saw a gorgeous old house there I'd have loved to restore. I've often said that if I had to live in Germany, it would have to be in the east. One reason for this is that the old buildings are mostly still there and are being restored. In West Germany, too many of the old buildings have been torn down and replaced with boring, modern, ten-story boxes. Even though many West German cities have maintained an "old town" area where one can find great restaurants and shops, those cities are just not nearly as appealing.

Another reason I'd need to live in the east is that things make more sense to me there. I visited Dresden with my friend Christel. We had a great time together. One very interesting difference from the west was in the attitudes of the servers in restaurants and the salespeople in the stores. In the west, you are treated as though you are intruding by patronizing their establishments. Waiters will be curt if not outright rude, and they will sling your food on the table. You are expected to pass your empty plates to the edge of the table to make it easier for them. This may be because there is no real tipping—service is supposedly included in the cost of the meal. People leave a bit of pocket change on the table, but it is no incentive for the servers. Likewise, the people who work in the stores are not especially interested in helping you. You bag your own groceries at the supermarket.

I was delighted, then, to see how they operated in Dresden. Waiters were polite and salespeople were helpful, and they were all friendly. They liked to test their English on me, so when I asked for something in German, they'd answer in English. And when they did speak to me in German, they called me by the informal "*Du*" rather than the formal "*Sie*." As an *Ami*,[90] this made me feel welcome and at home, especially since "*Du*" is regularly used between young people, whether they know each other or not. A typical West German would probably be offended.

Distanz is a thing to the Germans, too. They are all about shaking hands. I was at a party one time in Germany, and everyone lined up in a circle and went around shaking everyone else's hands, saying their last names. That outstretched hand, I came to realize, is not stretched

[90] American

out in welcome, but shouts clearly, "Keep your distance!" I'm guessing that this may be the origin of the phrase "at arm's length."

After our divorce, I saw X2 again for the first time in seven years at our grandson's high school graduation party. Driving there, I thought about how I should maybe stick out my hand when I saw him, then decided that that would be too much of a snub. And, honestly, for me it would have been. I'm a hugger, and anyway, I don't like touching other people's hands. I never know where those hands have been.

Of course, the minute X2 saw me, out came his hand. I almost laughed, except that when I took, it, I had something of a visceral reaction to touching him. I wasn't expecting it at all, and I quickly and instinctively pulled back my hand. His hand no longer belonged in mine. Later, though, we met outside for a smoke and talked for half an hour. It was okay. I was pleased and relieved to discover that I don't miss him at all.

I adored my neighbor Flo. She was in her early eighties and she was quite a character. She also had the dumbest luck when it came to me. Invariably, when she called me, I'd be in the shower or on the toilet or otherwise unable to get to the phone. I'm a napper. One afternoon Flo called, waking me from a dead sleep, asking me to come over and help her with something. The next afternoon, at exactly the same time, she again called, again waking me, to apologize for waking me the day before.

Flo was on some medication for a while that made her a bit crazy. Her husband had run out to the store, leaving her asleep in her bed. She woke up groggy from the meds and thought that someone was in her bathroom. This was in February, there was snow on the ground, and it was freezing outside. She ran, barefoot and in nothing but her nightgown, across the grass to my front door. Of course I was in the shower. I heard the dogs barking, but I thought it was just UPS dropping off a package. When I was out of the shower, the doorbell rang again, and there stood a policeman asking whether I'd seen any strangers around. When I hadn't answered the door, Flo had run to the next house and the lady there called the police.

Flo called regularly to check up on me. Initially, I tried to outdo her, and then I realized that the best gift I could give her was to be someone she could love and look after. As a several-time cancer survivor suffering from side effects of chemotherapy, having someone need her gave her a sense of still being useful. She always said that I was the best neighbor, but it was she who was the best neighbor.

Dear Flo passed away suddenly, just as I was in the final editing stages of this book. I will always hear her voice on the phone saying, "Hi, Cris, it's Flo next door," even though I knew it was she calling (thanks to Caller ID), and had answered, "Hi, Flo." We ended every phone call with, "I love you." Those were the last words we spoke to each other. And I am reminded again of just how precious are those who love us. Thank you, Flo, for loving me.

In the early 1980s, my friend Sue was living in Miami, Florida. One Christmas during that time, the temperature where I live was 70 degrees instead of the freezing and snowy conditions we're used to in December. My phone rang, and the voice on the other end said, "You're welcome."

"For what?" I asked. "For the nice Miami weather I sent you for Christmas," said Sue.

The very next year, temperatures were at a record low in Miami on Christmas. Sue didn't have a furnace in the house where she lived, but she did have a fireplace. Many of her friends who lived on boats in the anchorage were there trying to stay warm. Of course I had to call Sue and say, "You're welcome."

It seems to me that there are too many geniuses out there who get hired by software manufacturers, then get busy attempting to justify their jobs. They do this by fixing what's not broken and calling it upgrading. Before I wised up, I would always get whatever upgrade came along for any software I had. Then I figured it out—if the program was working fine as it was, why upgrade it? In a number of cases, when I did upgrade, I had to relearn how certain procedures I regularly used worked in the new version. It was not unusual for the new procedure to require an additional step or two. On one occasion, a procedure I used and needed had disappeared altogether.

The worst was the time I got a new PC. A program I'd been happily using for years without getting updates no longer worked on the new version of Windows. OK, so I caved and bought the new version of the software. Oh, but wait! It would not let me transfer my data directly from the old version to the new, several-generations-later version. I had to find an interim version, transfer the data to it, and then transfer it again from there to the newest version.

I just know that somebody stays awake at night thinking up these things. It's called planned obsolescence and they even admit to it.

Another set of geniuses works in marketing. They are obsessed with "new and improved." Once again, the old product is often just fine as it is, and the new version isn't quite as good. They no longer make the older version available, so I am stuck either using the less desirable new product or searching for another brand that still does the job. I am convinced that "new and improved" really means that they've reformulated the product in such a way as to make it cheaper to manufacture. But that's okay. They raise the price to make up for it.

Even worse than that is when a company arbitrarily discontinues a product I love. Poof! Gone! This happened one time with a candle company that had a store in the mall I frequent. They had an absolutely delicious-smelling lemon meringue pie candle. Not only could you smell the lemon, you could smell the crust. I bought these candles regularly for several years, both for myself and as gifts.

So one day I cruised into the store to buy a few more of them, only to find that they had been discontinued. Instead, there was an entire new (and of course "improved") line of candles, none of which appealed to me at all. The sales girl mentioned that the company wasn't doing well. I wrote to their headquarters, suggesting that it might serve them better to stick with a great candle than to discontinue it. I received the usual polite blow-off "we're sorry you were inconvenienced" letter. Sure enough, several months later, the store had closed.

If I were the boss of the world, companies would be required to maintain a stock of the *not* "new and improved" and discontinued items, for say, ten years. I would be perfectly happy purchasing these items directly from the manufacturer if necessary. After ten years, the manufacturer would have found out that I'm not the only one who prefers the discontinued item. They could even put those products back on the shelf and market them as "new and improved."

I don't have this problem with my favorite nail polish brand, though. There are only so many shades of any color. If my favorite is discontinued, and it will be, all I have to do is wait a year or two and it's back with a new name.

If I were to write advertising copy, I would create at least one ad stating that a product was *not* "new and improved," rather that it was just as wonderful as it had always been. If this idea ever catches on, perhaps it will rescue at least one of my favorite items from the geniuses.

I had the same problem with television. I got tired of the shows I liked best being cancelled. When they took *Journey To The Unknown* off the air in 1969, after only one season, I turned off the TV and didn't turn it back on for twenty-five years. I finally started watching again when DVRs were invented. I do like being able to watch a show when I want to and especially being able to fast forward through the commercials.

It's almost to the point where I'm tempted to write a letter to every company who produces a product or a TV show I like, giving them advance warning that the product or show won't last because I like it. I often tell the people behind me in any line that they'd best find another, because it's a good bet that the register will jam or someone in front of me will need to waste ten minutes squabbling over a price.

I'm not typically a violent person, but if there were one person I'd cheerfully shoot, it would be the guy who put the cyanide in the Tylenol years ago. That was the start of it. From that day on, I haven't been able to get *anything* out of the package.

Just recently I bought some of that cream we elderly women use to "tighten" the skin on our faces. I couldn't get the lid off. After putting on my reading glasses, I was finally able to spot the tiny transparent piece of tape that secured the lid. I removed it with the help of my trusty tweezers. I *still* couldn't get the lid off. It was screwed on so tightly that I had to use my rubber lid twister, and even then it wasn't easy. You'd think that products aimed at us elderly women might be accessibly packaged. You'd think.

Medicine containers are the worst. They call them "childproof," except that when you need to open one, you grab the nearest kid. And let's not forget those stiff, molded, clear plastic packages they put around smaller items to make them too big to easily steal. Get out the X-acto knife. I keep a pair of pliers in my kitchen so that I can get hold of the foil seal that stands between me and my orange juice. I could open a resale shop just to sell my assortment of tools for opening things.

It's wearying. Add the techno-creeps with their viruses and worms and identity theft. I dunno. Creeps and geniuses. What would we do without them?

If you use email, you've probably received at least one email that contains a link that you are told to open. It will come from someone you know, but they will not know they sent it. You may even have sent a few of these yourself without knowing it. Opening the link will get you in trouble, and most people are smart enough not to do so. The first time I caught this bug, whatever it was, my computer was sending out a link for the purchase of a male enhancement product. I got lots of emails from people telling me that it was happening, but the funniest was from a guy I know who should have known it was bogus, but apparently didn't. He replied thanking me for the information, but saying that he already had an overseas source for the product.

However, I've come to realize that, just as no one wakes up in the morning wondering what he or she can do to make my day better, no one wakes up in the morning wondering what he or she can do to make my day worse, either. I'm just not that important. I hope the identity thieves believe me.

I refuse to "feel" guilty. Guilt itself is not a feeling[91]. It's a state of being. Either we're guilty or we're not. The *result* of actual guilt is the feeling. When we're actually guilty of something, what we feel is remorse. I'm willing to feel remorse when it's valid. The dictionary defines guilt secondarily as a feeling of self-reproach, but I don't buy

---

[91] Guilt n. 1. the state of having done a wrong or committed an offense. 2. a feeling of self-reproach from believing that one has done a wrong. WEBSTER'S NEW WORLD DICTIONARY.

it. Dictionaries these days seem to get updated based on the way words are (mis)used instead of their actual meaning.

The point is, if we're not actually guilty of something, what's the sense in beating ourselves up? Yet we hear it all the time. *"I feel so guilty!"* I was astounded at the number of times I heard this (mostly from women) when I was in Grief Support after Jason died. None of them had caused the death of her loved one. I don't get it.

The only thing I can think of is that when someone we love dies, we want so desperately to make some kind of sense out of what's happened. We feel so utterly powerless. Perhaps that "feeling" of guilt creeps in and fools us into a false sense of control or power—as if, had we done something differently, we could have prevented the death.

I saw in the newsletter at our motor home resort in Naples that I'd been caught. Someone wrote, "I can walk around the park on any given day and see someone hugging a royal palm." I don't know if anyone else hugs palm trees, or is willing to admit it if they do, but I suspect it is I who was seen hugging mine.

We don't have palm trees up north. I already mentioned my first trip to California where I saw live palm trees for the very first time. I was so thrilled that I hugged the first one I could get my arms around, despite its being a scrawny thing, right there outside the terminal door, surviving in spite of the exhaust fumes. It still bid me a fine welcome. I've loved palm trees ever since.

Some years later, on our first trip to Florida, I astounded X2 by hugging the first palm tree I came across, which happened to be in a rest area along the highway. He didn't know whether to laugh or cry, but since he'd already married me, he wisely just added it to the growing list of my "idiosyncrissys" and learned to live with it.

I love my trees up north too, but it's hard to hug an Austrian Pine, so here I mostly just stroke needles and talk to them. I do know a tall, fifty-year-old oak tree that's a great hug though.

Then there's the four-way stop sign. There are two kinds of people in the world: those who think stop signs are really stay signs, and those, who like me, want to get on with it. The stay sign people like to sit there as long as possible, motioning everyone else in sight to go before they do. This may work for them, but not for the person who's behind them. Too often it is I. When I finally get to the front of the line, I smile at all the people who want to stay and I go.

I am in the minority of people who love traffic circles, also called roundabouts. There aren't many left, but there is still one in the town where I grew up, and there are several in Hilton Head. For the locals, it's the Hilton Head National Sport—yes, even bigger than golf and tennis—finding new ways to get where you wanted to go, without going around Sea Pines Circle. People don't know what to do when they come to a traffic circle. I always got a kick out of watching (and watching out for) all the people who seemed to be unable to merge, but instead sat there waiting for someone to let them in. This seems to be an epidemic, people expecting and waiting for someone to let them in, not only at traffic circles, but when entering a highway or when a lane ends. Apparently, merging is no longer taught in Driver's Ed.

Case in point: several days a week I head to my local Curves to work out. The road I take narrows from four to two lanes right after a traffic light. I always make sure I am in the left lane by that time, and I watch what happens next. Invariably, someone is going more slowly than the rest of us, is in the right lane, and hugs the white line at the side for as long as possible. Then he or she moves over into the left lane without benefit of a turn signal, let alone a glance in the side-view mirror. These people simply assume that someone will let them in, that someone's *supposed* to let them in. Of course, someone always does, if only in self-defense.

I've begun to realize that I have to choose my companions carefully. One day I was with an extremely negative woman and an extremely positive man, both at the same time. An interesting contrast. The woman is irrelevant outside of reminding me of what I don't want to be. The man's name was Cy, and he said two things that I found memorable and quotable.

He said, "I don't just allow a person his dignity, I insist on it." Then he said, "I don't hold anyone responsible for the acts of his forbears and I won't allow anyone to hold me responsible for the acts of mine." This guy had class, and his is the kind of thinking I need to be exposed to. He was from Birmingham, Alabama, and the conversation was about racial attitudes, but it's a concept that's transferable to life in general. I remember seeing in "Dear Abby" or "Ann Landers" something to the effect of, "Class is the ability to give without diminishing the receiver."

One of the things I learned about in therapy was "charges." A "charge" can be loosely defined as an experience from earlier in life that affects one's perception of something that's happening in the now. You've probably noticed that one of my major "charges" is feeling like I don't fit in. And, as I've said, I decided early on that if I couldn't fit in, I'd make a science out of it. After sixty-some years, that's not changed much, and much of the time I don't even particularly want to fit in. The quandary continues, though, with my alternately wishing I could fit in and working as hard as ever not to. I think that's called self-sabotage.

I hate it when someone says, "We all do." I ordered some Mary Kay Cleansing Creme from a lady I found in the phone book. Well, wait a minute. I didn't find *her* in the phone book. I found her ad. Anyway, it seemed I was always running out of the cleanser, and I commented to her, "It's like I eat this stuff." To which she replied, "We all do." The irony, if you didn't catch it, is that her saying that to me implied that in that way, at least, I do in fact fit in.

I pretty much like who I am. That's basically true, but it's also true by default. I look at other people and there's no one else I'd rather be. Perhaps it's just that I've been me for all these years and I've gotten used to myself. But when I'm tempted to wish I were someone else, I have to quickly remind myself that if I were that person, I'd have to take their faults and problems along with what I perceive to be good about them or their lives. I've not found many lives I'd want to trade mine for.

Fortunately, I've been blessed with enough people who love me and get me and appreciate who I am. It's not as much a matter of fitting in with them as it is simply being accepted. It's really more in the world at large where I get in trouble. Now, of course not everyone fits into every possible scenario or with everyone else in the world. If it were that simple, I could easily just pick my people and my scenarios, and probably manage to fit in more often than I do. If only.

But it's not that simple. Life likes to thrust us into situations despite our best attempts at being in control.

When X2 and I started having Germans staying at the house with us, they would always look at me as though I were crazy. I didn't do things the way they did—I didn't cook, didn't garden, etc. And they all do things the same way, so it was an ongoing and repeating pattern. I felt like a misfit in my own home. X2 didn't help. He was one of them. Of course, I never fit in when we went to Germany, either. It finally occurred to me that I never really fit in with X2, that I was never welcome in his life, either in Germany or in our home. The visiting Germans just took their cue from him.

At one point, early in our marriage, I'd told him that I would not go to Germany with him again unless he found a way to be able to still be my husband when we were with his mother, and not just her son. He was stuck in the middle between us and he never did figure out how to handle it. I came in second every time. *Mutter* controlled with cooking. When we were in Germany, we couldn't go anywhere for more than an hour or so because it was always time to go back to the house for lunch, coffee, or dinner.

Jason had a girlfriend whose mother was a passionate anti-smoker. One time I invited the girlfriend and her family to dinner. After we'd eaten, I started to light a cigarette, and the mother actually asked me whether I was really going to smoke. In my own house! I sweetly suggested that, if she didn't like my smoking, she was welcome to wait outside until I'd finished. I am aware that being a smoker does contribute to my being a misfit. This may be a big piece of why I find it so hard to quit.

As a smoker, I get the occasional "Shame on you" from someone. I don't usually smack the person, but I want to. I don't allow anyone to shame me. No one has the right to shame anyone else. If you're someone who feels it's your sacred duty to shame other people, it's not. Stop it.

Fitting in, or not, is definitely an issue for me as a Christian, and it's definitely a quandary. This is a bit hard to describe; I'm still trying to figure it out myself. I grew up with clear definitions of what "good" should look like, and that brand of "good" never seemed to work for me. I always felt a sense of falseness to that "goodness." I didn't trust it and I still don't. To me, truth and authenticity are of much greater importance. I always gravitated towards those who weren't so "good." They seemed to me to be more honest. If I fit anywhere, it is usually with the misfits.

Long before I started reading the Bible and learned the term, I perceived the "goodie-goodies" of the world as Pharisees, people who were proud of their "goodness," thinking it to be of themselves, even as they never even got close to understanding true goodness. It was all about obeying the rules and looking good on the outside, while judging those who didn't measure up. I've never had any desire to be one of them.

But I do know many formerly "good" people who have been touched and changed by Christ. I can trust them, because I know they know it's God's goodness in them, not their own. Still, I often feel like a fraud when I am with them. I still don't quite fit. That's the "charge."

Then there are those like me, with whom God's had a bit more of a challenge. I remain the reprobate, perhaps stubbornly, even as I am fully open to His work in my life. Fortunately, other people don't decide the truth about me. God does.

Certainly God uses "good" people, but He also uses reprobates like me. My message, my ministry, seems to be "If God can love someone like Crissy, He can love anyone."

The irony is that, as a Christian, I don't fit in well in the world either. What's a reprobate to do? The real truth, I suppose, is that we're all reprobates. Some of us just happen to be saved.

You know what really makes me crazy? People who are sick but insist on going out into the world to spread their germs to anyone within range. That's bad enough, but then there are those who go out of their way to tell you how sick they are. I don't want to know. I just wish they'd stayed home. X2 and I had shared birthday parties every year. One time a woman came who was clearly sick, made a point of giving me all the details, and then stating that, sick as she was, she just couldn't miss our party. Apparently she thought she was doing us a favor. She wasn't, and we never invited her again. Then there was the woman who went on a mission trip with a whole bunch of people from our church, including our pastor, who had a busy speaking schedule. The woman had the stomach flu. By the time the plane landed, everyone else had it too. Most of them spent the entire time running to the bathroom and very few were able to do what they'd gone on the trip to do. This, as they say on Facebook, is a special kind of stupid.

I'VE ALWAYS SAID . . .

It's my friend Michael T. who's always said, "I've always said . . . ," followed by something witty or ironic. I've borrowed the concept from him. The following are things that I have always said. I haven't heard or read them elsewhere that I can remember. I apologize to anyone who said any of them first or thinks they did.

There are people in this world who will always love me, and there's nothing I can do to change their minds. There are people in this world who will never love me, and there's nothing I can do to change their minds.

You can educate an idiot, but he'll still be an idiot.

I may have a Teflon brain, but I have a sticky heart.

God likes to put people in my life who annoy me. It's funny how they're always just like me.

If you want all those people out there for whom you've left messages to call you back, try taking a nap.

If you work, you have money, but no time to spend it, and if you don't work, you have plenty of time to shop, but no money. I don't know which is worse.

When you have enough money, time becomes more valuable than prices.

If it weren't for last minutes, nothing would ever get done.

It's OK for a man to go out to play tennis in rumpled shorts—he just looks like he has a good sex life.

You may use my material as long as you laughed when I said it!

Where have you been all your life?

75% of something is better than 100% of nothing.

Success is figuring out how to have your cake and eat it too.

A lot of seemingly nice people turn out to be closet jerks.

Silence can be a great weapon.

Hugs can also be a great weapon.

It's just stupid to get a ticket for speeding towards a red light.

Some people are dead but don't have the sense to lie down.

I deal with nuts every day of my life; I don't need them in my brownies. (This may be my best line ever).

I've never liked the way the world operates to begin with, and then it goes and changes the rules on me.

Must be my turn to change the toilet paper roll.

I'm butt-deep in catchup. I always said this when I'd get home from a trip and I'd be stuck to my desk chair for a week catching up.

One of the benefits of not cooking is that when my husband got hungry, he'd take me out to dinner!

I know why God gave us ears. What better place to stick a pencil?

Miss this at your own risk, something I say regularly during worship services at church.

There's always something to be depressed or upset about . . . but why bother?

I always pray for God's will in my life, but I seldom pray for it to come through someone else's mouth.

I could quit smoking if all the idiots in the world would suddenly disappear, if only because I'd disappear too.

No matter where I am or what I'm doing, there's always somewhere else I'm not, and something else I'm not doing.

I've tried for years to figure out how to be two places at once, but with limited success.

No, it's not Alzheimer's! It's just information overload.

No matter how much I pay for things, they still don't work.

Mondays should be cancelled for lack of interest.

Keep Tuesdays. We need them to sort out all the messes that seem to get made on Mondays.

Solving any problem always manages to create at least one new one.

I'd rather he be a philatelist than a philanderer. (As it turned out, he was both).

There are those people who will always think I'm a turkey . . . they may even be right.

If you think God's good in the good times, just wait till you see how good He is through the bad times.

Life is tough, but without God, it's impossible!

Being nice is usually costly.

Some things aren't worth the saliva to spit them out.

Some people take themselves quite seriously, regardless of my inability to do so.

God takes Himself seriously.

I can't remember exactly where it was written that life shouldn't be any fun, but wherever it was, I erased it.

If you can't cry it out, whisper it out. To God.

There are people who practice religion to whom it has never occurred that God might be real.

I am once again engaged to be a mother-in-law.

I AM A PROPHET
Crissy Shreve

I am a voice in the wilderness.
I have been given a gift . . .

I have been given a heart that wants Him above all things,
I have been given eyes that recognize the work of His hand,
I have been given ears that hear the very voice of God,
I have been given a mind that can understand His Word and His ways,
I have been given a soul that is a tiny, tiny piece of His own,
And I have been given a voice to shout of His goodness.
I never know when He will whisper in my ear,
Put this aside, that which you meant to do today.
Do this for Me.
Tell them.

Tell them that I love them.
You know I do, because I've shown my love to you.

Tell them that they need me.
You know, because you know how much you need Me.

Tell them that I'm good.
You know, because I've been so good to you.

Tell them that I'm gracious.
You know, because you live in my grace.

Tell them I'm alive.
You know, because you have seen Me in action.

Tell them I'm here.
For them, just as I've always been for you.

Tell them they don't have to earn my love.
You know. You have not earned it.

Tell them that they are welcome in my presence.
You know, you have been coming to Me for years.

Tell them I'm waiting for them to call on Me.
You know, because when you called, I answered.

You are My voice.

TELL THEM.

CHAPTER FORTY-ONE

THE GOSPEL ACCORDING TO CRISSY

"You are writing a gospel, a chapter each day,
By deeds that you do, by words that you say.
Men read what you write, whether faithless or true.
Say, what is the gospel according to you?"[92]

—Richard Johnson, song lyrics

I don't have a theology degree. I do have thirty-plus years attending one of the best Bible-teaching churches in this country. But my real credential is that I've spent that same thirty-plus years walking hand-in-hand with my Lord, watching Him at work in my life and in the lives of others. Watching Him keep the promises He makes in the Bible. Watching Him being absolutely faithful and trustworthy.

It bears repeating: *You couldn't convince me that God isn't real and isn't all He says He is in the Bible. I've simply seen too much.*

My "Gospel" is not about religion. I cringe when someone calls me religious. Religious is the last thing I am. I am a Christ-follower. I don't do it perfectly or even well, but it is who I am. That's the point. It's not about what I do; it's about what Jesus did on the cross.

Becoming a Christ-follower is an individual choice, unlike being born into a religion or even being born to Christian parents. It's choosing to believe the God of the Bible. Once someone chooses to believe, it all begins to make sense. Those who have not chosen to

---

[92] http://www.johnsonfamilymusic.com/lyrics/the_gospel_according_to_you.
html.

believe can't see it. It doesn't make any sense when seen only through human eyes.

The Bible says, "Taste and see that the Lord is good."[93] God allows us to wander and he pursues us. When we are ready to listen, He shows up. When a person chooses to trust Jesus for his or her salvation, things start to happen. One is that he or she receives at least one gift from God called a spiritual gift. There are many of them, and they are always in tune with the way the person is wired up with talents and passions.

My gift is prophecy. That does not mean that I can foretell the future. It means that I have been uniquely gifted to understand God's heart and to communicate His words and His ways effectively and in a culturally relevant way. I am strongly aware that, prior to trusting Christ, my understanding of God was pretty much nonexistent, and what little understanding I did have was faulty. That all changed drastically, and I had volitionally very little to do with it. That alone is enough to convince me that God is real.

I could almost end right there, but of course I won't. I want to introduce you to my God. I want you to see Him through my eyes, hear Him in my words, feel Him in your heart, know Him even as I have known Him. Much of the reason for this book is to demonstrate how God has loved me, his little reprobate, faithfully, for as long as I've known Him, and even before, regardless of my behavior, and regardless of whatever circumstances in which I found myself throughout my life.

I can't say it enough. It's all about *Who He is*. The dichotomy is this: "God demonstrates his own love for us in this: While we were still sinners, Christ died for us."[94] He loves reprobates. He uses reprobates. We're all reprobates. We're all He's got. Amazing. Only God.

As I was watching the movie *The Passion of The Christ*, it struck me that Jesus didn't just cave and go to the cross. He *insisted* on it. For *me*. He knew I needed it. He could easily have said no. Instead, He chose to do His Father's will. And as He Himself is God, it was His will too.

I can just hear you saying, "Wait a minute! Jesus is God? I thought He was just God's Son."

---

[93]   Psalms 34:8
[94]   Romans 5:8 NIV

This is one of my favorite subjects, and it is perhaps the concept most misunderstood by Christians and non-Christians alike. It dismays me how seldom the deity of Christ is taught in churches. At Christmas we sing, "Hark the Herald Angels Sing,"[95] which proclaims this: "Veiled in flesh the Godhead see, Hail the incarnate Deity," and "Jesus our Emmanuel." The word *Emmanuel* means God with us.

It is a hard concept for us humans to get. We can't quite grasp how anyone could be fully God *and* have been fully man at the same time. But God's not limited to what we can understand. Even so, it's not really all that hard. Christ's humanness came from his very mortal mother Mary, and his Godness came from being fathered by God through the Holy Spirit.

We read in the Old Testament that in God's eyes, only innocent blood is a sufficient sacrifice for the forgiveness of sin. Animals, often lambs and birds, were used. But that sacrifice needed to be repeated regularly because it was only a temporary fix and only for a particular person or group of persons until the next time they sinned. [96] Added to that was the Jewish Day of Atonement, *Yom Kippur*, which was meant to cover any unnoticed sins for which the Israelites had not offered a sacrifice.[97]

Jesus Christ is called The Lamb. He was sinless, and as such, His innocent blood is sufficient. The blood of no ordinary mortal man could have sufficed. Only the blood of God Himself could *once and for all* overcome sin.

The Jewish temple contained an inner room called the Holy of Holies.[98] Only the high priest could enter this room, and then only once a year. The room was separated from the outer room by a veil, which represented our separation from God. As Jesus died on the cross, that veil was split. This is huge. From that moment forward, we have been able to approach God directly, through Jesus Christ.

Jesus claimed to be God. He said, "I and the Father are one." The Jews believed He meant it; they wanted to stone Him. He said, "I have shown you many great miracles from the Father. For which of these

---

[95] "Hark the Herald Angels Sing," Christmas Carol written in 1739, by Charles Wesley, brother of John Wesley, founder of the Methodist Church.
[96] Hebrews 9
[97] ISAIAH 53 EXPLAINED, Mitch Glaser, 2010, Chosen People Productions.
[98] Matthew 27:51, Hebrews 10:20

do you stone me?" "We are not stoning you for any of these," replied the Jews, "but for blasphemy, because you, a mere man, claim to be God."[99]

Jesus, God Himself, left behind all the comfort and glory of heaven to come to us, only to be rejected by so many. He knew that would be so, and still He came. As C. S. Lewis pointed out, Jesus is either a liar, a lunatic, or He's Lord. That's what we all need to decide for ourselves, one way or the other.

Some pretend there is no God. Others believe He exists but want nothing to do with Him. But if Jesus says He's God, it seems to me that we ought to at least consider what that means if it's true.

I have an atheist friend. He says he has no problem with the idea of a divine creator, but that he stumbles over the question of who created the divine creator. This thinking attempts to limit God to human understanding.

I liken it to eternity, in the sense of infinity. I remember when I first realized that there is no end to space. It just goes on forever in every direction. This is easily proven by the question, "What comes after space?" The only possible answer is more space. In the same way, God is eternal and infinite. He simply is. He always was and He always will be. If He'd needed a creator, He wouldn't be God!

The atheist seems to think God needs his permission to exist. Ironically, God allows the atheist to exist. And *loves* him. I recently saw a great bumper sticker that said, "God doesn't believe in atheists." But it seems to me that atheists must believe in God to some degree— why else would they work so hard to deny His existence?

It has been said that an honest atheist will admit that he just doesn't want God cramping his style. Aldous Huxley made a

---

[99] John 10:30-33

statement to that effect,[100] as did philosopher Mortimer Adler, who admittedly rejected religion because [he] did not wish to live up to its standards."[101]

I agree! By that definition—having to live up to the standards of religion—I too reject it, not only because I don't wish to live up to its standards, but because I *cannot*. But that does not equate to rejecting God Himself. The beauty of being a Christ-follower is that I don't have to live up to the standards of any religion. I am not atheistic, but I am absolutely areligious, if that's a word.

God doesn't interfere in our lives—He enriches them. There's nothing out there that even begins to compare to life with God in it—certainly not life without Him in it.

There is a foundational confusion of religion with God. Religion is not about God, and more importantly, God is not about religion. We don't need to kick God out of our world, but we might do well to lose religion.

I'm just saying.

Truth does not necessarily affect perception. The Bible puts it this way: "The fool has said in his heart, 'There is no God.'"[102] One can tell himself anything he wants; it's when he believes himself that he gets in trouble.

Then there are those who do believe God exists but don't want any part of Him. Once again, it's that foundational misunderstanding, that confusion of God with religion. I don't want any part of religion

---

[100] "I had motives for not wanting the world to have meaning; consequently assumed it had none, and was able without any difficulty to find satisfying reasons for this assumption. The philosopher who finds no meaning in the world is not concerned exclusively with a problem in pure metaphysics; he is also concerned to prove there is no valid reason why he personally should not do as he wants to do . . . For myself, as no doubt for most of my contemporaries, the philosophy of meaninglessness was essentially an instrument of liberation. The liberation we desired was simultaneously liberation from a certain political and economic system and liberation from a certain system of morality. We objected to the morality because it interfered with our sexual freedom." Aldous Huxley, "Confessions of a Professed Atheist," Report: Perspective on the News, Vol. 3, June, 1966, p.19.

[101] Mortimer J. Adler, Philosophy at Large (New York: Macmillan, 1977), 316 as quoted in James S. Spiegel, The Making of an Atheist: How Immorality Leads to Unbelief (Chicago: Moody Publishers, 2010), 85.

[102] Psalms 14:1

either, but I sure can't imagine living without God, although untold millions of people do it. And it even works for a while—at least until someone they love is lying in a hospital bed or they themselves are facing death. Remember the members of Congress singing "God Bless America" in the wake of 9-11?

God's love is free for the asking. Salvation is a gift that cannot be earned. Christ already paid the bill. For years a friend of mine insisted that she was good enough to go to heaven. I'll admit that she's a pretty good person—she really is, but she's not good enough. She's a sinner just like I am, just like you are. She's not capable of being good enough because there is no good enough. Neither am I. Neither are you. God's standards are above our reach. Because He knows that's true, He provided an escape route. He came in skin to us to save us from ourselves.

Perhaps you've heard the story of "Aunt Jane."[103] It's about a conversation at her funeral. She was a good woman—it was agreed by all—always kind to people, etc. *Surely* she had gone to heaven—hadn't she? But then someone asked whether she'd known Jesus. Well, no, turns out she'd never want anything to do with Him and had let that be known.

The question, then, is this: Why would someone who never wanted anything to do with God in this life even want to spend eternity with Him?

Once again, the wisest statement I've ever heard is, "I would rather live my life as if there is a God and die to find out there isn't, than to live as if there isn't, and die to find out there is."[104]

Many have said that Christianity is a crutch, to which someone cleverly responded, "Yes, because we're all crippled."[105] The irony is that those who don't want God really think they don't need Him. I've never met a human person who isn't weak, only those who don't know they are. It's only a matter of time until their supposed strength is tested. The antidote to human weakness is God's strength. With His

---

[103] This story has been often quoted. The above is my paraphrased version. I heard it in a sermon, I think from Lee Strobel, but have not found a written source.

[104] Albert Camus (1913-1960)

[105] I can't find an exact source for this on the Internet. The statement that Christianity is a crutch has a number of sources.

vast store of strength to be tapped, why do puny humans insist on settling for only what little they can do on their own?

Those who don't want God think Christians are stupid and are to be pitied. I'm tempted to say, well, let's see who gets the last laugh. Tempted, but when the final shoe drops, no one will be laughing—not they, not I, and certainly not God. Truth does need to affect perception, because unpopular as it may have become to talk about it, hell hasn't gone away.

But hell is the last thing God desires for anyone. Perhaps the most well known verse in the Bible is John 3:16, which says, "For God so loved the world that he gave his one and only Son, that whoever believes in him shall not perish but have eternal life." It is the following verse 17 that banishes fear of the sledgehammer. "For God did not send his Son into the world to condemn the world, but to save the world through him." This is Jesus speaking, by the way.

God's waiting for his beloved children to come to Him. When we do, if He wants our behavior to change, He changes our hearts, and over time, those behaviors we cling to will no longer be so desirable. There is no loss when there is no desire.

For a lot of people, a major stumbling block is, as they say, "The church only wants my money." It's a favorite excuse to stay home. I get that. Now, it's true and it's even reasonable that churches need money to survive, just as does any other entity. I wonder, though, is this a problem with the churches or in our own hearts? I think it's probably some of both.

If our attitude is that it's our money, we're not going to easily part with it. And if we don't find value in learning about God, praising Him, and being with others who feel the same, all functions of the church, why would we want to support it? God Himself, however, doesn't want our money; He wants our hearts. If we love and embrace God, and we still don't find Him in a particular church, it's probably not the right church. When we find the right church and find value in being there, we logically would want to support it, for our own sakes and for the sake of others.

The Old Testament principle of giving was the tithe—ten percent.[106] That's a fine guideline, but the New Testament principle

---

[106] Malachi 3:10, Deuteronomy 14:22

is that God loves a cheerful giver.[107] If we don't want to give it, He doesn't want it.

Still, it's all God's money, whether we like to think so or not. He's given us the ability to earn it, whatever that looks like. When we give some of it back to Him, He wants it to be in gratitude, not grudgingly or under compulsion.[108]

Here's the biggie, though. When we care about and invest in His work, He gives us even more. It's been said, "You can't out give God."[109] Still, it starts in the heart. Jesus rebuked the Pharisees[110] for tithing yet disregarding the more important things of God such as justice and love.[111]

This is not, however, meant to sound like "prosperity theology." I'm not trying to tell you that the way to get rich is to become a Christian, although I do utterly trust in His provision.

Back to the question of why God allows things to happen. The whole world wondered why He allowed 9-11. And there is no question that He did allow it; if He hadn't, it wouldn't have happened. Again, I find it helps to recognize that we don't know what God *didn't* allow. He gave us free will, and in that, He allows us to do pretty much whatever we want to do. There are consequences to that. At the same time, because He loves his creation, He limits the consequences, individually and universally. If he didn't, the world would have ceased to exist long ago.

When my great-granddaughter was murdered, I couldn't come up with any reason whatsoever why God might have allowed it to happen. The words to a song on Christian radio helped me with that: "I won't keep searching for answers that aren't here to find."[112] It had to be enough for me that it wasn't okay with Him. So much of what goes on in our world is not okay with Him. And yet He keeps on being God and He keeps on being good. I can hang on to that even in the darkest moments.

---

[107]   2 Corinthians 9:7-8, 10-12
[108]   ibid
[109]   ibid
[110]   A Pharisee was a member of an ancient Jewish sect that emphasized strict interpretation and observance of the Mosaic law. www.thefreedictionary.com
[111]   Luke 11:42
[112]   Building 429, "Where I Belong."

We all like our free will. When we ask why God allows things to happen, we also have to ask ourselves whether we really want Him pulling strings and controlling everything we do. I don't think we do. We might better ask why *we* allow things to happen.

When we question why God allowed something, we also ought to perhaps consider what we would have done or what we would have liked God to do in the situation. Unless we are arrogant in the extreme, we can quickly conclude that we don't know all that He knows. We don't know a fraction of it. Can you just imagine what it would be like if you ran the world? Or, worse, if I did? It wouldn't be very good for me to have that responsibility with my limited resources, and it certainly wouldn't be good for the world.

God doesn't *make* bad things happen. He doesn't need to. But He does use what He allows. This can be a hard concept to grasp, especially when He's allowed something like my son to die unexpectedly at age 32. Jason's death was the result of a number of choices that he and others made. One small change in any of those choices would have meant he'd still be with us.

Jason trusted Christ for his salvation. He is at home with God. I'm quite sure he'd not choose to come back here even if he could. And I know that he will be there to greet me when I arrive. This is the only possible comfort for a mother who's lost a son.

Brent, who was in the accident with Jason, has come to recognize that he'd not have made it through the experience without God.

A number of people commented that I'd made it through Jason's death because of my faith. They saw God in action in my life. But it wasn't my faith; it was my faithful God. His presence with me was palpable, and perhaps the most powerful experience I've ever had.

So why free will? Here's what I think. Imagine that I said to you, "Hey, I'll give you a billion[113] dollars if you will love me." I just bet you'd say, "Oh, baby, I will *so* love you." So I give you the billion, but how do I know you *really* love me? How do I know you're not just pretending because you want the money?

God could so easily have made us puppets on strings. He could have made us to love Him and to have no choice about it. But God is relational. That's why He created us in the first place, to be in

---

[113] When I first started using this analogy years ago, I said a million dollars, but a million dollars just isn't what it used to be.

relationship with Him. *He wants us to choose Him.* He not only wants us to choose Him, He wants to be with us. What am I, who am I, that the Creator of the universe would want my company? Forever! Astoundingly, He does.

Heaven can be defined as eternity with God. Hell can be defined as eternity without Him. The fire and brimstone, although very real, are secondary. Without God, life in eternity would be . . . well, hell. Forever.

A friend once said something noteworthy to me. When I asked her why she believed that we'd live forever, she said, simply, "Energy doesn't die."[114] Back to my seventh grade science teacher saying, "Everything is made up of electricity (energy)—shocking isn't it?" We are then, in essence, energy. If one were to ponder scientifically the question of what happens to us when we die, this would seem to be a place to start. If we are eternal, then what? Secondary to that thought, if energy can be neither created nor destroyed, then where does it come from?

I've spent enough time looking at the basic premises of various religions to wonder what could possibly be the appeal of any of them. Some misunderstand and therefore completely misrepresent God as He presents Himself in the Bible; some have no God at all; some have several powerless "deities." These religions all require a lot of work towards no desirable end that I can determine.

None of their founders or prophets claimed to be God. None of them sacrificed anything for their followers. All of them died. None were resurrected—as I recently heard someone say on the radio, their bones can all be dug up. None of them answers prayer. None of them has any strength or power to offer. They all simply fall short of having any value, either in this life or into eternity.

People get mad at Christians for saying that only they have the key to eternal life, but it was Jesus Himself who said that He is the only way to God the Father. "Whoever believes in him is not condemned, but whoever does not believe stands condemned already because he

---

[114] The first law of thermodynamics is often called the Law of Conservation of Energy. This law suggests that energy can be transferred from one system to another in many forms. Also, it cannot be created or destroyed. www.physicalgeography.net/fundamentals/6e.html

has not believed in the name of God's one and only Son."[115] "I am the way, and the truth, and the life; no one comes to the Father, but through Me."[116]

I've so often heard people say that they'd rather go to hell because all their friends will be there. I think that's nuts. I've got a lot of great friends, but there's not one of them I'd rather be with than God.

My pastor presented an interesting perspective on hell not long ago—that we enjoy a reasonable degree of general protection in this life because God, in His love for His creation, does limit what He allows. That protection will not be available in hell. God will not be there. It will not be pretty. Like when I was in the cave and we turned off our headlamps and experienced the utter absence of light, hell is the utter absence of God.

Those friends will not be our friends in hell; they'll be betrayers and back-stabbers. They'll lie to us and steal from us. There will be nothing to stop them. We won't even have the luxury of dying to escape them.

---

[115] John 3:18
[116] John 4:16

"And heaven meets earth like a sloppy wet kiss,
And my heart turns violently inside my chest.
I don't have time to maintain these regrets,
When I think about the way . . . that He loves us."[117]

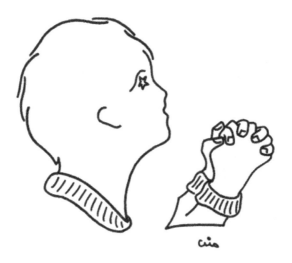

---

[117] "How He Loves," John Mark McMillan. Some of the above lyrics are from an alternate version.

ACKNOWLEDGEMENTS

A number of friends and family members previewed BMom for me and gave me good and honest feedback.

Thanks and love to Mike, Marge, Mary, Jan H., Nancy, Jennifer, Doug, Louise, Jo and Lou.

Special thanks to Beth, who did a masterful job of editing for grammar and the like, and to Jan S. who checked out my German.

Thanks also to everyone at Author House for guidance and encouragement in pulling it all together.

I am grateful to the great poets in our world—Donna Dickey Guyer, Robert Frost, and Edna St. Vincent Millay, along with many others who have inspired me over the years. And to those who write song lyrics.

Above all, thank You, my good and gracious Lord, for everything—just the way it is.